Immigration Law and Practice in the United Kingdom

First Supplement to Sixth Edition

Ian A Macdonald QC
Garden Court chambers

Ronan Toal
Garden Court chambers

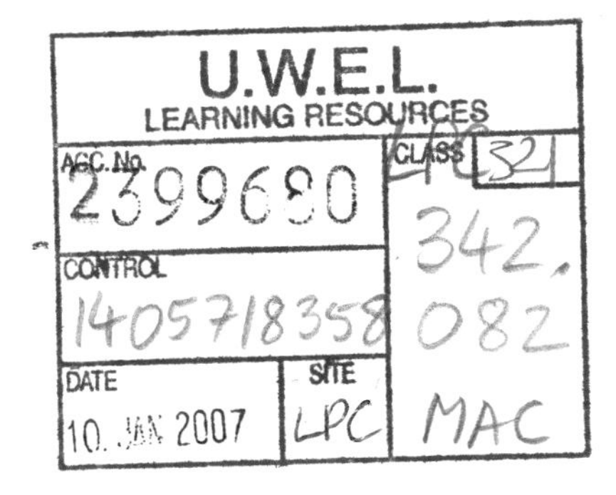

Members of the LexisNexis Group worldwide

United Kingdom	LexisNexis Butterworths, a Division of Reed Elsevier (UK) Ltd, Halsbury House, 35 Chancery Lane, LONDON WC2A 1EL, and RSH, 1–3 Baxter's Place, Leith Walk, EDINBURGH EH1 3AF
Argentina	LexisNexis Argentina, BUENOS AIRES
Australia	LexisNexis Butterworths, CHATSWOOD, New South Wales
Austria	LexisNexis Verlag ARD Orac GmbH & Co KG, VIENNA
Benelux	LexisNexis Benelux, AMSTERDAM
Canada	LexisNexis Canada, MARKHAM, Ontario
Chile	LexisNexis Chile Ltda, SANTIAGO
China	LexisNexis China, BEIJING and SHANGHAI
France	LexisNexis SA, PARIS
Germany	LexisNexis Deutschland GmbH, MUNSTER
Hong Kong	LexisNexis Hong Kong, HONG KONG
India	LexisNexis India, NEW DELHI
Italy	Giuffrè Editore, MILAN
Japan	LexisNexis Japan, TOKYO
Malaysia	Malayan Law Journal Sdn Bhd, KUALA LUMPUR
Mexico	LexisNexis Mexico, MEXICO
New Zealand	LexisNexis NZ Ltd, WELLINGTON
Poland	Wydawnictwo Prawnicze LexisNexis Sp, WARSAW
Singapore	LexisNexis Singapore, SINGAPORE
South Africa	LexisNexis Butterworths, DURBAN
USA	LexisNexis, DAYTON, Ohio

Published by LexisNexis Butterworths

A CIP Catalogue record for this book is available from the British Library.

ISBN for this volume

ISBN 10: 1 4057 1835 8

ISBN 13: 978 1 4057 1835 6

Typeset by Letterpart Ltd, Reigate, Surrey

Printed and bound in Great Britain by William Clowes Limited, Beccles, Suffolk

Visit LexisNexis Butterworths at www.lexisnexis.co.uk

Note

In this Supplement **the Immigration, Asylum and Nationality Act 2006** is referred to as 'IAN 2006'.

Preface

At the time that we decided to write this supplement, our assumption was that it would be quite short and would mainly consist of an account of the most recent primary legislation – the Immigration, Asylum and Nationality Act 2006 ('IAN 2006'). However, although only a year and a half has passed since the 6th edition of this book was written, there has been a huge amount of law-making quite apart from IAN 2006. Major pieces of European legislation ('The Citizens' Directive' and the asylum 'Qualification Directive') have been implemented by domestic Regulations and Rules; there have been 12 changes to the Immigration Rules; the Civil Partnership Act 2004 came into force on 5 December 2005, necessitating consequential amendments to the Immigration Rules; the Adoption and Children Act 2002 ('the 2002 Act') came into force on 30 December 2005 and revoked most of the Adoption (Intercountry Aspects) Act 1999 which had previously governed this area. The courts have been busy too. The House of Lords has decided seven immigration and asylum cases;[1] few days have passed without the Court of Appeal and the Administrative Court giving at least one judgment on the subject and the Asylum and Immigration Tribunal (the 'AIT') has made about 170 reported determinations.

A selection of the themes that can be identified includes the following.

First of all there is the creation of important new rights of residence under European Community law including the right to permanent residence for EU citizens and their family members who have resided legally for five years in a

1 *R (on the application of Bagdanavicius) v Secretary of State for the Home Department* [2005] UKHL 38 (article 3 claims based on fear of non-state violence); *R (on the application of Khadir) v Secretary of State for the Home Department* [2005] UKHL 39 (scope of the power to detain pending removal); *Szoma v Secretary of State for the Department of Work and Pensions* [2005] UKHL 64 (meaning of 'lawfully present'); *R (on the application of Limbuela) v Secretary of State for the Home Department* [2005] UKHL 66 (article 3 claims based on destitution consequent upon withdrawal of state welfare support); *A v Secretary of State for the Home Department (No 2)* [2005] UKHL 71 (admissibility of evidence obtained by torture); *Januzi v Secretary of State for the Home Department* [2006] UKHL 5 (internal flight / relocation in the context of refugee convention claims); *Fornah v Secretary of State for the Home Department* [2006] UKHL 46 (decided too recently for inclusion in the text) a woman from Sierra Leone with a well-founded fear of being persecuted there in the form of genital mutilation as part of an initiation rite had that fear for reasons of her membership of a particular social group and so was a refugee. In the linked case of *K v Secretary of State for the Home Department* [2005] EWCA Civ 1655, persecution of an individual for reasons of her membership of a third person's family was held to be persecution for reasons of membership of a particular social group even if the third person was not being persecuted for a refugee convention reason.

member state[2] and the right to 'subsidiary protection status' for those at risk of 'serious harm' in their home countries.[3]

Secondly, procedural and substantive requirements for obtaining leave to enter and remain in the UK have become more demanding, for example, by imposing a visa requirement on anyone, other than a few overseas British nationals, wishing to stay for more than six months and by extending the qualifying period for obtaining settlement for a person in the UK in a work-related category from four to five years.

Thirdly, there have been a variety of developments, making immigration status and (in certain circumstances) British citizenship far less secure and far more contingent upon the exercise of executive discretion. They include: the creation of a power to take away citizenship if the Secretary of State is satisfied that 'deprivation is conducive to the public good';[4] a power to remove a person's right of abode if the Secretary of State 'thinks it would be conducive to the public good' for the person to be removed;[5] amendment of the immigration rules to make the deportation of foreign national prisoners the rule rather than the exception, when they have finished their prison sentences;[6] giving recognized refugees an initial five years rather than indefinite leave to remain to those recognized as refugees; instituting a process of 'active review' for those with refugee status, exceptional leave to remain, humanitarian protection and discretionary leave, including the use of a wide range of 'unacceptable behaviours' as reference points.[7]

The machinery of immigration control has been further extended by IAN 2006 to include the imposition of civil penalties[8] and criminal liabilities on employers who employ a person who does not have the right immigration status to take the job;[9] by empowering the Secretary of State or an immigration officer to require production of a passenger list for arriving and departing ships and aircraft (including the particulars of passengers who are not subject to immigration control);[10] by enabling the police to require the owner or agent of a ship or aircraft to provide information about all passengers and crew,[11] irrespective of whether they are subject to immigration control or whether the information is needed for an immigration purpose; by providing for the sharing of information between the Secretary of State, the police and Revenue and Customs,[12] for the disclosure of information by them to the intelligence services,[13] and by the police to foreign police forces[14] and by extending the powers of immigration officers to examine those departing from the UK and to detain them for up to 12 hours pending examination.[15]

2 Directive 2004/38/EC, art 16.
3 Directive 2004/83/EC, art 18.
4 IAN 2006, s 56.
5 IAN 2006, s 57.
6 HC 395, para 364 as substituted by HC 1337.
7 See the Asylum Policy Instructions on Refugee Leave, Humanitarian Protection and Active Reviews.
8 IAN 2006, ss 15–19, not yet in force.
9 IAN 2006, ss 21–22, not yet in force.
10 IAN 2006, s 31, not yet in force.
11 IAN 2006, s 32, not yet in force.
12 IAN 2006, s 36.
13 IAN 2006, s 38.
14 IAN 2006, s 39.
15 IAN 2006, s 42, commenced 31 August 2006.

Fourthly, the effect of IAN 2006 is to make significant curtailments of rights of appeal so that there will no longer be a right of appeal against a refusal of entry clearance, unless the entry clearance application was made for limited family purposes or the appeal is on human rights or race discrimination grounds.[16] There will be no appeal against a refusal of leave to enter unless the person holds an entry clearance and seeks entry for that purpose or appeals on refugee Convention, human rights or race discrimination grounds.[17]

Fifthly, there has been much litigation about the scope of an appeal to the tribunal (formerly the Immigration Appeal Tribunal, now the Asylum and Immigration Tribunal) and to the Court of Appeal when the issue is whether the original decision contained a material error of law.[18] The Court of Appeal has repeatedly stated that in relation to issues of fact and judgment it will give considerable deference to the conclusions reached by the specialist, fact finding tribunal.[19] Nevertheless, a substantial proportion of the cases heard by the Court of Appeal have been concerned with the propriety of the tribunal's factual findings, e.g. its approach to assessing the plausibility of a claim[20] and its approach to medical and expert evidence when assessing the credibility of a witness.[21] However, the limitation of reconsideration by the tribunal and appeals to the Court of Appeal to cases where there is an error of law leaves ample scope for 'radical' error (Sedley LJ's word – he had in mind errors of fact)[22] and consequent, serious risk of harm to those wrongly refused asylum.

Sixthly, the conduct of the Home Office has repeatedly shown a disregard or even disdain for the rule of law. It ranges from prolonged inactivity in response to an application for leave to remain, indicative of a breakdown in the management of immigration control and properly described as a 'public disgrace'[23] to a practice of 'spiriting away' asylum seekers by detaining and removing them before they are able to obtain legal advice and access to the courts.[24] The 'Afghan hijackers' case[25] provides a striking instance of governmental contempt for the rule of law. In that case, a panel of adjudicators made a decision requiring that the claimants be granted discretionary leave to remain. The government disliked the decision and therefore defied the order of the tribunal. Sullivan J held that it 'would strike at the heart of the independent appeal system ... if the Secretary of State felt free to deliberately circumvent an adverse decision of the tribunal simply because he disagreed with the outcome on the merits'. Not only did the government fail to implement the panel's decision; it rewrote the discretionary leave policy in an

16 IAN 2006, s 4, not yet in force.

17 IAN 2006, s 6, not yet in force.

18 In relation to appeals to the Immigration Appeals Tribunal under Nationality, Immigration and Asylum Act 2002, s 101 (now repealed) and reconsideration by the Asylum and Immigration Tribunal of its own decisions under s 103A.

19 E.g. *Akaeke v Secretary of State for the Home Department* [2005] EWCA Civ 947.

20 *HK v Secretary of State for the Home Department* [2006] EWCA Civ 1037 and *Y v Secretary of State for the Home Department* [2006] EWCA Civ 1223.

21 *Mibanga v Secretary of State for the Home Department* [2005] EWCA Civ 367.

22 See Sedley LJ's judgment in *Reka v Secretary of State for the Home Department* [2006] EWCA Civ 552.

23 *Akaeke v Secretary of State for the Home Department.*

24 *R (on the application of Karas) v Secretary of State for the Home Department* [2006] EWHC 747 (Admin).

25 *R (on the application of S) v Secretary of State for the Home Department* [2006] EWHC 1111 (Admin), upheld in *S v Secretary of State for the Home Department* [2006] EWCA Civ 1157.

attempt to legitimize its inactivity. That conduct was described by Sullivan J as 'an abuse of power by a public authority' and he went on to say 'It is particularly disturbing that this was not simply the conduct of a junior official, that the process was authorized, if not initiated "at the highest level" '. All of the judges involved in the case 'attracted a degree of opprobrium' (to use the words of the Court of Appeal) including Sullivan J whose judgment (upheld by the Court of Appeal) was characterized by the Prime Minister as 'an abuse of common sense'.

Seventhly, contrary to the fulminations of politicians against the Human Rights Act and its application by the courts, judges have been most anxious that human rights should fetter governmental discretion in only the most exceptional cases. So much has been established by *Huang*[26] in article 8 cases, but the same relativist principle has established itself in the realm of the unqualified right not to be subject to torture, inhuman or degrading treatment or punishment. Thus, in cases where there is a fear of non-state violence in the destination country, the question whether removal would breach article 3 is to be answered not by reference to the nature and severity of the harm feared but by reference to the steps taken by the receiving state to protect from the harm.[27] In health cases, it has been acknowledged that the courts would not hesitate to find the removal of an HIV sufferer to a country where she would not receive treatment to be inhuman treatment if HIV was a rare affliction but have contrived reasons to find otherwise because of 'the sheer volume of suffering now reaching these shores'.[28]

The intention is that this supplement should update the original text so as to state the law as of 9 October 2006. Where we have used an earlier date we state this in the text.

The authors wish to thank Amarjit Ahluwalia, Kathryn Cronin, Katie Forster, Stephanie Harrison, Anne Kariithi, Tania Poscotis, Desmond Rutledge, Sadat Sayeed, William Toal, Frances Webber, and all the staff at LexisNexis Butterworths who have assisted with their usual professionalism.

Ian Macdonald QC and Ronan Toal
Garden Court chambers
London
7 November 2006

[26] *Huang v Secretary of State for the Home Department* [2005] EWCA Civ 105.
[27] *R (on the application of Bagdanavicius) v Secretary of State for the Home Department* [2005] UKHL 38.
[28] Sedley LJ in *T v Secretary of State for the Home Department* [2005] EWCA Civ 1421.

Contents

Table of Statutes

Table of Statutory Instruments

Table of Immigration Rules

Table of Conventions and Agreements

Table of European Legislation

Table of Cases

A

B

C

D

PARA

H

I

J

PARA

K

L

M

PARA

R (on the application of Rahman) v Entry Clearance Officer [2006] EWHC 1755 (Admin), [2006] All ER (D) 143 (Jun) 18.69
R v Governor of Durham Prison, ex p Singh [1984] 1 All ER 983, [1984] 1 WLR 704, [1983] Imm AR 198, 128 Sol Jo 349, [1981] LS Gaz R 1764 .... 3.37D, 17.13
R (on the application of A, D and Y) v Hackney London Borough Council [2005] EWHC 2950 (Admin), [2005] All ER (D) 251 (Dec) 13.175, 13.177, 13.178
R v Immigration Appeal Tribunal, ex p Antonissen: C-292/89 [1991] ECR I-745, [1991] 2 CMLR 373, ECJ 7.67, 7.120
R (on the application of Lekstaka) v Immigration Appeal Tribunal [2005] EWHC 745 (Admin), [2005] All ER (D) 222 (Apr) 8.89B
R v Immigration Appeal Tribunal and Surinder Singh, ex p Secretary of State for the Home Department: C-370/90 [1992] 3 All ER 798, [1992] ECR I-4265, [1992] 3 CMLR 358, [1993] 1 FCR 453, [1993] 1 FLR 798, [1993] Fam Law 272, [1992] Imm AR 565, [1993] 21 LS Gaz R 45, ECJ 7.55, 7.60, 7.87F
R v Javaherifard and Miller [2005] EWCA Crim 3231, [2006] Imm AR 185, (2006) Times, 20 January, [2005] All ER (D) 213 (Dec) 3.5, 6.7, 14.40
R (on the application of Badhu) v Lambeth London Borough Council [2005] EWCA Civ 1184, [2006] 1 WLR 505, [2006] HLR 122, (2005) Times, 19 October, [2005] All ER (D) 164 (Oct) 8.98, 13.184
R (on the application of Kimani) v Lambeth London Borough Council [2003] EWCA Civ 1150, [2004] 1 WLR 272, [2003] 3 FCR 222, [2003] 2 FLR 1217, [2003] Fam Law 811, [2004] HLR 207, [2003] 37 LS Gaz R 32, (2003) Times, 6 August, [2003] All ER (D) 16 (Aug) 13.178
R (on the application of B) v London Borough of Southwark [2006] EWHC 2254 (Admin), [2006] All ER (D) 83 (Sep) 13.178
R v Makuwa [2006] EWCA Crim 175, [2006] 1 WLR 2755, [2006] Crim LR 911, (2006) Times, 28 April, [2006] All ER (D) 324 (Feb) 14.38
R (on the application of C) v Merton London Borough Council [2005] EWHC 1753 (Admin), [2005] 3 FCR 42, [2005] All ER (D) 221 (Jul) 12.117
R (on the application of Gillan) v Metropolitan Police Comr [2006] UKHL 12, [2006] 2 WLR 537, (2006) Times, 9 March, 150 Sol Jo LB 366, [2006] All ER (D) 114 (Mar) 8.39
R v Navabi [2005] EWCA Crim 2865, (2005) Times, 5 December, [2005] All ER (D) 151 (Nov) 14.33, 14.38
R (on the application of Akyuz) v Same [2006] EWCA Civ 541, [2006] ICR 1314, [2006] All ER (D) 274 (May) 7.66, 7.154
R (on the application of K) v Same [2006] EWHC 980 (Admin), 150 Sol Jo LB 743, [2006] All ER (D) 300 (May) 17.35, 18.137
R (on the application of Ozturk) v Same [2006] EWCA Civ 541, [2006] ICR 1314, [2006] All ER (D) 274 (May) 7.66, 7.154
R (on the application of Abbasi) v Secretary of State for Foreign and Commonwealth Affairs [2002] EWCA Civ 1598, [2003] 3 LRC 297, (2002) Times, 8 November, [2002] All ER (D) 70 (Nov) 12.102
R (on the application of Al Rawi) v Secretary of State for Foreign and Commonwealth Affairs [2006] EWHC 972 (Admin), [2006] NLJR 797, (2006) Times, 19 May, [2006] All ER (D) 46 (May); affd [2006] EWCA Civ 1279, [2006] All ER (D) 138 (Oct) 12.102
R v Secretary of State for the Home Department, ex p Adan [2001] 2 AC 477, [2001] 1 All ER 593, [2000] All ER (D) 2357, [2001] 2 WLR 143, (2000) Times, 20 December, 145 Sol Jo LB 15, HL 12.20B
R (on the application of Ahmadzai) v Secretary of State for the Home Department [2006] EWHC 318 (Admin), [2006] All ER (D) 19 (Mar) 12.153
R (on the application of Ajoh) v Secretary of State for the Home Department [2006] EWHC 1489 (Admin), 150 Sol Jo LB 667, [2006] All ER (D) 235 (May) 8.89A
R (on the application of Anufrijeva) v Secretary of State for the Home Department [2003] UKHL 36, [2004] 1 AC 604, [2003] 3 All ER 827, [2003] 3 WLR 252, [2003] Imm AR 570, [2003] 33 LS Gaz R 29, (2003) Times, 27 June, [2003] All ER (D) 353 (Jun) 15.49

PARA

R

S

Decisions of the European Court of Justice are listed below numerically. These decisions are also included in the preceding alphabetical list.

Chapter 1

INTRODUCING IMMIGRATION LAW

OUTLINE OF CURRENT IMMIGRATION AND ASYLUM LAW

The Immigration Act 1971

1.21

[Penultimate sentence:]

Section 3C of the Immigration Act 1971 has been amended by IAN 2006, s 11 so that the new statutory leave only continues pending an in-country appeal against refusal.

[Final sentence:]

Section 31A of the Immigration Act 1971 has been repealed and replaced by IAN 2006, s 50.

The Asylum and Immigration Act 1996

1.24

[NB:]

Sections 8 and 8A of the Asylum and Immigration Act 1996 will be replaced when ss 21 and 23 of the IAN 2006 come into force (see 14.82A ff).

The Immigration and Asylum Act 1999

1.26

[Footnote 2:]

Section 5 of the Immigration and Asylum Act 1999 and s 122 of the NIAA 2002 will be repealed and replaced by IAN 2006, s 50 and Sch 2 when they come into force but this is a consolidating measure and there will be no change in the fees regime.

1.27

[NB:]

The power to take and arrange for the taking of fingerprints will be widened when ss 28 and 29 of the IAN 2006 come into force. See 3.35 below.

The Race Relations (Amendment) Act 2000

1.30

[Add at end:]

Under the Race Relations (Immigration and Asylum) (Comparison of Fingerprints and Photographs) Authorisation 2004, the IND could compare the fingerprints of asylum seekers from Iraq, Turkey, Iran, Somalia and Sudan against other governments' fingerprint databases of asylum seekers, failed asylum seekers and those granted some form of status. It also allowed the IND to compare the photographs of asylum seekers from these countries with visa application forms completed by individuals from the same countries.[1] In March 2006 this was revoked and replaced by a new authorisation, extending these powers to a list of ten nationalities, comprising Afghanistan, Eritrea, Iran, Somalia, India, Iraq, Sudan, Nigeria, China and Ethiopia and enabling the IND to check the fingerprints of asylum applicants from these countries with other governments' databases. The idea of the authorisation is to help the IND identify individuals who have claimed asylum, or enjoy some form of status, in a safe third country who subsequently claim asylum in the UK.[2] Another authorisation was made for a six month period in January 2006 in the light of evidence of fraudulent Zimbabwean applications for indefinite leave to remain in the UK on grounds of UK Ancestry lodged prior to 25 October 2004.[3] The aim was to enable staff in the IND to subject these applications to more rigorous investigation than applications from persons of other nationalities, for the purpose of detecting fraudulent applications. In addition, the annual report of the independent Race Monitor appointed under s 19E of the Race Relations Act 1976 (as amended) deals with the likely effect of authorizations and on how they operate in practice. In October 2006 an authorisation regarding the UK China Graduate Work Experience Programme was made under s 19D of the Race Relations Act 1976 (as amended) to enable Chinese graduates up to the age of 30 to participate in the Programme otherwise than in accordance with the Immigration Rules. The pilot began in mid-October 2006. See further the special provisions for tourism from China at 9.20B below.

1 Until 18 November 2005, 61 asylum applicants, excluding dependants, from these five countries whose fingerprints were checked entered the UK despite having an outstanding asylum claim, or status, in a safe third country.

2 Letter of Minister of State to ILPA (2.3.06). The provision of the previous authorisation under which the Asylum Screening Unit compared the photographs of applicants from 'top five' countries against visa application forms to identify any who travelled here on legitimate documents issued by a safe third country, as all nationalities are now subject to this examination. See 14.21 below.

3 Letter of Minister of State to ILPA (16.01.06).

1.32

[Add at end:]

The purpose of s 57A(1) of the Race Relations Act 1976, as amended, is to prevent there being inconsistent decisions in an immigration appeal under Pt V of the 2002 Act on the one hand, and in the County Court on the other. It is also to encourage, wherever possible, the making of discrimination decisions arising in the context of immigration before a Tribunal versed in immigration affairs. However, it was held *Emunefe v Secretary of State for the Home Department*[1] that once there is no longer an immigration appeal which is pending or could be brought, the possibility of inconsistent decision ceases to exist and, on the plain language of the statute, there is no bar to making a discrimination claim in the County Court.

1 [2005] EWCA Civ 1002, [2005] INLR 587.

Stereotyping

1.32A

[Add new paragraph:]

The issue of stereotyping and making generic assumptions has been raised in two recent court decisions. In *Q v Secretary of State for the Home Department*[1] in the Court of Appeal, Sedley LJ warned that reference to the asylum screening interview by way of a generic assumption that asylum seekers, given the opportunity, will be coached in false claims and/or will confabulate their account of events, so that the screening interview by anticipating this process affords 'the best evidence' suggests a stereotypical and negative attitude to asylum seekers as a class. In *AA (Bangladesh)*,[2] the AIT issued a powerful warning against deciding an application for entry clearance on the basis of general assumptions or stereotypes. They said it was quite wrong for an Entry Clearance Officer to assume that because the sectors based work permit scheme offers the applicant an opportunity, during the year that he is lawfully employed under it, to make what may by his standards be a considerable amount of money, that the application was being made only in order to enable the applicant to overstay. That was equivalent to an assumption that anyone who has the opportunity to commit an offence will do so. The poverty of the country from which the applicant comes was not of relevance to the Entry Clearance Officer's decision.

1 [2006] EWCA Civ 351 (9 March 2006).
2 [2006] UKAIT 00026.

The Nationality, Immigration and Asylum Act 2002

1.37

[Footnote 1:]

Section 31A of the Immigration Act 1971 will be replaced by IAN 2006, s 50 when it comes into force, but this is a consolidating measure and there will be no substantial change in the fees regime.

[Footnote 2:]

NIAA 2002, s 122 will be repealed and replaced by IAN 2006, s 50 and Sch 2 when they come into force but this is a consolidating measure and there will be no change in the fees regime.

[Footnote 5:]

The Immigration (Provision of Physical Data) Regulations 2003, as amended, have been revoked and replaced by the Immigration (Provision of Physical Data) Regulations 2006, SI 2006/1743, which came into force on 4 July 2006.

The Asylum and Immigration (Treatment of Claimants, etc) Act 2004

1.38

[Footnote 1:]

Section 8 of the Asylum and Immigration Act 1996 (criminal offence by employers) will be repealed when s 21 of the IAN 2006 comes into force.

The Civil Partnership Act 2004

1.38A

[Add new text:]

The Civil Partnership Act 2004 came into force on 5 December 2005. Civil partnerships are a new legal relationship which can be registered by two people of the same sex and give couples legal recognition for their relationship. From December 5 2005 the immigration rules have been amended so as to put civil partners on the same footing as spouses for immigration purposes. The 96 rule amendments made by HC 582 are to ensure that civil partners and proposed civil partners are afforded the same treatment as spouses and fiancés throughout.

The Immigration, Asylum and Nationality Act 2006

1.38B

[Add new paragraph:]

The Immigration, Asylum and Nationality Act 2006 ('IAN 2006') received the royal assent on 30 March 2006. The government began to implement its provisions in June, with full implementation not expected until 2008. The Act is arranged under six headings:

- **Appeals.** The main changes to the Appeal system are the new restrictions on appeals against refusals of entry clearance to dependants and family visitors and by holders of entry clearance who are refused entry at a port of entry. There are other modifications, including some controversial changes to appeal rights in national security deportations. All of the changes are dealt with in the chapter 18 alterations;
- **Employer sanctions.** A new scheme of civil penalties is to be introduced for employers who employ people who have no right to work or no right to work for that employer. There is also a more measured criminal sanction which is no longer an offence of strict liability and will

eventually replace section 8 of the Asylum and Immigration Act 1996. This is dealt with in the changes to chapter 14;

- **Information.** Vast new information-gathering and information sharing powers are introduced, which is aimed at creating a more integrated and co-operative machinery of border control;
- **Claimants and applicants.** There is a hotch potch of changes under this heading, including modifications of local authority powers to provide support and housing for asylum seekers, powers to enable the Secretary of State to regulate the provision of goods and services for those in section 4 housing and to make "integration loans" more accessible to both refugees and other categories of migrant. There also minor changes to nationality law;
- **Miscellaneous.** This widens the power to arrest pending deportation (section 53); introduces a statutory construction of Article 1(F)(c) of the Refugee Convention (section 54); directs the AIT on how to deal with the Secretary of State's certificates of non-application of the Refugee Convention (section 55); widens the power to deprive of British citizenship (section 56); introduces a new power to deprive of someone of the right of abode (section 57); brings in a new requirement of "good character" for the over 10's in order to qualify for registration as a British citizen; and allows detainees to be employed at less than the minimum wage;
- **General.** This contains the usual end of statute things like money, commencement, territorial reach and citation. The two schedules deal with consequential amendments and repeals.

Commencement

1.38C

[Add new paragraph:]

The Immigration, Asylum and Nationality Act 2006 (Commencement No 1) Order 2006 SI 2006/1497 brings the following provisions of the new Act into effect on 16 June 2006:

- **section 10** (s 110 of Nationality, Immigration and Asylum Act 2002 enabling the Secretary of State for the Home Department to make grants to advisory and welfare organizations ceases to have effect);
- **section 30** (amending Immigration Act 1971, s 3(9) re proving the right of abode. It permits the right of abode to be proved by an ID card issued under the ID Cards Act 2006);
- **section 43** (amending various provisions relating to the accommodation of asylum seekers and failed asylum seekers);
- **section 48** (amends Immigration and Asylum Act 1999, s 10 with the effect that when a person is notified of a decision to give directions for his or her removal under that section, the decision has the effect of invalidating any leave previously given to the person);
- **section 56** (introduces extremely broad new powers for the Secretary of State to deprive a person of citizenship simply on the ground that such deprivation is 'conducive to the public good');

- **section 60** (enabling the Secretary of State to pay expenses in connection with the Act.

On 30 June 2006 **section 45** came into effect, amending existing provisions relating to 'integration loans'.

Subject to Art 4, Art 3 of the Immigration, Asylum and Nationality Act 2006 (Commencement No 2) Order 2006 (SI 2006/2226) brings the following provisions of the new Act into effect on 31 August 2006:

- **section 1** (new right of appeal for people who are no longer recognised as refugees but allowed to stay);
- **section 2** (separate right of appeal against a decision to remove);
- **section 3** (limitation on grounds of appeal under new s 83A of NIAA 2002);
- **section 5** (limitation on the right of appeal against refusal of entry clearance for failure to provide documents);
- **section 6** (widening restrictions on right of appeal against refusal of leave to enter);
- **section 7** (restricting appeals to SIAC in deportations on national security grounds);
- **section 11** (amends continuation of leave provisions under IA 1971, s 3C and enacts new s 3D);
- **section 14** (consequential amendments) together with all the provisions of **Sch 1** (except para 11);
- **section 19** (code of practice for the imposition of penalties on employers who engage in unlawful employment);
- **section 23** (discrimination: code of practice for employers specifying how to avoid contravening the Race Relations laws);
- **section 27** (documents produced or found during immigration examination of passengers);
- **section 28** (fingerprinting of immigration detainees);
- **section 29** (attendance of asylum-seekers and their dependants for fingerprinting);
- **section 40** (searches: contracting out);
- **section 41** (miscellaneous supplemental matters to s 40, including appointment of a Monitor);
- **section 42** (power to obtain further information from embarking passengers);
- **section 46** (inspection of detention facilities by HM Chief Inspector of Prisons' (HMCIP));
- **section 49** (capacity to make nationality application);
- **section 53** (power to arrest pending deportation where notice has not yet been given to the prospective deportee);
- **section 54** (refugee convention: construction of Art 1(F)(c) in relation to terrorism);
- **section 55** (refugee convention: certification that an appellant is not entitled to the protection);
- **section 59** (detained persons: national minimum wage does not apply);
- **section 61** (repeals) together with **Sch 3**, to the extent that they relate to the entries in that Schedule listed in Schedule 2 to this Order.

Nationality Act 2006 listed in Sch 1. Article 4 makes transitional provision in relation to a number of the sections being brought into force.

UK and EU law

1.40

[NB:]

The Immigration (European Economic Area) Regulations 2006, SI 2006/1003 implement in domestic law Directive 2004/38/EC of the European Parliament and the Council of 29 April 2004 on the right of citizens of the Union and their family members to move and reside freely within the territory of the Member States. The Directive is now the main piece of subordinate legislation governing free movement rights in the EU. It has amended or replaced all the key Regulations and Directives in this area. The Directive amends Regulation (EEC) No 1612/68 and repeals Directives 64/221/EEC, 68/360/EEC, 72/194/EEC, 73/148/EEC, 75/35/EEC, 90/364/EEC, 90/365/EEC and 93/96/EEC. These repealed Directives were implemented by the Immigration (European Economic Area) Regulations 2000, as amended ('the 2000 Regulations'). The 2000 Regulations are now repealed and replaced by The Immigration (European Economic Area) Regulations 2006, SI 2006/1003, which came into force on 30 April 2006. For more details see chapter 7.

FEES

1.42A

[Add new paragraph:]

Fees for applications, work permits, certificates and passports now feature as an important element in immigration control, particularly as the amount charged has increased spectacularly beyond the rate of inflation. Clearly the policy behind this is to try to recoup as far as possible the cost of administration.[1] There is now little constraint on who can be charged and how much. The charging of all fees is regulated by statute and subordinate legislation. Fees must be set in accordance with these measures,[2] and throughout the book we refer to various current charges made under different Regulations or Orders in Council, as the case may be, always with a warning to check the up to date position.[3] Despite the comprehensive and clear nature of these measures, concern has been expressed by the independent monitor that as a result of out sourcing elements of the administration of visas, applicants at overseas posts are having to pay extra money to commercial agencies in order to get a visa for a visit or short term study.[4] By 2004 an estimated million visa applications were made in this way, almost half of all visa applications. The commercial agencies carrying out these functions charge compulsory additional fees, which vary from an additional £3.60 in Bangladesh to £8.20 in Ghana and £17.85 in Jordan, an effective increase in the cost of a visa by between 7% and 38%. There is no power to charge these fees under the Consular Fees Order and as these commercial agencies are operating under contract with the UK authorities, it is certainly arguable that the charges are unlawful.[5]

1 The government's stated aim is to deliver a self-financing managed migration programme by 2008, where possible, to reduce reliance on the public purse and to generate income to support the ongoing modernisation of immigration services: Explanatory Memorandum to the Immigration (Application Fees) Order 2005 at para 7.1.

2 It should not be thought that Silber J was suggesting that fees could be levied without statutory authority or a proper Regulation, when he stated in *R (on the application of Baiai) v Secretary of State for the Home Department* [2006] EWHC 1035 (Admin), [2006] All ER (D) 142 (May) at para 29: 'If the Secretary of State had imposed, as he was and is quite entitled to do, a proportionate system of scrutiny for sham marriages, it seems that there could have been no valid and rational objection to a charge of £135 for it'.

3 Domestic fees and charges (except for passports) are fixed by Regulations made under statute, overseas fees and charges and fees for passports, which are fixed by the Foreign Office are done by Orders in Council. See, for example, 2.21 (certificates of entitlement); 3.15 (entry clearance); 4.10 (applications for leave to remain and variations of leave); 9.51 and 9.54 (students).

4 Since 2003 a number of overseas posts have adopted exclusive arrangements whereby applications for visas can only be made via out-sourced commercial agencies: Report by the Independent Monitor, November 2005 (UK visas), para 27.

5 See Monitor Report, para 28.

1.42B

[Add new paragraph:]

On the other hand, the government has been concerned that they are not getting enough. Their complaint is that 'fees for immigration applications are currently charged at a level which reflects the administrative cost of providing a service up to the point of making and conveying a decision but does not deal with either the recovery of past deficits or the cost of providing an appeals function for those who seek leave to remain or variation of the conditions of their leave to enter or remain in the UK. Under s 102 of the Finance (No 2) Act 1987 government bodies are given a power to specify functions and matters which can be taken into account when exercising their power to fix a fee or charge. In relation to immigration and nationality, this power has been extended by s 22 of the Asylum and Immigration (Treatment of Claimants, etc) Act 2004 to enable fees to be set at a level exceeding the administrative costs, and reflecting the benefits deemed likely to accrue to successful applicants. In the Immigration (Application Fees) Order 2005 (SI 2005/582) the Secretary of State decided, when the Home Office set the fees for applications for leave to remain, for variation of leave, for immigration employment documents and so forth, that they would take into account not only the cost of appeals, but also the need to recover past deficits incurred in previous years in relation to the processing of these various immigration applications.

1.42C

[Add new paragraph:]

The Consular Fees Act 1980 allows fees to be charged for costs incurred overseas for such things as visas and passports. The Consular Fees Act 1980 (Fees) Order 2005 (SI 2005/2112), which came into force on 27 July 2005, and the Consular Fees Act 1980 (Fees) (No 2) Order 2005 (SI 2005/3198), which came into force on 4 November 2005, provide that the very considerable cost of issuing biometric passports[1] and of performing certain other passport functions will be passed on to the consumer. On the domestic front, s 51 of the IAN 2006 will consolidate the fee fixing power for immigration and nationality services under one statutory power. At present the power is scattered amongst the different immigration and nationality statutes.[2] Apart from Consular Fees Act 1980 each of these statutory provisions will be repealed by Sch 2 to the IAN 2006, when it and s 51 of the Act come into force.

1 Following the events of 11 September 2001 a decision was taken to incorporate micro-chips containing biometric identifiers into passports. This followed the introduction of biometric passports in legislation passed by the US in 2003. The Foreign Office will stop issuing the current form of digital machine-readable passports early in financial year 2006/07 and the rollout of new biometric passport systems will begin. The fees for issuing these passports will include the full cost of providing them during two financial years. The fees to be charged are set out in a separate Order in Council, the Consular Fees Order 2005 (SI 2005/1465), as amended by the Consular Fees (Amendment) Order 2005 (SI 2005/3182) and the Consular Fees (Amendment) Order 2006 (SI 2006/1912).

2 Fees are currently levied for a range of immigration applications under the following powers: (1) Applications for leave to remain in the UK and applications for the variation of leave to enter or remain in the UK (s 5(1)(a)(b) of the IAA 1999); (2) Applications for the transfer of limited or indefinite leave stamps into a new document (s 5(1)(c) of the IAA 1999); (3) Applications for leave to remain for holders of immigration employment documents, such as a work permit (s 122(1) of the NIAA 2002); (4) Applications for immigration employment documents such as a work permit (s 122(1) of the NIAA 2002); (5) Applications for citizenship (s 41(2) of the British Nationality Act 1981); and (6) Applications for a certificate showing the applicant has a right of abode in the UK (s 1 of the Consular Fees Act 1980 and s 10 of the NIAA 2002). Section 52 (1) of the IAN 2006 preserves the existing arrangement whereby fees for consular functions, as defined in the Consular Relations Act 1968, are set under the powers in the Consular Fees Act 1980. Once s 51 comes into force any orders already made under s 102 of the Finance (No 2) Act 1987 with reference to the powers to charge fees for immigration and nationality applications which are repealed in Sch 2 are to be read as if they refer to the charging powers in s 51: IAN 2006, s 52(2).

The Immigration Rules

1.48

[NB:]

Since the date covered by the 6th edition (5 April 2005) there have been 12 changes to the Immigration Rules, which were laid before parliament as follows: HC 104 on 15 June 2005; HC 299 on 12 July 2005; HC 582 on 24 October 2005; HC 645 on 9 November 2005; HC 697 on 21 November 2005; HC 769 on 19 December 2005; HC 819 on 23 January 2006; HC 949 on 1 March 2006; HC 1016 on 30 March 2006; HC 1053 on 20 April 2006; HC 1337 on 19 July 2006; and CM 6918 on 18 September 2006. We are all running in order to keep up.

1.51

[NB:]

The debate about the legal status of the Immigration Rules has been given a twist by the enactment of s 50 of the IAN 2006. This section will give the Secretary of State the power to use the immigration rules to prescribe the procedures to be followed in making applications for leave to remain and variations of leave from. This novel way of proceeding will replace s 31A of the Immigration Act 1971 which requires a statutory instrument to set out the procedures for making immigration applications for leave, variations of leave and so forth, and s 25 of the AI(TC)A 2004 which dealt with applications for permission to marry. So are the rules still rules of practice with consequences in appeals and judicial review or are they now, at least in part, to be regarded as delegated legislation?[1]

Note that s 8A of the Asylum and Immigration Act 1996 (power to make a Code of Practice) has been replaced by s 23 of the IAN 2006, which came into force on 31 August 2006.[2]

1 When prescribed application forms were first made compulsory in 1996, it was done under the immigration rules (HC 395, para 32, as amended by HC 329, effective from 3 June 1996). In *R v Secretary of State for the Home Department, ex p Immigration Law Practitioners Association* [1997] Imm AR 189, Collins J held that the statutory power under s 3(2) of the Immigration Act 1971 was broad enough to allow the Secretary of State to redefine how an application should be made.

2 Immigration, Asylum and Nationality Act 2006 (Commencement No 2) Order 2006, SI 2006/2226.

Chapter 2

RIGHT OF ABODE AND CITIZENSHIP

THE RIGHT OF ABODE

Restrictions on the right of abode

2.8

[NB:]

The Football Spectators' Act 1989 is amended by the Identity Cards Act 2006, s 39(1) and (2) to ensure that a requirement to surrender a passport includes a requirement to surrender an ID card, able to be used as a travel document. A similar amendment is made to the Criminal Justice and Police Act 2001, where courts can issue travel restriction orders in cases of serious drug offenders leaving prison: s 39(3) and (4).

HONG KONG AND THE RIGHT OF ABODE

2.20

[Footnote 5:]

In 2005, 3593 gratis UK residence permits (UKRPs) were issued, mainly to students: 6-monthly report on Hong Kong July-September 2005 (Cm 6751) at para 73.

PROVING ENTITLEMENT TO RIGHT OF ABODE

2.21

[NB:]

Section 39 of the Immigration Act 1971 has been reformatted by s 30 of the Immigration, Asylum and Nationality Act 2006 (IAN 2006),[1] which makes a number of amendments to the documents that can be used to prove a right of abode. The full list now is:

(a) A UK passport describing the person as a British citizen;
(b) A UK passport describing that person as a British subject with the right of abode in the UK;
(c) An ID card issued under the Identity Cards Act 2006 describing that person as a British citizen;
(d) An ID card issued under that Act describing the person as a British subject with the right of abode in the UK; or
(e) A certificate of entitlement.

In substance what the amendment does is to remove the now redundant reference to a passport issued to a 'citizen of the United Kingdom and colonies', as this category has not existed since 1 January 1993, when the British Nationality Act 1981 came into force.

1 In force on 16 June 2006: Immigration, Asylum and Nationality Act 2006 (Commencement No 1) Order 2006, SI 2006/1497.

Deprivation of the right of abode

2.22A

[Add new paragraph:]

Section 57 of IAN 2006 inserts a new s 2A into the Immigration Act 1971,[1] which confers on the Secretary of State a power to make an order removing a right of abode in the UK, where that right is derived from possession of citizenship of another Commonwealth country and it is conducive to the public good to remove or exclude that person from the UK. The Secretary of State may also make an order revoking the deprivation (s 57(3)). Section 57(2) provides a right of appeal against the decision to deprive a person of their right of abode, either to the Asylum and Immigration Tribunal (AIT) or to the Special Immigration Appeals Commission (SIAC).[2]

1 In force on 16 June 2006: Immigration, Asylum and Nationality Act 2006 (Commencement No 1) Order 2006, SI 2006/1497.
2 Section 57(2) inserts a new s 82(2)(b) of NIAA 2002.

BECOMING A BRITISH CITIZEN

Becoming a British citizen after commencement

Birth in the UK or an Overseas Territory

2.44

[NB:]

As originally enacted, subject to the provision made by s 47 for legitimation following the parents' marriage, the British Nationality Act 1981 did not confer any nationality status or entitlement on the basis of the relationship between a father and his illegitimate child. Amendments made to the British Nationality Act 1981 by s 9 of the NIAA 2002 have now come into force and will enable such benefits to flow to the child where either (a) the father is named in a birth certificated issued within one year of the birth of the child, or (b) he is identified as such by s 28 of the Human Fertilisation and Embryology Act 1990, or (c) he satisfies prescribed requirements as to proof of paternity. In the latter case, the requirements to be satisfied are those prescribed by regulations made by the Secretary of State under the newly in force s 50(9A) and (9B) of the British Nationality Act 1981.[1] The new provisions will have effect in relation to a child born on or after 1 July 2006.[2] The expectation is that a person whose claim or entitlement under the 1981 act is subject to satisfaction of the prescribed requirements as to proof of paternity will submit the requisite proof with his or her application for a UK passport or, as the case may be, with his or her application for registration by entitlement under the 1981 Act.

[1] Section 9 of the NIAA 2002 and British Nationality (Proof of Paternity) Regulations 2006 (SI 2006/1496), made under s 50(9B). The regulations came into force on 1 July 2006 (the Nationality, Immigration and Asylum Act 2002 (Commencement No 11) Order 2006 (SI 2006/4918).

[2] Commencement Order, as above, and NIAA 2002, s 162(5).

Descent

2.52

[Footnote 2:]

Detailed provisions relating to designated service are now contained in the British Citizenship (Designated Service) Order 2006, SI 2006/1390.

Registration

2.53

[NB:]

Section 58 of IAN 2006 will require most applicants for British nationality by registration to satisfy the Secretary of State that they are 'of good character' before nationality may be granted.[1] Exceptions will continue to be made where the applicant has an entitlement to registration deriving from the 1961 UN Convention on the Reduction of Statelessness or is entitled to registration as a BC under s 4B of the British Nationality Act 1981 which gives registration entitlements to certain British overseas citizens, British subjects and British protected persons without other citizenship, or is aged below 10 on the date of the application.[2]

[1] IAN 2006, s 58(1). At present such a requirement applies only to those seeking to acquire British nationality by naturalisation: see 2.55 below.

[2] IAN 2006, s 58(3).

Naturalisation

2.54

[NB:]

Regulation 8 of the EEA Regulations 2000 have now been replaced by reg 15 of the Immigration (European Economic Area) Regulations 2006, SI 2006/1003. They supersede the remainder of the text after the reference to footnote 12. The new Regulation sets out those who have a permanent right of residence. It includes EEA nationals and members of their families who have resided in the UK under the new regulations for a continuous period of five years. See further chapter 7.

2.55

[NB:]

Regulations to deal with knowledge of life in Britain have now been made. The British Nationality (General) (Amendment) Regulations 2005 (SI 2005/2785) amend the British Nationality (General) Regulations with effect from 1 November 2005 (1 May 2006 in the Channel Islands and the Isle of Man) to make provision for determining whether a person has sufficient knowledge of the English language and to make provision for determining whether a person has sufficient knowledge about life in the United Kingdom for the purposes of such an application. Copies of the citizenship materials for ESOL Learners pack referred to in reg 3 can be obtained from www.esol-citzenship.org or from EfES publications, Prolog, PO Box 5050, Annersley, Nottingham NG15 ODJ; tel: 0845 602 2260; email: dfes@prolog.uk.com.

[Footnote 2 – add:]

BNA 1981, s 49 now gives the Secretary of State a discretion to waive the 'full capacity' requirement, if it is the applicant's best interests: IAN 2006, s 49. The provision also applies to renunciation and resumption of citizenship. Section 49 came into force on 31 August 2006: Immigration, Asylum and Nationality Act 2006 (Commencement No 2) Order 2006, SI 2006/2226.

Deprivation of citizenship

2.61

[NB:]

(i) The deprivation criteria have been widened by s 56 of IAN 2006, which amends s 40(2) of the British Nationality Act 1981.[1] The existing criteria that the person concerned had done something which was 'seriously prejudicial to the vital interests of the UK or a British overseas territory' has been replaced with the criterion that it is conducive to the public good to deprive the person of his or her British nationality. The current limitation that a deprivation order may not be made on this basis if it would make the person stateless continues to apply. Section 56(2) enables the AIT, on an appeal against deprivation of nationality, to receive evidence in private.[2]

(ii) Under s 40(3) of the British Nationality Act 1981, as originally enacted, persons who were registered or naturalised as a BC might be deprived of their citizenship if they had shown themselves 'by act or speech to be disloyal or disaffected towards Her Majesty'.[3] In *R (on the application of Hicks) v Secretary of State for the Home Department*[4] H was an Australian citizen who had been seized in Afghanistan and was being held at Guantanamo Bay by the United States authorities. He satisfied the conditions for British citizenship by descent from his mother under the British Nationality Act 1981, s 4C and, accordingly, applied for registration as a British citizen. The Secretary of State proposed to grant British citizenship but at the same time to make an order depriving H of citizenship under s 40 of the 1981 Act. The Court of Appeal held that the deprivation would not be lawful since the conduct of H in Afghanistan, where he was alleged to have trained with terrorists, could not constitute disloyalty or disaffection towards the United Kingdom, for the purposes of the British Nationality Act 1981, s 40(3)(a) as originally enacted, a state of which he was not then a citizen, to which he owed no duty and on which he made no claim.[5]

1 In force on 16 June 2006: Immigration, Asylum and Nationality Act 2006 (Commencement No 1) Order 2006, SI 2006/1497.
2 BNA 1981, s 40A(3)(e), inserted by IAN 2006, s 56(2).
3 BNA 1981, s 40(3)(a), before repeal by NIAA 2002, s 4.
4 [2006] EWCA Civ 400, [2006] All ER (D) 173 (Apr).
5 The Court of Appeal held that s 40(3)(a) of the 1981 Act, as originally enacted, did contemplate circumstances in which conduct before grant of citizenship could provide grounds for revocation of citizenship, as did its statutory predecessors. An allegiance might also arise, the breach of which might constitute disloyalty or disaffection, without the person being a citizen: *Joyce v DPP* [1946] AC 347, [1946] 1 All ER 186, 31 Cr App Rep 57, 115 LJKB 146, 174 LT 206, 62 TLR 208, HL, considered.

THE RIGHT TO A BRITISH PASSPORT

A prerogative power

2.66

[NB:]

The Consular Fees Act 1980 has been amended by s 36 of the Identity Cards Act 2006 to allow flexibility in the setting of fees for the carrying out of consular functions which includes the setting of passport fees (for more details see para 1.42C of this supplement, above). Different levels of fees may be set for different cases. The most important gain is that it provides a statutory basis for the issue of free passports, which has already been introduced for those born on or before 2 September 1929. The bad news is that other applicants will have to pay more in order to subsidise these zero charges. Section 39 of the Identity Cards Act 2006 makes a series of amendments to existing legislation to enable the ID card, as a highly reliable form of proof of identity, to be used in the widest range of circumstances and to facilitate its use as a travel document. But there are restrictions too, so that where travel restrictions are imposed by a criminal court, they will in future apply to both the passport and the identity card: Identity Cards Act 2006, s 39(1) and (2). See also 2.8 above.

Identity cards

[Add new paragraph:]

Under the Identity Cards Act 2006 provision is made for the issue of identity cards to all UK residents and individuals, who have resided in the UK, for example, or are proposing to enter the UK. Initially the scheme will not be compulsory except for a few categories of person. If people want an identity card they will have to apply for it and their personal details will then be entered on the National Identity Register and they will be issued with an ID card (s 2). However, some persons' details may be entered into the register without their permission, such as failed asylum seekers who have not applied for and ID card, but whose information, including biometric data, was available. The idea of this is to ensure that if a failed asylum seeker applies to stay in the UK again using a different identity, his or her previous status as a failed asylum seeker will have been recorded (s 2(4)). The Act also creates a creeping form of compulsion. Section 4 gives the Secretary of State the power to designate documents for the purposes of the Act, for example passports.[1] Once a passport is designated, anyone applying for one must also apply at the same time for an ID card, unless he or she already has one (see s 5(2)). This requirement, however, does not apply until 1 January 2010. Until then individuals applying for a British passport can choose to 'opt out' of being issued with an ID card. But the 'opt out' does not apply to the register. All individuals who apply for a passport will be required to be entered onto the register once the passport becomes a designated document (s 6(7)). The power to designate documents will apply to any other documents issued by a Minister of the Crown, a government department, a Northern Ireland department, the National Assembly for Wales, or any other person who carries out statutory functions on behalf of the crown, such as residence permits for foreign nationals. In their case the ID card and resident document are likely to be contained in one document (s 6(1) and (2)). But this is not likely to happen in the case of a British passport where a separate ID card is likely to be issued alongside the new passport.

1 This must be done by order which will be subject to affirmative resolution in parliament. These documents are referred to in the Act as 'designated documents'. Persons responsible for issuing designated documents are referred to in the Act as 'designated documents authorities'.

Chapter 3

CONTROL OF ENTRY

INTRODUCTION

3.1

[NB – Footnote 3:]

Nationality, Immigration and Asylum Act 2002 (Juxtaposed Controls) Order 2003 (SI 2003/2818), has been amended by Nationality, Immigration and Asylum Act 2002 (Juxtaposed Controls) (Amendment) Order 2006.

[NB – Footnote 5:]

The Immigration (Provision of Physical Data) Regulations 2003 as amended have been revoked and replaced by the Immigration (Provision of Physical Data) Regulations 2006, SI 2006/1743, which came into force on 4 July 2006.

3.5

[NB:]

In *R v Javaherifard*[1] the Court of Appeal explained that s 11 has no application to entry by land; that those who disembark from a boat otherwise than at a port enter on disembarkation, as do those who disembark at a port which has no designated immigration area; and that s 11 does not apply to those who have already entered the UK overland or on an earlier disembarkation.

1 [2005] EWCA Crim 3231, (2006) Times, 20 January, [2005] All ER (D) 213 (Dec).

ENTRY CLEARANCE

Who needs entry clearance

3.10

[NB:]

Malawi has been added to the list of visa countries and Croatia has been taken off it by rule changes in HC 949 which took effect on 2 March 2006. Citizens of Malawi will also need a transit visa if passing through Britain.

[NB – Footnote 3:]

Section 3C of the Immigration Act 1971 has been amended by IAN 2006, s 11, so that, on an application to vary leave, leave will only be extended pending a decision on the application to vary or pending an in-country appeal. Section 11 of IAN 2006 came into force on 31 August 2006: Immigration, Asylum and Nationality Act 2006 (Commencement No 2) Order 2006, SI 2006/2226.

TRANSIT VISAS

3.11

[NB:]

Malawi has been added to the list of countries whose nationals require transit visas (Immigration (Passenger Transit Visa) (Amendment) Order 2006, SI 2006/493).

[NB – Footnote 1:]

Add Malawi to the list of transit visa countries: Immigration (Passenger Transit Visa) (Amendment) Order 2006, SI 2006/493.

3.12

[NB:]

The changes in the Immigration Rules in HC 645 are important. They represent the second phase of changes to UK entry clearance requirements. The initial phase came into effect on 13 November 2003. This made entry clearance mandatory for non-visa nationals wishing to stay in the UK for more than six months, who were nationals of 10 countries: United States, Canada, South Africa, Singapore, Malaysia, South Korea, Hong Kong (but not British Nationals (Overseas)), Japan, Australia and New Zealand. They were known as 'specified nationals'. They have now gone and HC 395, Appendix 3 in which the countries of specified nationals was listed was deleted by HC 645. The second phase came in on 13 November 2005 and from this date all non-EEA non-visa nationals seeking leave to enter for a period of more than six months require prior entry clearance.[1] The second phase is designed to accompany the implementation of what the Home Office describe as a 'more secure EU uniform residence permit for third country nationals', a format agreed under EC Regulation 1030/2002. One advantage of the new scheme for those planning a long stay in the UK is that prior entry clearance not only provides greater certainty of their status but will also be less expensive than applying for a resident's permit in the UK.[2] These new provisions will not apply to the five categories of British national, who do not have a right of abode in the UK, British Nationals (Overseas), BOTCs, BOCs, BPPs and persons who under the British Nationality Act 1981 are British subjects.[3] Because of their special status they will continue to be able to travel to the UK without prior entry clearance and apply for leave to enter the UK on arrival. Non-visa nationals seeking to come to Britain for a period not exceeding six months as a visitor or for some other purpose, for which prior entry clearance is not required, will be able to do so without obtaining any prior entry clearance.[4] British Nationals (Overseas) and other categories of British Nationals without a right of abode can come to the UK for any purpose for which prior entry clearance is not required and even if they are seeking leave to enter for more than six months they will be granted leave for a period of up to six months (HC 395 para 23B, inserted by HC 645).

1 HC 395, para 24, as amended by HC 645.
2 Explanatory Memorandum to HC 645, para 7.

[3] HC 395, para 24(2), as amended by HC 645.
[4] HC 395, para 23A, as substituted by HC 645.

The application

3.16

[Delete the last 2 sentences and insert:]

Applicants, applying to posts in any country, may be required to provide a record of their fingerprints and photographs of their faces. For this to be done they may be required to attend a British Diplomatic mission or Consular post, a Diplomatic mission or Consular post of another state, or other premises nominated for their fingerprints or photographs to be taken.[8] A failure to provide fingerprints or a facial photograph entitles the entry clearance officer to treat the application as invalid.[9]

[Footnote 8 should now read:]

The Immigration (Provision of Physical Data) Regulations 2003, as amended, have been revoked and replaced by the Immigration (Provision of Physical Data) Regulations 2006, SI 2006/1743, which came into force on 4 July 2006. The Regulations apply to any person applying for entry clearance and not just to applications in particular countries, as before – these countries were Congo, Djibouti, Eritrea, Ethiopia, Holland, Kenya, Rwanda, Sri Lanka, Tanzania, Uganda and Vietnam. The same safeguards for children under 16 apply, as before, under reg 4 of the new Regulations.

[Footnote 9 should now read:]

SI 2003/1875, reg 5 has now been replaced by SI 2006/1743, reg 7. An application is not be invalid if the applicant is a refugee, seeking leave to enter the United Kingdom, and presents a convention travel document endorsed with an entry clearance for that journey to the UK. The application will not be treated as invalid but it may be refused if he does not provide a record of his fingerprints or a photograph of his face as required: reg 7(2) and (3).

The Channel Tunnel

3.26 & 3.27

[NB:]

The Channel Tunnel (International Arrangements) Order 1993 and the Channel Tunnel (Miscellaneous Provisions) Order 1994 have been further amended by the Channel Tunnel (International Arrangements) (Amendment) Order 2006 (SI 2006/2626), and the Channel Tunnel (Miscellaneous Provisions) (Amendment) Order 2006 (SI 2006/2627), respectively. The Orders were made on 29 September 2006.

3.28

[NB:]

The Nationality, Immigration and Asylum Act 2002 (Juxtaposed Controls) (Amendment) Order 2006, amends the Nationality, Immigration and Asylum (Juxtaposed Controls) Order 2003, SI 2003/2818, which privatises the power search vehicles in a UK control zone at a juxtaposed control at Calais, Dunkerque or Boulogne, and to detain and persons hidden inside and provides for the taking of fingerprints under s 141 of the Immigration and Asylum Act 1999 in a UK control zone at these same locations.

EXAMINATION AT THE POINT OF ENTRY

Who is examined

3.35

[NB:]

The power of immigration officers to examine and detain documents is amended by s 27 of IAN 2006 by deleting Sch 2, para 4(2A) of the Immigration Act 1971 and substituting a new para 4(4). The amendment enables immigration officers to require incoming passengers to provide biometric information (such as fingerprints or features of the iris) in order to ascertain whether the passenger in question is the rightful holder of the passport or other document produced.[1]

Amendment is also made to s 141 of the Immigration and Asylum Act 1999 which allows police, immigration officers and other authorised officials to fingerprint passengers. The amendments enable fingerprints to be taken and stored from a person who has been detained as well as arrested under Sch 2 of the 1971 Act.[2] Section 29 of IAN 2006 contains further provisions relating to attendance at specified places for fingerprinting under s 142 of the Immigration and Asylum Act 1999.

1 Immigration Act 1971, Sch 2, para 4(5), inserted by IAN 2006, s 27, which came into force on 31 August 2006: Immigration, Asylum and Nationality Act 2006 (Commencement No 2) Order 2006, SI 2006/2226.

2 IAN 2006, s 28, which came into force on 31 August 2006: Immigration, Asylum and Nationality Act 2006 (Commencement No 2) Order 2006, SI 2006/2226.

[Delete the sentence before footnote 7 and insert:]

Those seeking leave to enter who present a UN convention travel document endorsed with entry clearance may be required by an immigration officer to provide a record of fingerprints and a photograph of their face.[7]

7 The Immigration (Provision of Physical Data) Regulations 2003, as amended, have been revoked and replaced by the Immigration (Provision of Physical Data) Regulations 2006, SI 2006/1743, which came into force on 4 July 2006.

[NB – Footnote 8:]

Directive 2004/38/EC (the 'Citizens' Directive) of 29 April 2004 on the right of citizens of the Union and their family members to move and reside freely within the territory of the Member States, has replaced 68/360/EEC and 73/148/EEC as from 30 April 2006. See chapter 7, below.

Passenger information

3.36

[NB:]

IAN 2006, s 31 will make yet further amendments to the most amended provision of all the immigration laws, para 27 of Sch 2 to the Immigration Act 1971 to enable the collection of passenger lists and crew information in advance of the arrival of a ship or aircraft into the UK and not just on arrival. The duty to provide this information will be placed on owners and agents and not just captains.

Temporary admission

3.37A

[Add new paragraph:]

Temporary admission has been the subject of some scrutiny in three important recent decisions of the House of Lords and Court of Appeal:

- *Szoma v Secretary of State for the Department of Work and Pensions* [2005] UKHL 64, [2006] 1 AC 564, [2006] 1 All ER 1, [2005] 3 WLR 955;
- *R (on the application of Khadir) v Secretary of State for the Home Department* [2005] UKHL 39, [2006] 1 AC 207, [2005] 4 All ER 114, [2005] 3 WLR 1; and
- *S v Secretary of State for the Home Department (sub nom R (on the application of GG) v Secretary of State for the Home Department)* [2006] EWCA Civ 1157, [2006] All ER (D) 30 (Aug).

3.37B

[Add new paragraph:]

Under para 16 of Sch 2 to the Immigration Act 1971 the following non-British persons are liable to be detained:

(i) **pending** examination and **pending** a decision to give or refuse leave to enter, if they are seeking leave to enter para 16(1);
(ii) **pending** examination **and pending** a decision to cancel their leave to enter or remain, where they arrive at a port of entry with that leave and it is suspended by an immigration officer (para 16(1A) read with para 2A);
(iii) **pending** a decision to remove or **pending** removal from the UK on reasonable suspicion that they are someone in respect of whom removal directions can be given, because the person has been refused leave to enter (para 8), is an illegal entrant (para 9), is an overstayer or breacher

of conditions attached to his or her leave (Immigration and Asylum Act 1999, s 10(7)); or is the member of the family of any of these (Sch 2, para 10A).

Temporary admission may be given to any of the above persons under Sch 2, para 21 of the Immigration Act 1971. Section 67 of NIAA 2002 has made it clear that even those awaiting removal on a long-term basis, in the circumstances set out in that section, should ordinarily do so under the temporary admission regime.

3.37C

[Add new paragraph:]

Temporary admission is a bit of a hybrid animal. It is half way between leave to enter or remain and detention. But for those who have arrived in the UK and have not been given leave to enter, it means they are deemed not yet to have entered the UK under the deeming provisions of s 11 of the Act (see 3.5 of the main text). The purpose of the deeming provision has been a matter of some debate. Is it to protect someone given temporary admission from being prosecuted for entering the UK without leave under s 24(1)(a) of the 1971 Act? In *Kaya v Haringey London Borough Council*[1] the Court of Appeal took this line, drawing on the speech of Lord Bridge in *Musisi*[2] In *Szoma v Secretary of State for the Home Department*[3] the House of Lords said they were wrong. The deeming provision was to exclude the person given temporary admission from the rights (in particular the right to seek an extension of leave) given to those granted leave to enter.[4] Lord Brown at para 25 said it would be quite wrong to carry the fiction beyond its originally intended purpose so as to deem a person in fact lawfully here not to be here at all.[5]

1 [2001] EWCA Civ 677, [2002] HLR 1, [2001] All ER (D) 15 (May).
2 One of the cases decided in *Bugdaycay v Secretary of State for the Home Department* [1987] AC 514, [1987] 1 All ER 940, [1987] 2 WLR 606, [1987] Imm AR 250, HL.
3 [2005] UKHL 64, [2006] 1 AC 564, [2006] 1 All ER 1, [2005] 3 WLR 955 (the case was about whether a person on TA was 'lawfully present' for the purposes of the Social Security Consequential Amendment Regulations 2000, SI 2000/263, and was eligible for welfare benefits).
4 Lord Brown said at para 24 that *Re Musisi* was rightly decided but for the wrong reasons.
5 This decision is in line with the ECtJ which has rejected the fiction of temporary admission in *R (on the application of Yiadom) v Secretary of State for the Home Department: C-357/98* [2000] ECR I-9265, [2001] All ER (EC) 267, [2001] 2 CMLR 132, [2000] All ER (D) 1760, ECJ in holding that the safeguards against expulsion of those enjoying Treaty rights apply equally to those physically in the country for a period of time pending a decision on admission. See further 3.5 of the main text.

3.37D

[Add new paragraph:]

The other two cases are concerned with the increasing use and length of temporary admission, which can mean that people remain physically in the UK for years, and may have married and had children, but still do not get leave to enter. In *Khadir*[1] the Appellant was Iraqi Kurd who came to the UK clandestinely in the back of a lorry and unsuccessfully claimed asylum. He came from the Kurdish Autonomous Area ('KAA') of northern Iraq and in that area would have no well-founded fear of persecution. But there was a problem. Although he would be safe in the KAA, the Secretary of State had no safe means of enforcing his return there. He claimed he should stop being on temporary admission and should be granted leave to enter. The House of Lords ruled against him. He still remained liable to detention under para 16 of Sch 2 of the Immigration Act 1971 **pending** removal. The House held that 'pending' meant 'until'. Lord Brown drew a distinction between liability to be detained and the exercise of the power. So persons are 'liable to be detained' within the meaning of Sch 2 where the power to detain them exists even if it would not be a proper **exercise** of that power actually to do so. This distinction between the **existence** of a power and its **exercise** meant the House was able to distinguish the case law which says that it is unlawful to detain someone pending removal if there is no reasonable prospect of removal.[2] The result is not entirely satisfactory, because it means that 'pending' is used as a preposition (meaning 'until') for the purpose of its existence, but as adjectivally for the purpose of its proper exercise by continuing to detain. But there is a certain practicality in the decision, because the House also recognizes that if there comes a point where there is no realistic prospect of removal then leave should be given. In *S v Secretary of State for the Home Department (sub nom R (on the application of GG) v Secretary of State for the Home Department)* (the Afghan highjack case),[3] the story was different. The Appellants could not be removed to Afghanistan because there they would face torture, imprisonment and death. A panel of three adjudicators had ruled to this effect on 8 June 2004. At that point the men unquestionably qualified under paras 2.6 and 5.1 of the Discretionary Leave API for a grant of six months' Discretionary Leave. For a long time afterwards the Secretary of State did nothing. Then he changed the text of the API to give himself a new power to enable the men to be '*kept or placed on temporary admission or temporary release*'. In a powerful and scathing judgment the Court of Appeal held that temporary admission under para 21 did not extend to this kind of situation. The case was entirely distinguishable from *Kadir,* because here there was no possibility of removal. Furthermore, it was beyond the powers of the Secretary of State to introduce a new category of 'persons temporarily admitted' without Parliamentary sanction. Leave to enter needed to be given.

1 *R (on the application of Khadir) v Secretary of State for the Home Department* [2005] UKHL 39, [2006] 1 AC 207, [2005] 4 All ER 114, [2005] 3 WLR 1.

2 *R v Governor of Durham Prison, ex p Singh* [1984] 1 All ER 983, [1984] 1 WLR 704 at 706, QB; *Re Mahmod (Wasfi Suleman)* [1995] Imm AR 311, QB; *R (on the application of I) v Secretary of State for the Home Department* [2002] EWCA Civ 888, [2002] All ER (D) 243 (Jun), [2003] INLR 196; and *Tan Te Lam v Superintendent of Tai A Chau Detention Centre* [1997] AC 97, [1996] 4 All ER 256, [1996] 2 WLR 863, 140 Sol Jo LB 106, PC.

3 [2006] EWCA Civ 1157, [2006] All ER (D) 30 (Aug).

GENERAL GROUNDS FOR REFUSING ENTRY CLEARANCE OR LEAVE TO ENTER

The mandatory and discretionary grounds

3.50

[NB:]

In *RM (Kwok On Tong: HC 395 para 320) India*[1] it was held that only the first seven sub-paras of para 320 prevent the claimant succeeding. Under the later subparagraphs, although the presumption is clearly against entry clearance, there is no bar on a grant of entry clearance. A grant of entry clearance would not, therefore, conflict with the Rules.

An Immigration Judge is, therefore, entitled to allow an appeal even if he or she considers that one (or more) of the later subparagraphs apply to the case.

1 [2006] UKAIT 00039 (18 April 2006).

Excluded persons under international obligations

3.70

[NB:]

The schedule to the Immigration (Designation of Travel Bans) Order 2000 has been replaced by the schedule to the Immigration (Designation of Travel Bans) (Amendment) Order 2005, SI 2005/3310, which came into force on 6 December 2005. The later amendment order in SI 2003/3285 has been revoked by the 2005 Order. The effect of substituting the schedule is to add to, and delete from, the list of designated instruments, which consist of Resolutions of the UN Security Council and Common Positions adopted by the Council of Europe relating to terrorist organisations, and to make some technical amendments to the list. In the new schedule one of the UN resolutions relating to Al-Qua'ida and the Taliban (Resolution 1455 (2003)) of 17 January 2003 has been deleted.

[NB – Footnote 4:]

The most recent version of the schedule is contained in SI 2005/3310.

RIGHTS OF APPEAL

3.76

[NB:]

Sections 88, 90 and 91 of NIAA 2002 have now been replaced by a new s 88A by s 4 of IAN 2006. The new section limits all appeals against refusal of entry clearance to human rights and race discrimination grounds, with the exception of family visitors and people wishing to join dependants in the UK, who retain a full right of appeal. But regulations can now be made which will define in detail the relationships, degree of dependency and circumstances which count for these categories. In particular, regulations may specify that the UK sponsor should be lawfully settled in the UK, or that individuals involved should have resided together for a certain length of time.[1] For applicants who are refused entry clearance in any other category there will remain a right of appeal on both human rights and race discrimination grounds.[2]

Section 43 of IAN 2006 provides that the Secretary of State must lay a report before parliament on the operation of the entry clearance system and the effect of removing rights of appeal within three years of the commencement of s 4.

[Footnote 1 should now read:]

Nationality, Immigration and Asylum Act 2002, ss 82, 88 and 89, as amended by IAN 2006, ss 5 and 6.

[Footnote 2 – add at end:]

At end of footnote add: Monitoring is now extended to refusals of entry clearance that carry only a limited right of appeal: s 23(1) of IAA 1999, as amended by IAN 2006, s 4(2).

1 NIAA 2002, s 88A (2), as amended by IAN 2006, s 4.
2 NIAA 2002, s 88A(3), as amended by IAN 2006, s 4.

Chapter 4

CONTROL AFTER ENTRY

EXTENDING AND VARYING LEAVE

4.2

[NB:]

Phase 2 of the Home Office scheme to require everyone who wishes to stay in the UK for longer than six months to obtain prior entry clearance came into force on 13 November 2005 by the rule changes in HC 645. The category of 'specified nationals' has gone and all non-visa nationals who are seeking to come to the UK for more than six months now have to seek prior entry clearance. An exception is made for British Nationals (Overseas) and other categories of British nationals without a right of abode in the UK (HC 395, para 24(2), as substituted by HC 645). With an entry clearance, they will not need to apply for a UK residence permit. The entry clearance is in the form of a vignette or sticker placed in the passport at a visa-issuing post overseas. British nationals without the right of abode who wish to stay for more than six months will be given six months leave to enter and advice to apply to the Home Office for leave to remain which will be in the form of a residence permit (HC 395 para 24, as substituted by HC 645).

Leave to remain

4.5

[NB – Footnote 4:]

Section 3C of the Immigration Act 1971 has been amended by IAN 2006, s 11, which came into force on 31 August 2006: Immigration, Asylum and Nationality Act 2006 (Commencement No 2) Order 2006, SI 2006/2226.

[NB – Footnote 8:]

HC 395, para 23A has been amended by HC 645 which took effect on 13 November 2005.

Variation of leave to enter or remain

4.6

[NB – Footnote 3:]

Where leave is revoked, s 3D of the Immigration Act 1971, as inserted by IAN 2006, s 11(5), now extends the person's leave during any period when that person can bring an in-country appeal against the revocation (ignoring any possibility of an appeal out of time with permission) or an in-country appeal against it is pending. See also notes at 5.11.

Applying for variation of leave

4.7

[NB:]

At present applications for leave to remain or a variation of leave by non-EEA nationals must in general be made on compulsory prescribed application forms under the provisions of s 31A of the Immigration Act 1971. In future, the way in which these applications are to be made and the forms which are to be used will be prescribed in the Immigration Rules.[1] The Immigration (Leave to Remain) (Prescribed Forms and Procedures) Regulations 2005 have now been replaced by the Immigration (Leave to Remain) (Prescribed Forms and Procedures) (Amendment) 2006, SI 2006/1548 which came into force on 22 June 2006. The forms prescribed by these regulations are largely the same as the forms prescribed by the earlier ones although there are changes to existing questions and new questions have been added to reflect rule changes affecting certain categories of applicant. There are also two new categories of applicant: overseas qualified nurse or midwife, and visiting religious worker or religious worker in a non-pastoral role, for whom forms are prescribed.

1 These are cosmetic changes brought about by IAN 2006, s 50(1) and (2); s 31A is repealed (s 50(3)). Section 50 was not yet in force as at 1 October 2006.

[NB – Footnote 4:]

Immigration Act 1971, s 31A remains in force but will eventually be replaced by IAN 2006, s 50, For references to the Immigration (Leave to Remain) (Prescribed Forms and Procedures) Regulations 2005 substitute the Immigration (Leave to Remain) (Prescribed Forms and Procedures) Regulations 2006, SI 2006/1421, as corrected by Amendment Regulations 2006/1548. Regulations 3(2), 9(3) and 12(3) of SI 2006/1421 exempt asylum claimants and their dependants and EC Association Agreement applicants from using a number of these forms.

[NB – Footnote 5:]

Immigration (Leave to Remain) (Prescribed Forms and Procedures) Regulations 2005, SI 2005/771 are replaced by Immigration (Leave to Remain) (Prescribed Forms and Procedures) Regulations 2006, SI 2006/1421, as corrected by SI 2006/1548.

[NB – Footnote 6:]

The Immigration (Leave to Remain) (Prescribed Forms and Procedures) (Amendment) Regulations 2004, SI 2004/581 and Immigration (Leave to Remain) (Prescribed Forms and Procedures) Regulations 2005, SI 2005/771 are now revoked and replaced by Immigration (Leave to Remain) (Prescribed Forms and Procedures) Regulations 2006, SI 2006/1421, as corrected by SI 2006/1548.

[NB – Footnote 7:]

Immigration (Leave to Remain) (Prescribed Forms and Procedures) Regulations 2005, SI 2005/771 are now replaced by Immigration (Leave to Remain) (Prescribed Forms and Procedures) Regulations 2006, SI 2006/1421, reg 13.

4.8

[NB – Footnote 1:]

Immigration (Leave to Remain) (Prescribed Forms and Procedures) Regulations 2005, reg 13(1)–(3) have been revoked and replaced by SI 2006/1421, reg 14(1)–(3).

[NB – Footnote 7:]

Immigration (Leave to Remain) (Prescribed Forms and Procedures) Regulations 2005, reg 14 is now revoked and replaced by Immigration (Leave to Remain) (Prescribed Forms and Procedures) Regulations 2006, SI 2006/1421, reg 15.

4.9

[NB – Footnote 3:]

SI 2005/771, reg 14 has now been revoked and replaced by SI 2006/1421, reg 15.

Fees

4.10

[In second sentence s 5 of the Immigration and Asylum Act 1999 will be replaced by s 51 of IAN 2006 when that section comes into force, but it will be a change of name rather than of substance.]

[In the third line the reference to s 52 of the Asylum and Immigration (Treatment of Claimants etc) Act 2004 should read s 42.]

4.11

[NB – Footnote 1:]

For the Immigration (Leave to Remain) (Prescribed Forms and Procedures) Regulations 2005, SI 2005/771, reg 23(2)(c) read SI 2006/1421, reg 14(2)(b).

Leaving the UK

4.14

[NB – Footnote 1:]

For Immigration (Leave to Remain) (Prescribed Forms and Procedures) Regulations 2005, SI 2005/771 read Immigration (Leave to Remain) (Prescribed Forms and Procedures) Regulations 2006, SI 2006/1421, as amended by SI 2006/1548.

[NB – Footnote 3:]

For a statutory continuation of leave after revocation, see 4.6 above and notes at 5.11 on the new Immigration Act 1971, s 3D, inserted by IAN 2006, s 11(5).

Variation of leave by statute

4.17

[NB:]

Section 11 of IAN 2006, which came into force on 31 August 2006,[1] amends s 3C of the Immigration Act 1971 which currently extends leave to enter or remain in the UK if that leave would otherwise expire while an application for renewal is being considered and for such time as an appeal against a decision to curtail or refuse to vary leave could be brought or is pending. The new s 3D(2)(b), (c) makes it clear that leave will only be extended when an in-country appeal may be brought or is pending. It is often not possible to decide an application for an extension of leave to remain until after the period of leave has expired. One potential problem with the present drafting of s 3C is that it only expressly provides for an application to be regarded as having been decided when notice of such decision is given in accordance with regulations made under s 105 of the Nationality, Immigration and Asylum Act 2002. The Regulations made under s 105 are the Immigration (Notices) Regulations 2003 and provide for notice of those decisions which give rise to a right of appeal to the Asylum and Immigration Tribunal. The Regulations do not provide for notification of any decision which does not give rise to such a right of appeal. On a literal interpretation of s 3C(6) this would mean that an application for further leave was not to be regarded as having been decided where the decision on the application was not appealable. A decision to grant the application or a decision to refuse the application where the applicant continues to enjoy leave under the initial grant would not give rise to a right of appeal. The Immigration (Continuation of Leave) (Notice) Regulations 2006, SI 2006/2170, which came into force on 31 August 2006, remove the possibility on this construction being placed on s 3C by providing that an application is to be regarded as having been decided either when a notice of an appealable decision is given under the Immigration (Notices) Regulations 2003 or when written notice of an unappealble decision is given in accordance with s 4(1) of the Immigration Act 1971.

Section 3C(6) of the 1971 Act is replaced by a new provision allowing the Secretary of State to make regulations to define when an application is decided and what types of notice may do so, thus terminating leave extended by s 3C.[2]

1 Immigration, Asylum and Nationality Act 2006 (Commencement No 2) Order 2006, SI 2006/2226.

2 IAN 2006, s 11(4).

4.18

[NB:]

Note that s 3C of the Immigration Act 1971 referred to in the first sentence of the paragraph has been amended by IAN 2006, s 11 and a new s 3D has been inserted to allow extensions of leave following curtailment or revocation of a leave to enter or remain.

The 'no switching' rule

4.26

[NB:]

No visitors, entering the UK on or after 1 July 2006, can now switch to student (see 9.25 below). As regards doctors, dentists and student nurses and midwives, it should be noted that the rules have been radically recast.[1] There are now two intermediate 'stepping stone' categories to full work permit or similar status. The first is the *SEGS* scheme, whose requirements have recently been liberalised (see below at 10.109). The second allows students who have obtained qualifications in Scotland to switch to the *Fresh Talent: Working in Scotland Scheme* under HC 395, paras 143A to 143F (see 10.110A below). Those admitted in a temporary capacity can stay on under the marriage or civil partnership rules at HC 395, para 295D, as amended by HC 582, and those admitted for marriage or civil partnership may stay for contact with children under HC 395, para 248A, as amended by HC 582.

1 See 9.45ff below for doctors and dentists; and 10.30Aff for overseas nurses and midwives. As regards transitional provisions for doctor visitors being allowed to follow certain courses, see 9.45C below.

[NB – Footnote 3:]

HC 395, para 98(i) has been repealed by HC 302. There is now no scope for switching to working holiday maker under the rules.

General grounds for refusing variations and curtailing leave

4.27

[NB:]

Ground (9) for refusing an extension of leave is a failure to produce within a reasonable time documents or other evidence required by the Secretary of State to establish a claim to remain under the rules. This has now been amended by HC 104 to include information as well as documents or other evidence. This additional ground for refusing an application could arise where the applicant has failed to provide information requested on the application form or where the applicant has failed to provide information requested in addition to that already provided in the application form.

4.28

[NB:]

Where leave is curtailed and there is an in-country right of appeal,[1] a new s 3D inserted by s 11(5) of IAN 2006 now extends the 'curtailed' or revoked leave so long as an in-country appeal against revocation or curtailment may be brought or is pending. It replaces the provisions of s 82(3) of the NIAA 2002, which used a different mechanism to achieve the same result, namely, that curtailment or revocation should not take effect while an appeal could be made or was pending. The only difference now is that this operates only if it is an in-country appeal.

1 See Nationality, Immigration and Asylum Act 2002 Act, s 82(3)(e).

Recourse to public funds

4.32

[For 'spouse' in the penultimate line, read 'spouse and civil partner'.]

REGISTRATION WITH THE POLICE

4.37

[NB:]

A requirement to register with the police should not be imposed on a civil partner under HC 395, paras 326(2), 9(iv), as amended by HC 582.

CONTROL OF DEPARTURE

Right to depart – Immigration Officers' powers

4.42

[NB:]

There have been big changes in the power of Immigration Officers to examine departing passengers. Currently this can only be done to establish nationality and identity. Now s 42 of IAN 2006 has amended paras 3 and 16 of Sch 2 to the Immigration Act 1971 to cover three additional kinds of information:

- whether the passenger's entry to the UK was lawful;
- whether the passenger has complied with any conditions of his or her leave in the UK;
- whether the passenger's return to the UK is prohibited or restricted.[1]

If a cursory investigation into these matters is not enough, the Immigration Officer can require the passenger to submit to further examination by giving him or her written notice And can detain him or her for a maximum of 12 hours pending the completion of that further examination.[2] Section 42(4) states that para 21 of Sch 2 to the 1971 Act, which makes provision for temporary admission, does not apply to the detention of departing passengers. This has presumably been done on the basis that a maximum of 12 hours detention does not make temporary admission necessary. These powers must be so exercised as not to infringe EEA national right to free movement under community law.

1 IAN 2006, s 42(2).
2 IAN 2006, s 42(3).

Chapter 5

SETTLEMENT AND RETURN

SETTLEMENT

Residence in breach of the immigration laws

5.9

[NB – Footnote 3:]

Mark v Mark has now been upheld in the House of Lords: [2005] UKHL 42, [2005] INLR 614.

Consequences of being settled

5.11

[NB:]

Where revocation of indefinite leave attracts an in-country right of appeal[1] a new s 3D of the Immigration Act 1971[2] will extend the revoked leave and replace the provisions in s 82(3) of the NIAA 2002, which use a different mechanism to achieve the same result, namely, that curtailment or revocation should not take effect while an appeal is pending.

1 See NIAA 2002, s 82(2)(f).
2 Inserted by IAN 2006, s 11(5).

[Footnote 3 – add at end:]

The right of appeal against removal under NIAA 2002, s 82(2)(g) now applies to a decision to remove by way of directions under the Act of 2000, s 10(1)(ba) (IAN 2006, s 2). This will give the person a separate right of appeal at each of the two decision stages: the first at the revocation stage and the second at the stage when the decision to remove is taken. The Home Office explain that this separation of appeal rights is considered necessary in light of the importance of refugee status (Explanatory Notes on IAN 2006, para 16). No decision to remove will be taken while an appeal against revocation is pending.

Settlement under the Immigration Rules

5.13

[NB:]

Although categories like student and working holiday do not directly lead to settlement, they may now do so indirectly by the loosening of the previous inflexibility of switching. For example, students can now enter the world of work in a variety of ways, if they have the right qualifications (see 9.30) and working holiday makers can do much the same (see 9.67). There are also three intermediate categories of employment or training which are stepping stones to settlement categories. These are: the *SEGS* scheme (see 10.109 below); the *Fresh Talent: Working in Scotland Scheme* (see 10.110A below); and overseas qualified nurses or midwives (see 10.30B below).

All references to 'spouses' should now read 'spouses and civil partners': see changes set out in HC 582 which took effect on 5 December 2005.

Footnotes 2 and 3 should be deleted. HC 395, para 98 referred to in fn 3 was deleted by HC 302.

5.14

[NB:]

For all employment related categories of entry to the UK the qualifying period for settlement ('indefinite leave to remain') is now five years.[1] This means that they will have to spend five years working in the UK before being eligible to apply for settlement. According to the Home Office this brings the UK in line with the European norm for these purposes.[2]

1 HC 1016 which took effect on 3 April 2006. Footnotes 1–8 of the main text have to be amended accordingly.

2 Explanatory Memorandum to the Statement of Changes in Immigration Rules laid on 30 March 2006 (HC 1016). See also 5.16 below.

5.15

[NB:]

For the reference to settlement after four years, amend to 'four or five years'.

5.16

[NB:]

Directive 2004/38/EC consolidates the provisions made in a number of repealed EC Directives, but it also introduces a new permanent right of residence in a host Member State, which generally applies after five years residence, provided that during this period the individual has been exercising a Treaty right (ie employment, self-employment, studying or self-sufficiency). Regulations 15 and 18 of the Immigration (EEA) Regulations 2006, which came into force on 30 April 2006, transpose this right into UK domestic law and apply it to all EEA nationals and their family members. HC 395, para 290A is amended[1] so that an EEA national who holds a registration certificate or a document certifying permanent residence issued under the 2006 EEA Regulations[2] is to be regarded as present and settled in the United Kingdom. See further chapter 7.

1 HC 1053.

[2] This includes an EEA national who holds a residence permit issued under the Immigration (European Economic Area) Regulations 2000 which is treated as if it were such a certificate or document by virtue of Sch 4 to the 2006 EEA Regulations.

5.17

[NB:]

The reference to 'bereaved spouses' should read 'bereaved spouse and civil partners': see changes set out in HC 582, which took effect on 5 December 2005.

Chapter 6

COMMON TRAVEL AREA, CREW MEMBERS AND EXEMPTED GROUPS

COMMON TRAVEL AREA

The Irish exceptions

Leave required

6.7

[NB:]

In *R v Javaherifard* [2005] EWCA Crim 3231, [2006] Imm AR 185, the Court of Appeal held that entry to the UK occurred at the point where someone crossed the border from the Republic into Northern Ireland and not at the point where they first present a passport. Section 11, which deals with entry into the United Kingdom has no application to entry by land, only to entries by boat and ship. Although the provision in s 11(2) in relation to the Common Travel Area and local journeys has the effect of making the Act generally neutral in relation to such journeys, it was necessary to exclude them from s 11(1) because someone arriving by ship or air from within the Common Travel Area could otherwise never disembark in law and thus could never enter or be an illegal entrant. Such a person could also move from UK port to UK port until he or she found one where there was no actual control and then enter after a local journey.

Immigration laws in the Islands

6.11

[NB:]

The fate of the Isle of Man's first asylum seeker could lie in the hands of Lieutenant Governor. At the moment, if an asylum seeker arrives in the Island via the common travel area, the rule is they are shipped back to the UK or Ireland. It is more complicated in the case of those who may arrive from outside the CTA. As the Island is not a state for the purposes of asylum and has no asylum legislation, it cannot provide asylum in its own right.

Chapter 7

EUROPEAN COMMUNITY LAW AND RELATED OBLIGATIONS

INTRODUCTION

7.1

[NB:]

The main changes which have taken place since the 6th edition have been the accession of two further states to the European Union, Bulgaria and Romania and the implementation of the Citizens' Directive[1] into UK domestic law by the deadline date of 30 April 2006 through the Immigration (European Economic Area) Regulations 2006.[2] The Citizens' Directive merges into a single instrument all the legislation on the right of entry and residence for Union citizens, consisting of two regulations and nine directives. There are some important new provisions, but for the most part the Citizens' Directive codifies and simplifies. So a very large number of references in the chapter need to be revised (i) to fit in with the Directive and (ii) to take into account the new domestic transposition of the Directive into domestic law through the 2006 Regulations. The 2006 Regulations replace the 2000 Regulations which they revoke (except for the provisions on posted workers which are required to make sense of the Swiss posted worker provisions). All the various amendments to the 2000 Regulations are also revoked though the Immigration (Swiss Free Movement of Persons) (No 3) Regulations 2002 are retained for posted workers. It should be noted that the 2006 Regulations are designed to implement the Directive, not the other way around. If the Regulations are not in conformity with the Directive (and EU law in general) then it is the Regulations which must be struck down and EU law which is to prevail. We deal below with one major area where we think that the Regulations are out of step with community law.

1 Directive 2004/38/EC of the European Parliament and of the Council of 29 April 2004 on the right of citizens of the Union and their family members to move and reside freely within the territory of the Member States, amending Regulation (EEC) No 1612/68 and repealing Directives 64/221/EEC, 68/360/EEC, 72/194/EEC, 73/148/EEC, 75/34/EEC, 75/35/EEC, 90/364/EEC, 90/365/EEC and 93/96/EEC on 30 April 2006 (reg 38). It came into force on 30 April 2004, and had to be implemented by Member States on 30 April 2006.

2 SI 2006/1003.

ACCESSION OF NEW MEMBER STATES

7.5

[NB:]

The European Union (Accessions) Act 2006 approves the Treaty of Accession of Bulgaria and Romania to the EU on 1 January 2007. Section 2 of the Act gives the Secretary of State the power to make regulations about free movement rights for nationals of those two countries. No regulations have yet been made.

Registration scheme for workers in accession period

7.12

[NB:]

The government announced in May 2006 that the registration scheme would continue after 1 May 2006, noting that applicants have helped fill vacancies in parts of the economy experiencing shortages of labour.

SCOPE OF FREE MOVEMENT RIGHTS

Territorial scope

7.53

[NB:]

The reference to the Immigration (European Economic Area) Regulations 2000, SI 2000/2326, should now be read as a reference to the Immigration (European Economic Area) Regulations 2006, SI 2006/1003, and footnote 1 should be amended accordingly. The new Regulations, like the 2000 regulations, do not address the question of the territorial scope of the EC Treaty, but deal with an initial right of residence of an EEA national and an extended right of residence of a 'qualified person' purely in terms of the personal scope of the Treaties. Initial admission under reg 11 and an extended right of residence under reg 14 give effect in UK domestic law to the right of admission and right of residence only as regards the UK.

PERSONAL SCOPE (1) NATIONALS

EU and EEA nationals

7.54

[NB:]

The Citizens' Directive, which has consolidated and codified much of the subsidiary legislation on free movement makes it clear that the free movement of workers only applies to 'union citizens, which it defines as 'any person having the nationality of a Member State.'[1] The Directive repealed Council Directive (EEC) 68/360, referred to in **footnote 1** as from 30 April 2006.[2]

1 Directive 2004/38/EC, Art 2(1).
2 See n 1 above, Art 38(2).

7.55

[NB:]

All references to the Immigration (European Economic Area) Regulations 2000, SI 2000/2326, should now be read as a reference to the Immigration (European Economic Area) Regulations 2006, SI 2006/1003 ('the 2006 Regulations'). The definition of 'qualified person' is now contained in SI 2006/1003, Regulation 6, and footnote 1 should be changed accordingly. Under the 2006 Regulations no family member is a 'qualified person' and the sentence in the main text prior to footnote 4 and footnote 4 should be deleted. It should also be noted that the *Surinder Singh*[1] situation is now dealt with by reg 9 of the 2006 Regulations (see 7.60 of this supplement below) which no longer uses the fiction that a 'qualified person' is a 'EEA national', but instead uses the fiction that a 'UK national' is an 'EEA national.' Despite these niggly changes our comments in the main text about EEA Regulations remain valid.

1 *R v Immigration Appeal Tribunal and Surinder Singh, ex p Secretary of State for the Home Department: C-370/90* [1992] 3 All ER 798, [1992] ECR I-4265.

UK nationals for EC purposes

7.60

[NB:]

The *Surinder Singh* situation is now dealt with by reg 9 of the 2006 Regulations.[1] The effect of the Regulation is to apply the *Surinder Singh* principle to the family of returning UK nationals who have been workers or self employed in another EEA state. It does so by treating a UK national for these limited purposes as an EEA national.[2] There is no corresponding provision in the Citizens' Directive.[3] However, the Regulation makes very narrow provision for UK nationals who may be exercising community rights and there is, for example, no provision for the *Carpenter*[4] type of situation, where a UK national was held to be exercising community rights by providing services in another EU Member State while retaining UK residence. The 2000 Regulations required that where a UK citizen was seeking to bring a non-EEA national family member with him or her on return from another Member State, that family member must be lawfully resident in an EEA State.[5] This requirement is not repeated in the new Regulation. But lawful residence in an EEA State is one of the alternative requirements for the issue of an EEA family permit by an entry clearance officer under reg 12 of the 2006 Regulations, although its importance is likely to be greatly diminished in the light of the fact that Art 6 of the Citizens' Directive creates a new right of residence for up to three months 'without any conditions or any formalities' and it would be very difficult for the Secretary of State to disprove an assertion of lawful residence at least for this period (see 7.61 below).

1 See para 7.59, fn 1 above (*Surinder Singh*). The Immigration (European Economic Area) Regulations 2006, SI 2006/1003.

2 SI 2006/1003, reg 9(1) and 9(3), whereby the UK national is to be treated as holding a valid passport issues by an EEA State.

3 Directive 2004/38/EC.

[4] *Carpenter v Secretary of State for the Home Department: C-60/00* [2003] QB 416, [2002] ECR I-6279, [2003] All ER (EC) 577, [2003] 2 WLR 267.

[5] SI 2005/47, reg 2, amending SI 2000/2326, reg 11(2)(b).

Non-nationals

7.61

[NB:]

Non-nationals are normally outside the personal scope of the Treaty but, as always, there are exceptions. In the main text we refer to the first of these as 'family members of qualified persons'. This is slightly misleading. Under the Citizens Directive[1] family members of all EU members travelling from one member state to another have a new right residence for up to three months 'without any conditions or any formalities'. For a stay of longer than three months the right applies to family members of qualified persons under the 2006 Regulations.[2]

[1] Directive 2004/38/EC, Art 6, transposed into UK domestic law by Immigration (European Economic Area) Regulations 2006, SI 2006/1003, reg 13.

[2] SI 2006/1003, reg 14.

Internal situations

7.64

[NB:]

In *Ali v Secretary of State for the Home Department*[1] the Court of Appeal found that the rights under Art 18 are expressly stated to be subject to 'the limitations and conditions laid down in this Treaty and by the measures adopted to give it effect' and that this included the various Directives which contain restrictions on the right of residence.

[1] [2006] EWCA Civ 484, [2006] 3 CMLR 326.

PERSONAL SCOPE (2) WORKERS

7.66

[NB:]

In *R (on the application of Payir) v Seretary of State for the Home Department; R (on the application of Ozturk) v Same; R (on the application of Akyuz) v Same*[1], the Court of Appeal found that students and au pairs were workers within the meaning of European law, but this did not necessarily mean that they were eligible to benefit from the Turkish Association Agreement after spending one or more years in 'legal employment' as that term was to be construed in European law. The case was referred to the European Court for a ruling.

[1] [2006] EWCA Civ 541, [2006] ICR 1314.

7.67

[NB:]

Under Art 6 of the Citizens' Directive all EU nationals (and thereby all EEA nationals) get a three months' right of residence irrespective of the purpose of their entry. At the end of the three months, they have aright to remain longer if they are workers. Workers includes job seekers, as defined in *Antonissen.*[1] There is also an additional safeguard contained in Art 14(4)(b) of the Directive, which provides that where Union citizens entered the territory of the host Member State in order to seek employment, they should not be expelled for as long as they can provide evidence that they are continuing to seek employment and that they have a genuine chance of being engaged. The Directive also covers the situation of those who have been on short fixed term contracts or have been in employment for periods of more than or less than one year.[2] These community rights have been transposed into UK domestic law by the 2006 Regulations,[3] which have replaced the 2000 Regulations as from 30 April 2006.

1 *R v Immigration Appeal Tribunal, ex p Antonissen: C-292/89* [1991] ECR I-745, [1991] 2 CMLR 373 at para 10, ECJ.
2 Directive 2004/38/EC, Arts 7(3) and 14.
3 The Immigration (European Economic Area) Regulations 2006, SI 2006/1003, reg 6(2). Regulation 6(2)(b) may not on first sight appear to be a faithful reproduction of the Directive, but it should be noted that sub-paras (a), (b), and (c) are alternatives, not cumulative.

[Delete footnote 10]

PERSONAL SCOPE (3) ESTABLISHMENT

7.70

[NB:]

Council Directive 73/148 was repealed by the Citizens' Directive on 30 April 2006 and its provisions have been incorporated into the Directive in a short and simplified form.[1] The provisions of the 2000 Regulations have been replaced by those of the 2006 Regulations.[2]

1 Directive 2004/38/EC, Art 7.
2 Immigration (European Economic Area) Regulations 2006, SI 2006/1003, reg 6.

[Delete footnote 2]

PERSONAL SCOPE (4) PROVISION AND RECEIPT OF SERVICES

Providing services

7.73

[NB:]

Council Directive (EEC) 73/148, which dealt with services, as well as the right of establishment, was repealed by the Citizens' Directive on 30 April 2006,[1] and all references to Council Directive (EEC) 73/148 in the text and footnotes should be read accordingly. But the Directive is silent on the provision and receipt of services. No reference is made to them. Instead the Directive creates a new right for all union citizens and their families to travel to another member state and reside there for up to three months without any limitation on the purpose of the visit.[2] All those who wish to travel either to provide or receive services will therefore be covered by the new right. If they wish to stay longer, (i) they may have to register their presence with the authorities; and (ii) they will only be able to stay on, if they are self employed or exercising a right of establishment. The case law still holds good that, if something more permanent than a temporary visit is intended, the provisions relating to establishment or workers will apply.[3] These new rights are transposed into UK domestic law for all EEA citizens by the 2006 Regulations.[4] Under reg 11 an EEA national must be admitted to the United Kingdom if he produces on arrival a valid national identity card or passport issued by an EEA State, and is then is entitled to reside in the United Kingdom for a period not exceeding three months under reg 13.

1 Directive 2004/38/EC, Art 38.
2 See n 1 above, Art 6.
3 *Steymann v Staatssecretaris van Justite: 196/87* [1988] ECR 6159, [1989] 1 CMLR 449, ECJ. See further *EC Commission v France: 220/83* [1986] ECR 3663, [1987] 2 CMLR 113, ECJ (co-insurance services); *Rush Portuguesa Lda v ONI: C-113/89* [1990] ECR I-1417, [1991] 2 CMLR 818, ECJ.
4 Immigration (European Economic Area) Regulations 2006, SI 2006/1003, regs 13 and 14.

7.74

[NB:]

The same comments as at 7.73 apply to this paragraph and all references to Council Directive (EEC) 73/148 in the text and footnotes should be read accordingly.

Receiving services

7.77

[NB:]

The same comments as at 7.73 apply to this paragraph and all references to Council Directive (EEC) 73/148 in the text and footnotes should be read accordingly.

PERSONAL SCOPE (5) STUDENTS, THE SELF-SUFFICIENT AND THE RETIRED

Students

7.80

[NB:]

The position regarding students has been altered in form, if not in substance, by the Citizens' Directive becoming fully effective as from 30 April 2006. First, the fact that students may be recipients of services is of little help to their situation in view of the repeal of the service provisions of Council Directive 73/148 and their non-replacement in the Citizens' Directive (see 7.73 above). Secondly, Council Directive 93/96 has been repealed and its provisions replaced by the much simpler provisions of the Citizens' Directive.[1] Thirdly, the 2000 Regulations, which transposed community law into UK domestic law have been replaced by the 2006 Regulations.[2] Although Arts 10 and 11 of Regulation (EEC) 1612/68 on the rights of workers families have been repealed and replaced by the Citizens' Directive, Art 12 of 1612/68, dealing with the educational rights of workers' children has been left unrepealed.[3]

1 Directive 2004/38/EC, Art 7(1)(c) and (d).
2 Immigration (European Economic Area) Regulations 2006, SI 2006/1003. Students are defined in reg 4(1)(d) and are 'qualified persons' under reg 6 and entitled to extended free movement rights under reg 14.
3 Directive 2004/38/EC, Art 38.

7.81

[NB:]

Council Directive 93/96 has been repealed and its provisions replaced by the much simpler provisions of the Citizens' Directive. All references to Council Directive 93/96 in the main text and footnotes should be deleted. Now All Union citizens have the right of residence on the territory of another member State for more than three months, as a student, if they fulfil two main conditions.[1] First, they must be enrolled at a private or public establishment, accredited or financed by the host Member State on the basis of its legislation or administrative practice, for the principal purpose of following a course of study, including vocational training. Secondly, they must have comprehensive sickness insurance cover in the host Member State and assure the relevant national authority, by means of a declaration or by such equivalent means as they may choose, that they have sufficient resources for themselves and their family members not to become a burden on the social assistance system of the host Member State during their period of residence. These provisions of the Directive have been transposed into UK domestic law by the Immigration (European Economic Area) Regulations 2006.[2] Thus students are defined in reg 4(1)(d) and are listed as 'qualified persons' under reg 6 and are thereby entitled to extended free movement rights under reg 14. It should also be noted that if a union citizen has been studying as only a secondary purpose and work has been his or her principal purpose, he or she has better rights than as a student alone.

1 Directive 2004/38/EC, Art 7(1)(c).
2 SI 2006/1003.

7.82

[NB:]

Council Directive 93/96 has been repealed and its provisions regarding family members of students have been replaced by the much simpler provisions of the Citizens' Directive.[1] Under it students, who fulfil the requirements of Art 7(1)(c) can be joined by a spouse or civil partner and dependent children but do not enjoy the rather more generous family provisions for workers and the self-sufficient.[2] These provisions have been transposed into domestic law by the 2006 Regulations.[3] All references to Council Directive 93/96 in the main text and footnotes (wrongly referred to as 93/936) and to the 2000 Regulations should be deleted.

1 Directive 2004/38/EC, Art 7(1)(d).
2 See n 1 above, Arts 2(2) and 7(4).
3 Immigration (European Economic Area) Regulations 2006, SI 2006/1003, reg 7(1) and (2). For extended family members who can join a student, see reg 7(4) and 7.87E of this supplement below.

The self sufficient

7.83

[NB:]

Council Directive 90/364 has been repealed and its provisions replaced by the much simpler provisions of the Citizens' Directive. All references to Council Directive 90/364 in the main text and footnotes should be deleted. Now All Union citizens shall have the right of residence on the territory of another Member State for more than three months if they have sufficient resources for themselves and their family members not to become a burden on the social assistance system of the host Member State during their period of residence and have comprehensive sickness insurance cover.[1] These provisions have been transposed into domestic law by the 2006 Regulations.[2]

1 Directive 2004/38/EC, Art 7(1)(b).
2 Immigration (European Economic Area) Regulations 2006, SI 2006/1003, reg 4(1)(c) and are 'qualified persons' under reg 6 and entitled to extended free movement rights under reg 14.

7.84

[NB:]

Council Directive 90/364 has been repealed and its provisions regarding family members of students have been replaced by the much simpler provisions of the Citizens' Directive.[1] All references to Council Directive 90/364 in the main text and footnotes and to the 2000 Regulations should be deleted. Now the family members who can join the self-sufficient are a spouse or civil partner and any dependent descendants (children or grandchildren) of that person or of the spouse or civil partner and any of their dependent relatives in the ascending line (parents and grandparents).[2] These provisions have been transposed into domestic law by the 2006 Regulations.[3]

1 Directive 2004/38/EC, Art 7(1)(d).
2 See n 1 above, Art 2(2).
3 Immigration (European Economic Area) Regulations 2006, SI 2006/1003, reg 7(1). For extended family members who can join a self sufficient person, see regs 7(3) and 7.87E of this supplement below.

The retired

7.85

[NB:]

Council Directive 90/365 has been repealed and its provisions replaced by those of the Citizens' Directive. All references to Council Directive 90/365 in the main text and footnotes should be deleted. Commission Regulation (EC) No 635/2006 of 25 April 2006 also repeals Regulation (EEC) No 1251/70, which deals with the right to permanent residence of retired and incapacitated workers and frontier workers and with family rights. Its provisions have been replaced by the Citizens' Directive. The result is a complicated and somewhat laborinthine set of provisions, in this case rather easier to follow in the 2006 regulations, which is the Secretary of State's best effort to transpose them into UK law. Now the right of permanent residence in the host Member State can be enjoyed before completion of a continuous period of five years of residence by:

(a) **Retirement** – Workers or self-employed persons who retire from work, having reached the age laid down by the law of that Member State for entitlement to an old age pension or workers who cease paid employment to take early retirement, provided that they have been working in that Member State for at least the preceding twelve months and have resided there continuously for more than three years.[1] The conditions as to length of residence and employment do not apply if the worker's or the self-employed person's spouse or civil partner is a national of the host Member State or has lost the nationality of that Member State by marriage to that worker or self-employed person.[2] This is matched by reg 5(2) of the 2006 Regulations.[3]

(b) **Incapacity** – Workers or self-employed persons who stop working as a result of permanent incapacity and who have either (i) resided continuously in the host Member State for more than two years; or (ii) the incapacity is the result of an accident at work or an occupational disease that entitles him to a pension payable in full or in part by an institution in the host Member State.[4] The condition as to length of residence does not apply if the worker's or the self-employed person's spouse or civil partner is a national of the host Member State or has lost the nationality of that Member State by marriage to that worker or self-employed person.[5] This is matched by reg 5(3) of the 2006 Regulations.[6]

(c) **Frontier workers** – Workers or self-employed persons who, after three years of continuous employment and residence in the host Member State, work in an employed or self-employed capacity in another Member State, while retaining their place of residence in the host Member State, to which they return, as a rule, each day or at least once a week.[7] This is matched by reg 5(4) of the 2006 Regulations.[8]

(d) **Frontier workers** – Who do not qualify for permanent residence in the host state under (c) above, because they cannot satisfy the condition of three years' prior residence and employment in the host state, may qualify under (a) or (b) above by treating their employment in the other member State as if it had taken place in the host member State.[9] This is transposed by reg 5(5) of the 2006 Regulations by reference to the UK (the host country) and another EEA country in a much clearer and understandable way than in the Directive.[10]

(e) **Family members** – Where workers and the self employed acquire permanent residence in one of the above ways, their family members, irrespective of nationality, are entitled to the same thing.[11] Family members may also acquire the right of permanent residence, if the worker or self-employed person dies while still working but before acquiring permanent residence, but there are three conditions which must be fulfilled: either (i) the worker or self-employed person had resided continuously on the territory of that Member State for two years at the time of his or her death; (ii) the death resulted from an accident at work or an occupational disease; or (iii) the surviving spouse lost the nationality of that Member State following marriage to the worker or self-employed person.[12]

In calculating the period spent in employment, periods of involuntary unemployment, periods not worked for reasons not of the person's own making, and absences from work or cessation of work due to illness or accident are to be regarded as periods of employment.[13]

1 Directive 2004/38/EC, Art 17(1)(a). If the law of the host Member State does not grant the right to an old age pension to certain categories of self employed persons, the age condition shall be deemed to have been met once the person concerned has reached the age of 60.
2 Immigration (European Economic Area) Regulations 2006, SI 2006/1003.
3 Directive 2004/38/EC, Art 17(2).
4 SI 2006/1003, Art 17(1)(b). If such incapacity is the result of an accident at work or an occupational disease entitling the person concerned to a benefit payable in full or in part by an institution in the host Member State, no condition shall be imposed as to length of residence.
5 Directive 2004/38/EC, Art 17(2).
6 Immigration (European Economic Area) Regulations 2006, SI 2006/1003, reg 5(3).
7 Directive 2004/38/EC, Art 17(1).
8 Immigration (European Economic Area) Regulations 2006, SI 2006/1003.
9 Directive 2004/38/EC, Art 17(1)(a). The Directive says that, for the purposes of entitlement to the rights referred to in points (a) and (b), periods of employment spent in the Member State in which the person concerned is working should be regarded as having been spent in the host Member State.
10 Immigration (European Economic Area) Regulations 2006, SI 2006/1003, reg 5(6).
11 Directive 2004/38/EC, Art 17(3).
12 Directive 2004/38/EC, Art 17(4).
13 Directive 2004/38/EC, Art 17(1); Immigration (European Economic Area) Regulations 2006, SI 2006/1003, reg 5(7).

MEMBERS OF THE FAMILY

Overview

7.86A

[Add new paragraph:]

Under the Citizens' Directive all Union citizens have the right to enter another Member State by virtue of having an identity card or valid passport. Family members, whether they have or do not have the nationality of a Member State, enjoy the same rights as the citizen who they have accompanied. There are three categories of family member. The first list is the same as under Art 10 of Regulation 1612/68 with the addition of civil partners.[1] It consists of spouses and civil partners, and direct descendants under 21 or dependent and dependent direct relatives in the ascending line of the union citizen and his or her spouse or civil partner. There are the same limitations for students – only dependent children and no ascending line relatives. The second list, referred to as extended family members in the 2006 Regulations,[2] is catered for in Art 3(2)(a) and (b) of the Directive. These are (i) family members not falling under the definition in Art 2(2) (the first list) who, in the country from which they have come, are dependants or members of the household of the Union citizen having the primary right of residence; (ii) family members, who have serious health problems which strictly require the personal care of the Union citizen; and (iii) a partner, who is neither spouse nor civil partner, with whom the Union citizen has a durable relationship, duly attested. Under the Directive the host Member State shall facilitate their entry and residence 'in accordance with its own national legislation'.[3] The third category arises after residence in the host Member State has occurred. They are referred in the 2006 Regulations as a 'Family Member who has retained a right of residence'.[4] Subject to certain conditions set out in the Directive, the death of the Union citizen, his or her departure from the host Member State, divorce, annulment of marriage or termination of partnership does not affect the right of family members who are not nationals of a Member State to continue residing in the Member State in question. These include the widowed, orphaned or abandoned after one year's residence, and parents of children (ie *Baumbast*[5] cases) but the parent must have actual custody. These people can acquire a permanent right of residence. Family members, irrespective of their nationality, who acquire the right to reside will be entitled to engage in economic activity on an employed or self-employed basis.

1 Directive 2004/38/EC, Art 2(2).
2 Immigration (European Economic Area) Regulations 2006, SI 2006/1003, reg 8.
3 Directive 2004/38/EC, Art 3(2).
4 The Immigration (European Economic Area) Regulations 2006, SI 2006/1003, reg 10.
5 *Baumbast v Secretary of State for the Home Department: C-413/99* [2002] ECR I-7091, [2002] 3 CMLR 599, [2003] ICR 1347, ECJ.

7.86B

[Add new paragraph:]

Under the Directive no visa or equivalent formality may be imposed on union citizens, including family members. They need only an identity card or passport. Non-national family members shall only be required to have a a short-stay visa[1] or its national equivalent or a valid residence card, presumably one issued by any Member State.[2] Where the persons concerned do not have travel documents, the host Member State must afford them every facility in obtaining the requisite documents or having them sent.[3] Family members of Union citizens who are union citizens need only apply for a registration certificate,[4] and those who are not nationals of a Member State must apply for a residence card, which is valid for five years and remains so, despite temporary absences from the host Member State, as set out in the Directive.[5]

1 Regulation 539/2001, in which neither the UK nor Ireland participated.
2 Directive 2004/38/EC, Art 5(2). They must also have a valid passport: Art 5(1).
3 Directive 2004/38/EC, Art 5(4).
4 Directive 2004/38/EC, Art 8.
5 Directive 2004/38/EC, Arts 9, 10 and 11.

7.86C

[Add new paragraph:]

Union citizens acquire the right of permanent residence in the host Member State after a five-year period of uninterrupted legal residence, provided that an expulsion decision has not been enforced against them. This right of permanent residence is no longer subject to any conditions.[1] The same rule applies to family members who are not nationals of a Member State and who have lived with a Union citizen for five years.[2] Subject to decisions on grounds of public policy, public security and public health, the right of permanent residence is lost only in the event of more than two successive years' absence from the host Member State. The Directive also recognizes, in certain circumstances, the right of permanent residence for Union citizens who are workers or self-employed persons and for family members before the five-year period of continuous residence has expired, subject to certain conditions being met,[3] and a right of permanent residence for non-national family Members who have retained a right of residence.[4]

1 Directive 2004/38/EC, Art 16(1).
2 Directive 2004/38/EC, Art 16(2).
3 Directive 2004/38/EC, Art 17.
4 Directive 2004/38/EC, Art 18.

7.87D

[Add new paragraph:]

These provisions relating to the entry and residence of family members and the formalities to be gone through are transposed into the 2006 Regulations, following very closely the requirements of the Directive, except with regard to the entry and residence of third country national family members, where there is what, in our view, is a serious divergence of principle. Under the 2006 Regulations EEA nationals are admitted to the UK on production of a passport or identity card irrespective if they are family members or coming for some other purpose (reg 11). If they are extended family members, their credentials will be examined for the first time when they apply for a registration certificate and reg 16(5) and (6) gives immigration officials their first opportunity to conduct an extensive examination of their personal circumstances and to issue a certificate. This provision is clearly drafted with Art 3(2) of the Directive in mind, whose wording is consistent with the task of determining whether someone is within the extended family category being a matter for determination of each Member State's domestic administration.

7.87E

[Add new paragraph:]

Non-nationals are subjected to a different regime. Non-national family members coming to the UK and/or the EEA for the first time are only admitted under reg 11(2) if they have a passport and an 'EEA family permit' issued in accordance with reg 12. This is where the controversy arises. Under reg 12(1)(b) the family member who is accompanying the EEA national to the United Kingdom or joining him or her there must either:

(i) be lawfully resident in an EEA State; or
(ii) would meet the requirements in the immigration rules (other than those relating to entry clearance) for leave to enter the United Kingdom as the family member of the EEA national; or
(iii) in the case of direct descendants or dependent direct relatives in the ascending line of his spouse or his civil partner, as the family member of his spouse or his civil partner, were the EEA national or the spouse or civil partner a person present and settled in the United Kingdom.

What this Regulation is seeking to do is:

(a) to impose a condition of prior lawful residence in the EEA – a matter of doubt and controversy under community law, with some support from the ECJ decision in *Akrich*[1] and the opinion of the A-G in *Jia*;[2]
(b) to apply UK domestic law to all non-national family members making their first visit to the territory of the EEA – also a matter of doubt and controversy under community law; and
(c) by applying UK immigration law parents and grandparents under 65, for example, will need to show that the most exceptional circumstances apply to their situation and children of single parents will have to show that their parent in the UK has sole responsibility.[3]

1 *Secretary of State for the Home Department v Akrich: C-109/01* [2004] QB 756, [2004] All ER (EC) 687, (2003) Times, 26 September, ECJ.
2 This is discussed at 7.60 in the main text and in this Supplement.
3 See HC 395, paras 317(e) and 297(1)(e). The extent of the discretion under the previous Regulations (SI 2000/2326), reg 10(2) was very wide as can be seen from the recent decision of AIT: *SY (EEA Regulation 10(1) – Dependancy Alone Sufficient) v Sri Lanka* [2006] UKAIT 00024, but kept closely to the text of the now repealed Art 10(2) of Regulation 1612/68.

7.87F

[Add new paragraph:]

In the new regime for family reunion, the Citizens' Directive marks out a clear demarcation line between the competence of Community law and that of the domestic law of the Member States. First, the Preamble to the Directive sets out the principles. Paragraph 5 says: 'The right of all Union citizens to move and reside freely within the territory of the Member States should, if it is to be exercised under objective conditions of freedom and dignity, be also granted to their family members, irrespective of nationality.' Secondly, the substantive provisions of the Directive make it clear:

- (i) who in community law are members of the family (Art 2);
- (ii) that it is their right to join or be with the union citizen who is exercising his or her free movement rights;
- (iii) what the procedures will apply and what documentation will be needed to make good the community rights given to family members by the Directive; and
- (iv) that the admission of further possible family members (not within the definition in Art 2 but defined in very broad terms in Art 3) whose admission is also a community right but is initially to be determined using domestic immigration law procedures, but with a strong nudge from Community law to facilitate entry where appropriate.

In this respect the creation of community rights is set within a larger framework of community competence than the mere reach of the Citizens' Directive. We have already highlighted the *Surindar Singh* situation[1] at 7.60 and shown that the reach of community law goes much wider than the Directive as in the case of *Carpenter*,[2] where a UK national was held to be exercising treaty rights by providing services in other EU Member States while retaining his UK residence. In this connection the case of *Morson v Jhanjan*[3] has also set a very clear, if contentious, boundary to community competence (at 7.62 above). Not all union citizens can have their family reunion rights adjudicated by community law. There needs to be a community law element to the case which brings it within the competence of community law, such as an exercise of free movement rights by moving from the territory of one Member State to that of another. Once the community element is established community law, not domestic law, applies. It is a clear boundary, not a very satisfactory one in view of the added importance of union citizenship, but clear and well established in the case law. In our view, there is a similarly clear boundary between community and domestic law over the right of family members who are not EEA citizens to join a union citizen who is exercising his or her free movement rights under the Directive. But others would have it differently. In *Jia*[4] the A-G has given an opinion that the first admission of a family member who is not a citizen of the Union is a matter to be decided by the domestic law of each Member State and once he or she has been lawfully admitted into the EEA, then and then only does community law take over. He bases his opinion in part on the reasoning of the Court in *Akrich*.[5] In our view his opinion runs against the grain of principle, against the limits of competence set by the Citizens' Directive, against the distinction drawn by *Morson and Jhanjan*,[6] and against the prevailing case law of the ECJ.[7] The A-G wants to set new boundaries. He is not alone. He has the backing of the UK and Dutch governments. The Secretary of State has gone one stage further. He has incorporated his minority ideas into the 2006 Regulations for determining the entry and admission of spouses and children and other family members to join their partners and parents who have exercised their free movement rights. This is not a correct transposition of the Directive and will no doubt have to be litigated sooner or later. Meanwhile we await the judgment of the ECJ in *Jia*.

[1] *R v Immigration Appeal Tribunal and Surinder Singh, ex p Secretary of State for the Home Department: C-370/90* [1992] 3 All ER 798, [1992] ECR I-4265, [1992] 3 CMLR 358, ECJ.

[2] *Carpenter v Secretary of State for the Home Department: C-60/00* [2003] QB 416, [2002] ECR I-6279, [2003] All ER (EC) 577, [2003] 2 WLR 267, ECJ.

[3] *Morson and Jhanjan v Netherlands: 35/82 and 36/82* [1982] ECR 3723, [1983] 2 CMLR 221, ECJ.

[4] Case C-01/05 *Jia v Migrationsverket* (*Opinion of AG Geelhoed of 27.4.06*).

[5] *Secretary of State for the Home Department v Akrich: C-109/01* [2004] QB 756, [2003] ECR I-9607, [2004] All ER (EC) 687, [2004] 2 WLR 871, ECJ. A returned illegally to the United Kingdom, and married a British woman. After having worked in Ireland for six months, the couple attempted to return to the United Kingdom, invoking the rights granted to the spouses of Community workers by Art 10 of Regulation No 1612/68, as interpreted by the Court in *Surindar Singh*. Here, the Court held that, in order to benefit from the rights provided for in Art 10 of Regulation No 1612/68, the national of a non-Member State, who is the spouse of a citizen of the Union, must be lawfully resident in a Member State when he moves to another Member State to which the citizen of the Union is migrating or has migrated.

[6] In *Jia* the A-G recategorises the *Morson v Jhanjan* principle as a chance factor which is both arbitrary and unjust (para 75) as it creates inequality in respect of Community citizens who have not exercised this right and in respect of third-country nationals who do not have the privilege of being the relative of a migrant Community citizen. But it is not, on present community jurisprudence, a chance factor. Moving from one state to another is an exercise of community rights and is the key factor for bringing the case within community competence.

[7] *Carpenter v Secretary of State for the Home Department: C-60/00* [2003] QB 416, [2002] ECR I-6279, [2003] All ER (EC) 577, [2003] 2 WLR 267, [2002] 2 CMLR 1541, [2003] 2 FCR 711, (2002) Times, 20 July, [2002] All ER (D) 182 (Jul), ECJ; *Mouvement contre le racisme, l'antisémitisme et la xénophobie ASBL v Belgium: C-459/99* [2002] ECR I-6591, [2003] 1 WLR 1073, [2002] 3 CMLR 681, [2002] All ER (D) 113 (Aug), ECJ, where the Court stated that the right of a third–country national, married to a Member State national, to enter the territory of the Member States derives under Community law from the family ties alone; moreover, a Member State is not permitted to refuse issue of a residence permit and to issue an expulsion order against a third-country national who is able to furnish proof of his identity and of his marriage to a national of a Member State on the sole ground that he has entered the territory of the Member State concerned unlawfully. *European Commission v Spain: C-157/03* [2005] All ER (D) 164 (Apr), ECJ, decided more than a year after *Akrich*, the Court again adopted the approach followed in MRAX that the right to enter the territory of a Member State by a third-country-national who is the spouse of a national of a Member State derives from the family relationship alone. It was wrong for Spanish legislation to require a third country national, who is a member of the family of a Community national, to apply for a residence visa at the Spanish consulate in their last place of domicile, as a precondition for obtaining a residence permit.

Spouse

7.88

[NB:]

The issue of marriages of convenience, which is discussed in the main text, has now been largely resolved by the coming into force of the Citizens' Directive and it seems that the controversy over the attempt to exclude 'a party to a marriage of convenience' from the family reunion provisions of community law in Immigration (European Economic Area) Regulations 2000 has by now runs its course. The same definition has been re-enacted in the 2006 Regulations which have also extended it to civil partnerships.[1] Now the Home Secretary is on firmer ground. Under the heading of 'Abuse of rights' Art 35 of the Citizens' Directive provides that Member States may adopt the necessary measures to refuse, terminate or withdraw any right conferred by the Directive in the case of abuse of rights or fraud, such as marriages of convenience. The Article then adds that any such measure must be proportionate and subject to the procedural safeguards provided for in Arts 30 and 31. Thus the right to exclude 'a party to a marriage of convenience' is given, but it exercise is subject to two of the key procedural safeguards of the replaced Council Directive 64/222 and must be a proportionate exercise of national power.

1 Immigration (European Economic Area) Regulations 2006, SI 2006/1003, reg 2(1): 'civil partner' does not include a party to a civil partnership of convenience; 'spouse' does not include a party to a marriage of convenience.

Civil Partners

7.88A

[Add new paragraph:]

In Chapter 11 we deal with civil partners in UK domestic immigration and family law (see 11.1 below). Now the Citizens' Directive has for the first time extended community law to include civil partners as family members. In Art 2(2)(b) a family member now includes 'the partner with whom the Union citizen has contracted a registered partnership, on the basis of the legislation of a Member State, if the legislation of the host Member State treats registered partnerships as equivalent to marriage and in accordance with the conditions laid down in the relevant legislation of the host Member State.' Provision is also made for partners who are unmarried or who are not civil partners but are in durable relationships in Art 3(2)(b), implemented in the 2006 Regulations by regs 7(1)(a) and 8(5).

7.90

[NB:]

Although the issue of marriages of convenience has now been largely resolved by the coming into force of the Citizens' Directive and the 'Abuse of rights' Article contained in it (Art 35), there is still no definition and the discussion in the main text is still relevant.

7.94

[NB:]

Council Regulation (EEC) 1251/70 and Directive (EEC) 75/34 have both been replaced by the Citizens Directive and the 2000 EEA Regulations, SI 2000/2326 have been superseded by the Immigration (European Economic Area) Regulations 2006, SI 2006/1003.

Descendants: children

7.95

[NB:]

The 2000 EEA Regulations, SI 2000/2326 have been replaced by the Immigration (European Economic Area) Regulations 2006, SI 2006/1003, and references to it should be deleted. Regulation 1612/68, Arts 10 and 11 have been repealed and replaced by the Citizens' Directive 2004/38/EC.

7.96

[NB:]

Regulation 1612/68, Arts 10 and 11 have been repealed and replaced by the Citizens' Directive 2004/38/EC. See now Art 2. Note that Art 12 has not been repealed.

[Footnote 5:]

The Immigration (European Economic Area) Regulations 2000, SI 2000/2326 have been superseded by the Immigration (European Economic Area) Regulations 2006, SI 2006/1003.

7.98

[NB:]

Regulation 1612/68, Arts 10 and 11 have been repealed and replaced by the Citizens' Directive 2004/38/EC.

7.99

[NB:]

Regulation 1612/68, Arts 10 and 11 have been repealed and replaced by the Citizens' Directive 2004/38/EC. Note that Art 12 has not been repealed.

Other family members

7.101

[NB:]

Other family members are now dealt with by Directive 2004/38/EC , Art 3 and the 2000 EEA Regulations, SI 2000/2326 have been superseded by the Immigration (European Economic Area) Regulations 2006, SI 2006/1003. See regs 8 (extended family) and 12 (issue of EEA family permit). In reg 12 one of the conditions for the issue of an EEA family permit is that family members will be accompanying the EEA national to the United Kingdom or joining him or her there and will either be (i) lawfully resident in an EEA State; or (ii) would meet the requirements in the immigration rules (other than those relating to entry clearance)[1] for leave to enter the United Kingdom as the family member of the EEA national.[2] As we have already indicated we do not think that this is a valid transposition of the provisions of the Directive, since it is based on the view that national law, not community law, should deal with a third country national's first entry into the EEA, a matter discussed at 7.87E–7.87F above.

1 Under HC 395, para 317 the following relatives must show, amongst other things, the most exceptional circumstances before qualifying for entry: a parent or grandparent under 65, a son, daughter, sister, brother, uncle or aunt over the age of 18.

2 In the case of direct descendants or dependent direct relatives in the ascending line of the EEA national's spouse or civil partner, the person has to meet the requirement of the immigration rules for leave to enter as the family member of the EEA national's spouse or civil partner, were the EEA national or the spouse or civil partner a person present and settled in the United Kingdom: Immigration (European Economic Area) Regulations 2006, SI 2006/1003.

7.102

[NB:]

For references to the Immigration (European Economic Area) Regulations 2000, SI 2000/2326, now read Immigration (European Economic Area) Regulations 2006, SI 2006/1003 and for references to Council Regulation (EEC) 1612/68 now read Directive 2004/38/EC.

7.103

[NB:]

As regards the case of *McCollum*,[1] note that under the Citizens' Directive (Directive 2004/38/EC) and under the implementing Regulations (Immigration (European Economic Area) Regulations 2006, SI 2006/1003, provision is now made for civil partnerships, whereby same sex partners are treated as members of the family (see 7.88A above) and provision is also made for partners who are unmarried or who are not civil partners but are in durable relationships in Art 3(2)(b), implemented in the 2006 Regulations by regs 7(1)(a) and 8(5).

1 *R v Secretary of State for the Home Department, ex p McCollum*, CO 589/99, 24 January 2001, CA.

7.104

[NB:]

Regulation 10 of the Immigration (European Economic Area) Regulations 2000 has been replaced by reg 12 of Immigration (European Economic Area) Regulations 2006, SI 2006/1003.

Dependency

7.105

[NB:]

Regulation 10 of the Immigration (European Economic Area) Regulations 2000 has been replaced by reg 12 of Immigration (European Economic Area) Regulations 2006, SI 2006/1003 and Art 10 of Council Regulation (EEC) 1612/68 has been superseded by Directive 2004/38/EC. None of the new measures define dependency, and the discussion in the main text remains relevant.

7.106

[NB:]

Although Art 10 of Council Regulation (EEC) 1612/68 and the 2000 Regulations have now been replaced, the Directive 2004/38/EC (the Citizens' Directive) may simplify and codify but there is still the comprehensive code referred to in the main text.

MATERIAL SCOPE (1) FREE MOVEMENT RIGHTS

Abolishing discrimination and other obstacles to free movement

Non-discrimination

7.108

[NB:]

Article 24(1) of Directive 2004/38/EC (the Citizens' Directive) sets out the principle of non-discrimination as regards free movement rights spelt out in the Directive as follows:

> 'Subject to such specific provisions as are expressly provided for in the Treaty and secondary law, all Union citizens residing on the basis of this Directive in the territory of the host Member State shall enjoy equal treatment with the nationals of that Member State within the scope of the Treaty. The benefit of this right shall be extended to family members who are not nationals of a Member State and who have the right of residence or permanent residence.'

In *European Parliament v European Council Case*,[1] the ECJ considered allegations from the European Parliament that Directive 2003/86/EC, which deals with the right of minor children of third country nationals respects fundamental rights and, in particular the right to respect for family life under Art 8 of the ECHR and contains useful material on the best interests of the child and discrimination on the grounds of age.

1 *C-540/03* [2006] 2 FCR 461, [2006] All ER (D) 320 (Jun), ECJ.

MATERIAL SCOPE (2) RIGHT TO LEAVE, ENTER AND RESIDE

Right to leave own country

7.114

[NB:]

Council Directives (EEC) 68/360 (workers) and 73/148 (self-employed) which require Member States to grant workers the right to leave their territory have now been replaced by Directive 2004/38/EC, Art 4 and all footnotes should be amended accordingly.

Right to enter

7.115

[NB:]

The Immigration (European Economic Area) Regulations 2006[1] now include Switzerland. All the rights to enter in the main text are now covered by Directive 2004/38/EC and the implementing 2006 Regulations.[2] All references in the text and footnotes to Council Directives (EEC) 68/360, and 73/148 and to SI 2000/2326 should be deleted. Under Art 5 of the Citizens' Directive, all Union citizens have the right to enter another Member State by virtue of having an identity card or valid passport. For stays of less than three months, that is the only requirement.[3] Under no circumstances can an entry or exit visa be required. Where the citizens concerned do not have travel documents, the host Member State must afford them every facility in obtaining the requisite documents or having them sent. Family members who do not have the nationality of a Member State enjoy the same rights as the citizen who they have accompanied. They may be subject to a short-stay visa requirement.[4]

Although there is no specific mention of entering to provide or receive services, they are covered by the new right given to all union nationals to enter and remain for three months whatever the purpose of their visit upon production of a passport and identity card. Under the Immigration (European Economic Area) Regulations 2006,[5] the transposed requirements are contained in regs 11 (entry) and 12 (the short stay visa requirement for non-EEA nationals called an 'EEA family permit'). Although it is not referred to in the 2006 Regulations, reg 12 is subject to the important requirement in Art 5(2) that 'Member States shall grant such persons every facility to obtain the necessary visas. Such visas shall be issued free of charge as soon as possible and on the basis of an accelerated procedure'.

1 SI 2006/1003, reg 2(1).
2 Immigration (European Economic Area) Regulations 2006, SI 2006/1003.
3 The host Member State may in addition require the persons concerned to register their presence in the country within a reasonable and non-discriminatory period of time.
4 Under Regulation (EC) No 539/2001, which the UK does not subscribe to, or under national law. Residence permits will be deemed equivalent to short-stay visas.
5 SI 2006/1003.

7.116

[NB:]

The entitlement to enter under UK domestic law is now governed by the Immigration (European Economic Area) Regulations 2006 (SI 2006/1003) and all references to the 2000 Regulations in the main text and footnotes should be deleted. The main provisions are outlined at 7.87E above. Assuming the person has the requisite documents needed for automatic entry they may still be refused entry. Under reg 19, if exclusion is justified on grounds of public policy, public security or public health and in the case of family members, if they are not accompanied by the EEA national or coming to join him or her or the EEA national has no right to reside under the Regulations. Regulations 22 and 24 incorporate the powers of examination, detention and temporary admission under Sch 2 to the Immigration Act 1971 for those seeking admission or refused admission who are family members of EEA nationals or EEA nationals who might fall to be excluded from the UK on public policy grounds. The A-G's opinion in *Commission v Spain has been upheld by the Court.*[1]

[1] *European Commission v Spain: C-157/03* [2005] All ER (D) 164 (Apr), ECJ.

Right of residence

7.117

[NB:]

The Immigration (European Economic Area) Regulations 2006, SI 2006/1003 have replaced the 2000 EEA Regulations and Council Directives (EEC) 68/360 and 73/148 have now been replaced by Directive 2004/38/EC. All references in the text and footnotes to these provisions should be deleted. With the coming into force of the Citizens' Directive there has been a change in the documentation given to Union citizens and members of their families who exercise their free movement rights under the Directive. First, Union citizens no longer get a residence permit as confirmation of their right of residence. Under the new regime there are registration certificates (Art 8) and a document certifying permanent residence (Art 19) for union citizens, and a residence card (Art 9) and a permanent residence card (Art 20) for family members. These requirements of the Directive are matched in the Immigration (European Economic Area) Regulations 2006. Registration certificates (reg 16), residence cards (reg 17) and documents certifying permanent residence and permanent residence cards (reg 18) are all covered.

[Footnote 20:]

The references to Directive 64/221 (EEC) should now be a reference to Directive 2004/38/EC (The Citizens' Directive). Article 5 of Directive 64/221 (EEC) has been repealed, but in the Citizens' Directive the six-month time limit is expressly retained for the obtaining of first residence cards (Art 10) and permanent residence cards (Art 20) for family members and for revocation of an expulsion decision (Art 32).

Registration certificate

7.117A

[Add new paragraph:]

Where registration is required, the deadline may not be less than three months from the date of arrival. A registration certificate must be issued immediately and should contain the name and address of the person registering (Art 8(2)). Under the Directive the documentation needed to obtain a registration certificate will vary depending on the particular free movement right being exercised. Member States may only require that:

- *workers and the self employed* present a valid identity card or passport, a confirmation of engagement from the employer or a certificate of employment, or proof that they are self-employed persons;
- *the self-sufficient* present a valid identity card or passport and provide proof that they satisfy the conditions laid down for self sufficiency;
- *students* present a valid identity card or passport, provide proof of enrolment at an accredited establishment and of comprehensive sickness insurance cover and the declaration or equivalent means to show they have sufficient funds. Member States may not require this declaration to refer to any specific amount of resources.

In determining what are 'sufficient resources', member States must not lay down a fixed amount, but must take into account the personal situation of the person concerned. In all cases the funds needed should be no higher than the threshold below which nationals of the host Member State become eligible for social assistance, or, where this criterion is not applicable, no higher than the minimum social security pension paid by the host Member State (Art 8(4)).

Family members of Union citizens, who are themselves Union citizens, may also be issued a registration certificate and will be required to produce the following documents:

(a) a valid identity card or passport;
(b) a document attesting to the existence of a family relationship or of a registered partnership;
(c) where appropriate, the registration certificate of the Union citizen whom they are accompanying or joining;
(d) in cases of direct descendants or ascendants, documentary evidence that they meet conditions laid down for their qualifying as 'family members';
(e) in cases of extended family members falling under Art 3(2)(a) of the Directive, a document issued by the relevant authority in the country of origin or country from which they are arriving, certifying that they are dependants or members of the household of the Union citizen, or proof of the existence of serious health grounds which strictly require the personal care of the family member by the Union citizen;
(f) in cases of partners who have not married or entered into a civil partnership (Art 3(2)(b)), proof of the existence of a durable relationship with the Union citizen.

These provisions have been transposed into UK domestic law by reg 16 of the Immigration (European Economic Area) Regulations 2006.[1] In the case of extended family members who are EEA nationals, the Secretary of State uses the registration process as the means of exercising the discretion given to Member States under Art 3(2)(b) and (c) of the Directive to facilitate the entry of extended family members in accordance with its national legislation.[2]

1 SI 2006/1003.
2 SI 2006/1003, reg 16(5) and (6).

Duration of first residence permit

7.118

[Delete paragraph]

Renewal of residence permit

7.119

[Delete heading and whole paragraph EXCEPT for second and third sentences and footnotes 2 and 3.]

[NB:]

Under the 2006 Regulations the broad rule is that a qualified person is entitled to reside in the United Kingdom for so long as he or she remains a qualified person (reg 14(1)) and family members of a qualified person are entitled to reside for so long as they remain family members of the person through whom they qualify for a residence card (see reg 14(2)). Both the Directive[1] and the 2006 Regulations[2] make detailed provision to ensure that a worker or self employed person remains qualified despite periods of sickness or unemployment.

1Directive 2004/38/EC.

2Immigration (European Economic Area) Regulations 2006, SI 2006/1003, reg 6(2).

Public funds and voluntary unemployment

7.120

[NB:]

The decision in *Antonissen*[1] has been incorporated into the Directive[2] by Art 14(4)(b) which provides that an expulsion measure may in no case be adopted against Union citizens or their family members if the Union citizens entered the territory of the host Member State in order to seek employment. This continues to be the case so long as the Union citizens can provide evidence that they are continuing to seek employment and that they have a genuine chance of being engaged. These measures are also reproduced in the

2006 Regulations.[3] A jobseeker is included in the list of 'qualified persons' in reg 6(1) and is defined in reg 6(4). As regards recourse to public assistance, the position is made somewhat simpler by the creation of the three month 'no questions asked' period of residence now given to all union citizens travelling to another member state. Under Art 14(1) they retain that right of residence provided they do not become an unreasonable burden on the social assistance system of the host Member State. Article 14(3) provides that expulsion should not be the automatic consequence of a Union citizen's or his or her family member's recourse to the social assistance system of the host Member State. Once someone finds work or self employment they should not be penalised because they have had recourse to social assistance (Art 14(4)(a)). These measures are also reproduced in the 2006 Regulations.[2] A jobseeker is included in the list of 'qualified persons' in reg 6(1) and is defined in reg 6(4). As regards public funds the Directive also provides that the host Member State shall not be obliged to confer entitlement to social assistance during the first three months of residence or, where appropriate, the longer period provided for in Art 14(4)(b), nor shall it be obliged, prior to acquisition of the right of permanent residence, to grant maintenance aid for studies, including vocational training, consisting in student grants or student loans to persons other than workers, self-employed persons, persons who retain such status and members of their families (Art 24(2)). This Article has to be read in the light of the ECJ case law referred to in the main text, which are not overridden by the Directive.

1 *R v Immigration Appeal, ex p Antonissen* [1991] ECR I-745, [1991] 2 CMLR 373, ECJ.
2 Directive 2004/38/EC.
3 Immigration (European Economic Area) Regulations 2006, SI 2006/1003.

Permanent residence in the UK

7.121

[NB:]

The Citizens' Directive[1] has now made clear provision for permanent residence as a right. Article 16 provides that Union citizens who have resided legally for a continuous period of five years in the host Member State shall have the right of permanent residence there. It is an unconditional right. The same right will also apply to family members who are not nationals of a Member State and have legally resided with the Union citizen in the host Member State for a continuous period of five years. Article 16(3) of the Directive and reg 3(2) of the 2006 Regulation provide that continuity of residence is not broken by temporary absences not exceeding a total of six months per year, by absences of a longer duration for compulsory military service, or by one absence of a maximum of 12 consecutive months for important reasons such as pregnancy and childbirth, serious illness, study or vocational training, or a posting in another Member State or a third country. Subject to public policy reasons, Art 16(4) makes it clear that once acquired, the right of permanent residence can only be lost through absence from the host Member State for a period exceeding two consecutive years. Permanent residence may in some cases be acquired in a shorter period than this as we have described in relation to retirement and incapacity at 7.85 above. Under Art 12 family members retain their right of residence in the event of the death or departure from the host member state of the Union citizen if they meet certain conditions contained in the Article and the same applies under Art 13 in the event of divorce, annulment of marriage or termination of registered partnership. Nationals of member States acquire permanent residence if they become entitled to any of the free movement rights set out in Art 7. Different conditions apply to non-nationals. If they manage to keep their right of residence by meeting these conditions for a period of five years they will acquire permanent residence under Art 18. These provision have been transposed into the 2006 Regulations.[2]

1 Directive 2004/38/EC.
2 Immigration (European Economic Area) Regulations 2006, SI 2006/1003, regs 15 and 18.

7.122

[NB:]

The position regarding permanent residence has been greatly clarified by the Directive 2004/38/EC as set out in the previous paragraph and by regs 15 and 18 of the Immigration (European Economic Area) Regulations 2006, SI 2006/1003. Because of the changes references to Immigration (European Economic Area) Regulations 2000 and to the Immigration Rules should be deleted.

7.123

[NB:]

The position of workers and their families under the changes made in Directive 2004/38/EC and the Immigration (European Economic Area) Regulations 2006, SI 2006/1003 have already been documented above at 7.85.

7.124

[Delete paragraph]

7.125

[Delete paragraph]

Appeals against adverse decisions of UK immigration authorities

7.126

[NB:]

The right of appeal against an adverse EEA decision is now contained in Pt 6 of the Immigration (European Economic Area) Regulations 2006.[1] The appeal lies to the Asylum and Immigration Tribunal, except where it raises interests of national security; or the interests of the relationship between the United Kingdom and another country, when it lies to SIAC. For further details see 18.17 of this Supplement.

1 SI 2006/1003.

TERMINATION OF THE RIGHT TO RESIDE: CESSATION OF ENTITLEMENT AND EXCLUSION

Cessation and public policy

7.128

[NB:]

Note that Directives 68/360 or 73/148 have been repealed and replaced by Directive 2004/38/EC ('The Citizens' Directive').

7.129

[NB:]

The Immigration (European Economic Area) Regulations 2000 have been replaced by the 2006 Regulations and these give the Secretary of State similar powers to those under the 2000 Regulations. Under reg 19(3) there is a power to remove those who have ceased to have a right to reside and under reg 20(2) there is power to revoke and refuse to renew residence documentation, if the person has ceased to have a right to reside.[1]

1 In *DA (EEA, Revocation of Residence Permit) Algeria* [2006] UKAIT 00027, the Tribunal held that where the worker had left the UK there was nothing inconsistent with EU legislation in bringing to an end the derivative rights of the worker's family. This type of decision would need to be revised in the light of the new legislation.

7.130

[For the reference to the 'Immigration (European Economic Area) Regulations 2000' substitute a reference to the 'Immigration (European Economic Area) Regulations 2006'.]

Implementation of the public policy proviso

7.132

[NB:]

The references to Directive 64/221 (EEC), which has been repealed, should now be a reference to Directive 2004/38/EC (The Citizens' Directive), Chapter VI and the Immigration (European Economic Area) Regulations 2006 have now replaced the Immigration (European Economic Area) Regulations 2000. Regulation 21 of the 2006 Regulations deals with decisions taken on the grounds of public policy, public security and public health and keeps close to the language of the Directive.

7.132A

[Add new paragraph:]

The Directive does not simply reproduce the text of Directive 64/221; it also incorporates changes and clarifications of community law by the case law of the European Court. This is most clear from the text of Art 27 which sets out the general principles of the old Directive. It enables Member States to restrict the freedom of movement and residence of Union citizens and their family members, irrespective of nationality, on grounds of public policy, public security or public health, but they can only do these things 'subject to the provisions of this Chapter'. These powers are not absolute. First, these grounds shall not be invoked to serve economic ends. Secondly, measures taken on grounds of public policy or public security shall comply with the principle of proportionality and shall be based exclusively on the personal conduct of the individual concerned. Previous criminal convictions shall not in themselves constitute grounds for taking such measures. Moreover, the personal conduct of the individual concerned must represent a genuine, present and sufficiently serious threat affecting one of the fundamental interests of society. Justifications that are isolated from the particulars of the case or that rely on considerations of general prevention shall not be accepted. Thirdly, careful provision is made for inquiries of other Member States in order to ascertain whether the person concerned represents a danger for public policy or public security, when issuing a registration certificate or a residence card. Fourthly, when someone has been expelled on grounds of public policy, public security, or public health from one Member State provision, the Member State which issued the passport or identity card to the person expelled must allow the holder of the document who to re-enter its territory without any formality even if the document is no longer valid or the nationality of the holder is in dispute. Article 28 deals with protection against expulsion. First, in a paragraph which is reminiscent of the ECHR decision in *Boultif*,[1] it is incumbent upon a Member State, which is considering making an expulsion decision on grounds of public policy or public security, to take into account such factors as how long the individual concerned has resided on its territory, his/her age, state of health, family and economic situation, social and cultural integration into the host Member State and the extent of his or her links with the country of origin. Secondly, the host Member State may not take an expulsion decision against Union citizens or their family members, irrespective of nationality, who have the right of permanent residence on its territory, except on serious grounds of public policy or public security. Thirdly, an expulsion decision may not be taken against Union citizens, except if the decision is based on imperative grounds of public security, as defined by Member States, if they:

(a) have resided in the host Member State for the previous 10 years; or
(b) are a minor, except if the expulsion is necessary for the best interests of the child, as provided for in the United Nations Convention on the Rights of the Child of 20 November 1989.

Articles 30 and 31 contain important provisions about notification of decisions and procedural safeguards. Article 32 deals with revocation of expulsion or exclusion orders. Article 33 makes important provision about deportation orders against union citizens. First it makes it clear that expulsion orders may not be issued by the host Member State as a penalty or legal consequence of a custodial penalty, unless they conform to the requirements of Arts 27, 28 and 29. Secondly, if an expulsion order is enforced more than two years after it was issued, the Member State is required to check that the individual concerned is currently and genuinely a threat to public policy or public security and must assess whether there has been any material change in the circumstances since the expulsion order was issued. These are very clear indications and are in marked contrast to the deportation policy recently outlined under UK domestic law. See 15.1 and 15.30 below.

1 *Boultif v Switzerland (Application 54273/00)* [2001] 2 FLR 1228, [2001] ECHR 54273/00, ECtHR.

7.133

[NB:]

In *European Commission v Spain*[1] the ECJ held that Spain had breached its obligations under Arts 1–3 of Directive 64/221 by refusing entry into the Schengen area to third country nationals, solely on the basis of an SIS alert, without first verifying whether their presence would be constitute a genuine present and sufficiently serious threat to one of the fundamental interests of socity.[1]

1 *Case C-503/03* [2006] ECR I-1097, ECJ.

7.134

[NB:]

The references to Directive 64/221 (EEC), which has been repealed, should now be a reference to Directive 2004/38/EC (The Citizens' Directive), Chapter VI and the Immigration (European Economic Area) Regulations 2006 have now replaced the Immigration (European Economic Area) Regulations 2000.

7.135

[NB:]

The references to Directive 64/221 (EEC) should now be a reference to Directive 2004/38/EC (The Citizens' Directive), Chapter VI.

Public health

7.142

[NB:]

The references to Directive 64/221 (EEC) should now be a reference to Directive 2004/38/EC (The Citizens' Directive), Chapter VI. Article 29 deals with public health and the need to restrict free movement only if there is a risk from diseases with epidemic potential and other infectious diseases or contagious parasitic diseases and sets out the measures which can be taken. It mirrors the previous position set out in the main text.

Procedural safeguards

7.143

[NB:]

The references to Directive 64/221 (EEC) should now be a reference to Directive 2004/38/EC (The Citizens' Directive), Chapter VI.

Reasons

7.144

[NB:]

The reference to Directive 64/221 (EEC) should now be a reference to Directive 2004/38/EC (The Citizens' Directive), Chapter VI.

Review and appeal

7.145

[NB:]

The reference to Directive 64/221 (EEC) should now be a reference to Directive 2004/38/EC (The Citizens' Directive), Chapter VI.

Appeal to the Asylum and Immigration Tribunal

7.149

[NB:]

The reference to Directive 64/221 (EEC) should now be a reference to Directive 2004/38/EC (The Citizens' Directive), Chapter VI.

National security cases

7.150

[NB:]

The right of appeal is still to SIAC under the Immigration (European Economic Area) Regulations 2006, SI 2006/1003. See regs 26 and 28.

RIGHTS UNDER ASSOCIATION AGREEMENTS

7.151

[NB:]

Note that EC Association Agreements and HC 395, paras 211 to 223 will become redundant once Bulgaria and Romania become members of the EU in 2007. Until then initial admission will usually be for two years, not 12 months, and qualification for settlement now takes five, not four years.[1]

1 HC 395, paras 215 and 222, as amended by HC 1016 as from 3 April 2006.

Turkish Association Agreement

7.154

[NB:]

In *R (on the application of Payir) v Seretary of State for the Home Department; R (on the application of Ozturk) v Same; R (on the application of Akyuz) v Same*[1], the Court of Appeal want to test the ECJ's resolve with a novel point intended to curtail Turkish worker rights under the Turkish Association Agreement and at the same time to counter the crude 'bludgeon', as one member put it, of European Court interpretations in these worker right cases. The issue in the case is whether Turkish students, who are working to pay their fees, and a Turkish au pair are by law entitled to the benefit of Art 6(1) of Decision No 1/80 of the Association Council, which provides that a Turkish worker duly registered as belonging to the labour force of a Member State is entitled to increasing access to the Member State's labour market after one, three and four years of legal employment. In *Birden*[2] the ECJ said that 'the legality of the employment presupposes a stable and secure situation as a member of the labour force of a Member State and, by virtue of this, implies the existence of an undisputed right of residence (para 55).' In *Ozturk* it was conceded that the students, who each had part time jobs, and the au pair were workers. They were also quite lawfully in the UK and there was nothing illegal about the work they were doing. But the Court of Appeal queried whether they were engaged in an effective and genuine economic activity which could be classed as 'legal employment' within the meaning of Art 6(1), if their admission to the UK had an 'overarching social purpose' inconsistent with the beneficiaries of the scheme being 'integrated into the labour force of [the] Member State' (para 27). Laws LJ said he sought to suggest that within the Member States there may be regimes involving work which possess an autonomous claim to public merit, different from but no less valid than the claims enjoyed by the ideal of free movement within the labour markets of the EU (para 28). He thought there was good reason to put the matter on the basis that students and au pairs are not in legal employment because they were not in 'a stable and secure situation as [members] of the labour force'. The Court decided to refer the case to the ECJ for a ruling. Perhaps it should be renamed *R (by the application of Sophistry) v Bludgeon.*

1 [2006] EWCA Civ 541, [2006] ICR 1314.
2 *Birden v Stadtgemeinde Bremen: C-1/97* [1998] ECR I-7747, [1999] 1 CMLR 420, ECJ.

Family members from Turkey

7.159

[NB:]

In *OY (Ankara Agreement; Stanstill Clause; Workers Family) Turkey*[1] the Tribunal held that the standstill clause in the Ankar Agreement does not restrict Member States' ability to regulate control of entry of family members to those national rules in force at the time of accession to the EC.

1 [2006] UKAIT 00028.

Chapter 8

HUMAN RIGHTS LAW

Home Office policy

8.32

[In the text after footnote 2 add:]

Current Home Office policy on discretionary leave and humanitarian protection is described in this supplement at paras 12.174 ff.

ECHR PRINCIPLES

8.39

[At the end of the text add:]

The policy whereby discretionary leave could be withheld from a person who otherwise qualified on Art 8 grounds if Ministers 'decide in view of all the circumstances of the case that it is inappropriate to grant any leave' conferred a discretion that was so broad and open ended that it was not 'in accordance with the law' within the meaning of Art 8(2).[1] For an interference with a protected right to be 'in accordance with the law' there would also have to be adequate legal safeguards against abuse,[2] including scrutiny of the measure by an independent and impartial body competent to review all the relevant questions of fact and law and to determine its lawfulness, even in the context of national security.[3]

1 *R (on the application of S) v Secretary of State for the Home Department* [2006] EWHC 1111 (Admin).

2 *R (on the application of Gillan) v Metropolitan Police Comr* [2006] UKHL 12, [2006] 2 WLR 537, (2006) Times, 9 March.

3 *Lupsa v Romania (Application 10337/04)* [2006] 2 FCR 685, [2006] ECHR 10337/04, ECtHR.

Territoriality

8.43

[Add at end:]

The tribunal has held that a person outside the jurisdiction cannot normally rely upon Convention rights to claim an entitlement to entry clearance; the exception to that principle is where an applicant for entry clearance relies upon Art 8 in relation to family life with someone who is within the jurisdiction.[1]

1 *H (Somalia)* [2004] UKIAT 00027; and *Moon* (USA) [2005] UKIAT 00112.

Right to life

8.46

[In the text, delete the sentence following footnote 7 (which says: 'Thus, unless expulsion means that death is a 'near certainty', the European Court will find a violation of Article 3, but not of Article 2') and substitute the following:]

However, the European Court of Human Rights has now held that a real risk of being executed upon deportation was sufficient to establish a breach of Art 2.[1]

1 *Bader v Sweden* (2005) App. No. 13284/04.

Exposure to torture or inhuman or degrading treatment or punishment

8.47

[NB:]

On the nature and extent of the international and common law prohibition of torture, see *A v Secretary of State for the Home Department (No 2)* [2005] UKHL 71, [2006] 2 AC 221, [2006] 1 All ER 575.

8.48

[Add at end:]

In *Said v Netherlands* the Court reversed the negative credibility findings relied on by the authorities to refuse asylum and held that removal of the applicant to Eritrea would breach Art 3 because of the risk of torture and inhuman or degrading treatment as an army deserter and dissident[1]. Similarly in *N v Finland*[2] the Court reversed the national authorities' negative credibility assessment and held that removal of the applicant would breach Art 3. The Court did so after hearing oral evidence from the applicant and other witnesses.

1 (2005) App No 2345/02.
2 (2005) App No 38885/02.

8.51

[Add at end:]

The House of Lords has now held that in a non-state agent case it is not enough to show that the returnee faces a real risk of being subjected to sufficiently serious harm; failure by the receiving state to provide reasonable protection from the violence of non-state actors must also be shown.[1] Surprisingly, therefore, the question whether a person's removal is compatible with Art 3 is to be answered not by reference to whether the removing, signatory state would breach its obligations under the Convention by acting in such a way as to expose the person to real risk of sufficiently serious harm but by reference to whether the recipient state would breach its Art 3 obligations, such obligations being purely notional in the case of non-signatory states.

1 *R (on the application of Bagdanavicius) v Secretary of State for the Home Department* [2005] UKHL 38, [2005] 2 AC 668, [2005] 4 All ER 263.

Application of Article 3 to illness

8.53

[In the text before the sentence containing footnote 14 add the following:]

To establish a breach of Art 3 by reference to the consequences of removal for a person's health, an exceptional case would have to be shown.[1]

[At the end of the paragraph add the following:]

The Court of Appeal has subsequently held that the 'real risk of a significantly increased risk of suicide' was sufficient to establish a breach of Art 3 only on the particular facts of that particular case; what has to be established is a real risk that removal of the person would cause him or her to commit suicide.[2] Whilst confirming that in principle such a claim could succeed, the approach elaborated by the Court of Appeal has made it extremely difficult for such a claim to succeed in practice.[3]

1 *T v Secretary of State for the Home Department* [2005] EWCA Civ 1421, (2005) Times, 23 December. Although Art 3 is an absolute right, the court in *ZT* made it quite clear that whilst it would have 'little hesitation' in holding that removal of an HIV sufferer to a country where the illness is not treatable would breach Art 3 if the disease was a rare condition, it would not find such a breach because the reality is that there is a substantial number of sufferers.

2 *J v Secretary of State for the Home Department* [2005] EWCA Civ 629, [2005] All ER (D) 359 (May).

3 *J v Secretary of State for the Home Department* (fn 2 above); and *R (on the application of Tozlukaya) v Secretary of State for the Home Department* [2006] EWCA Civ 379, [2006] All ER (D) 155 (Apr).

Domestic application of D

8.54

[Footnote 1 – add:]

Ibrahim v Secretary of State for the Home Department [2005] EWCA Civ 1816, [2005] All ER (D) 202 (Dec) – conditions in Somalia were such that returning a vulnerable and traumatized woman would breach Art 3 because of her extreme resourcelessness.

8.55

[Add at end:]

The House of Lords has now approved the decision of the majority of the Court of Appeal in *Limbuela*.[1] Lord Hope[2] and Baroness Hale[3] disapproved Laws LJ's 'spectrum analysis' as introducing considerations of proportionality into the absolute prohibition required by Art 3. Even in relation to acts and omissions pursuant to legitimate government policy the state is obliged to refrain from conduct that causes suffering of the necessary degree of severity. Lord Brown[4] found much of Laws LJ's analysis useful, not because it was helpful to place Art 3 complaints on a spectrum but because it highlighted the need to look at cases in the round.

1 *R (on the application of Limbuela) v Secretary of State for the Home Department* [2005] UKHL 66, [2006] 1 AC 396, [2005] 3 WLR 1014.
2 [2005] UKHL 66 at para [53] ff.
3 [2005] UKHL 66 at para [77].
4 [2005] UKHL 66 at para [89].

Slavery and forced labour

8.56

[Add at end:]

A minor, compelled to perform domestic work for a family for 15 hours per day, seven days per week was thereby held in servitude contrary to Art 4; amongst the means relied on to compel her to work was manipulation of her fear of the police owing to her unlawful immigration status.[1]

1 *Siliadin v France (Application 73316/01)* (2005) 20 BHRC 654, ECtHR.

Detention

8.58

[Add at end:]

A majority of the European Court of Human Rights (3:4) upheld the decision of the House of Lords in *Saadi*.[1] The issue was whether an asylum seeker who presented no risk of absconding could lawfully be detained for reasons of administrative convenience connected with processing his asylum claim, given that Art 5(1)(f) only permitted detention 'to prevent his effecting an unauthorized entry into the country'. The Court held that detention of a person who had not been granted leave to enter or remain could be considered as aimed at preventing unlawful entry simply by virtue of the fact that leave had not been granted. Moreover, there was no requirement that detention should be a 'necessary' means to the end of preventing unlawful entry. Whereas for a person authorized to be at large in a country, deprivation of his or her liberty required a reasonable balance to be struck between the interests of the individual and those of society, no such balance had to be struck for an immigrant who was not 'authorised' to be on the territory. 'All that is required is that the detention should be a genuine part of the process to determine whether the individual should be granted immigration clearance and/or asylum and that it should not otherwise be arbitrary, for example on account of its length'.[2] The Court did find a breach of Art 5(2) because of the failure to provide adequate reasons for the detention.

1 *Saadi v United Kingdom (Application No 13229/03)* (2006) Times, 3 August, [2006] All ER (D) 125 (Jul), ECtHR.
2 *(Application No 13229/03)* at para [45].

Family and private life

8.80

[In the text after footnote 14 add:]

Moreover, it is not enough to consider existing family life; the state must also have regard to potential family life and refrain from inhibiting the development of a real family life in the future.[1]

[Add at end:]

Where family members have lived apart for a considerable period of time Art 8 may entitle them to be reunited rather than merely to maintain their existing level of contact, particularly where their separation was caused by duress,[2] but even where it was freely chosen.[3]

[Footnote 14 – add:]

See also *Krasniqi v Secretary of State for the Home Department* [2006] EWCA Civ 391, (2006) Times, 20 April – relationship between two women protected by Art 8, given their traumatic histories; their emotional and mental fragility; the nature of the love and support they offered each other and their shared experience of bringing up a child together. In *R (on the application of Katshunga) v Secretary of State for the Home Department* [2006] EWHC 1208 (Admin), [2006] All ER (D) 71 (May) Gibbs J held that the adult claimant could establish that her removal would breach Art 8 by reference to her relationship with her adult brother upon whom she was particularly dependant owing to her own and her family's traumatic history and her consequent mental illness. See also *Mukarkar v Secretary of State for the Home Department* [2006] EWCA Civ 1045, (2006) Times, 16 August, [2006] All ER (D) 367 (Jul) – the tribunal had been entitled to conclude that refusing leave to remain to a father who was in poor health and dependant upon his family in the UK for support breached Art 8.

1 *R (on the application of Fawad Ahmadi) v Secretary of State for the Home Department* [2005] EWCA Civ 1721, [2005] All ER (D) 169 (Dec).
2 *Tuquabo-Tekle v Netherlands (Application No 60665/00)* [2005] 3 FCR 649, [2006] 1 FLR 798, [2006] Fam Law 267, [2005] ECHR 60665/00, ECtHR; *R (on the application of Yussuf) v Secretary of State for the Home Department* [2005] EWHC 2847 (Admin), [2005] All ER (D) 105 (Nov); *H (Somalia)* [2004] UKIAT 00027.
3 *Sen v Netherlands* (2003) 36 EHRR 7.

8.83

[In the text after footnote 3 add:]

The same principles were applied in *Tuquabo-Tekle* where it was held to be a breach of Art 8 not to allow an Eritrean national and former asylum seeker, resident in the Netherlands, to bring her 15 year old daughter to join her.[1] Similar principles were applied in the context of refusal to renew the residence permit of a Turkish national who was the husband and father of Turkish citizens resident in the Netherlands.[2] Particular weight was attached to the fact that for the children to join their father in Turkey, given that they had always lived in the cultural and linguistic environment of the Netherlands and attended school there, would mean a 'radical upheaval' for them which they could not 'realistically be expected' to undergo. These principles were further developed in *Da Silva and Hoogkamer* where it was held that Art 8 required the state to permit the mother of a young child, a citizen of the state, to reside there, notwithstanding that the mother had been unlawfully present throughout her stay in the state and conceived the child at a time when she had no entitlement to reside there.[3] The decisive consideration for the Court was the far reaching consequences for the family life between the mother and daughter that would result from the mother's expulsion given that the child would not be permitted by her father (who had a parental responsibility order) to accompany the mother.

1 *Tuquabo-Tekle v Netherlands (Application No 60665/00)* [2005] 3 FCR 649, [2006] 1 FLR 798, [2006] Fam Law 267, [2005] ECHR 60665/00, ECtHR.

2 *Sezen v Netherlands (Application No 50252/99)* [2006] 1 FCR 241, [2006] ECHR 50252/99, ECJ.

3 *Da Silva v Netherlands (Application No 50435/99)* [2006] 1 FCR 229, [2006] ECHR 50435/99, ECtHR.

8.85

[Add at end:]

The Court applies the same criteria to assessing the proportionality of expelling an individual who has been in a country since a young age (eg 10) as it applies to a second generation immigrant, ie the nature and gravity of the offence committed by the individual; the length of stay in the host country; the family ties and the social ties established in the host country by receiving schooling and spending the 'decisive years' of his or her youth there.[1]

1 *Radovanovic v Austria* (2004) App. No. 42703/98.

8.86

[Add at end:]

Through residence in a country an individual develops 'the personal, social and economic ties that make up the private life of every human being'[1] so that to refuse an application for residence or to expel the person would be an interference with private life. Moreover, merely to refrain from removing may be insufficient respect for private life; the Convention provides practical and effective protection for rights, not merely theoretical protection and that may entail the positive obligation to confer status (including a permanent right of residence) so as to enable a person to exercise the right in question without interference.[2] In the case of long resident and well integrated individuals, reasons of a particularly serious nature would be required to justify such an interference.[3]

1 See *Sisojeva v Latvia* (2005) App no. 60654/00; *Slivenko v Latvia (Application 48321/99)* [2004] 2 FCR 28, [2003] ECHR 48321/99, 15 BHRC 660, ECtHR.

[2] *Sisojeva* at para 104–5.
[3] *Sisojeva* at para 107–8.

Article 8 in the domestic courts

8.89

[Add at end:]

In *Ekinci* the Court of Appeal held that removing a Turkish citizen married to a British woman would not breach Art 8 because after removal he could apply for entry clearance to rejoin his wife in the UK. It was not open to him to argue in an appeal against removal that since he would probably be refused entry clearance, his removal would breach Art 8; any breach of his human rights resulting from refusal of entry clearance could be litigated in an appeal against that refusal.[1] The tribunal has treated the decision in *Ekinci* as a statement of generally applicable principle. However, declining as a matter of principle to consider whether removal of a family member would breach Art 8 because of problems that might subsequently arise in gaining readmission is inconsistent with Strasbourg jurisprudence.[2] Moreover, the Court of Appeal has held that *Ekinci* was a decision on its own facts and did not purport to lay down any general proposition of law[3]. It has been said that for the purpose of deciding whether a case is 'truly exceptional', 'the question is not whether the case against removal is outside the general run of human experience: it is whether it stands out from the general run of cases for non-removal on family or private life grounds, almost all of which tend to evoke sympathy'.[4]

[1] *R (on the application of Ekinci) v Secretary of State for the Home Department)* [2003] EWCA Civ 765, [2003] All ER (D) 215 (Jun); and *LH (Jamaica)* [2006] UKAIT 00019.
[2] For example, *Sezen v Netherlands (Application No 50252/99)* [2006] 1 FCR 241, [2006] ECHR 50252/99, ECJ. There the government sought to justify an interference with family life on the basis that the deportee could apply for permission to return. The Court was unimpressed with that because of the absence of an indication from the government as to when and under what conditions such an application would succeed.
[3] *Mukarkar v Secretary of State for the Home Department* [2006] EWCA Civ 1045, (2006) Times, 16 August, [2006] All ER (D) 367 (Jul).
[4] By Sedley LJ in *Krasniqi v Secretary of State for the Home Department* [2006] EWCA Civ 391, (2006) Times, 20 April.

Article 8 – delay

8.89A

[Add new paragraph:]

The relevance of delay on the part of the state in determining a claim to enter or remain in the UK has been further considered by the Courts and Tribunal. Substantial administrative delay that brings consequences other than the bare passage of time is a matter that the decision maker is obliged to consider, but there is no distinct principle whereby the existence of such delay is determinative of the judgment on proportionality.[1] The delay need not cause substantial prejudice[2] and the weight to be given to it in an individual case is a matter for the decision maker.[3] Substantial weight might be given to delay where, in consequence, the claimant was refused instead of being granted leave to remain and thereby lost the procedural right he would have gained to make an in-country application for leave to remain as a spouse. That procedural right would have obviated the interference with his family life caused by the refusal of leave to remain[4]. Significantly less weight would be given where the delay had no such consequence and where there was not even a claim to interference with family life but at most, a tenuous claim based on private life.[5] Whilst the existence of delay does not avoid the need to identify 'exceptional circumstances' before finding a breach of Art 8,[6] the fact of unreasonable delay may be the factor that makes a case 'truly exceptional'.[7]

1 *Strbac v Secretary of State for the Home Department* [2005] EWCA Civ 848, [2005] All ER (D) 121 (Jul).

2 *Akaeke v Secretary of State for the Home Department* [2005] EWCA Civ 947, (2005) Times, 23 September, [2005] All ER (D) 409 (Jul); and *Senthuran v Secretary of State for the Home Department* [2004] EWCA Civ 950, [2004] 4 All ER 365, [2004] 3 FCR 273. In a case where the Home Office had delayed for nearly two years in determining an application for leave to remain by the spouse of a British citizen, Collins J said of the argument that the couple had suffered no consequent prejudice that it lacked merit and humanity: 'It must be obvious that the longer the husband and wife and their family are able to remain in this country and put down roots in this country, the more hard it will be for them to be uprooted and for the family life to be interfered with in the way that is suggested': *R (on the application of Ajoh) v Secretary of State for the Home Department* [2006] EWHC 1489 (Admin), [2006] All ER (D) 235 (May).

3 See *Akaeke v Secretary of State for the Home Department* (fn 2 above).

4 *Shala v Secretary of State for the Home Department* [2003] EWCA Civ 233, [2003] All ER (D) 407 (Feb).

5 See *Strbac v Secretary of State for the Home Department* (fn 1 above).

6 *Janosevic v Secretary of State for the Home Department* [2005] EWCA Civ 1711, [2005] All ER (D) 247 (Dec).

7 See *Akaeke v Secretary of State for the Home Department* and *R (on the application of Ajoh)*. The tribunal has considered the question of delay in *MB (Croatia)* [2005] UKIAT 00092; *GS (Serbia and Montengro)* [2005] UKAIT 00121; *MM(Serbia and Montenegro)* [2005] UKAIT 00163.

Article 8 – policies

8.89B

[Add new paragraph:]

Policies other than those contained in the immigration rules are relevant to determining whether an interference with a right protected by Art 8 can be justified as proportionate. On the one hand, it has been said that when the Court of Appeal in *Huang* talked about the immigration rules striking the balance between private right and public interest, it must also have had in mind the various policies and concessions that supplement the rules.[1] Thus a case would only have to be shown to be 'truly exceptional' in order to establish a breach of Art 8 if it fell outside the policies and concessions as well as the rules. On the other hand, the Court of Appeal has adopted the approach that if a person might qualify under a policy, that would be a reason to characterise his or her case as 'truly exceptional'.[2] Moreover, even if a person does not qualify within the strict terms of a policy, he or she is entitled to rely upon its rationale to establish a 'truly exceptional' case.[3] In this context, to decide whether Art 8 is breached an immigration judge has to do more than merely determine whether the decision maker has properly applied any relevant policy;[4] the immigration judge has to apply the policy him or herself to determine whether the appellant falls within the policy[5] or its rationale[6] or spirit[7] or meets most if not all of the policy's criteria.[8]

1 See *Huang v Secretary of State for the Home Department* [2005] EWCA Civ 105; and *MB (Croatia)* [2005] UKIAT 00092.

2 *R (on the application of Tozlukaya) v Secretary of State for the Home Department* [2006] EWCA Civ 379, [2006] All ER (D) 155 (Apr).

3 *Shkembi v Secretary of State for the Home Department* [2005] EWCA Civ 1592, [2005] All ER (D) 323 (Nov); and *R (on the application of Lekstaka) v Immigration Appeal Tribunal* [2005] EWHC 745 (Admin), [2005] All ER (D) 222 (Apr). Such reliance for the purpose of informing the Court's judgment on proportionality is to be distinguished from an impermissible attempt to have the Court enlarge a policy so as to establish an enforceable right for the benefit of a person to whom the policy does not apply as in *Mongoto v Secretary of State for the Home Department* [2005] EWCA Civ 751.

4 Generally speaking, the limit of the tribunal's jurisdiction when considering whether a decision was 'not in accordance with the law' owing to failure to give effect to a relevant policy: *Abdi (Dhudi Saleban) v Secretary of State for the Home Department* [1996] Imm AR 148, CA.

5 *Baig v Secretary of State for the Home Department* [2005] EWCA Civ 1246.

6 See *Shkembi* (fn 3 above).

7 See *Lekstaka* (fn 3 above).

8 *Miao v Secretary of State for the Home Department* [2006] EWCA Civ 75, [2006] All ER (D) 215 (Feb).

8.90

[In the text after footnote 4 add:]

The Court of Appeal has acknowledged that the British citizenship of a child is a relevant factor for the purpose of deciding whether removal of the child's non-citizen mother breaches Art 8.[1]

1 *Nguyen v Secretary of State for the Home Department* [2006] EWCA Civ 414, [2006] All ER (D) 380 (Mar).

Article 8 – health

8.92

[Add at end:]

Whilst a case based upon the effect on a person's health of removal from the UK could in principle fail under Art 3 but succeed under Art 8, in practical terms the test to be satisfied was high if not impossible to meet.[1]

1 *T v Secretary of State for the Home Department* [2005] EWCA Civ 1421, (2005) Times, 23 December. In respect of HIV sufferers who face removal, only something markedly exceeding the level of suffering inherent in being removed to a want of treatment would qualify a person for protection. See also *SN v Secretary of State for the Home Department* [2005] EWCA Civ 1683.

The right to marry and found a family

8.97

[Add at end:]

The scheme under Asylum and Immigration (Treatment of Claimants etc) Act 2004, s 19 whereby a person subject to immigration control requires the permission of the Secretary of State in order to marry in the UK has now been held to breach Arts 12 and 14 of the Convention.[1] It was held that the state could legitimately interfere with the right to marry in order to prevent sham marriages being contracted for the purpose of avoiding immigration control. However, the statutory scheme which required a person to have leave to enter or remain of a particular duration in order to qualify for permission to marry was not rationally connected to that objective: there was no rational basis for the presumed connection between the length of a person's leave to enter or remain and the genuineness of a marriage; there was no rational basis for the assumption (apparent from the exemption from the requirement to obtain permission to marry for those marrying in the Church of England) that Anglican marriages were not sham whereas other religious marriages might be (permission being required for any other kind of religious marriage); the scheme arbitrarily disregarded evidence tending to show the genuineness of a prospective marriage (eg children of a relationship, cohabitation, property) and it allowed no capacity for making representations that permission be granted other than in relation to compelling compassionate circumstances making it unreasonable for the couple to marry abroad. It was also held that the scheme was disproportionate (because it attached insufficient importance to Convention rights), notwithstanding that it was enacted by the legislature in the field of 'broad social policy', an area in which the Court would always be reluctant to intervene.

1 *R (on the application of Baiai) v Secretary of State for the Home Department* [2006] EWHC 823 (Admin), 2006] 3 All ER 608, [2006] 2 FCR 131.

Non-discrimination

8.98

[Add at end:]

The requirement that a person subject to immigration control and wishing to have a religious wedding ceremony obtain permission to marry from the Home Office whereas a person subject to immigration control and wishing to have an Anglican wedding ceremony did not require such permission was held to discriminate on grounds of religion in relation to Art 12.[1] Differential treatment of applicants for assistance under the Housing Act 1996 according to whether their dependant children were British was held to be in breach of Art 14 in conjunction with Art 8.[2]

1 *R (on the application of Baiai) v Secretary of State for the Home Department* [2006] EWHC 823 (Admin), 2006] 3 All ER 608, [2006] 2 FCR 131.

2 *R (on the application of Morris) v Westminster City Council; R (on the application of Badhu) v Lambeth London Borough Council* [2005] EWCA Civ 1184, [2006] 1 WLR 505, [2006] HLR 122.

Protection of property – Protocol 1, Art 1

8.99A

[Add new paragraph:]

Exclusion from the UK could be challenged on the ground that it interfered with the applicant's right to the peaceful enjoyment of his possessions in circumstances where the applicant was outside the UK but his property (in the form of a contractual right to receive medical treatment) was in the UK.[1]

[1] *R (on the application of Murungaru) v Secretary of State for the Home Department* [2006] EWHC 2416 (Admin).

HUMAN RIGHTS APPEALS

8.104

[Add at end:]

To ignore the impact of an appellant's removal upon the family left behind, even though the family were not appellants would be 'hopelessly blinkered'.[1] By contrast, in the context of an appeal under Immigration and Asylum Act 1999, s 65 the Court of Appeal held that the adjudicator had erred in law by giving undue weight to the impact of the appellant's removal on his mother, given that the appellate jurisdiction was to consider the human rights of the appellant.[2]

[1] At least in the case of an appellant caring for his seriously ill but settled brother: *R (on the application of Fawad Ahmadi) v Secretary of State for the Home Department* [2005] EWCA Civ 1721, [2005] All ER (D) 169 (Dec).

[2] *Betts v Secretary of State for the Home Department* [2005] EWCA Civ 828, [2005] All ER (D) 77 (Jul). See also *CM (Jamaica)* [2005] UKIAT 00103 and para 18.49 of the main text.

8.105

[Add at end:]

In an appeal against deportation, the tribunal should consider first whether the decision to deport is in accordance with the immigration rules before deciding whether deportation would breach Art 8.[1]

[1] *CM (Jamaica)* [2005] UKIAT 00103; and *CW (Jamaica)* [2005] UKIAT 00110.

8.109

[NB:]

This paragraph needs to be read in the light of current Home Office policy with regard to discretionary leave and humanitarian protection, described at paras 12.174 ff of this supplement.

[Add at end:]

Successfully establishing in an appeal that removal from the UK would breach the ECHR establishes not merely a right not to be removed but also an entitlement to leave to enter or remain in the UK.[1]

1 *S v Secretary of State for the Home Department (sub nom R (on the application of GG) v Secretary of State for the Home Department)* [2006] EWCA Civ 1157, [2006] All ER (D) 30 (Aug).

GOING TO EUROPE

Procedure

8.111

[Footnote 6 – add:]

See also *N v Finland* (2005) App No 38885/02 where the Court heard oral evidence in order to make its own assessment of the credibility of an asylum seeker from the Democratic Republic of Congo.

Chapter 9

VISITS, STUDY AND TEMPORARY PURPOSES

INTRODUCTION

9.1

[Footnote 4:]

The schedule to the Immigration (Designation of Travel Bans) Order 2000 has been replaced by the schedule to the Immigration (Designation of Travel Bans) (Amendment) Order 2005, SI 2005/3310, which came into force on 6 December 2005. One of the UN resolutions relating to Al-Qua'ida and the Taliban (resolution 1455 (2003)) of 17 January 2003 has been deleted from the schedule.

9.2

[NB:]

Phase 2 of the Home Office's scheme for compulsory prior entry clearance for all non-visa nationals who seek entry into the UK for more than six months has been brought into force by the rule changes in HC 645. There is no longer a category of 'specified nationals' and the requirement for prior entry clearance now applies to all non-visa nationals except British nationals who do not have a right of abode.[1] Non-visa nationals coming for a visit do not need prior entry clearance.[2]

1 These are, British Nationals (Overseas), BOTCs, BOCs, BPPs and persons who under the British Nationality Act 1981 are British subjects: HC 395, para 24(2), as inserted by HC 645. See 3.12 above.
2 HC 395, para 23A, inserted by HC 645.

9.3

[NB:]

Marriage visitors now include those coming to enter into a civil partnership ceremony in the UK under HC 395, para 56D, as amended by HC 582 as from 5 December 2005.

9.4

[NB:]

Marriage visitors now include those coming to enter into a civil partnership ceremony in the UK under HC 395, para 56D, as amended by HC 582 as from 5 December 2005.

The IDI on 'special classes of visitor' in Chapter 2, Annex B, have been updated in February 2006. Much is as before, but there are changes and some are new entries. Reference should be made to the full IDI. The classes dealt with and their paragraph numbers are as follows:

1. academic visitors;
2. visitors under the UK/China ADS Memorandum of Understanding (dealt with at **9.20** below and under HC 395, paras 56G-56I, inserted by HC 486 which came into effect on 5 April 2005);
3. appellants seeking leave to attend their appeal hearings (see below);
4. visiting archaelogists;
5. business visitors (dealt with in main text);
6. carers;
7. child minders for relatives;
8. court reporters coming to take formal depositions (who should obtain work permits);
9. Doctors coming for PLAB tests (dealt with at 9.45C below);
10. entertainers and sportspersons who may be admitted as visitors (see below);
11. marriage visits (dealt with in chapter 11 of main text);
12. parents with children at school here;
13. persons coming for job interviews;
14. visitors from country A coming to the UK to seek visas for country B, including settlement visas. We expand on two of these categories.

Appellants coming to the UK to attend their appeals. Although they have no right to enter for the sole purpose of attending the appeal, appellants can be admitted as visitors if they can satisfy the immigration officer that they will leave the UK regardless of the outcome of their appeal or if they qualify for entry in some other capacity.

Entertainers and sportspersons. The IDI distinguishes between amateurs and professionals. It is alright for amateurs to be given board and lodgings and reasonable expenses, but not appearance money, fees or sponsorship or cash prizes. Amateur sportspersons can join amateur clubs, provided that the team is represented wholly or predominantly by amateur players and they are not being paid by the club in cash or in kind other than board and lodging and reasonable expenses arising from sporting activity (for example reasonable sponsorship of equipment) and provided they are not giving coaching (IDI Ch 17, s 8, para 3.3). Professionals can come as visitors for personal appearances and promotions such as signing album covers, television chat shows, the publication of a book, negotiating contracts, discussing sponsorship deals etc, provided no performance other than a private audition or trial is involved. Professional sportspersons can come in as visitors to take part in a specific event or tournament, such as the British Open Golf or Wimbledon tennis, or series of events as individual competitors or as members of overseas touring rugby, soccer or cricket teams, or a boxer coming for one fight. Amateurs or professionals may also come to take part in specific one-off charity sporting events, testimonials, benefit and exhibition matches, even though they may be joining UK-based teams, provided that they do not receive payment other than for travelling and other expenses.

9.5

[NB:]

Marriage visitors now include those coming to enter into a civil partnership ceremony in the UK under HC 395, para 56D, as amended by HC 582 as from 5 December 2005.

General rules on admission

9.7

[Footnote 2:]

IDI Ch 2, s 1, para 2.6 (Feb 2006) says that leave of only three months should be given to holders of Council of Europe travel documents and passengers with a passport stamped with an authorised visa, signaling a specified period of leave, should be given that period.

Maintenance and accommodation

9.13

[Footnote 3:]

The reference to the 1987 Housing Benefit (General) Regulations should be replaced with the Housing Benefit Regulations 2006, SI 2006/213, reg 10.

Visits for family reasons, civil partnership ceremonies and marriage

9.14

[NB:]

Visits to Britain for civil partnership ceremonies now rank alongside weddings and the same rules apply, as set out in the paragraph: see HC 395, para 56D, as amended by HC 582 as from 5 December 2005.

Child visitors

9.14A

[Add new paragraph:]

HC 819, which took effect on 12 February 2006, inserts a number of new rules relating to child visitors. The main changes are as follows:

(1) Children travelling alone and applying for entry as visitors will have to meet all the visitor requirements as they do at present in the Immigration Rules. In addition, they will now have to show that there are

arrangements in place for their arrival in the UK and will also need to identify the parent or guardian normally responsible for them in their home country.

(2) This means that in the case of a child, who subsequently comes to the attention of the caring or educational services, there will be a record of their family or carers, both prior to, and immediately after, their arrival. If the provision of these gives cause for concern, then entry to the UK may be refused or further investigation will need to take place.

(3) Children who are accompanying an adult, whether a family member or not, and seeking entry as visitors, will have to meet all the requirements of the Visitor Rules. In addition, they will have to give details of the accompanying adult so that the nature of the journey and the relationship can be established. Children from countries whose nationals require a visa to the UK will have to produce, in order to be admitted, a visa or entry clearance that names the accompanying adult in an identifiable way, and will only be admitted to the UK on the same occasion as this adult.

(4) If the provisions of this information or the information itself gives cause for concern, either when provided or at the point of entry, then entry to the UK may be refused and further investigation may have to take place. The information and identities provided will be a record that may be assessed, if the child subsequently comes to the attention of the caring or educational services.

The concern which has prompted these rules is the concern that minors are brought to the UK for trafficking purposes or that the accompanying adult disappears and the children then claim asylum.

Extension of stay as a visitor

9.19

[NB:]

Where child visitors wish to have an extension of stay, within the maximum six-month period allowed for visits, they will have to be able meet the cost of their return or onward journey, be under the age of 18, can demonstrate that there are suitable arrangements for their care in the UK and that they have a parent or guardian in their home country or country of habitual residence who is responsible for their care.[1]

1 HC 395, para 46D, inserted by HC 819 with effect from 12 February 2006.

Visiting religious workers

9.20A

[Add new paragraph:]

It has long been recognised that religious communities in the UK face difficulties in recruiting sufficient numbers of priests from within the UK. Now a new category of visitor has been created by rule changes in HC 769, which took effect from 9 January 2006. The new rule deals with two categories of religious workers, who perform vital religious duties rites within their communities, but who do not preach to a congregation.[1] A *visiting religious worker* must be an established religious worker based overseas, is less schooled in the faith than a religious worker in a non-pastoral role, and can only get an aggregate of six months' leave.[2]

A *religious worker in a non-pastoral role* needs to show much greater training, and gets an initial 12 months,[3] which can be extended to two years.[4] Neither category will not be required to speak English.[5]

1 These are defined as: (i) a *visiting religious worker* who is a person coming to the UK for a short period to perform religious duties at one or more locations in the UK; and (ii) a *religious worker in a non-pastoral role* who is a person employed in the UK by the faith he or she is coming here to work for, and whose duties include performing religious rites within the religious community, but not preaching to a congregation: HC 395, para 177A, as inserted by HC 769.
2 HC 395, paras 177B–E, as inserted by HC 769.
3 HC 395, para 177B and 177C, as inserted by HC 769.
4 HC 395, para 177A, as inserted by HC 769.
5 A religious worker in a non-pastoral role must be joining a local religious community where at least one full-time member of staff has a sufficient knowledge of English.

Visitors from China

9.20B

[Add new paragraph:]

HC 486 created a new category of 'ADS visitor'[1] or those seeking to enter the UK under the terms of the Memorandum of Understanding (MoU) on visa and related issues concerning tourist groups from the People's Republic of China to the United Kingdom.

The new rule is intended to regulate outward tourism from China to the UK by providing a mechanism for issuing visas for groups of Chinese tourists to authorised travel agents. The new category is necessary because the terms of the MoU differ from the existing requirements for visitors under the Immigration Rules. ADS visitors will have to meet the requirements for ordinary visitors at para 41(ii)–(vii) of HC 395, but in addition, applicants must be Chinese nationals; must be genuinely seeking entry as a visitor for a maximum period of 30 days; must intend to enter, travel and leave the UK as part of a group and will not be permitted to extend their stay beyond the maximum 30 day period.[2] In conjunction with these Rules changes, the Immigration (Leave to Enter and Remain) (Amendment) Order 2005, which came into force on 5 April 2005, provides that visas issued pursuant to the MoU shall have effect as single entry visas and have effect as leave to enter on one occasion unless endorsed as dual entry visas; in which case they shall have effect as leave to enter on two occasions.[3]

1 Approved Destination Status, created by The UK/China ADS Memorandum of Understanding (MoU) which was signed on 21 January 2005.
2 In order to prevent ADS tourists being able to extend their stay by applying for an extension in another visitor category, amendments are also being made to HC 395, para 44 (extension of stay as an ordinary visitor); para 54 (extension of stay as a visitor for private

medical treatment) and para 56A (leave to enter or remain for a parent of a child at school). As to the exemption under s 19 of the Race Relations Act 1976, s 19, see 1.20 above.

3 SI 2005/1159.

Visitors in transit

9.21

[Footnote 8:]

For the list of amendments after SI 2005/492 add the Immigration (Passenger Transit Visa) (Amendment) Order 2006, SI 2006/493.

Visitors – switching categories

9.25

[NB:]

The switching rules from visitor to student have been changed yet again. Previously, as we have explained in the main text, non-visa nationals who were admitted to the UK as visitors could be granted leave as a student if they had been accepted on a course of degree level or above. All other visitors (visa nationals, and non-visa nationals accepted for courses below degree level) were prohibited from gaining leave as a student without having the necessary entry clearance. HC 1016 now removes[1] the more favourable Rules for non-visa national visitors who have been accepted for courses of degree level or above, so that they too must have entry clearance as a student or prospective student before they will be allowed to gain leave as a student. There is an exception. Non-visa nationals who were granted leave to enter as a visitor before 1 July 2006 will not be subject to this Rules change and will continue to enjoy the same rights as before.[2]

1 HC 395, para 60(i), as substituted by HC 1016, with effect from 3 April 2006.
2 HC 395, para 60(i)(b).

The list of specified nationals from non-visa countries who were required to have an entry clearance if they were seeking entry to the UK for more than six months has now gone. Now all non-visa nationals require entry clearance in these circumstances. See 3.12 above

[Footnote 5:]

HC 395, para 98(i) has been repealed by HC 302. There is now no scope for switching to working holiday maker by visitors or anyone else under the rules.

9.26

[NB:]

A visitor may switch to leave as an unmarried partner, but cannot do so to leave as a civil partner or a married partner under HC 395, para 284 (i), as amended by HC 582 as from 5 December 2005.

STUDENTS

Student nurses

9.44A

[Add new paragraph:]

Student nurses and midwives who qualify in the UK can go straight into work permit employment, but with nurse and midwives who have qualified overseas, their entry into the UK labour market has been much more fraught and uncertain. Under the old supervised practice programme, overseas qualified nurses and midwives would apply to the Nursing and Midwifery Council (NMC) for pre-registration and then enter the UK as either student nurses or as work permit holders. However, neither route was entirely appropriate as a period of supervised practice is simply a bridge to employment in the UK. The requirements of the student nurse rules relating to intentions to leave are inappropriate as the whole idea of the supervised practice course was to prepare and shunt the nurses into employment as quickly as possible. On the other hand, it is a requirement of the work permit rules that a person is capable of taking the employment in question. Strictly, this requirement cannot be met until a nurse has completed supervised practice and been fully registered with the NMC. Now the situation has been dealt with by the creation by HC 645, which took effect on 30 November 2005, of an intermediate category of permit free employment while the nurse or midwife gets his or her adaptation training, before switching into work permit employment. We deal with this at 10.30A ff.

Postgraduate doctors and dentists

9.45

[Delete the whole of para 9.45 and replace with new paras 9.45–9.45D:]

Graduate doctors and dentists may both wish to spend time in the UK training for further qualifications at basic or higher specialist level. For a long time the Immigration Rules have catered for these needs under the student rules, although much of what is being done is clearly in the nature of employment training, and other doctors and dentists in non-training posts at the same grades as those covered by this category are in fact working under work permits. That policy has now been dramatically recast in the latest round of rule changes contained in HC 1016, which took effect on 3 April 2006.[1] The changes make a lot of sense. What is properly classified as on the job training is now moved into employment and the basic training is kept under the student rules. But why now? The government say that, first, the needs and the structure of the health service and medical training programmes have changed considerably since this category was introduced. Secondly, the number of places in UK medical and dental schools has increased, meaning that there are now more UK graduates seeking relevant training posts. There is therefore no longer a need for a specific category in the Immigration Rules to enable doctors and dentists to train in the UK for many years, prior to either leaving the UK or switching into an employment or self employment category.[2]

[1] There was another set of rules, HC 974, laid before parliament on the same day and coming into force on the same day in almost identical terms to HC 1016. They can be ignored.
[2] IDI Ch 3, s 6 (Jul 2006): Explanatory Memorandum to HC 1016.

9.45A

With effect from 3 April 2006, the revised rules for Postgraduate Doctors and Dentists only provides for those doctors and dentists who have completed their medical or dental studies in the UK[1] to take their Foundation Programme in the UK.[2] They qualify to take the Foundation Programme and nothing else. The Foundation Programme consists of one year at Pre-Registration House Officer level and one year at Senior House Officer level and was introduced on 2 August 2005 for doctors (although it will not be made compulsory until August 2007).[3] The previous rules for Postgraduate Doctors and Dentists covered training at the following levels:

- Foundation Programmes;
- Basic Specialist Training;[4]
- Higher Specialist Training.[5]

Work permits can now be issued for training posts at these grades, if all the relevant requirements are met (see chapter 10 below).[6] Those left in the student trainee category are still considered as trainees for this period, and are expected to leave the UK at the end of their training,[7] unless they have been able to switch into work permit employment or one of the other categories of leave as set out in the Rules.[8] Consequently, this category does not lead to settlement and any period spent in Foundation training will not count towards settlement, if a graduate later switches into a settlement category of employment or self employment.[9] Other non-EEA doctors and dentists will still be able to come to the UK. However, those taking up a Senior House Officer or Specialist Registrar post (or equivalent grades at either level) will now be considered as in employment for immigration purposes, and will need to meet the requirements of the work permit or other employment schemes. The same applies for to those wanting to undertake a Foundation Programme in the UK but who do not meet the requirements of the revised immigration rules introduced by HC 1016. According to the IDI, the new arrangements apply for all posts at these grades.[10] There has previously been confusion about which of these posts are recognised training posts (and therefore eligible for leave as a Postgraduate Doctor or Dentist), and which posts at the same grade are not recognised as training posts, even where filled by trainee doctors or dentists (and where a work permit is therefore required). Since the changes to the rules for Postgraduate Doctors and Dentists, there is no longer any distinction between training and non-training posts for immigration purposes.

[1] The applicant must have successfully completed and obtained a recognised UK degree in medicine or dentistry from either: (a) a UK publicly funded institution of further or higher education; or (b) a UK bona fide private education institution which maintains satisfactory records of enrolment and attendance: HC 395, para 70(i), as inserted by HC 1016. Secondly, they must previously have spent the final academic year of their above studies as an ordinary student, a student nurse, doing resits of their exams, or writing up a thesis, and

have been enrolled as an ordinary student for at least one other academic year (aside from the final year) of their studies: Ibid, para 70(ii).

2 HC 395, para 70(iii) and (iv), as inserted by HC 1016. Pre-Registration House Officer is now the first year of the Foundation Programme.

3 IDI Ch 3, s 6 (Jul 2006).

4 This refers to Senior House Office (SHO) and equivalent grades: IDI Ch 3, s 6 (Jul 2006).

5 This refers to Specialist Registrar and equivalent grades. The General Practice Vocational Training Scheme (GPVTS) is also considered as higher specialist training: IDI Ch 3, s 6 (Jul 2006).

6 Those caught by the change of rules are not catered for in the immigration rules, but should consult the very full list of interim and transitional measures in the IDI to safeguard their positions: IDI Ch 3, s 6 (Jul 2006), pp 26–31.

7 Ibid, para 70(vi), as inserted by HC 1016.

8 These are: (a) a doctor or dentist undertaking a period of clinical attachment or a dental observer post; (b) a work permit holder; (c) a highly skilled migrant; (d) someone intending to establish themselves in business; or (e) an innovator. See HC 395, para 70(vi), as inserted by HC 1016.

9 IDI Ch 3, s 6 (Jul 2006).

10 IDI Ch 3, s 6 (Jul 2006).

9.45B

Leave can be granted as a Postgraduate Doctor or Dentist when **all** the requirements of paras 70 (leave to enter) or 73 (extension of stay) of HC 395 are met. Entry into the training may be made by those who have finished their degree and then left the UK, in which case they will need an entry clearance under para 70. Alternatively they may still be in the UK with leave in the one of the student categories identified in para 70, in which case they will switch into training under para 73 without any need to leave the country or get an entry clearance. Some applicants may have undertaken a short period of clinical attachment or dental observer post[1] after their studies but before the Foundation Programme starts. They too may switch under para 73. But someone who is in the UK with any other category of leave (including those who are in the UK as the dependant of another migrant) will not qualify to switch and will need to leave the country to obtain an entry clearance. The Foundation Programme lasts 24 months. Leave can be granted for a maximum of 26 months initially – this is to allow one month either side of the Foundation Programme.[2] Applicants who need further time to complete the Programme can then be granted a further period of leave up to a maximum of three years in total.[3]

1 Under HC 395, paras 75G–75M.

2 HC 395, para 71, as amended by HC 1016.

3 Ibid, para 73. Some migrants may need extra time to complete their Foundation Programme, for example because they have been ill or need to re-take part of it. Previous periods of leave may complicate the calculation of leave to be given at the three different stages: entry clearance, leave to enter; leave to remain and anyone concerned should consult the very helpful table in IDI Ch 3, s 6 (Jul 2006).

9.45C

Before any doctor can practise medicine in the United Kingdom they must register with the General Medical Council (GMC). Doctors who qualify overseas and wish to register must first pass the test of the Professional and Linguistic Assessment Board (PLAB) to demonstrate their knowledge of English and their medical expertise. The PLAB test has two parts – part one can be taken in the UK or abroad, but part two can only be taken in the UK. Applicants can apply for leave to enter to take either or both parts of the test in the UK. Leave to enter will be for a period of six months extendable on application to a maximum of 18 months, under the visitor rules (see 9.7 in the main text). Doctors who come to the UK to take the PLAB Test may also undertake periods of clinical attachment during their leave. This involves observation only and not treatment of patients and so does not breach the prohibition on employment. Doctors who pass the PLAB Test are allowed to switch into certain other categories. They may apply for leave to remain to undertake a period of clinical attachment, as a postgraduate doctor or trainee general practitioner, as a doctor employed in the UK with a valid work permit, or as a General Practitioner under the highly-skilled migrant Programme.[1]

1 HC 395, paras 75A–F, inserted by HC 346 from 15 March 2005. See IDI Ch 3, s 7 (Mar 05). Transitional provisions allow doctors who entered the UK as visitors before that date specifically to take the test to be granted extensions up to the maximum of 18 months allowed under the rules and to benefit from the new switching provisions: IDI Ch 3, s 7, para 1.2.

9.45D

A period of stay of up to 12 months is available under the visitor rules for a clinical attachment or as a dental observer, for graduates from medical or dental schools.[1] Clinical attachments may also be undertaken by successful PLAB examinees, and by doctors and dentists in the UK who are work permit holders.[2] The post must be unpaid and involve observation only.[3] The general requirements of the visit rules for visitors (see 9.7 above) must be complied with, except for the intention to leave, which is in the alternative to the grant of leave for further training or work as a doctor or dentist.[4]

1 HC 395, para 75G–M as inserted. These studies need not have been undertaken in the UK.
2 HC 395, para 75K(i).
3 HC 395, para 75G(ii).
4 HC 395, para 75G(iii) and 75K(iv). See also IDI Mar 05, Ch 3, s 8. Transitional arrangements benefit those admitted as visitors before the rule change for similar purposes: IDI Ch 3, s 8, para 1.2.

Spouses and children of students and prospective students

9.46

[NB:]

Civil partners, as well as spouses, of students are admitted in line with the student partner's or spouse's leave under HC 395, para 76, as amended by HC 582 as from 5 December 2005.

Duration of leave

9.51

[Replace fn 8:]

The fees charged to students for a visa or entry clearance are contained in the Consular Fees Order 2002, SI 2002/1672 and are currently set at £36. The big increase in fees comes when the student gets to the UK and needs an extension of leave (see 9.54 below).

Extensions for students and student nurses

9.52

[Footnote 11 – add:]

In *WR (Student: Regular Attendance; Maximum Period) Jamaica* [2005] UKAIT 00170, [2006] Imm AR 177 the Tribunal held that 'regular' in the context of HC 395, para 60(iv) meant 'sufficiently often, habitual or frequent' to meet the demands of the particular course, which was a question of fact in each case and there was no fixed percentage, but the greater the attendance the more likely that it would satisfy the rule.

[Footnote 13 – add:]

In *TB (Student application, variation of course, effect) Jamaica* [2006] UKAIT 00034 (06 April 2006) the AIT found that, where a student had chosen, prior to the date of decision, to take a course falling into a different student leave category so that at the date of decision it was clear she had abandoned any intention of following the course for which she had applied for an extension of stay, the nature of the change was such that she could not comply with the requirements of the Immigration Rules in relation to the course for which she had initially applied.

[Footnote 15 – add:]

In *SW (Paragraph 60 (v): meaning of 'including') Jamaica* [2006] UKAIT 00054 the AIT have taken a hard line on the need to pass exams,holding that whatever other evidence of progress is provided, the applicant is required to show that she has both taken and passed any 'relevant examinations'. No other cases were cited or discussed.

9.54

[Footnote 1:]

The 2005 Regulations (SI 2005/771) have been revoked and replaced by the Immigration (Leave to Remain) (Prescribed Forms and Procedures) Regulations 2006, SI 2006/1421, as corrected by SI 2006/1548.

Changing from student status

9.61

[Footnote 5:]

HC 395, para 98(i) has been repealed by HC 302. There is now no scope for switching to working holiday maker by students or anyone else under the rules. Overseas doctors admitted for the PLABS test may switch into other categories either as employees under the work permit scheme or become a GP under the Highly Skilled Migrants Scheme (see 9.45 above). Graduate students, who meet the requirements of the Scheme, may also seek and take work under 'The Fresh Talent: Working in Scotland Scheme' (see 10.111A below).

AU PAIRS

The requirements

9.63

[Requirement (iii) should now read:]

(iii) is unmarried and is not a civil partner;

WORKING HOLIDAYMAKERS

9.65

[NB:]

Prior to an amendment of the immigration rules relating to working holidaymakers (WHM) by HC 302 in February 2005, the WHM Rules referred to leave being granted on arrival in the UK for a period not exceeding two years.[1] The amendments in HC 302 were silent on the maximum period of stay. HC 104, which became effective on 6 July 2005, then made it clear that the two-year period starts from the date when the entry clearance became valid for use, not from the date of arrival in the UK. Then came HC 645 on 13 November 2005, which accidentally deleted Annex 3 to the Rules, which contained the list of countries whose nationals were eligible for working holidays in the UK. Finally, there was HC 697, one week later on 22 November 2005, which reinstated the list 'inadvertently deleted.' We hope this is the final jinx on working holidaymakers. They deserve a better break.

1 HC 395, paras 96 and 98 (as printed in the 5th edn of this work).

Working holiday

9.67

[NB:]

Working holiday makers can switch into employment in an occupation listed on the Work Permits (UK) shortage occupations list: HC 395, para 131D, as amended by HC 302.

[Footnote 4 should read:]

HC 395, para 131D, as amended by HC 302.

Chapter 10

WORKING, BUSINESS, INVESTMENT AND RETIREMENT IN THE UK

INTRODUCTION

10.1

[NB:]

In March 2006 the government announced a five tier points based system as one of the central plank of its managed migration system[1] as follows:

- **TIER 1 – Highly skilled individuals to contribute to growth and productivity.** The most highly skilled individuals, and people with large sums of money to invest, should qualify for entry or leave to remain under Tier 1. The aim is to target the migrants who are most likely to maximise growth and productivity. So points would need to be allocated and weighted according to evidence as to which factors are most closely related to economic success.[2]
- **TIER 2 – Skilled workers with a job offer; and workers to meet specific overseas requirements.** Tier 2 should offer an entry route to skilled individuals with a job offer where there is a labour market demand. A points system could allow for a migrant with a verified job offer not on the shortage list to reach the points threshold by a combination of salary, skills and/or regional need.[3]
- **TIER 3 – Limited numbers of workers to fill low skill shortages.** Tier 3 should provide for some specific low skill schemes, if needed. As set out in the five year plan, the Government is not convinced that there is a need for low skill migration schemes for non-EEA nationals, following EU enlargement.
- **TIER 4 – Students: increasing exports and improving the education sector for the UK.** Tier 4 would provide for students. Students already have to meet a range of tests such as whether they have a place at a bona fide educational institution; whether they have sufficient funds to support themselves and whether they are primarily coming to the UK to study. These tests will form the basis of a points system.
- **TIER 5 – Other temporary categories: visiting workers, selected development schemes and youth mobility/cultural exchange.** There are a number of specific provisions in the current system for people to work in the UK for a short time or to work as part of a holiday which could be considered for taking forward into the new system as Tier 5: visiting workers, selected development schemes, youth mobility/cultural exchange, and business visitors.

Tiers 1 and 2 would lead to permanent residence after five years residence and fulfilling other requirements. The others would not, but in some cases, for instance, students graduating and finding work in a shortage area, people on the *Fresh Talent: Working in Scotland* scheme, or post-doctoral researchers, could move quickly into Tiers 1 or 2. The government would require different attributes and behaviour from migrants according to tier. They would have different entitlements according to tier, for example to work with or without restriction; or to be joined by family.

At present nothing is worked out, as the above brief sketch, taken from the government's consultation document, shows. Only time will tell whether the scheme is some kind of bureaucratic utopianism or something which is workable in any way.

1 *A Points-Based System: Making Migration Work for Britain*, Cm 6741.
2 See suggested points table at Cm 6741, p 23.
3 See suggested points system at Cm 6741, p 26. The brochure runs out of suggested points tables after Tier 3.

WORKERS (1): NON-WORK PERMIT EMPLOYEES

10.5

[NB:]

Settlement may only be obtained in the following categories of non-permit employment listed in the main text and since 3 April 2006 this now takes five, not four, years of continuous employment:

- overseas journalists and broadcasters (HC 395, para 142(i), as amended by HC 1016);
- sole representatives (para 150(i), as amended above);
- private servants in diplomatic households (para 158(i), as amended above);
- domestic workers (para 159G(i), as amended above);
- overseas government employees (para 167(i), as amended above);
- ministers of religion, missionaries and members of religious orders (para 176(i), as amended above);
- operational ground staff of overseas airlines (para 184(i), as amended above);
- Commonwealth citizens with grandparental connections (para 192(ii), as amended above).

Overseas journalists and broadcasters

10.10

[NB:]

Initial admission will now usually be for two years, not 12 months, and qualification for settlement now takes five, not four years.[1]

1 HC 395, paras 137 and 142, as amended by HC 1016 as from 3 April 2006.

Sole representatives

10.15

[NB:]

Initial admission will now usually be for two years, not 12 months, and qualification for settlement now takes five, not four years.[1]

[1] HC 395, paras 145 and 150, as amended by HC 1016 as from 3 April 2006.

Private servants in diplomatic households

10.16

[NB:]

Initial admission will now usually be for two years, not 12 months, and qualification for settlement now takes five, not four years.[1]

[1] HC 395, paras 153 and 158, as amended by HC 1016 as from 3 April 2006.

Domestic workers

10.18

[NB:]

Initial admission will now usually be for two years, not 12 months, and qualification for settlement now takes five, not four years.[1]

[1] HC 395, paras 159B and 159G, as amended by HC 1016 as from 3 April 2006.

10.20

[NB:]

The validity of this paragraph may be in doubt once s 8 of the Asylum and Immigration Act 1996 is repealed when s 21 of IAN 2006 comes into force. There is nothing in the Act to suggest that the new civil penalty or the new criminal offence do not apply to employment in a person's private household: see 14.82 below.

Overseas government employees

10.21

[NB:]

Initial admission will now usually be for two years, not 12 months, and qualification for settlement now takes five, not four years.[1]

[1] HC 395, paras 162 and 167, as amended by HC 1016 as from 3 April 2006.

Ministers of religion, missionaries and members of religious orders

10.24

[NB:]

Initial admission will now usually be for two years, not 12 months, and qualification for settlement now takes five, not four years.[1]

[1] HC 395, paras 171 and 176, as amended by HC 1016 as from 3 April 2006.

Generally applicable requirements

10.28

[NB:]

Initial admission will now usually be for two years, not 12 months, and qualification for settlement now takes five, not four years.[1]

[1] HC 395, paras 171 and 176, as amended by HC 1016 as from 3 April 2006.

Operational ground staff of overseas airlines

10.30

[NB:]

Initial admission will now usually be for two years, not 12 months, and qualification for settlement now takes five, not four years.[1]

[1] HC 395, paras 179 and 184, as amended by HC 1016 as from 3 April 2006.

Overseas Nurses Programme

10.30A

[Add new paragraph:]

Before being able to practice their profession in the UK, overseas trained nurses and midwives must be registered with the Nursing and Midwifery Council (NMC). From 1 September 2005, overseas qualified nurses seeking to register with the NMC were expected to do so through the NMC's Overseas Nurses Programme.[1]

After 1 September 2006, it will be compulsory for them to do so. Under the old supervised practice programme, overseas qualified nurses and midwives would apply to the NMC for pre-registration and then enter the UK as either student nurses or as work permit holders (see 9.44A above). Under the old system all the applicant had to do was to produce a letter from the approved placement setting (ie the hospital or nursing home) confirming their acceptance and provided the setting was on the accredited supervised practice list (nurses) or the accredited midwife adaptation list, he or she would be given a work permit, if applied for, and would then obtain leave to enter either as a student nurse or as a work permit holder.[2]

1 In fact, from 1 September 2005, anyone applying for registration with the NMC will be required to do so through the NMC's Overseas Nurses Programme. Only those who applied before that date had an option to go through the old route: IDI Ch 4, s 7 (Jan/06).

2 From April to August 2005, the NMC issued dual-decision assessment letters. This means that applicants who applied to the NMC before September 2005, and were issued with a decision letter between April and August 2005 were offered a choice of how to become fully registered with the NMC. They could either proceed through the Overseas Nurses Programme or complete the required period of supervised practice in the old supervised practice system, provided that they could complete the placement by 31 August 2006. NMC decision letters are valid for two years. Applicants who were issued with a decision letter from before April 2005 also had the choice of how to become registered with the NMC even though they did not have a dual-decision assessment letter. As long as their decision letter has not expired, applicants may proceed under the Overseas Nurses Programme even though their decision letter does not make specific reference to it. Anyone concerned about the transitional and parallel arrangements during the transitional period up to September 2006 should consult the IDI Ch 4, s 7 (Jan/06).

10.30B

[Add new paragraph:]

The new programme was created so that every overseas qualified nurse or midwife can be assessed to a uniformly high standard before achieving registration with the NMC.[1] Under it, all overseas qualified nurses seeking to register with the NMC will either be required to undertake a 20-day period of protected learning time to orientate them to UK health care practice, or to undertake a period of supervised practice in a practice setting that has been audited and quality assured by an education provider approved by the NMC.[2] Where an overseas qualified nurse is only required to undertake the 20-day period of protected learning and has an offer of employment, they will immediately qualify for the issue of a work permit , and will not need to undertake a period of supervised practice, and should not be granted leave to enter or remain as an overseas qualified nurse or midwife under this heading. But the nurses who are required by the NMC to complete a period of supervised practice should be admitted, or given leave to remain, under a new permit-free employment category as an overseas qualified nurse or midwife.[3] Once they have completed the programme they can qualify for the grant of a work permit.[4]

Under the rules leave can be granted as a supervised practice nurse or midwife when all of paras 69M (leave to enter) or 69P (extension of stay) of the Immigration Rules are met. Leave may be granted for a period up to 18 months, depending on the applicant's needs.[1] People with leave to remain in the following categories may switch into the overseas nurses programme as a supervised practice nurse or adaptation midwife:

- a student; or
- a prospective student;[2] or
- a student nurse; or
- a working holidaymaker who has been in the UK at least twelve months.

- by a temporary concession, nurses who have switched from work permit into this programme.[3] Applicants who are in the UK with any other category of leave will not qualify to switch into leave as an overseas qualified nurse or midwife whilst in the UK.

Once leave in this category has been granted, overseas qualified nurses and midwives are permitted to take employment for a maximum of eight weeks prior to the commencement of their courses, at the approved educational institute or service provider where they are to be trained.[4] Once their course has commenced, there is no restriction on the number of hours worked, if this is a necessary part of the course and has the agreement of the education institution concerned.[5] In these circumstances no further approval is required from the Home Office.

Nurses and midwives admitted in this category may also engage in supplementary employment without requiring further authorisation from the Home Office, provided:

(a) the type of work is similar in nature and at the same level as the work which the individual is undertaking in the practice setting;
(b) it does not exceed 20 hours per week; and
(c) it is not entered into through an employment or recruitment agency.[6]

1 HC 395, paras 69N (leave to enter) and 69Q (extension of stay), as inserted by HC 645, with effect from 30 November 2005. See also IDI Ch 4, s 7 (Jan/06), p 2.
2 IDI Ch 4, s 7 (Jan/06), p 2.
3 HC 395, paras 69M–69R, as inserted by HC 645; and HC 395, para 131B, as amended by HC 645 with effect from 30 Nov 2005.
4 HC 395, para 131B, as amended by HC 645.
5 HC 395, paras 69N and 69Q.
6 HC 395, paras 82–87.
7 IDI Ch 4, s 7 (Jan/06).
8 See n 7 above.
9 See n 7 above.
10 See n 7 above.

Persons with UK ancestry

10.33

[NB:]

From 3 April 2006, initial admission will be for up to five years, not four years as before.[1] This mirrors a wider change in the Immigration Rules as part of the government's 'Five Year Strategy for Asylum & Immigration', requiring those in employment routes, leading to settlement, to spend five years working in the UK before they can apply for settlement.

1 HC 395, para 187, as amended by HC 1016.

10.34

[NB:]

Qualification for settlement now takes five, not four years.[1]

1 HC 395, para 192, as amended by HC 1016 as from 3 April 2006.

Family members

10.35

[NB:]

Civil partners as well as spouses and unmarried partners enjoy the benefits of family reunion. The same rules apply as for spouses under HC 395, paras 194 and 195, as amended by HC 582 as from 5 December 2005.

WORKERS (2): WORK PERMIT EMPLOYEES

The main work permit scheme

Entry to the UK with a work permit

10.54

[NB:]

Qualification for settlement for those in work permit employment now takes five years, not four as before.[1]

1 HC 395, para 134, as amended by HC 1016 as from 3 April 2006.

Switching to approved employment

10.57

[NB:]

Switching to approved employment is now also available to those who have successfully been through the Overseas Nurses Programme[1] and to those who have been part of 'The Fresh Talent: Working in Scotland scheme'.[2]

1 HC 395, para 131B, as amended by HC 645: see 10.30Aff above.
2 HC 395, paras 131H, 132 and 133: see 10.110A below.

Family members

10.62

[NB:]

Civil partners as well as spouses and unmarried partners enjoy the benefits of family reunion. The same rules apply as for spouses under HC 395, paras 194 and 195, as amended by HC 582 as from 5 December 2005.

SECTORS-BASED SCHEME

10.63

[NB:]

Participants on the Sectors Based Scheme (SBS) must be aged between 18 and 30. Although this requirement is currently one of the criteria in the work permit guidance, it was only recently incorporated into the Immigration Rules.[1] This amendment to the Rules is intended to ensure that decisions made by Work Permits (UK) caseworkers and entry clearance officers are consistent. Such consistency was not much in evidence in the only reported decision on the working of the Scheme. In *AA (Bangladesh)*[2] the Tribunal was concerned with refusals of entry clearance after Work Permits UK had approved the issue of work permits. They held entry clearance applications cannot properly be refused on the basis of generalities that may originate from a disapproval of the scheme and a suspicion of abuse. Assumptions based on poverty were of no relevance. How long the Scheme will last is a matter of some conjecture. However, following a review of the Scheme, the government announced in June 2005 that the SBS would cease operating in the hospitality sector, but would continue until June 2006 in the food processing sector. The scheme was introduced on 1 May 2003 and provided for the issuance of work permits for low skilled vacancies in the hospitality and the food-processing sectors.

1 HC 645, para 135I(ii), as substituted by HC 645, para 15.
2 [2006] UKAIT 00026.

THE TRAINING AND WORK EXPERIENCE SCHEME (TWES)

Admission of families

10.75

[NB:]

Civil partners as well as spouses and unmarried partners enjoy the benefits of family reunion. The same rules apply as for spouses under HC 395, paras 122 to 127, as amended by HC 582 as from 5 December 2005.

BUSINESS AND THE SELF-EMPLOYED

Introduction and history

10.76

[NB:]

As from 31 July 2006, applications considered by the Business Casework Unit (BCU), which was transferred to Work Permits UK in 2003, will be processed by a new team, Leave to Remain 7. The new contact details are: Leave to Remain 7, Work Permits (UK), PO Box 3468, Sheffield S3 8WA. Telephone enquiries: 0114-274-3045.

Business status

Extensions and settlement

10.97

[NB:]

Initial admission will now usually be for two years, not 12 months and in order to obtain settlement a business person now needs to have spent a continuous period of five years in the United Kingdom in this capacity, not four years as before.[1] All references in the main text to four years should be read accordingly.

1 HC 395, paras 204 and 209, as amended by HC 1016 as from 3 April 2006.

Business status under the EC Association Agreements

10.99

[NB:]

Note that EC Association Agreements and HC 395, paras 211 to 223 will become redundant once Bulgaria and Romania become members of the EU in 2007. Until then initial admission will usually be for two years, not 12 months, and qualification for settlement now takes five, not four years.[1]

1 HC 395, paras 215 and 222, as amended by HC 1016 as from 3 April 2006

Writers, composers and artists

10.103

[NB:]

Initial admission will now usually be for two years, not 12 months, and qualification for settlement now takes five, not four years.[1]

1 HC 395, paras 233 and 238, as amended by HC 1016 as from 3 April 2006.

THE NEW BRAINS OF BRITAIN

Innovators

10.106

[NB:]

Initial admission will now usually be for two years, not 18 months, and qualification for settlement now takes five, not four years.[1]

1 HC 395, paras 210B and 210G, as amended by HC 1016 as from 3 April 2006.

THE HIGHLY SKILLED MIGRANT PROGRAMME (HSMP)

10.107

[NB:]

Initial admission will now usually be for two years, not 12 months, and qualification for settlement now takes five, not four years.[1] But the rather extravagant aggregation of work experience allowed to a skilled migrant by the wording of the old para 135G(i) has now gone. The amended paragraph now reads:

> '(i) has spent a continuous period of 5 years in the United Kingdom, of which the most recent period must have been spent with leave as a highly skilled migrant (in accordance with paragraphs 135A to 135F of these Rules), and the remainder must be made up of leave as a highly skilled migrant, leave as a work permit holder (under paragraphs 128 to 133 of these Rules), or leave as an Innovator (under paragraphs 210A to 210F of these Rules); and'.

In November 2006 the HSMP Programme was reviewed by the Home Office. First, there are the changes to the criteria which have to be met in order to get into it. The revised HSMP criteria will allow applicants to score points against the following criteria:

- qualifications;
- previous earnings;
- prior UK experience as a student or employee;
- age; and
- participation in an MBA scheme.

A mandatory English language requirement has also been added to the programme, when an initial application is made and again at extension stage. Most of these changes will be effected in policy documents and do not require amendment to the Immigration Rules.[2] The second change is to the Immigration Rules, which have been amended by HC 1702, which are mainly concerned with extensions of leave.[3] Instead of having to show that they have taken all reasonable steps to become lawfully economically active in the UK (as they do under current rules), applicants will now have to show that they can meet a points test similar to that required of applicants who are applying for a HSMP approval letter. The points criteria for extension applications are set out in new Appendices 4 and 5 to the Immigration Rules. These robust new rules now allow the Home Office to refuse incomplete applications and ones where they have a reasonable doubt about the veracity of a document produced in support of a claim.[4]

1 HC 395, paras 135B and 135G, as amended by HC 1016 as from 3 April 2006.

2 For more detailed information on the new HSMP criteria, see www.workingintheuk.gov.uk

3 HC 395, paras 135D–135F were deleted as from 8 November 2006, not to be replaced until 5 December 2006, when all the other changes took place. One rule has not been replaced. Previously, those with existing leave to do the Professional and Linguistic Assessment Board (PLAB) test (which allows overseas doctors to practise in the UK) or a clinical attachment have been able to switch into HSMP provided that they have received a HSMP approval letter using the Priority Application Process for General Practitioners. As the Home Office are removing the GP Priority provision as part of the changes to the points criteria, people who have leave in these categories will not now be able to switch into HSMP. There will be published concessionary arrangements for those who have been

granted a HSMP approval letter under the Priority Application Process before the publication of the new rule changes in HC 1702.

4 HC 395, paras 135GA and 135HA, as amended by HC 1702.

SCIENCE AND ENGINEERING GRADUATE SCHEME (SEGS)

10.109

[NB:]

SEGS already enables overseas students who have been awarded an undergraduate degree (at 2:2 or above), a Master's degree or PhD in a subject which is approved by the Department for Education and Skills for the purposes of this scheme to work in the UK for up to 12 months after their studies and they can switch into other immigration categories to continue to work in the UK beyond this 12 months. HC 1016, which took effect on 3 April 2006, makes changes which apply to all Master's degree and PhD students commencing their studies in the UK on or after 1 May 2006. They will now be eligible to apply for SEGS regardless of the subject they have studied.[1] This new provision is part of measures the government is taking to make the UK a more attractive study destination and to encourage more international students to come to the UK to study. There are separate provisions in place to enable those overseas students already studying in the UK to work here after their studies. The Scheme does not of itself lead to settlement, but is a stepping-stone to other categories, such as work permit employment, which do.

1 HC 395, para 1350 (ii)(b), as substituted by HC 1016.

FRESH TALENT: WORKING IN SCOTLAND SCHEME

10.110A

[Add new paragraph:]

'The Fresh Talent: Working in Scotland scheme' is a new immigration category intended to counter Scotland's falling population by encouraging people to consider living and working in Scotland. It will make it easier for non-EEA nationals who have studied in Scotland to stay on after their studies and to switch into a relevant immigration category to start working or continue working in Scotland.[1] The Scheme does not of itself lead to settlement, but is a stepping-stone to other categories, such as work permit employment, which do. It came into force on 22 June 2005. Those who have been awarded an HND, or a UK recognised undergraduate degree, Master's degree, or PhD, by a relevant Scottish institution,[2] will be eligible to apply for leave under the scheme up to 12 months after they complete their qualification.[3] They will have to have shown a commitment to Scotland both by choosing to study there and by living in Scotland for an appropriate period of time during their studies.[4] Participants of the Fresh Talent: Working in Scotland scheme will be given up to two years of leave during which they can take any type of employment (paid or unpaid), self employment or business without having to make a separate application for a work permit or other permission from the Home Office. Participants will also have to show that they can accommodate and maintain themselves and any dependants without recourse to public funds,[5] and intend to leave the United Kingdom if, on expiry of their leave under this scheme, they have not been granted leave to remain in the United Kingdom either:

(a) as a work permit holder; or
(b) under the highly skilled migrant programme; or
(c) as a person intending to establish themselves in business; or
(d) as an innovator.[6]

The Immigration Rules have also been amended by HC 104 to enable participants in the Fresh Talent: Working in Scotland scheme to switch into any of the work categories (a) to (d) above. They may also combine working under this scheme and working under the Science and Engineering Graduates Scheme[7] provided that the amalgamated period of stay in the two schemes does not exceed two years.

The Scottish Executive will also be publishing reports on the monitoring of the scheme on their website.

1 HC 395, para 143A (iii), inserted by HC 104.
2 HC 395, para 143A (i).
3 HC 395, para 143A (v).
4 HC 395, para 143A (ii).
5 HC 395, para 143A (vi).
6 HC 395, paras 131H, 132 and 133 (work permits); 135DH, 135E and 135F (highly skilled migrants); 206G, 207 and 208 (business); 210DH, 210E and 210F ((innovators). These rules are all printed as amended in the main text.
7 See HC 395, paras 135O–135T. The maximum stay under this scheme is 12 months: see 10.109–10.110.

INVESTMENT AND SELF-SUFFICIENCY

Investors

10.114

[NB:]

Initial admission will now usually be for two years, not 12 months, and qualification for settlement now takes five, not four years.[1] Someone switching from one of the other permitted categories will not be able to aggregate time spent in the other category.

1 HC 395, paras 225 and 230, as amended by HC 1016 as from 3 April 2006.

Retired persons of independent means

10.115

[NB:]

Initial admission and an extension of stay for someone switching from one of the other permitted categories can now be for up to five years, not four, and qualification for settlement now takes a minimum of five, not four years.[1]

1 HC 395, paras 264, 267 and 269, as amended by HC 1016 as from 3 April 2006.

Family members of business, self employed, investors and retired people

10.120

[NB:]

Civil partners as well as spouses and unmarried partners enjoy the benefits of family reunion. The same rules apply as for spouses.[1]

1 HC 395, paras 240–245 (spouses and children of business persons, investors, writers, composers and artists), 271–276 (spouses and children of retired persons of independent means), as amended by HC 582 as from 5 December 2005.

Chapter 11

FAMILIES, PARTNERS AND CHILDREN

INTRODUCTION

11.1

[NB:]

This chapter also deals with the ground breaking statutory enactment of a new family status of civil partnerships and its ramifications in immigration law. The Civil Partnership Act 2004 finally came into force on 5 December 2005. Civil partnerships are a new legal relationship which can be registered by two people of the same sex and give couples legal recognition for their relationship. It is a long and detailed Act, which incorporates civil partnerships into many areas of law. Its scope is much beyond the subject matter of this work. But the Act also makes changes to immigration law, which we describe in this chapter. From 5 December 2005 the Immigration Rules have been amended so as to put civil partners on precisely the same footing as spouses for immigration purposes. The 96 or so rule amendments made by HC 582[1] and HC 1016[2] are to ensure that civil partners and proposed civil partners are afforded the same treatment as spouses and fiancés throughout. In this chapter we highlight the main changes. The second major change has been in the field of inter country adoptions. The Adoption and Children Act 2002 ('the 2002 Act') came into force on 30 December 2005 and revoked most of the Adoption (Intercountry Aspects) Act 1999 which had previously governed this area. Then there is the Children and Adoption Act 2006 which received Royal Assent on 21 June 2006, but which has not yet come into force. It makes a number of provisions about intercountry adoption, including a statutory framework for the suspension of intercountry adoption from specified countries where there are concerns about adoption practices in that country.

1 The main amendments came into effect on 5 December 2005.
2 HC 1016, para 25, taking effect on 3 April 2006. The main changes to the Immigration Rules to include provision for civil partners came into effect on 5 December 2005. Due to an oversight, the term 'proposed civil partner' was not included in para 284(i). In practice, applications have not been penalised because this term was not included but this amendment now brings 'proposed civil partners' in line with 'fiances'. New IDI are at ch 8, s 2 and Annexes H and K (Mar/06). Annex H contains a list of recognised foreign civil partnerships.

11.3

[NB:]

This overview of rule changes since the coming into force of the Human Rights Act 1998 now has to incorporate the new status of civil partnerships. As from 5 December 2005 HC 582 and HC 1016 incorporate civil partners and civil partnerships into the definitions of 'a parent' and 'sponsor' in HC 395, para 6. Where 'spouse' appears in the rules, the words 'civil partner' is added. The same goes for references to 'marriage' and 'wedding'. In each case 'civil partnership' is added. Thus in the overview of the rules, we find that civil partners are afforded the same treatment as spouses in relation to bereavement,[1] access to children of former partnerships,[2] admission as the partner of a refugee,[3] and rules on public funds.[4] The downside is that they are also subject to the same restrictions on varying their leave after entering into a civil partnership if on the last admission they were granted leave of less than six months.[5]

1 HC 395, para 287(b), as amended by HC 582, para 24(g). IDI, ch 8, s 2, para 5.
2 HC 395, para 248A(vii), as amended by HC 582, para 15.
3 HC 395, paras 352A–F, as amended by HC 582, paras 37 and 38.
4 HC 395, para 6A, the definition of 'sponsor' having been amended by HC 582, para 1(c).
5 HC 395, para 284(i), as amended by HC 582, para 24. See also *FB (HC 395, para 284: 'six months') Bangladesh* [2006] UKAIT 00030 (16 March 2006); and 11.68 below.

[Footnote 12:]

Note that s 25 of the Asylum and Immigration (Treatment of Claimants etc) Act 2004 will cease to have effect when IAN 2006, s 50(3) comes into force (s 50 was not yet in force as at 1 October 2006).

IDI

11.3A

[Add new paragraph:]

Some of the IDI dealing with family members have been updated. Some have not. The following sections have been updated as of Mar/06: Chapter 8 section 1 (spouses), Chapter 8 section 3 (fiancé(e)s), Chapter 8 section 4 (victims of domestic violence), and Chapter 8 section 9 (unmarried and same sex partners). Chapter 8 section 5A (children) was updated as at Jul/06. Chapter 8 section 5 (adopted children) and Chapter 8 section 6 (dependant relatives) have not been updated since the 6th edition. Chapter 8 section 2 (civil partnerships) is dated Mar/06 and is new.

Of the Annexes to chapter 8 (we omit annexes dealing with refusal formulae) there have been **changes** in the following:

- **Section 1 – Spouses**
  - Annex F – Family Members–Maintenance and accommodation (Mar/06)
- **Section 2 – Civil partnerships**
  - Annex H – Civil partnerships (Mar/06)
- **Section 3 – Fiance(e)s and proposed civil partners**
  - Annex K – Visits for marriage and forming a civil partnership (Mar/06)
- **Section 4 – Victims of domestic violence**
  - Annex AB – List of recognised domestic violence organisations (Mar/06)

- **Section 5 – Children/Adopted children**
  - Annex N – DNA testing and overage re-applicants (Jun/06)
- **Section 9 – Unmarried and same sex relationships**
  - Annex Z – Further guidance on the unmarried and same sex partners rules and required levels of documents (Mar/06)

In the following there have been **no changes**:

- **Section 1 – Spouses**
  - Annex B – Recognition of marriage and divorce
  - Annex C – Polygamous and potentially polygamous marriages
  - Annex D – Domicile
  - Annex E – Domestic violence–list of police forces and pro-forma letter
- **Section 3 – Fiance(e)s and proposed civil partners**
  - Annex J – Requirements to have met
  - Annex O – Children of fiance(e)s
- **Section 4 – Victims of domestic violence**
  - Annex P – General guidance
- **Section 5 – Children/Adopted children**
  - Annex M – General guidance Part 1 & Part 2–guidance on interpretation of the rules
  - Annex Q – Validity of adoptions under United Kingdom law and general guidance relating to adoption cases which fail to be considered under the Immigration Rules
  - Annex R – Adoptions not recognised as valid in the United Kingdom and 'De Facto' arrangements
  - Annex S – Children coming for adoption and children adopted through courts in the United Kingdom
- **Section 6 – Dependents relatives**
  - Annex V – Parents and grandparents
  - Annex W – Other relatives
  - Annex X – Village visits
  - Annex Y – Refusal formulae

11.5

[NB:]

The law on inter-country adoptions has been further updated by the coming into force of the Adoption and Children Act 2002 and the making of Regulations under it: see 11.99 ff.

DOMICILE

11.24

[Footnote 2:]

Mark v Mark has now been upheld in the House of Lords: [2005] UKHL 42, [2005] INLR 614.

11.27

[NB:]

Mark v Mark has now been upheld in the House of Lords: [2005] UKHL 42 [2005] INLR 614. It was held that unlawful presence is not a bar to obtaining a domicile of choice, but may be relevant to the factual question of whether or not the person has formed the required *animus manendi*. Similarly illegal residence is not a bar to establishing habitual residence for the purposes of s 5(2) of the Domicile and Matrimonial Proceedings Act 1973.

MARRIAGE

Spouses under 16

11.40

[NB:]

The immigration rule concerning young spouses, contained in HC 395, para 277, has been amended by HC 582 to include civil partners.

ADMISSION OF FAMILY MEMBERS AND PARTNERS

11.45

[NB:]

Family members now include civil partners (HC 395, paras 281 to 289, as amended by HC 582, as from 5 December 2006) one of whom may now be the sponsor (HC 395, para 6). They are also included in the rules relating to victims of domestic violence and bereavement, as the amendments to footnotes 5 and 6 show.

[Footnote 5:]

HC 395, para 289A has been amended to include civil partners by HC 582.

[Footnote 6:]

HC 395, para 287(b)(i)(b) has been amended to include civil partners by HC 582.

11.46

[NB:]

Where the rules allow children to join parents in the different categories described in this paragraph, there is a requirement that they be 'unmarried'. In each of these cases the rules have been amended by HC 582 to add the words 'and is not a civil partner'.[1] Civil partners also qualify for entry as partners of students, workers, business people and others mentioned in this paragraph of the main text, appropriate amendments having been made by HC 582 to HC

395, paras 76 to 78 (students), 89 (au pairs), 95 (working holiday makers),122 to 124, 125 (teachers and trainees), 194 to 197 (workers other than those in the Sectors-based scheme), 240 to 243 (business, self employed, investor, writer, composer and artist), 248A (person exercising right to access to child), 257 (family member of EEA national), 271 to 274 (retired persons of independent means), 276R to 276W, 276AD to 276AF, 276X, 276AA and 276AG (armed forces rules), 277 (under age relationships), 281 to 289 (spouses and civil partners of person settled in UK), 289A (victims of domestic violence), 289AA to 295O (fiancés, unmarried partners and bereaved partners), 349 and 352A to 352D (refugees) 356 (definition of family members and close relatives of those granted temporary protection under the Temporary Protection Directive 2001/55/EC), 365, 366, 367, 389 and 395B (family members of deportees and administrative removees). The footnotes to 11.46 should be read as amended.

[1] HC 395, paras 125(iii), 197(iii), 243(iii), 274(iii), 276X(iii), 276AA(iii), 276AG(iii), 297(iii), 298(iii), 301(iii), 303A(iii), 352D and 356(iv).

ENTRY CLEARANCE REQUIREMENTS

11.47

[NB:]

Family members now include civil partners and the references to immigration rules in the text and footnotes should be read as amended by HC 582, as set out at 11.46 above.

11.50

[NB:]

The six-month rule described in the main text now applies to civil partners: HC 395, para 284(i), as amended by HC 582.

[Footnote 2:]

HC 395, para 284 (i), is further amended by HC 582.

[Footnote 2 – add at end:]

See also *FB & Ors (HC 395 para 284: 'six months') Bangladesh* [2006] UKAIT 00030 (16 March 2006); and 11.68 below.

PRESENCE OF SPONSOR

11.51

[NB:]

Sponsor now includes a civil partner and a proposed civil partner: HC 395, para 6, as substituted by HC 582 as from 5 December 2005.

MAINTENANCE AND ACCOMMODATION

11.53

[NB:]

Family members now include civil partners and the references to immigration rules in the text and footnotes should be read as amended by HC 582, as set out at 11.46 above. 'Sponsor' now includes a civil partner and a proposed civil partner: HC 395, para 6, as substituted by HC 582 as from 5 December 2005. The IDI on maintenance and accommodation are now updated to Mar/06 at chapter 8, sections 1 and 2, and at Annex F and all references to IDI in the main text should be read as updated.

11.54

[NB:]

The references to spouses and unmarried partners should now include civil partners and the references to immigration rules in the text and footnotes should be read as amended by HC 582, as set out at 11.46 above. The IDI on maintenance and accommodation are now updated to Mar/06 at chapter 8, sections 1 and 2, Annex F and all references to IDI in the main text should be read as updated. In particular the updated IDI referred to in footnote 9 repeats the same heresy as before: Annex F, para 5.1, but the broad discretion given to immigration decision makers may prevent unnecessarily harsh decisions.

11.55

[NB:]

The references to spouses and unmarried partners should now include civil partners and 'sponsor' now includes a civil partner and a proposed civil partner: HC 395, para 6, as substituted by HC 582 as from 5 December 2005. The IDI on maintenance and accommodation are now updated to Mar/06 at chapter 8, sections 1 and 2, Annex F and all references to IDI in the main text should be read as updated.

[Footnote 2:]

The Social Security Administration Act 1992, s 78 has been amended by the Civil Partnership Act 2004, Sch 24, para 61 to include couple in a civil partnership.

[Footnote 2:]

The Social Security Administration Act 1992, s 105 has been amended by the Civil Partnership Act 2004, Sch 24, para 62 to include undertakings by a civil partner, who is a sponsor.

[Footnote 5:]

HC 395, paras 287, 294, 298 and 211 have been amended by HC 582 to include civil partners.

11.56

[NB:]

The references to spouses should now include civil partners and the references to 'sponsors' now includes a civil partners and a proposed civil partners: HC 395, para 6, as substituted by HC 582 as from 5 December 2005. IDI on maintenance and accommodation are now updated to Mar/06 at chapter 8, sections 1 and 2, Annex F and all references to IDI in the main text should be read as updated.

WHICH SPOUSES QUALIFY FOR ENTRY AND STAY?

Spouse under 18

11.60

[NB:]

The immigration rule concerning young spouses, contained in HC 395, para 277, has been amended by HC 582 to include civil partners.

Marriages of convenience and 'sham' marriages

11.63

[NB:]

The provisions requiring registrars to notify the Secretary of State of suspected sham marriages now apply to civil partnerships under the Civil Partnership Act 2004. Immigration and Asylum Act 1999, s 24A. The 'permission to marry' scheme referred to at 11.67 of the main text also extends to civil partnerships: see 11.67 below. The Immigration (European Economic Area) Regulations 2000, have now been replaced by the Immigration (European Economic Area) Regulations 2006, which like their predecessor, purport to exclude parties to marriages of convenience from the definition of spouse, and also now exclude parties to a civil partnership of convenience from the definition of civil partner: reg 2.

[Footnote 2:]

Note that s 25 of the Asylum and Immigration (Treatment of Claimants etc) Act 2004 ceases to have effect when IAN 2006, s 50(3) comes into force (s 50 was not yet in force as at 1 October 2006).

[Footnotes 6 and 7:]

Have been replaced by SI 2006/1003, reg 2, which also deals with civil partnerships of convenience.

'Intention to live together'

11.65

[NB:]

The references to spouses should now include civil partners and the references to fiancés should now include proposed civil partners, appropriate amendments having been made by HC 582 to HC 395, paras 281 to 289 (spouses and civil partners of person settled in UK), and 289AA to 292 (fiancés) and any of these rules referred to in the footnotes should be read as amended by HC 582, as set above.

In *GA ('Subsisting' marriage) Ghana*[1] a starred decision, the Tribunal held that the requirement in para 281(iii) that a marriage be 'subsisting' is not limited to considering whether there has been a valid marriage which formally continues. The word requires an assessment of the substance of the current relationship between the parties, rather than to its legal formality, and a decision as to whether in the broadest sense it comprises a marriage properly described as 'subsisting'.

1 [2006] UKAIT 00046.

Marriage in the UK: restrictions

11.67

[NB:]

The 'permission to marry' scheme has been adapted to apply to civil partnerships. Where two people wish to register as civil partners of each other and one of them is subject to immigration control, the person subject to immigration control must either (i) have an entry clearance granted expressly for the purpose of enabling him or her to form a civil partnership in the United Kingdom, (ii) have the written permission of the Secretary of State to form a civil partnership in the United Kingdom, or (iii) fall within a class specified by regulations.[1] The Immigration (Procedure for Formation of Civil Partnerships) Regulations 2005 make provision for applications for the written permission of the Home Secretary to form a civil partnership (a certificate of approval) for a set fee at £135.[2] The regulations also specify the registration districts in England and Wales at which persons subject to immigration control may give notice of a civil partnership.[3]

In the Administrative Court in *Baiai*[4] Silber J found that the system of 'certificates of approval' for marriage was incompatible with the EHCR, Art 12 because the regime is not rationally connected to the legislative objective – particularly unsatisfactory was the failure of the Secretary of State to consider or investigate whether marriages entered into in non-Anglican religious ceremonies should have been exempted from the certification requirements. Furthermore, the scheme constituted unfair and unjustifiable discrimination based on personal characteristics such as religion and nationality contrary to Art 12 read with Art 14. However, at a further hearing he found that his earlier judgment did not apply to those who were in the country illegally.[5]

1 Civil Partnership Act 2004, Sch 23. The exempt persons are those who are settled in the United Kingdom and those to whom Sch 3 to the Civil Partnership Act 2004 applies (registration by former spouses one of whom has changed sex): Immigration (Procedure for Formation of Civil Partnerships) Regulations 2005, SI 2005/2917, reg 4.

2 SI 2005/2917, reg 3. The fee has been determined on a cost recovery basis in accordance with Treasury guidelines: Explanatory Notes to the Regulation.

3 SI 2005/2917, reg 5 and Sch 2. According to the Explanatory Notes the restricted number of locations will enable the Immigration Service to target their intelligence and enforcement effort in order to tackle abuse of the immigration system via sham civil partnerships in England and Wales. In the context of marriage, there is less evidence of abuse in Scotland and Northern Ireland, therefore notice may be given there at any registration district.

4 *R (on the application of Baiai) v Secretary of State for the Home Department* [2006] EWHC 823 (Admin), [2006] 3 All ER 608, [2006] 2 FCR 131, [2006] Fam Law 535. See further 8.97 of this supplement.

5 *R (on the application of Baiai) v Secretary of State for the Home Department* [2006] EWHC 1454 (Admin), [2006] 4 All ER 555.

Leave to enter and remain

11.68

[NB:]

The references to spouses should now include civil partners and the references to fiancés should now include proposed civil partners, appropriate amendments having been made by HC 582 to HC 395, paras 281 to 289 (spouses and civil partners of person settled in UK), and 289AA to 292 (fiancés) and any of these rules referred to in the footnotes should be read as amended by HC 582, as set above.

In *FB (HC 395 para 284: 'six months') Bangladesh*[1] the Tribunal considered the terms of para 284(i) of the Immigration Rules, HC 395, which sets out the requirements for an extension of stay as the spouse of the person present and settled in the United Kingdom, unless on the last admission they were granted leave of less than six months other than as a fiance. They held that a person given leave to enter the United Kingdom for a period expiring on the day bearing the same date as the date of entry in the sixth month after entry is given leave for a period of six months and one day. Such a person is therefore not excluded from seeking to remain in the UK as a spouse under para 284(i) of HC 395 as amended by HC 538 on 1 April 2003. That period of six months and one day does not, however, extend beyond six months from the date of admission within the meaning of para 284(i) as amended by Cm 5949 (in force from 25 August 2003 to 1 October 2004). The leave of any such person is nevertheless extended by s 3C of the 1971 Act if he applies for variation; and in that case he too meets the requirements of para 284(i). The most recent change to para 284(i), Cm 6339, (taking effect on 1 October 2004) does, however, exclude such a person if leave of more than six months is prohibited by the Immigration Rules in his or her case.

1 [2006] UKAIT 00030, [2006] Imm AR 400.

11.69

[NB:]

The references to spouses should now include civil partners, appropriate amendments having been made by HC 582 to HC 395, paras 281 to 289 (spouses and civil partners of person settled in UK), and any of these rules referred to in the footnotes should be read as amended by HC 582, as set above.

Domestic violence rule

11.70

[NB:]

The references to a spouse should now include a civil partner, an appropriate amendment having been made by HC 582 to HC 395, paragraph 289A and the reference in footnote 1 to para 289A should be read accordingly.

HC 395, para 289A(iv) is an indication of the kind of evidence which is needed to establish that a spouse or partner has been subjected to domestic violence within a particular time frame and that this has led to the breakdown of the relationship. This is evidence required by the Secretary of State. The rule goes no further and any sensible interpretation of the words 'may be required by' is that the evidence must be such as to satisfy the Secretary of State that there is sufficient evidence to prove that there was domestic violence, that it took place within the two-year timeframe required by the rule, and that it caused the breakdown of the marriage. There is a clear commonality of interest between the Secretary of State and the victim of violence. When one goes to the IDIs (set out in the main text) the Secretary of State for the Home Department is saying: 'I prefer a court order or similar evidence, but that may not be possible, and, if it is not, acceptable evidence may take the form of more than one of these alternatives'. The guidance suggests a very considerable degree of flexibility, bearing in mind that this is a rule of evidence and not a policy statement. In one of the most off-the-wall determinations (starred to boot) in *RH (Para 289A/HC 395 – no discretion) Bangladesh*[1], the AIT held that question they had to decide was whether the Immigration Judge has a discretion to accept evidence that is not specified in the IDI. The answer was 'no'. There is a triple loss of perspective here. First rigidity replaces flexibility. Secondly, an issue of evidence has been classified as a question of discretion. Proof of the victim's plight is a matter of evidence not public law choices of alternative courses of action. The underlying policy of the rule is to help victims of domestic violence not to straightjacket them by misplaced legal sophistry. Thirdly, the end result is to elevate IDIs and other internal guidance documents into rules of law so far as appeals are concerned by the dubious proposition that if the immigration rules give a discretion, the internal guidance can fill this out, thereby investing the IDI with the same statutory force in an appeal as the immigration rule itself, and enabling the Secretary of State for the Home Department to circumvent Parliamentary scrutiny of his rule making power under s 3 of the immigration Act 1971. This case is one of the saddest examples of an abnegation of the duty to protect migrant women from the consequences of domestic violence within the context of a benign and compassionate immigration rule.

1 [2006] UKAIT 00043.

ADMISSION OF UNMARRIED AND SAME-SEX PARTNERS

11.71

[NB:]

There are new IDI at Annex Z dated as at Mar/06.

[Footnote 16:]

The Immigration Rules at HC 395, para 295D (iv) and (v), referred to in the main text and in footnote 16 have not been changed since the passing of the Civil Partnership Act 2004, which is now in force: see HC 582.

[Footnote 17:]

The 'permission to marry' scheme has been extended to civil partnerships: see 11.67 above.

11.73

[NB:]

The reference to spouses and unmarried partners should now include civil partners.

MARRIAGE BY OVERSTAYERS AND ILLEGAL ENTRANTS

11.74

[NB:]

The references to a spouse should now include a civil partner, appropriate amendments having been made by HC 582 and HC 1016 to HC 395, para 284 and the reference in footnote 1 to para 284 should be read accordingly.

In *Baiai*[1] the 'permission to marry' scheme was held in breach of Article 12 read with Art 14 of ECHR, because it discriminated on grounds of religion, but in a further hearing[2] the court held that this was not the case where the applicant's presence in the UK was unlawful. It is, therefore, unlikely that such persons would be given permission to marry or enter into a civil partnership. If they marry in the Church of England they do not need permission: see 11.67 above and in the main text.

1 *R (on the application of Baiai) v Secretary of State for the Home Department* [2006] EWHC 823 (Admin), 2006] 3 All ER 608, [2006] 2 FCR 131, [2006] Fam Law 535.

2 *R (on the application of Baiai) v Secretary of State for the Home Department* [2006] EWHC 1454 (Admin), [2006] 4 All ER 555.

ADMISSION OR STAY FOR THE PURPOSES OF CONTACT WITH RESIDENT CHILDREN

11.76

[NB:]

The references to a spouse should now include a civil partner, an appropriate amendment having been made by HC 582 to HC 395, para 248A (person exercising right to access to child) and the reference in the footnotes to para 289A should be read accordingly.

ADMISSION OF CHILDREN UNDER 18

Introduction

11.77

[NB:]

The IDI on children has been updated as at Jul/06 and a useful guide on DNA testing is at Annex N dated Jun/06. References in the text and footnotes of this section should be read accordingly.

Meaning of 'parent'

11.78

[NB:]

HC 582 has amended the definition of 'parent' in HC 395 to take account of civil partnerships as follows:

(i) after 'the stepfather of a child whose father is dead' insert '(and the reference to stepfather includes a relationship arising through civil partnership)'; and

(ii) after 'the stepmother of a child whose mother is dead' insert '(and the reference to stepmother includes a relationship arising through civil partnership'.

Section 9 of the NIAA 2002 has now been brought into force: see 2.44 of this supplement above.

11.79

[NB:]

Note the amended definition of parent in the previous paragraph.

Non-British children born in the UK

11.84

[NB:]

Children born in the UK who seek leave to enter or remain as the child of parents settled or being admitted for settlement in the UK under HC 395, para 305 must be unmarried and not a civil partner: HC 395, para 305 (iii), as amended by HC 582 and footnote 1 should be read accordingly.

Children under 18 with a UK-settled parent, parents or relative

11.86

[NB:]

The requirement that children be 'unmarried' has now been amended by HC 582 to add the words 'and is not a civil partner'. See HC 395, paras 297(iii), 298(iii) and 301(iii).

Children of fiancé(e)s

11.98

[NB:]

The requirement that children be 'unmarried' has now been amended by HC 582 to add the words 'and is not a civil partner'. See HC 395, para 303A(iii).

INTER-COUNTRY ADOPTION

11.99

[NB:]

The Hague Convention on Protection of Children and Co-operation in Respect of Intercountry Adoption (the Convention) has now come into force in **46** states and **three** others have signed but not yet ratified it.

[Footnote 2:]

Add to those who have ratified the Convention: Bolivia, Burkina Faso, Colombia, Costa Rica, Ecuador, El Salvador, Madagascar, Philippines and Thailand. **Remove** South Africa (it has not ratified the Convention only acceded to it).

[Footnote 3:]

Those who have signed but not ratified the Convention are the Russian Federation, Ireland and the United States of America. **Remove** Belgium and China from this list.

11.100

[Delete existing text and insert:]

The Adoption and Children Act 2002 ('the 2002 Act') came into force on 30 December 2005[1] and revoked most of the Adoption (Intercountry Aspects) Act 1999 which had previously governed this area. The only sections which will remain in force will be ss 1 and 2, which enabled the United Kingdom to ratify the Convention, s 7 which amended the British Nationality Act 1981, and Sch 1, which contains the text of the Convention. The 2002 Act replaces the Adoption Act 1976 ('1976 Act') and also incorporates most of the provisions of the 1999 Act. Intercountry adoptions in England and Wales have been regulated between 2003 and 30 December 2005 by two separate sets of regulations ('the 2003 Regulations'):

- the Intercountry Adoption (Hague Convention) Regulations 2003 (SI 2003/118), made under the 1999 Act which, together with the corresponding legislation in Scotland and Northern Ireland, enabled the UK to ratify the Convention on 1 June 2003; and
- the Adoption (Bringing Children into the United Kingdom) Regulations 2003 (SI 2003/1173), made under the transitional provisions in the 2002 Act which amended the 1976 Act, which apply to adoptions from non-Hague Convention countries or Convention Contracting States that have acceded to the Convention but the UK has raised an objection.

The 2003 regulations have now been repealed and replaced by the the Adoptions with a Foreign Element Regulations 2005 (SI 2005/392) ('the AFE Regulations'). The AFE Regulations provide for adoptions under the Convention and non-Convention adoptions and apply to bringing children into the UK and to removing children from the UK for the purposes of adoption. The AFE Regulations apply to these different cases as follows:

- Part 2, Chapter 1 sets out the requirements and conditions that must be met by prospective adopters and the functions conferred on local authorities where a child is brought into the UK in circumstances where s 83 of the 2002 Act applies;
- Part 2, Chapter 2 applies where a person or couple wishes to remove a child for the purposes of adoption under the law of a country or territory outside the British Islands under s 85 of the 2002 Act, other than under the Convention;
- Part 3, Chapter 1 applies where a person or couple habitually resident in the British Islands wish to adopt a child who is habitually resident in a Convention country outside the British Islands;
- Part 3, Chapter 2 applies where a person or couple habitually resident in a Convention country outside the British Islands wish to adopt a child who is habitually resident in the British Islands; and
- Part 3, Chapter 3 deals with miscellaneous provisions, modifications and offences relating to certain provisions in Part 3, Chapter 1.

The AFE Regulations need to be read with the Adoption Agencies Regulations 2005 (SI 2005/389), which make provision relating to the exercise by adoption agencies of their functions in relation to adoption. In particular, the

Adoption Agencies Regulations set out the procedure to be followed in respect of the assessment of prospective adopters including obtaining information and various reports. The IDI have not been updated and remain as before (chapter 8, section 5 and Annexes Q, R and S). Some updating can be expected in the near future. In June 2006 there came further legislation. The Children and Adoption Act 2006 which received Royal Assent on 21 June 2006, but which is not yet in force, makes a number of provisions about intercountry adoption, including a statutory framework for the suspension of intercountry adoption from specified countries where there are concerns about practices in connection with the adoption of children.

1 The Adoption and Children Act 2002 (Commencement No 9) Order 2005, SI 2005/2213. For a full list of all Voluntary Adoption Agencies See government adoption site at http://www.everychildmatters.gov.uk/adoption/ For up-to-date information on intercountry adoptions see http://www.dfes.gov.uk/intercountryadoption/

Convention adoption abroad

11.102

[NB:]

The Adoption and Children Act 2002 (Commencement No 10) (Transitional and Savings Provisions) Order 2005 (SI 2005/2897) makes transitional provisions where the adoption process was started before 30 December 2005 in relation to intercountry adoption cases. For Hague Convention cases in progress on 30 December 2005, Art 6 sets out a general rule, with exceptions, that any action or decision taken before that date under a provision of the Hague Convention Regulations shall, on or after that date, be treated as if it were an action or decision taken under the corresponding provision of Pt 3 of the AFE Regulations. Article 7 makes transitional provision concerning the conditions to be met by prospective adopters in non-Convention cases and specifies the extent to which the Adoption (Bringing Children into the United Kingdom) Regulations 2003 still apply. Apart from these transitional provisions this paragraph has been superseded by the AFE Regulations.

Convention and non-Convention adoptions in the UK

11.103

[NB:]

The same comments as in the previous paragraph apply here. The Intercountry Adoption (Hague Convention) Regulations 2003 (SI 2003/118) and the Adoption (Bringing Children into the United Kingdom) Regulations 2003 are no longer in force except by way of transitional provisions. The Adoption Act 1976 has been repealed and the main text and footnotes need to be amended accordingly.

[Footnote 1:]

For up-to-date information on intercountry adoptions, including local authority contacts and lists of Voluntary Adoption Agencies , see the government websites at 11.100, fn 1.

[Footnote 4:]

Under s 24(2) of the Adoption Act 1976 (now repealed), the court could not make an adoption order if there had been a contravention of the s 57 prohibition on making certain payments for adoption. Section 57, although repealed, has been replicated and expanded in section 95 of the Adoption and Children Act 2002 but the court is not precluded from making an adoption order in the event of contravention. Further, the 2002 Act gives greater emphasis to the paramount consideration of the child's welfare 'throughout his life'. It can be expected that the case law balancing welfare and public, including immigration, policy will continue to be important in such cases. See *Re H (A Minor) (Adoption Non-patrial)* (1938) FLR 85, (1982) 12 Fam Law 218, CA; *Re H (a minor) (adoption: non-patrial)* [1996] 4 All ER 600, [1997] 1 WLR 791, [1996] 2 FLR 187, [1996] Fam Law 602, [1996] 02 LS Gaz R 30, 140 Sol Jo LB 128, *sub nom Re A (a minor) (adoption: non-patrial)* [1996] 3 FCR 1, CA; *Re Adoption Application* [1992] 1 WLR 596, [1992] 1 FLR 341, [1992] Fam Law 241, *sub nom Re GD* [1992] 1 FCR 433; *Re J (a minor) (adoption: non-patrial)* [1998] 1 FCR 125, [1998] 1 FLR 225, [1998] Fam Law 130, CA; *Re B (adoption order: nationality)* [1999] 2 AC 136, [1999] 2 All ER 576, [1999] 2 WLR 714, [1999] 1 FCR 529, [1999] 1 FLR 907; *Re R (a minor) (inter-country adoptions: practice)* [1999] 4 All ER 1015, [1999] 1 WLR 1324, [1999] 1 FCR 418, [1999] 1 FLR 1042, [1999] Fam Law 289; *Re C (a minor) (adoption illegality)* [1999] Fam 128, [1999] 2 WLR 202, [1998] 2 FCR 641, [1999] 1 FLR 370, [1998] Fam Law 724.

11.104

[Footnote 2:]

Note that the definition of parent in the immigration rules has been amended by HC 582. See 11.78 above of this supplement.

The Adoption Act 1976 has been repealed and the main text giving rise to footnotes 8 and 9 should be deleted and replaced by the following, with new footnotes 8 and 9 inserted:

> 'If the prospective adopter is the parent, or the child was placed for adoption with the applicant by an adoption agency or in pursuance of an order of the High Court, he/she will have to have the child living with him or her for 10 weeks before an application for adoption can be made.[8] If the applicant is a step-parent of the child or a partner to the child's parent he/she has to wait for six months before lodging the adoption application. If the applicants are local authority foster parents the child will have to have lived with them for one year preceding the application. All other adopters have to have had the child living with them or with one of them if it is a couple for a period of three years (continuous or not) in the five years preceding the application'.[9]

[Footnote 8:]

Adoption and Children Act 2002, s 42(2)

[Footnote 9:]

Adoption and Children Act 2002, s 42(3), (4) and (5).

Designated overseas adoptions

11.105

[NB:]

The Adoption and Children Act 2002 (Commencement No 10) (Transitional and Savings Provisions) Order 2005, SI 2005/2897 makes transitional provisions where the adoption process was started before 30 December 2005 in relation to intercountry adoption cases. Article 7 makes transitional provision concerning the conditions to be met by prospective adopters in non-Convention cases and specifies the extent to which the Adoption (Bringing Children into the United Kingdom) Regulations 2003 still apply. Apart from these transitional provisions this paragraph has been superseded by the AFE Regulations. References in the paragraph to the 2003 Regulations should be read accordingly.

The Adoption Act 1976 has been repealed and references to it in the footnotes should be deleted as follows:

[Footnote 4:]

Delete 'See also Adoption Act 1976, s 56A' and insert 'See also Adoption and Children Act 2002, Sch 4, para. 12.'

[Footnote 6:]

Delete 'See also Adoption Act 1976, s 56A, as substituted by'. Retain remainder of text.

'Genuine transfer of parental responsibility …'

11.107

[Footnote 2 – add:]

The Intercountry Adoption Guide has not yet been updated to reflect the Adoption and Children Act 2002 which is now in force.

Legal adoption in or from a non-designated and non-convention country

11.109

[NB:]

The adopter will have to comply with the AFE Regulations which have now superseded the Adoption (Bringing Children into the United Kingdom) Regulations 2003.

The main text dealing with a single adopter should read as follows:

> 'A single adopter, or, if the application is being made by a married couple, one of them, will have to show that he or she is domiciled in the British Islands in order to apply to adopt a child in the British Islands and the applicant or both the prospective parents if it is a couple will also have to have been habitually resident in the British Islands for a year before the application.'[3]

3 Adoption and Children Act 2002, s 49(2) and (3).

Proposal for British child to be adopted abroad

11.115

[NB:]

The Adoption Act 1976 has been repealed; so references to it in the main text and footnotes have to be deleted. Note also the provisions of the AFE Regulations, where a person or couple habitually resident in the British Islands wish to adopt a child who is habitually resident in a Convention country outside the British Islands.

[After first two sentences delete and insert:]

Now prospective adopters must also apply for parental responsibility under **s 84(1) of the Adoption and Children Act 2002.**[1] In order to qualify for parental responsibility prospective adopters **would have to have spent the same amount of time habitually resident in the British Islands as they would have needed to qualify for an adoption order to be made in their favour in the British Islands.**[2] If **s 84 of the Adoption and Children Act 2002** is not complied with the act of removing the child from the United Kingdom will amount to a criminal offence under **s 85.**[3] This offence could be committed by the prospective adopters or a local authority.[4] However, where a child is subject to a care order, **s 85** does not apply.[5] If a child is not subject to a care order but is being accommodated under s 20 of the Children Act 1989 (or assisted under s 17 of the Children Act 1989) as the result of a freeing order or otherwise, **s 85** will still apply.[6]

1 Adoption and Children Act 2002, ss 85(2)(a), 84(1).
2 Adoption and Children Act 2002, s 84(2).
3 Adoption and Children Act 2002, s 85(6).
4 A person can include a body of persons corporate or incorporate: Interpretation Act 1978, s 1.
5 Adoption and Children Act 2002, s 85.

[6] *Re B (children) (adoption: removal from jurisdiction)* [2004] EWCA Civ 515, [2004] 2 FCR 129, [2004] All ER (D) 305 (Apr), *sub nom Re A (adoption: placement outside jurisdiction)* [2005] Fam 105, [2004] 3 WLR 1207, [2004] 2 FLR 337, [2004] Fam Law 560, *sub nom B v Birmingham City Council* (2004) Times, 10 June.

UNACCOMPANIED CHILDREN

11.116

[NB:]

Note the rule changes on child visitors contained in HC 819, which took effect on 12 February 2006. See 9.14A above in this supplement.

PARENTS, GRANDPARENTS AND OTHER DEPENDENT RELATIVES

The classes of admissible dependent relatives

11.123

[NB:]

The references to spouses, fiancés and unmarried partners should now include civil partners. The rule for parents or grandparents seeking to enter or remain in the UK which is set out in HC 395, para 317(i)(d) (category (iii) and footnote 6 in the main text) has now been changed by HC 582 to read:

> '(d) a parent or grandparent aged 65 or over who has entered into a second relationship of marriage or civil partnership but cannot look to the spouse, civil partner or children of that second relationship for financial support; and where the person settled in the United Kingdom is able and willing to maintain the parent or grandparent and any spouse or civil partner or child of the second relationship who would be admissible as a dependant;'

Chapter 12

REFUGEES, ASYLUM AND EXCEPTIONAL LEAVE

INTRODUCTION

United Nations High Commissioner for Refugees

12.13

[Add at end:]

The House of Lords approved significant parts of the UNHCR Guidelines on internal relocation[1].

[1] *Januzi v Secretary of State for the Home Department; Hamid v Same; Gaafar v Same; Mohammed v Same* [2006] UKHL 5, [2006] 3 All ER 305, [2006] 2 WLR 397.

12.14

[Footnote 6 – add:]

In *Golfa v Secretary of State for the Home Department* [2005] EWHC 2282 (Admin), [2005] All ER (D) 348 (Jun) Moses J, citing *Mhute v Secretary of State for the Home Department* [2003] EWCA Civ 1029, [2003] All ER (D) 229 (Jun) held that the decision maker was obliged to have regard to UNHCR recommendations relating to removal to a particular country but was not bound to follow them.

The European Union Qualification Directive

12.20A

[Add new paragraph:]

Article 63(1) of the Treaty Establishing the European Community required the Council to adopt 'measures on asylum, in accordance with the Geneva Convention ...and the Protocol ...relating to the status of refugees and other relevant treaties'. These measures were to include 'minimum standards with respect to the qualification of nationals of third countries as refugees'.[1] Pursuant to that provision the Council made the 'Qualification Directive'[2] which entered into force on the 20th day following its publication (on 30 September 2004) in the *Official Journal of the European Union.*[3] Article 38(1) of the Directive required Member States to 'bring into force the laws, regulations and administrative provisions necessary to comply with this Directive before 10 October 2006'. The UK has sought to comply with that obligation by means of the Refugee or Person in Need of International Protection (Qualification) Regulations[4] and by amendments to the Immigration Rules.[5] The Regulations apply to any application for asylum and any immigration appeal made or pending on or after 9 October 2006.[6] Although the amended immigration rules do not make express provision as to the time from which they apply, the President of the Asylum and Immigration Tribunal issued a *Practice Direction* on 9 October 2006 saying that the rules would be taken as applying to all applications and appeals pending on 9 October 2006 and thereafter. The *Practice Direction* also provides that the Tribunal would treat the grounds of appeal in appeals pending on 9 October 2006 as including such grounds as are needed to enable consideration of matters under the Regulations and Rules. Some of the specific provisions contained in the Directive and the implementing rules and Regulations are referred to below.

1 Article 63(1)(c).
2 Council Directive 2004/83/EC of 29 April 2004 on minimum standards for the qualification and status of third country nationals or stateless persons as refugees or as persons who otherwise need international protection and the content of the protection granted. The literature on the Directive includes: Anja Klug 'Harmonization of Asylum in the European Union – Emergence of an EU Refugee System?' (2004) 47 GYIL; *UNHCR Annotated Comments on the EC Council Directive 2004/83/EC of 29 April 2004* (Jan 2005); Jane McAdam 'The European Union Qualification Directive: The Creation of a Subsidiary Protection Regime' (2005) IJRL 461; Helene Lambert 'The EU Asylum Qualification Directive, its Impact on the Jurisprudence of the United Kingdom and International Law' (2006) 55 ICLQ 161.
3 Council Directive 2004/83/EC, Art 39.
4 SI 2006/2525.
5 CM 6918, amending HC 395.
6 SI 2006/2525, reg 1(2).

12.20B

[Add new paragraph:]

Among the issues that are likely to arise in the interpretation and application of the Qualification Directive are the following. First of all there is the issue of the relationship between the criteria for qualification for refugee status contained in the Directive and those contained in the Refugee Convention, as interpreted[1] by the Courts in the UK. The Directive acknowledges the Geneva Convention and Protocol as the 'cornerstone of the international legal regime for the protection of refugees'[2] and its substantive provisions quite closely reflect the Geneva Convention. However, the Directive does not purport to interpret refugee status as defined under the Geneva Convention; instead it contains an autonomous definition of a refugee[3] and imposes on Member States an obligation under the Directive rather than the Convention to recognise refugee status.[4] The Directive expressly recognises Member States' other obligations under international law to avoid refoulement[5] and confer refugee status.[6] Moreover, the purpose of the Directive is to set minimum standards[7] and it expressly acknowledges that Member States may introduce or retain more favourable standards.[8] It would seem, therefore, that in circumstances where the UK's interpretation of the Geneva Convention would lead to recognition of refugee status, such status would have to be recognised even if the person did not qualify under the Directive. However, many of the provisions in the Directive are expressed in mandatory terms.[9] Article 3 which permits Member States to introduce or retain more favourable standards contains the proviso 'in so far as those standards are compatible with this

Directive'. It will almost certainly be argued that where the UK's interpretation of the Geneva Convention is more generous than any of the mandatory requirements of the Directive, the UK interpretation will have to succumb to the Directive. Resolution of this issue is likely to entail consideration of whether a minimum standards Directive can operate so as to impose maximum standards; whether the proviso, contextually and purposively construed can legitimately limit the protection that would otherwise be provided by the UK and whether the proviso which applies to the standards for qualification for refugee status under the Directive has any application at all to the standards for qualification under the separate Geneva Convention regime. This issue may need to be decided in relation to: the capacity of non-state bodies to provide protection capable of obviating the need for refugee status[10] and whether membership of a particular social group requires *both* a shared, innate characteristic *and* social perception of group membership.[11] A second issue that is likely to arise concerns the effect of the Rules and the Regulations that purport to implement the Directive. One argument may be that the Rules and the Regulations are unlawful and should not be applied because although they faithfully implement what is contained in the Directive, they are nevertheless inconsistent with the Geneva Convention. Where such an argument arises, it will probably require reference to the ECJ for its resolution. Another argument, and one more capable of resolution in the UK Courts is that the Regulations and Rules are inconsistent with the Directive and therefore unlawful. It may be said that the Regulations are generally inconsistent with the Directive because whereas the Directive sets out the criteria for qualification as a refugee as defined under the Directive, the Regulations are intended to apply to claims to be a refugee as defined by the Geneva Convention.[12] If that is right, then the Regulations are ultra vires the statutory provision under which they were made which is limited to the making of regulations for the purpose of implementing Community obligations.[13] A more particular inconsistency between the Directive and the Regulations, making the latter potentially more restrictive than the former arises from the omission from reg 4(2) of the words 'inter alia' that appear in Art 7(2) of the Directive. The consequence of that omission is that there may be circumstances in which far less needs to be done by an asylum seeker's country of origin to provide sufficient domestic protection obviating the need for refugee status, if the Regulations are applied than if the Directive is applied.[14]

1 For the Convention having a single, autonomous meaning that is authoritatively determined by the Court see *R v Secretary of State for the Home Department, ex p Adan* [2001] 2 AC 477, [2001] 1 All ER 593, [2000] All ER (D) 2357, HL.
2 Preamble (3).
3 Art 2(c). The clearest difference between the Geneva Convention definition and the definition in the Directive is that is that the latter applies only to third country, i e non-EU nationals and stateless people. However, Art 9 is expressed as being interpretive of 'persecution within the meaning of Art 1A of the Geneva Convention.
4 Article 2(d).
5 Article 21(1).
6 Article 20(1).
7 Consolidated Version of the Treaty Establishing the European Community, Art 63(1)(c).
8 Directive, preamble (8) and Art 3.
9 Eg Art 7: 'Protection can be provided by …'; Art 9(1): 'Acts of persecution …must'; Art 10(1): 'member states shall …'; Art 12(1) and (2): 'A third country national or a stateless person is excluded …'

[10] Directive Art 7(1)(b) which mandates a lower standard of refugee protection than does the Geneva Convention as interpreted in *Gardi v Secretary of State for the Home Department* [2002] EWCA Civ 750, [2002] 1 WLR 2755, [2003] Imm AR 39 and *R (on the application of Vallaj) v A Special Adjudicator* [2001] EWCA Civ 782, [2001] INLR 342.
[11] As per Art 10(1)(d), by contrast to the position under the Geneva Convention as interpreted in the UK where the two are alternative tests.
[12] The Refugee or Person in Need of International Protection (Qualification) Regulations 2006, SI 2006/2525, reg 2.
[13] European Communities Act 1972, s 2(2).
[14] See further para 12.53 below.

THE DEFINITION OF REFUGEE

'Owing to a well-founded fear'

12.22

[In the text after footnote 1 add:]

If a person is at risk of being persecuted in his home country as a consequence of being returned there forcibly the risk would not make him or her a refugee if it was possible for the person, by returning voluntarily, to avoid the risk. The person would not be a refugee even if he or she refused to return voluntarily resulting in forcible removal and a real risk of being persecuted. That is because such a person cannot be said to be outside the country of nationality 'owing to well founded fear' as required by the refugee Convention definition. The person must have some other reason for making the choice not to return and it is the choice not to return that gives rise to the risk, not the risk that gives rise to the choice.[1]

[In the text, after footnote 4 add:]

The Qualification Directive acknowledges that a need for protection may arise as a result of events occurring after the applicant left the country of origin and that such events may include the applicant's own activities outside the country of origin.[2] However, the Qualification Directive permits refugee status to be withheld where the applicant has deliberately created a risk of persecution[3], eg by deliberately bringing him or herself to the hostile attention of his/her authorities. The implementing immigration rules make provision for 'sur place' claims but do not exclude 'bad faith' claims.[4]

[1] *AA v Secretary of State for the Home Department; LK v Secretary of State for the Home Department* [2006] EWCA Civ 401, [2006] NLJR 681, (2006) Times, 17 April.
[2] Council Directive 2004/83/EC, Art 5.
[3] Council Directive 2004/83/EC, Art 5(3).
[4] HC 395, para 339P, as inserted by HC 6918.

Well-founded

12.23

[In the text, after footnote 3 add:]

A person may still be at risk of being persecuted even if his account of past persecution has been rejected as unbelievable.[1] Moreover, where an asylum seeker's claim has been disbelieved, it would be wrong to treat a subsequent, alternative claim as being an abuse of process which should not therefore be considered;[2] 'the fact that a claim is inconsistent with the first claim made does not of itself deprive an applicant of the protection of the Refugee Convention or the European Convention on Human Rights'.[3]

[In the text, after footnote 6 add:]

The Qualification Directive provides that the fact that an individual has experienced persecution or serious harm in the past or direct threats of such persecution or harm is a 'serious indication' of current risk unless there are 'good reasons' to consider that such serious harm or persecution will not be repeated.[4]

1 *Daoud v Secretary of State for the Home Department* [2005] EWCA Civ 755, [2005] All ER (D) 259 (May), where Sedley LJ said: 'To claim falsely that you have been persecuted in the past because of your ethnicity does not mean that you may not face risks in future because of it'.

2 Which was the approach taken in the tribunal's starred determination *MY(Somalia)** [2004] UKIAT 00174. Ouseley J held that it would be an abuse of process to permit the appellant, whose claim to be Somali had been disbelieved, to advance a claim on the alternative basis, inconsistent with the first, that he would be at risk on return to Somalia for the reason that he was not Somali.

3 *Yusuf v Secretary of State for the Home Department* [2005] EWCA Civ 1554, 150 Sol Jo LB 90, [2005] All ER (D) 194 (Dec), the appeal from *MY (Somalia)* per Pill LJ.

4 Council Directive 2004/83/EC, Art 4(4), implemented by HC 395, para 339K, as inserted by HC 6918.

Refraining from acts exacerbating risk

12.32

[In the text, after footnote 6 add:]

However, having to alter behaviour and conceal sexuality in order to avoid being persecuted will not by itself amount to persecution unless the distress and suffering caused is so intense or prolonged that the person cannot reasonably be expected to tolerate it.[1] The decision maker would need to consider whether the person could reasonably be expected to tolerate living 'discreetly' not only in relation to sexual activity but more broadly in relation to sexual identity and whether the person could be expected to tolerate being unable to live openly with a partner.[2]

1 *RG (Colombia) v Secretary of State for the Home Department* [2006] EWCA Civ 57.

2 *J v Secretary of State for the Home Department* [2006] EWCA Civ 1238.

Internal relocation alternative

12.42

[Add at end:]

The House of Lords has now rejected the proposition that there is a presumption against the existence of an internal flight alternative where the state is the agent of the feared persecution.[1] In a case of persecution by the

State, whether there is an internal flight alternative is a question of fact which requires analysis of the nature of the State's involvement in the persecution. 'The more closely the persecution in question is linked to the State, and the greater the control of the State over those acting or purporting to act on its behalf, the more likely (other things being equal) that a victim of persecution in one place will be similarly vulnerable in another place within the State. The converse may also be true'.[2]

Article 8 of the Qualification Directive[3] relating to internal protection has now been implemented by the Immigration Rules.[4] The Directive and the rule both provide for a person to be disqualified from international protection if there is an 'internal flight alternative' but 'technical obstacles to return to the country of origin'; the disqualification is not applicable where return to some part of the country is possible but there are technical obstacles to return to the safe part of the country.

1 *Januzi v Secretary of State for the Home Department; Hamid v Same; Gaafar v Same; Mohammed v Same* [2006] UKHL 5, [2006] 3 All ER 305, [2006] 2 WLR 397.
2 *Januzi v Secretary of State for the Home Department* per Lord Bingham at para 21.
3 Council Directive 2004/83/EC.
4 HC 395, para 339O, as inserted by HC 6918.

12.43

[Add at end:]

That case[1] had decided that whether there was an internal flight alternative had to be determined according to whether basic norms of civil, political and socio-economic human rights were satisfied in the putatively 'safe area'. That approach has been rejected by the House of Lords.[2] The question is simply whether it would be unreasonable to expect the refugee to relocate within his or her country and it would be unreasonable if such relocation was 'unduly harsh'.[3] Lord Bingham commended the UNHCR Guidelines on International Protection of 23 July 2003 as providing 'valuable guidance' on the approach to reasonableness and undue harshness in this context.[4] They say that internal flight would not be reasonable if: deprivation of fundamental rights to the individual in the area of relocation would be sufficiently harmful to him or her; the person could not earn a living, access accommodation or obtain adequate medical care; the person faced economic destitution or existence below at least an adequate level of subsistence; the person could not 'sustain a relatively normal life at more than just a minimum subsistence level'; the person would be denied access to land, resources and protection because he or she does not belong to the dominant clan, tribe, ethnic or religious or cultural group in the area; the person was required 'to relocate to areas, such as the slums of an urban area, where they would be required to live in conditions of severe hardship'[5]. In order to determine whether a gay Palestinian could relocate within Lebanon it was necessary to take account of the legal ban on Palestinians owning property; accommodation being too expensive; the legal exclusion of Palestinians from many trades and professions; the difficulty of obtaining a work permit and the difficulties that would be faced by a homosexual living in a Muslim area of the country.[6] An internal flight alternative might be unreasonable if it depended upon an individual having to conceal some aspect of his or her identity or history and having to live with the consequent fear of discovery.[7]

[1] *Refugee Appeal No 71684/99* [2000] INLR 165, approved in *Canaj v Secretary of State for the Home Department, Vallaj v Special Adjudicator* [2001] EWCA Civ 782, [2001] All ER (D) 322 (May), [2001] INLR 342.

[2] *Januzi v Secretary of State for the Home Department; Hamid v Same; Gaafar v Same; Mohammed v Same* [2006] UKHL 5, [2006] 3 All ER 305, [2006] 2 WLR 397.

[3] *Januzi v Secretary of State for the Home Department* per Lord Bingham at para 15 and Lord Hope at para 47.

[4] *Januzi v Secretary of State for the Home Department* at para 20.

[5] *UNHCR Guidelines on International Protection* of 23 July 2003, cited in *Januzi v Secretary of State for the Home Department.*

[6] *HC v Secretary of State for the Home Department* [2005] EWCA Civ 893, [2005] All ER (D) 267 (Jul).

[7] *Hysi v Secretary of State for the Home Department* [2005] EWCA Civ 711, (2005) Times, 23 June, [2005] All ER (D) 135 (Jun).

12.44

[Footnote 3 – add:]

The appeal in *AE* did not proceed. Instead, the House of Lords dealt with the issues in *Januzi v Secretary of State for the Home Department; Hamid v Same; Gaafar v Same; Mohammed v Same* [2006] UKHL 5, [2006] 3 All ER 305, [2006] 2 WLR 397.

12.45

[Add at end:]

However, internal flight is only a legitimate issue in an appeal if proper notice that it is to be raised is given.[1] Moreover, notwithstanding that there is no formal burden of proof on the Home Office in relation to internal flight, an otherwise well-founded claim may only be rejected if the evidence satisfies the judge of fact that internal relocation is a safe and reasonable option.[2]

[1] *Daoud v Secretary of State for the Home Department* [2005] EWCA Civ 755, [2005] All ER (D) 259 (May).

[2] Sedley LJ's dissenting judgment in *Jasim v Secretary of State for the Home Department* [2006] EWCA Civ 342, (2006) Times, 17 May. The majority dismissed the appeal on the basis that the immigration judge had been entitled to find on the evidence that internal relocation was safe and reasonable.

Persecution

12.46

[Add at end:]

The Qualification Directive sets out a definition of 'acts of persecution'[1] in mandatory terms by which they must be '(a) sufficiently serious by their nature or repetition as to constitute a severe violation of basic human rights, in particular the rights from which derogation cannot be made under article 15(2) of the European Convention for the Protection of Human

Rights'[2] or '(b) be an accumulation of various measures, including violations of human rights which is sufficiently severe as to affect an individual in a similar manner as mentioned in (a)'. It lists various forms that acts of persecution may take (eg acts of physical or mental violence, legal, administrative, police or judicial measures which are discriminatory) but it is important to note that the list is illustrative, not exhaustive.[3] The individual's particular characteristics and circumstances including background, gender and age must be taken into account in order to determine whether the acts feared would amount to persecution or serious harm.[4]

1 Council Directive 2004/83/EC, Art 9(1), implemented by the Refugee or Person in Need of International Protection (Qualification) Regulations 2006, reg 5(1).
2 Ie ECHR Arts 2, 3, 4 and 7.
3 Council Directive 2004/83/EC, Art 9(2) and the Refugee or Person in Need of International Protection (Qualification) Regulations 2006, reg 5(2).
4 Council Directive 2004/83/EC, Art 4(3)(C), implemented by HC 395, para 339J(iii), as inserted by HC 6918.

[Footnote 10 – add:]

But see *Amare v Secretary of State for the Home Department* [2005] EWCA Civ 1600, [2005] All ER (D) 300 (Dec) where the Court of Appeal said that Professor Hathaway's definition had to be 'treated with a degree of caution' because it did not give a clear place to the requirement that the human rights violation had to be sufficiently serious by reference either to its intensity or duration. See also *RG (Colombia) v Secretary of State for the Home Department* [2006] EWCA Civ 57 applying what had been said obiter in *Amare*.

12.48

[Add at end:]

As examples of 'acts of persecution' the Qualification Directive refers to prosecution or punishment which is disproportionate or discriminatory,[1] denial of judicial redress resulting in a disproportionate or discriminatory punishment[2] and prosecution or punishment for refusal to perform military service in a conflict, where performing military service would include acts constituting crimes against peace, war crimes, crimes against humanity, serious non-political crime or acts contrary to the purposes and principles of the United Nations.[3]

1 Council Directive 2004/83/EC, Art 9(2)(c), implemented by the Refugee or Person in Need of International Protection (Qualification) Regulations 2006, reg 5(2)(c).
2 Council Directive 2004/83/EC, Art 9(2)(d), implemented by the Refugee or Person in Need of International Protection (Qualification) Regulations 2006, reg 5(2)(d).
3 Council Directive 2004/83/EC, Art 9(2)(e), implemented by the Refugee or Person in Need of International Protection (Qualification) Regulations 2006, reg 5(2)(e). The list of acts which performing military service would include comes from Art 12(2).

Persecution by non-state actors

12.51

[Add at end:]

The Qualification Directive identifies as 'actors of persecution' the state, parties or organisations controlling the state or a substantial part of the territory of the state and non-state actors. In the case of non-state actors, there must be a want of protection provided by the state or party before they can be treated as 'actors of persecution'.[1]

1 Council Directive 2004/83/EC, Art 6, implemented by the Refugee or Person in Need of International Protection (Qualification) Regulations 2006, reg 3.

12.53

[Add at end:]

Under the Refugee Convention only the State or an international body to which the functions and powers of the State have been transferred as a matter of international law is capable of providing 'protection' of a kind that obviates the need for international protection.[1] The Qualification Directive allows for such protection to be provided not only by the State but by parties or organisations, including international organisations, controlling the State or a substantial part of the territory of the State.[2] As for the quality of protection, the 'actors of protection' have to take 'reasonable steps' to prevent the persecution or serious harm, 'inter alia by operating an effective legal system for the detection, prosecution and punishment of acts constituting persecution or serious harm and the applicant must have access to such protection'.[3] The implementing Regulations are materially different in that they do not reproduce the phrase 'inter alia' used in the Directive.[4] The effect of that is that operation of an effective legal system becomes in the Regulation a sufficient rather than (as in the Directive) a necessary but not necessarily sufficient condition for the provision of protection. An example might be that a reasonable step that should be taken by an actor of protection to prevent a woman suffering domestic violence is the provision of women's refuges. The absence of such refuges might, under the Directive, establish that there is not sufficient domestic protection. However, under the Regulation, the provision of an effective legal system would be all that could be required of the asylum seeker's home country in order to establish sufficient protection there.

1 *R (on the application of Vallaj) v Special Adjudicator* [2001] EWCA Civ 782, [2001] INLR 342; *Gardi v Secretary of State for the Home Department* [2002] EWCA Civ 750, [2002] 1 WLR 2755, [2003] Imm AR 39.

2 Council Directive 2004/83/EC, Art 7(1), implemented by the Refugee or Person in Need of International Protection (Qualification) Regulations 2006, reg 4(1).

3 Council Directive 2004/83/EC, Art 7(2).

4 The Refugee or Person in Need of International Protection (Qualification) Regulations 2006, reg 4(2).

12.57

[In the text, after footnote 3 add:]

The issue is not whether the authorities are willing to provide protection but whether they are capable of providing the particular individual with adequate protection.[1]

1 *DK v Secretary of State for the Home Department* [2006] EWCA Civ 682.

12.60

[Add at end:]

The decision in *Fadli* was applied to both the asylum and human rights claims of a Sri Lankan intelligence officer fearing assassination by the LTTE. Newman J in *R (on the application of Gedara) v Secretary of State for the Home Department*[1] held that the State did not have a duty to protect him from the risk of harm resulting from his own actions in providing protection to fellow citizens so that that risk could not establish a claim to refugee status or under the ECHR.

1 [2006] EWHC 1690 (Admin), [2006] All ER (D) 99 (Jul).

'For reasons of'

12.64

[Add at end:]

The causal nexus between the feared persecution and the 'convention reason' required by the Qualification Directive is merely that there be 'a connection' between them.[1] Moreover, it is immaterial whether the applicant actually possesses the characteristic which attracts the persecution so long as the characteristic is attributed to the applicant by the actor of persecution.[2]

1 Council Directive 2004/83/EC, Art 9(3). The language of the implementing legislation is different. It provides that 'an act of persecution must be committed for at least one of' the Convention reasons: The Refugee or Person in Need of International Protection (Qualification) Regulations 2006, reg 5(3).

2 Council Directive 2004/83/EC, Art 10(2) and the Refugee or Person in Need of International Protection (Qualification) Regulations 2006, reg 6(2).

Religion

12.70

[Add at end:]

The Qualification Directive requires a broad interpretation of religion to include the holding of theistic, non-theistic and atheistic beliefs, the participation in or abstention from formal worship in private or in public, alone or in community with others, other religious acts of expressions of view or forms of personal or communal conduct based on or mandated by any religious belief.[1]

[1] Council Directive 2004/83/EC, Art 10(1)(b), implemented by the Refugee or Person in Need of International Protection (Qualification) Regulations 2006, reg 6(1)(b).

Nationality

12.71

[Add at end:]

The Qualification Directive also requires a broad interpretation of nationality so as to include membership of a group determined by its cultural, ethnic, or linguistic identity, common geographical or political origins or its relationship with the population of another state.[1]

[1] Council Directive 2004/83/EC, Art 10(1)(c), implemented by the Refugee or Person in Need of International Protection (Qualification) Regulations 2006, reg 6(1)(c).

Political opinion

12.72

[Add at end:]

The Qualification Directive includes within 'political opinion' 'the holding of an opinion, thought or belief on a matter related to the potential actors of persecution ...and to their policies or methods, whether or not that opinion, thought or belief has been acted upon by the applicant'.[1]

[1] Council Directive 2004/83/EC, Art 10(1)(e) and the Refugee or Person in Need of International Protection (Qualification) Regulations 2006, reg 6(1)(f).

Refusal to perform military service

12.75

[Add at end:]

The list of acts contained in the Qualification Directive and capable of amounting to acts of persecution includes 'prosecution or punishment for refusal to perform military service in a conflict where performing military service would include' crimes against peace, war crimes, crimes against humanity, serious non-political crimes or acts contrary to the purposes and principles of the United Nations.[1] The list of persecutory acts is illustrative, not exhaustive and the Directive does not pretend to identify all of the circumstances in which refusal to perform military service may result in being persecuted.

[1] Council Directive 2004/83/EC, Arts 9(2)(e), 12(2) and the Refugee or Person in Need of International Protection (Qualification) Regulations 2006, reg 5(2)(e).

Membership of a particular social group

12.78

[Add at end:]

According to the UNHCR Guidelines[1] cited in the original text there are two alternative tests for establishing the existence of a particular social group: 'shared characteristics' or 'social perception'. The Guidelines say 'a particular social group is a group of persons who share a common characteristic other than their risk of being persecuted, or who are perceived as a group by society'. By contrast, the Qualification Directive provides that the 'innate characteristics' test and the 'social perception' test are cumulative rather than alternative requirements for the existence of a particular social group.[2] The Directive expressly acknowledges that sexual orientation may be the common characteristic upon which a particular social group is based but excluding acts considered to be criminal in national law from the meaning of sexual orientation.[3] Surprisingly, and plainly at odds with the UK's interpretation of the Refugee Convention, the Directive says that gender may be relevant but is not by itself capable of constituting a particular social group.[4] Quite rightly the implementing Regulations do not give effect to this part of the Directive.[5]

1 *Guidelines on International Protection: 'Membership of a particular social group'* (7 May 2002) (HCR/GIP/02/02)
2 Council Directive 2004/83/EC, Art 10(1)(d) and the Refugee or Person in Need of International Protection (Qualification) Regulations 2006, reg 6(1)(e).
3 Council Directive 2004/83/EC, Art 10(1)(d), the Refugee or Person in Need of International Protection (Qualification) Regulations 2006, reg 6(1)(e) and the Refugee or Person in Need of International Protection (Qualification) Regulations 2006, reg 6(1)(e).
4 Council Directive 2004/83/EC, Art 10(1)(d).
5 See the Refugee or Person in Need of International Protection (Qualification) Regulations 2006, reg 6(1)(e) which reproduces that part of the Directive relating to sexual orientation but not the immediately following part about gender.

12.80

[In the text, after footnote 4 add:]

a woman in Ethiopia fearing forced marriage.[1]

[In the text, after footnote 13 add:]

The Court of Appeal, by a majority,[2] held that although a young woman from Sierra Leone had well founded fear of being persecuted in the form of female genital mutilation, it was not for reason of 'membership of a particular social group' because no group could be identified without reference to the feared persecution.[3] Women who had already been mutilated could not have the fear of being persecuted so that a reference to not having undergone female genital mutilation had to be introduced into the definition of the group and that amounted to defining the group by reference to the feared persecution. An appeal against that decision has been heard but not yet decided by the House of Lords.

[Footnote 15 – add:]

See also *RG (Ethiopia) v Secretary of State for the Home Department* [2006] EWCA Civ 339, 150 Sol Jo LB 473, [2006] All ER (D) 20 (Apr).

1 *RG (Ethiopia) v Secretary of State for the Home Department* [2006] EWCA Civ 339, 150 Sol Jo LB 473, [2006] All ER (D) 20 (Apr).

2 *Fornah v Secretary of State for the Home Department* [2005] EWCA Civ 680, [2005] 1 WLR 3773, [2005] 3 FCR 449, Auld and Chadwick LLJ, Arden LJ dissenting.

3 See para 12.78(ii) in the original text.

Cessation

12.84

[Add at end:]

The Qualification Directive[1] effectively reproduces the 'Cessation clauses' in Art 1C of the Refugee Convention except for the proviso whereby a statutory refugee could invoke 'compelling reasons arising out of previous persecution' to avoid the application of the Cessation clause. For refugee status to cease owing to a change of the circumstances in connection with which the person became a refugee, the change of circumstances must be of such a significant and non-temporary nature that the refugee's fear of persecution can no longer be regarded as well-founded.[2] The Directive obliges the Member State to revoke or refuse to renew refugee status if the person ceases to be a refugee and asylum had been sought after the Directive came into force.[3] In such circumstances, the Member State is required to demonstrate that the person has ceased to be a refugee.[4] In addition, refugee status is to be revoked, ended or not extended if the Member State shows that misrepresentation or omission of facts, including the use of false documents were decisive for the granting of refugee status.[5]

1 Council Directive 2004/83/EC, Art 11(1), implemented in the UK by HC 395, para 339A, as inserted by HC 6918.

2 Council Directive 2004/83/EC, Art 11(2), implemented in the UK by HC 395 para. 339A as inserted by HC 6918.

3 Council Directive 2004/83/EC, Art 14(1) and HC 395, para 339A(i)–(iv). Applicable, according to the Rules, where asylum was sought on or after 21 October 2004.

4 Council Directive 2004/83/EC, Art 14(2).

5 Council Directive 2004/83/EC, Art 14(3) and HC 395, para 339A(viii).

Exclusion

12.88

[Add at end:]

The Qualification Directive substantially reproduces[1] Art 1D of the Refugee Convention (exclusion of those receiving protection from other UN organisations).

1 Council Directive 2004/83/EC, Art 12(12) and the Refugee or Person in Need of International Protection (Qualification) Regulations 2006, reg 7(1).

Exclusion for criminal activity

12.90

[Add at end:]

The Qualification Directive reproduces the exclusion clause in Art 1F of the Refugee Convention (exclusion for war crimes, crimes against peace, crimes against humanity, serious non-political crimes and acts contrary to the purposes and principles of the UN) but with a number of substantial alterations and additions that broaden the scope of the exclusion.[1] Firstly, Art 1F(b) of the Refugee Convention excludes a person who 'has committed a serious non-political crime outside the country of refuge prior to his admission to that country as a refugee'. The Directive defines the phrase 'prior to his or her admission as a refugee' as meaning prior to the time of being issued with a residence permit based on the granting of refugee status.[2] Secondly, the Directive also provides that 'particularly cruel actions, even if committed with an allegedly political objective, may be classified as serious non-political crimes' for the purpose of the exclusion clause.[3] UNHCR's understanding of 'particularly cruel actions' is 'criminal acts which are particularly egregious'.[4] Thirdly, the Directive defines 'acts contrary to the purposes and principles of the United Nations' as being acts contrary to the Preamble and Arts 1 and 2 of the Charter of the United Nations.[5] This provision in the Directive may substantially broaden the scope for exclusion beyond the intention of Art 1F(c) in the Refugee Convention which was that it would apply to those who occupied positions of power in their countries.[6] The implementing Regulation does not reproduce that part of the Directive defining 'acts contrary to the purposes and principles of the United Nations'. The Directive obliges the member state to revoke, end or refuse to renew the refugee status of a person who is or should have been excluded from being a refugee.[7]

1 Council Directive 2004/83/EC, Art 12(2).
2 Council Directive 2004/83/EC, Art 12(2)(b) and the Refugee or Person in Need of International Protection (Qualification) Regulations 2006, reg 7(2)(b).
3 Council Directive 2004/83/EC, Art 12(2)(b) and the Refugee or Person in Need of International Protection (Qualification) Regulations 2006, reg 7(2)(a).
4 *UNHCR Annotated Comments on the EC Council Directive 2004/83/EC* (January 2005).
5 Council Directive 2004/83/EC, Art 12(2)(c).
6 *UNHCR Annotated Comments on the EC Council Directive 2004/83/EC* (January 2005).
7 Council Directive 2004/83/EC, Art 14(3) and HC 395, para 339A(vii), as inserted by HC 6918.

12.93

[At the end of sub-para (4), add:]

In relation to the obligation on an adjudicator to consider the possible applicability of the exclusion clauses, even if not raised by the Secretary of State, the Court of Appeal held that an adjudicator had erred in law by failing to consider whether an asylum seeker from Iraq should be excluded for 'serious non-political crimes' on account of his admitted involvement in detaining and torturing opponents of the Saddam Hussein regime.[1] The tribunal found a similar error where an adjudicator failed to consider whether

Art 1F applied to a member of the Jihad Islamic Movement who had been involved in its armed activities in Gaza, including a (failed) suicide bombing.[2]

1 *A (Iraq) v Secretary of State for the Home Department* [2005] EWCA Civ 1438, 149 Sol Jo LB 1492, [2005] All ER (D) 22 (Dec).
2 *AA (Palestine)* [2005] UKIAT 00104.

War crimes, crimes against humanity and crimes against the purposes and principles of the UN

12.94A

[Add new paragraph:]

Section 54 of the Immigration, Asylum and Nationality Act 2006 (which is not yet in force) introduces an obligatory, statutory interpretation of Article 1(F)(c) of the Convention.[1] Article 1(F)(c) excludes from the Convention a person of whom there are serious reasons for thinking that 'he has been guilty of acts contrary to the purposes and principles of the United Nations'. Section 54 of the Act provides that 'acts contrary to the purposes and principles of the United Nations' includes acts of committing, preparing or instigating terrorism and acts of encouraging or inducing others to commit, prepare or instigate terrorism, whether or not the acts amount to an actual or inchoate offence. Terrorism has the meaning given by s 1 of the Terrorism Act 2000.[2] It can be seen that this definition is potentially of extremely wide application.

1 Contrary to the principle that 'the Convention must be interpreted as an international instrument, not a domestic statute, in accordance with the rules prescribed by the Vienna Convention on the Law of Treaties' (*Januzi v Secretary of State for the Home Department; Hamid v Same; Gaafar v Same; Mohammed v Same* [2006] UKHL 5, [2006] 3 All ER 305, [2006] 2 WLR 397, per Lord Bingham, para. 4).
2 Which provides: (1) In this Act 'terrorism' means the use or threat of action where– (a) the action falls within subsection (2), (b) the use or threat is designed to influence the government or an international governmental organization or to intimidate the public or a section of the public, and (c) the use or threat is made for the purpose of advancing a political, religious or ideological cause. (2) Action falls within this subsection if it– (a) involves serious violence against a person, (b) involves serious damage to property, (c) endangers a person's life, other than that of the person committing the action, (d) creates a serious risk to the health or safety of the public or a section of the public, or (e) is designed seriously to interfere with or seriously to disrupt an electronic system. (3) the use or threat of action falling within subsection (2) which involves the use of firearms or explosives is terrorism whether or not subsection (1)(b) is satisfied. (4) In this section– (a) 'action' includes action outside the United Kingdom, (b) a reference to any person or property is a reference to any person, or to property, wherever situated, (c) a reference to the public includes a reference to the public of a country other than the United Kingdom, and (d) 'the government' means the government of the United Kingdom, of a part of the United Kingdom or of a country other than the United Kingdom. (5) In this Act a reference to action taken for the purposes of terrorism includes a reference to action taken for the benefit of a proscribed organization.

Serious non-political crime

12.95A

[Add new paragraph:]

Section 55 of the Immigration, Asylum and Nationality Act 2006[1] makes provision for a special procedure to be followed in asylum appeals[2] involving issues of exclusion. The Secretary of State may issue a certificate that Art 1F applies to the person or that Art 33(2)[3] applies on grounds of national security. If such a certificate is issued, the tribunal or SIAC must begin substantive deliberations on the asylum appeal by considering the statements in the Secretary of State's certificate.[4] If it agrees with those statements it must dismiss the asylum appeal before considering any other aspect of the case (eg the human rights grounds).[5] A similar procedure has already been established for asylum appeals where the Secretary of State has issued a certificate that the person may not claim the benefit of the refugee Convention because he or she has been convicted of a particularly serious crime.[6] If the Secretary of State issues a certificate on Arts 1F or 33(2) national security grounds and issues another certificate on 'particularly serious crime' grounds, the tribunal or SIAC must consider the Arts 1F or 33(2) (national security) certificate first and need only consider the 'particularly serious crime' certificate if it does not agree with the first certificate.[7]

1. Which came into force on 31 August 2006. See the Immigration, Asylum and Nationality Act 2006 (Commencement No 2) Order 2006, SI 2006/2226.
2. Ie appeals under Nationality, Immigration and Asylum Act 2002, ss 82, 83 or 101 or Special Immigration Appeals Commission Act 1997, s 2 in which the appellant claims that his or her removal would be contrary to the UK's obligations under the Refugee Convention. See Immigration, Asylum and Nationality Act 2006, s 55(2). This new procedure will replace the procedure presently applicable in appeals before SIAC where the Secretary of State certifies that Arts 1(F) or 33(2) apply – hence the repeal of Anti-terrorism, Crime and Security Act 2001, s 33 by IAN 2006, s 55(6).
3. 'The benefit of the present provision [ie non-refoulement of a refugee] may not, however, be claimed by a refugee whom there are reasonable grounds for regarding as a danger to the security of the country in which he is, or who, having been convicted by a final judgment of a particularly serious crime, constitutes a danger to the community of that country'. See further, para 12.97 ff in the original text.
4. IAN 2006, s 55(3).
5. IAN 2006, s 55(4).
6. Nationality, Immigration and Asylum Act 2002, s 72. See para 12.99 of the original text.
7. IAN 2006, s 55(5).

EXPULSION OF REFUGEES

12.99

[Add at end:]

The Asylum Policy Instruction on Refugee Leave identifies an extremely wide range of circumstances which may lead the government to rely on Art 33(2) to remove a refugee or, if that is not possible, to vary his or her leave to discretionary leave. The list includes: sentencing for an offence to more than two years' imprisonment; recommendation for deportation by a court; inclusion of the individual on the sex offenders register; where an extradition request is received either from the country from which asylum was sought or from a country which might refoule the refugee or where the Secretary of State considers that the refugee's presence is not conducive to the public good. A decision that the person's presence is not conducive to the public good may be made if the person 'engages in one or more unacceptable behaviours, whether in the UK or abroad'. Unacceptable behaviours includes using any medium of communication or any position of responsibility to express views foment, justify or glorify terrorist violence; seek to provoke others to terrorist acts; foment serious criminal activity or seek to provoke others to criminal acts or foster hatred which may lead to inter community violence in the UK.

The Qualification Directive enables Member States to revoke, end or refuse to renew refugee status if there are reasonable grounds for regarding the person to be a danger to the security of the state or, having been convicted of a particularly serious crime he or she constitutes a danger to the community.[1]

[1] Council Directive 2004/83/EC, Art 14(4) and HC 395, para 339A(ix) and (x).

CONSEQUENCES OF RECOGNITION

12.102

[In the text, after footnote 6 add:]

However, a person's recognition as a refugee does not entitle him to the diplomatic protection of the country that has granted asylum.[1]

[1] *R (on the application of Al Rawi) v Secretary of State for Foreign and Commonwealth Affairs* [2006] EWHC 972 (Admin), [2006] NLJR 797, (2006) Times, 19 May. Thus there was no obligation on the UK government even to consider making representations to the government of the USA on behalf of claimants recognized in the UK as refugees and detained in Guantanamo Bay; there was an obligation to consider making representations in respect of British citizens: *R (on the application of Abbasi) v Secretary of State for Foreign and Commonwealth Affairs* [2002] EWCA Civ 1598, (2002) Times, 8 November.

SUBSIDIARY PROTECTION

12.107A

[ADD NEW PARAGRAPH:]

The Qualification Directive creates a legal obligation on Member States to provide 'subsidiary protection' to third country nationals and stateless people who do not qualify as refugees but who face a real risk of suffering serious harm, who are not excluded from protection and to whom protection is not available in their home country.[1] Serious harm consists of the death penalty or execution, torture or inhuman or degrading treatment or punishment or serious and individual threat to a civilian's life or person by reason of indiscriminate violence in situations of international or internal armed conflict.[2] The provisions of the Directive relating to assessment of facts and circumstances,[3] international protection needs arising *sur place*,[4] actors of persecution or serious harm,[5] actors of protection[6] and internal protection[7] which are applicable to determination of refugee status also apply to the determination of entitlement to subsidiary protection. Eligibility for subsidiary protection ceases if there has been a significant, non-temporary change of circumstances of such a degree that protection is no longer required[8] and in such circumstances, the Member State is obliged to revoke, end or refuse to renew the status.[9] A person is excluded from subsidiary protection if he or she has committed a crime against peace, a war crime or a crime against humanity, a serious crime, has been guilty of acts contrary to the purposes and principles of the United Nations or constitutes a danger to the community or to the security of the Member State.[10] A person may be excluded from subsidiary protection if he or she committed one or more other crimes which would be punishable by imprisonment had they been committed in the member state and the person left his or her country of origin solely to avoid sanctions resulting from those crimes.[11]

1 Council Directive 2004/EC/83, Arts 2(e), 18 and HC 395, para 339C–339Q, as inserted by HC 6918 make provision for applications for subsidiary protection in the form of humanitarian protection.
2 Council Directive 2004/EC/83, Art 15.
3 Article 4.
4 Article 5.
5 Article 6.
6 Article 7.
7 Article 8.
8 Article 16.
9 Article 19(1).
10 Article 17.
11 Article 17(3).

UK PRACTICE ON ASYLUM

The application

12.108

[After the first sentence in the text, add:]

For the purpose of the appeals provisions, an asylum claim means a claim made by a person to the Secretary of State at a place designated him that to remove the person from the United Kingdom would breach the United Kingdom's obligations under the Refugee Convention.[1] Section 12 of the IAN 2006 (when it comes into force) will substitute a new definition of 'asylum claim' as meaning 'a claim made by a person that to remove him from or require him to leave the United Kingdom would breach the United Kindgom's obligations under the Refugee Convention'. In contrast to the current definition, it does not specify to whom the claim must be made, nor does it specify where it must be made. The new definition makes provision for subsequent claims to be disregarded in circumstances determined by the immigration rules. The provision also substitutes a new definition of 'human rights claim' in similar terms.

1 Nationality, Immigration and Asylum Act 2002, s 113(1).

Children

12.117

[Add at end:]

Such reasons would have to explain why the authority disagreed with expert evidence relied on by the applicant.[1]

1 *R (on the application of C) v Merton London Borough Council* [2005] EWHC 1753 (Admin), [2005] 3 FCR 42, [2005] All ER (D) 221 (Jul).

12.120

[Add at end:]

The Administrative Court has emphasized the importance of making special provision for determining asylum claims by children and held that failure by the Secretary of State to apply his own guidelines made the decision on a child's claim unlawful.[1]

1 *R (on the application of Mlloja) v Secretary of State for the Home Department* [2005] EWHC 2833 (Admin), [2005] All ER (D) 234 (Nov), Gibbs J.

Investigation of asylum claims

12.124

[Footnote 1 – add:]

The Court of Appeal in *C v Secretary of State for the Home Department* [2006] EWCA Civ 151, [2006] All ER (D) 122 (Feb) approved the statement in para 5.40 of the Asylum and Immigration Tribunal Guidelines that women may face additional problems in demonstrating that their claims are credible.

Safe third country cases

12.153

[Add at end:]

However, it would be unreasonable to return an asylum seeker to Austria, the country responsible for determining his claim, where there had been an unexplained delay of two years between the acceptance of responsibility by Austria and steps being taken to remove him there. In such circumstances, the asylum seeker was entitled to have his claim determined in the UK.[1]

1 *R (on the application of Ahmadzai) v Secretary of State for the Home Department* [2006] EWHC 318 (Admin), [2006] All ER (D) 19 (Mar).

ASYLUM APPEALS

Safe countries of origin

12.161

[NB:]

Mongolia (in respect of all persons) and Ghana and Nigeria (in respect of men) have been added to the 'white list' under Nationality, Immigration and Asylum Act 2002, s 94(4).[1]

[Add at end:]

IAN 2006, s 13 when it comes into force will enable the Secretary of State, by order, to exempt certain people from liability to certification of their asylum or human rights claims as clearly unfounded.[2] It will apply to people originally granted leave to enter or remain in circumstances specified in the order who have subsequently been refused a variation of leave or whose leave has been varied so that they have no leave to enter or remain. It may be that this provision will be used to enable those granted leave as unaccompanied asylum seeking children to appeal against a subsequent refusal of status, notwithstanding that their claims might otherwise be certified as clearly unfounded.

1 Asylum (Designated States) (No 2) Order 2005, SI 2005/3306 with effect from 2 December 2005.
2 Under Nationality, Immigration and Asylum Act 2002, s 94(1A) or (2).

Credibility

12.163

[Add at end:]

A person may be disbelieved entirely about his or her claimed history of persecution but still be found to be at risk of being persecuted in the future.[1]

1 *Daoud v Secretary of State for the Home Department* [2005] EWCA Civ 755, [2005] All ER (D) 259 (May).

12.170

[After first sentence in the text – add:]

The Court of Appeal has said that 'by restricting the remedial route of an appellant both within the Asylum and Immigration Tribunal and to the Court of Appeal to legal error, Parliament has increased the burden on the Secretary of State to give the most careful consideration to fresh claims'.[1]

[In text after footnote 1 – add:]

IAN 2006, s 13, when it comes into force will introduce a new definition of 'asylum claim' for the purpose of the appeals provisions. It makes provision for subsequent asylum claims (and human rights claims) to be disregarded in accordance with the immigration rules, thereby giving statutory expression to the long established practice.

[In text after footnote 2 – add:]

The requirement that there should be a realistic prospect of success is a low one and amounts to little more than that there is a reasonable chance that the claim might succeed.[2] If the eventual success of a claim depends upon the credibility of new evidence, the Secretary of State should not refuse to treat it as a fresh claim on the ground that he does not believe the evidence unless the evidence is not reasonably capable of belief.[3] The fact that the person making the fresh claim has previously been disbelieved by an immigration judge does not by itself mean that everything put forward thereafter must equally be disbelieved.[4]

1 *Kaydanyuk v Secretary of State for the Home Department* [2006] EWCA Civ 368, [2006] All ER (D) 26 (Apr).

2 *R (on the application of Rahimi) v Secretary of State for the Home Department* [2005] EWHC 2838 (Admin) (Collins J). Note that the Secretary of State has permission to appeal to the Court of Appeal against this decision.

3 *R (on the application of Rahimi) v Secretary of State for the Home Department* [2005] EWHC 2838 (Admin). However, in his later judgment in *R (on the application of Naseer) v Secretary of State for the Home Department* [2006] EWHC 1671 (Admin), [2006] All ER (D) 227 (Jun) Collins J took the view that in *Rahimi* he had imposed too strict a test and that the applicable test was whether the Secretary of State reasonably took the view that the fresh evidence could not be accepted. Bean J in a later judgment *R (on the application of Khail) v Secretary of State for the Home Department* [2006] EWHC 2139 (Admin), [2006] All ER (D) 80 (Aug) found himself bound by *R v Secretary of State for the Home Department, ex p Onibiyo* [1996] QB 768, [1996] 2 All ER 901, [1996] 2 WLR 490, CA to hold that it was not for the Court to determine whether there was a reasonable chance that the fresh claim would succeed; the issue was whether the Secretary of State had rationally concluded that it would fail.

4 *R (on the application of Naseer) v Secretary of State for the Home Department* [2006] EWHC 1671 (Admin), [2006] All ER (D) 227 (Jun) (Collins J).

Leave to remain

12.172

[Add at end:]

There have been very significant changes in the treatment of people recognized as refugees since the original text was written. Those recognized as refugees on or after 30 August 2005 will be granted five years leave to enter or remain rather than indefinite leave.[1] At the end of five years, the refugee will be eligible to seek indefinite leave to remain, subject to any review of his or her status and to any policies then applicable, including the likely introduction of a requirement to pass 'English language and knowledge of British life tests'. During the initial five years or upon application for indefinite leave to remain a person's refugee status may be subject to review which may in turn lead to the withdrawal of refugee status and the curtailment of the person's leave or refusal to grant further leave or to the variation of the person's leave if he or she qualifies on some other basis but not as a refugee (eg discretionary leave or humanitarian protection). If the Secretary of State decides to conduct a review, the person concerned must be informed in writing, told the reasons for the review and invited to make representations.[2] There are three 'triggers' for review of refugee status. The first is information relating to the activities of the individual which shows that: he or she no longer needs the protection of the refugee Convention;[3] that refugee status was obtained by deception; that the exclusion clauses in Art 1(F) of the Convention apply or that Art 33(2) applies.[4] The second 'trigger' is a Ministerial statement to the effect that circumstances in a particular country or part of a particular country have changed in a significant and non-temporary way so that all refugees or a specific group of refugees from that country or from part of that country no longer have well founded fear of being persecuted.[5] The third 'trigger' is an application by a refugee for further leave before the expiry of the original leave. In such cases, the review should not be in-depth and should involve no more than checking whether there should have been an earlier review in response to the first or second triggers.[6] If an individual applies late for an extension or does not apply at all there should be an 'in-depth review', including consideration (even in the absence of a ministerial statement) of whether there has been a change of circumstances in the country of origin such that the person no longer qualifies for refugee status. The burden of proof for a decision to withdraw refugee status is on the Secretary of State and 'clear evidence' is required.[7] If the Secretary of State decides to withdraw refugee status he then has to consider whether humanitarian protection or discretionary leave should be granted.[8]

1 Asylum Policy Instruction 'Refugee Leave'.
2 API, s 4.2.
3 Ie activities bringing the individual within Art 1(C)(1)–(4) including voluntary re-availment of the protection of the country or nationality; voluntary re-acquisition of a lost nationality; acquisition of a new nationality and protection; voluntary re-establishment in the country where persecution was feared: API, s 5.2.
4 See para 12.99 in the supplement above.
5 API, s 6, justified by reference to Art 1(C)(5)–(6).
6 API, s 7.
7 API, s 4.2.
8 API, s 8.

HUMANITARIAN PROTECTION AND DISCRETIONARY LEAVE

12.174

[Add at end:]

The Asylum Policy Instruction on Humanitarian Protection has been updated.[1] The eligibility criteria remain as in earlier instructions described in the original text. The criteria for exclusion are extremely broad. A person otherwise eligible will be excluded if: he or she has committed a crime against peace, a war crime or a crime against humanity as defined in the international instruments drawn up to make provision in respect of such crimes; has committed a serious crime in the UK or overseas (with a 'serious crime' meaning one for which a custodial sentence of at least 12 months has been imposed in the UK or a crime serious enough to exclude a person from being a refugee in accordance with Art 1F(b) of the Refugee Convention or conviction of an offence listed in an order made under s 72 of the Nationality,

Immigration and Asylum Act 2002); is included on the Sex Offenders Register; if their presence is deemed by the Secretary of State to be not conducive to the public good; if the person engages in 'unacceptable behaviours' whether in the UK or abroad (which include writing, producing, publishing or distributing material, public speaking, preaching, running a website or using a position of responsibility to express views which foment, justify or glorify terrorist violence, seek to provoke others to terrorist acts, foment or incite serious criminal activity or foster hatred which may lead to inter-community violence in the UK).

[Replace text from footnote 8 onwards with the following:]

There is also a new Asylum Policy Instruction on Discretionary Leave.[2] Discretionary leave should normally be granted: where removal of an applicant would breach Art 8 ECHR; where removal would breach Art 3 ECHR for reasons other than deliberately inflicted ill-treatment in the country to which the person is to be returned, eg owing to suffering due to a medical condition or severe humanitarian conditions ('eg absence of water, food or basic shelter'); where removal would breach some ECHR right other than Arts 3 or 8; to an unaccompanied child who does not qualify for asylum or humanitarian protection 'if there are inadequate reception arrangements in their own country'; in the case of a failed asylum seeker, where there are individual circumstances 'so compelling that it is considered appropriate to grant some form of leave' and in some cases where a person is excluded from refugee status or humanitarian protection. Previous policy was that a person excluded from refugee status or humanitarian protection would normally be granted discretionary leave if removal would be contrary to the ECHR. Current policy is that a person excluded from refugee status or humanitarian protection by application of Arts 1F or 33(2) of the Refugee Convention (or on analogous grounds in relation to humanitarian protection) will normally be kept or placed on temporary admission or temporary release unless Ministers decide, in the light of all the circumstances of the case, that it would be appropriate to grant up to six months discretionary leave.[3] In other circumstances (eg commission of an offence less serious than one justifying exclusion under Arts 1F or 33(2); where exclusion is considered conducive to the public good but for reasons other than national security or 'unacceptable behaviours'), an individual excluded from humanitarian protection may be granted discretionary leave for six months unless Ministers decide that they should be kept or placed on temporary admission. Mr Justice Sullivan held in the case concerning 'the Afghan hijackers'[4] that 'there is no freestanding power to grant temporary admission ***instead of*** granting leave to enter; as opposed to granting temporary admission ***while*** a decision to grant or refuse leave is under consideration, or following refusal while a decision to make removal directions is under consideration, or attempts are being made to implement those directions once they have been made'. That being the case, a decision to keep or place a person on temporary admission in the circumstances set out in the discretionary leave policy would be unlawful.

1 The current version was issued in August 2005.
2 Issued 12 January 2006.
3 API on discretionary leave (12 January 2006), s 2.6.

4 *R (on the application of GG) v Secretary of State for the Home Department* [2006] EWHC 1111 (Admin), (2006) Times, 14 June, [2006] All ER (D) 143 (May); *affd sub nom S v Secretary of State for the Home Department (sub nom R (on the application of GG) v Secretary of State for the Home Department)* [2006] EWCA Civ 1157, [2006] All ER (D) 30 (Aug).

Duration, revocation and settlement

12.175

[Replace the first sentence in the text with:]

Those granted leave on humanitarian protection grounds on or after 30 August 2005 should be granted five years in the first instance; those granted such leave before that date were normally granted leave for three years.[1] For those granted leave on humanitarian protection grounds before 30 August 2005, the procedures and criteria for granting settlement, active review and revocation of leave remain as described in the original text.[2] Where leave was granted on or after 30 August 2005 a person will be liable to active review during the currency of their leave in similar circumstances to those that would 'trigger' review of a person's limited leave as a refugee.[3] If a person applies for settlement before the end of five years' leave on humanitarian protection grounds, the application should be granted (subject to background, character and conduct checks) without 'an in-depth review to determine whether the individual is still entitled to humanitarian protection' unless a review should have been 'triggered' at an earlier stage but was not carried out.[4] If the application is made after the expiry of the initial leave a review would be carried out to determine whether the person continued to qualify for humanitarian protection. Those who were granted exceptional leave to remain for four years before 1 April 2003 should, on application, be granted indefinite leave to remain subject to background, character and conduct checks[5]. The API on discretionary leave makes detailed provision about duration and extension of discretionary leave and about review and revocation of leave.[6]

1 *API on Humanitarian Protection* (August 2005).
2 Those criteria and procedures are set out in the annex to the current API.
3 See para 12.173 above.
4 API, s 8.
5 *API on Humanitarian Protection* (August 2005), s 11.
6 *API on Discretionary Leave* (12 January 2006).

DEPENDANTS AND FAMILY REUNION

12.179

[In text after footnote 7 – add:]

The Court of Appeal has confirmed that the requirement in the refugee family reunion policy of 'compelling, compassionate circumstances' for the admission of family members other than spouse and minor children is less demanding than 'the most exceptional compassionate circumstances' required under the immigration rules.[1] The Asylum Policy Instructions on Family Reunion and on Dependants of Refugees are currently being reviewed.

[Add at end:]

The Qualification Directive requires Member States to ensure that family members of a person with refugee status or subsidiary protection are given benefits that include a residence permit, travel document, access to employment, education, social welfare and health care.[2] In this context, family members means, 'insofar as the family already existed in the country of origin', the spouse, unmarried partner and minor, unmarried, dependant children 'present in the same member state in relation to the application for international protection'.[3] The provision may be extended to 'other close relatives who lived together as part of the family at the time of leaving the country of origin and who were wholly or mainly dependent on the' person granted refugee status or subsidiary protection. The immigration Rules provide for the 'spouse, civil partner, unmarried or same sex partner or minor child accompanying a principal applicant' to be included in the asylum claim as his dependant and to be granted leave to enter or remain of the same duration as any leave granted to the principal applicant.[4] An question may arise in relation to the word 'accompanying' in the immigration rule and whether a family member who arrives after the principal applicant is also entitled to be given leave to enter or remain if the principal is given status. That is because of the subsequent provisions relating to family members seeking leave to enter as the spouse or other family member of a refugee which require the person to have entry clearance.[5] The Directive does not require family members to have entry clearance in order to benefit from the family unity provision and so to require family members who arrive after the principal applicant to have entry clearance would be inconsistent with the Directive.

1 *Miao v Secretary of State for the Home Department* [2006] EWCA Civ 75, [2006] All ER (D) 215 (Feb). The obiter dictum in *Senanayake v Secretary of State for the Home Department* [2005] EWCA Civ 1530, [2005] All ER (D) 215 (Nov) to the effect that the two tests were indistinguishable was said in Miao to be wrong.
2 Council Directive 2004/83/EC, Art 23.
3 Council Directive 2004/83/EC, Art 2(h).
4 HC 395, para 394, as inserted by HC 6918.
5 HC 395, para 352A–352F.

12.181

[Add at end:]

The marriage in the UK of a failed asylum seeker to a recognized refugee did not by itself create 'truly exceptional circumstances' such that removal of the failed asylum seeker would breach Art 8.[1]

1 *Chikwamba v Secretary of State for the Home Department* [2005] EWCA Civ 1779, [2005] All ER (D) 217 (Nov).

Chapter 13

ASYLUM SUPPORT, COMMUNITY CARE AND WELFARE BENEFITS

Leave given as the result of a maintenance undertaking

13.7

[Footnote 4 – add:]

See also the Commissioner's decision *CIS/1697/2004* as to whether a maintenance undertaking had been given.

Exemptions from 'subject to immigration control' test

Income-based jobseeker's allowance, income support, social fund payments, housing benefit, council tax benefit

13.12

[Add at end:]

The House of Lords allowed the asylum seeker's appeal in *Szoma v Secretary of State for the Department of Work and Pensions*.[1] It held that a person on temporary admission was 'lawfully present in the United Kingdom' within the meaning of para 4 of the Schedule to the Social Security (Immigration and Asylum) Consequential Amendments Regulations 2000, SI 2000/636. Thus nationals of the EEA Member States, Albania, Armenia, Moldova and Turkey present in the UK with temporary admission would not be treated as 'subject to immigration control' for the purpose of determining eligibility for income support, jobseeker's allowance, social fund payments, housing benefit, council tax benefit and state pension credit.

1 [2005] UKHL 64, [2006] 1 AC 564, [2006] 1 All ER 1.

Habitual residence

13.23

[For the reference in footnote 1 to the Housing Benefit (General) Regulations 1987, SI 1987/1971, reg 7A(4)(e) substitute the Housing Benefit Regulations 2006, SI 2006/213, reg 10(2).]

[For the reference to the Council Tax Benefit (General) Regulations 1992 SI 1992/1814, reg 4A(4)(e) substitute the Council Tax Benefit Regulations 2006, SI 2006/215, reg 7.]

[In addition, see Housing Benefit (Persons who have attained the qualifying age for state pension credit) Regulations, SI 2006/214, reg 10 and the Council

Tax Benefit (Persons who have attained the qualifying age for state pension credit) Regulations 2006, SI 2006/216 reg 7.]

[Footnote 4 – add:]

The rule was considered and applied by the Social Security Commissioners in *CIS/3573/2005* where they held that an EEA national resident in the UK who had not been economically active did not have right to reside in the UK and therefore was not 'habitually resident'.

13.24

[Add at end:]

Even if a decision maker finds that a person is not presently habitually resident, the decision maker is obliged to consider whether the person is likely to become habitually resident within the near future (ie within the next 13 weeks) and to make a prospective award if so satisfied.[1]

1 *Bhakta v Secretary of State for Work and Pensions* [2006] EWCA Civ 65, [2006] 10 LS Gaz R 26, (2006) Times, 20 March, [2006] All ER (D) 195 (Feb).

13.25

[For the reference in footnote 2 to the Housing Benefit (General) Regulations 1987, SI 1987/1971, reg 7A(4)(e) substitute the Housing Benefit Regulations 2006, SI 2006/213, reg 10(2).

[For the reference to the Council Tax Benefit (General) Regulations 1992, SI 1992/1814 substitute the Council Tax Benefit Regulations 2006, SI 2006/215, reg 7.]

[See also the Housing Benefit (Persons who have attained the qualifying age for State Pension Credit) Regulations, SI 2006/214, reg 10 and the Council Tax Benefit (Persons who have attained the qualifying age for state pension credit) Regulations 2006, SI 2006/216, reg 7.]

[For the reference in footnote 5 to the Housing Benefit (General) Regulations 1987, SI 1987/1971, reg 7A(4) and (5) substitute the Housing Benefit Regulations 2006, SI 2006/213, reg 10(3).]

Backdating benefits for refugees

13.26

[For the reference in footnote 8 to the Housing Benefit (General) Regulations 1987, SI 1987/1971, reg 7B and Schedule A1 substitute the Housing Benefit Regulations 2006, SI 2006/213, reg 10A and Sch A1.]

[For the reference to Council Tax Benefit (General) Regulations 1992 substitute the Council Tax Benefit Regulations 2006, SI 2006/215, reg 7A and Sch A1.]

[See also the Housing Benefit (Persons who have attained the qualifying age for State Pension Credit) Regulations, SI 2006/214, reg 10A and Sch A1 and

the Council Tax Benefit (Persons who have attained the qualifying age for state pension credit) Regulations 2006, SI 2006/216, reg 7A.]

13.27

[Add at end:]

IAN 2006, s 45[1] amends s 13 of the Asylum and Immigration (Treatment of Claimants etc) Act 2004 so as to extend eligibility for integration loans to classes of people (to be prescribed in regulations) in addition to recognized refugees.

1 Came into force on 30th June 2006 – see Immigration, Asylum and Nationality Act 2006 (Commencement No 1) Order 2006, SI 2006/1497.

Asylum support

13.34

[Add at end:]

The IAN 2006, s 43(1)[1] amended Immigration and Asylum Act 1999, s 99(1) so that local authorities can provide support on behalf of the Secretary of State under s 4 of the 1999 Act (failed asylum seekers and others on temporary admission, bail or released from detention) as well as under ss 95 and 98 (support for asylum seekers). IAN 2006, s 43(3)[2] amends Immigration and Asylum Act 1999, s 118(1)(b) so that local authorities can provide accommodation to persons supported under s 4 of the Act as well as those supported under s 95.

1 Which came into force on 16 June 2006 – The Immigration, Asylum and Nationality Act 2006 (Commencement No 1) Order 2006, SI 2006/1497.
2 Which also came into force on 16th June 2006: SI 2006/1497.

COMMON ASPECTS OF THE TWO SCHEMES FOR SUPPORT

'Asylum seekers' under the support schemes

Claim for asylum

13.40

[Add at end:]

IAN 2006, s 44 (not yet in force) enables the Secretary of State, by statutory instrument, to repeal the provisions[1] made under s 9 of the Asylum and Immigration (Treatment of Claimants etc) Act 2004 by which failed asylum seekers' families with children are made ineligible for support.

1 Nationality, Immigration and Asylum Act 2002, Sch 3, para 7A.

Claim for asylum has not been determined

13.44

[Add at end:]

Refusal of asylum is not, per se, an 'immigration decision' against which an appeal may be brought to the Asylum and Immigration Tribunal.[1] Therefore, if a person is refused asylum but no immigration decision against which the person could appeal is taken against him or her, the person ceases to be an asylum seeker and loses any eligibility for support that is contingent upon being an asylum seeker. The person does not regain the status of 'asylum seeker' even if there is a subsequent immigration decision against which an appeal is brought on asylum grounds.[2]

1 Because it is not one of the decisions listed in Nationality, Immigration and Asylum Act 2002, s 82(2) against which an appeal may be brought.

2 *R (on the application of M) v Slough Borough Council* [2006] EWCA Civ 655, (2006) Times, 13 June, [2006] All ER (D) 364 (May).

NATIONAL ASYLUM SUPPORT SCHEME (NASS)

Avoiding a breach of a person's Convention rights

13.57

[Add at end:]

The House of Lords dismissed the Secretary of State's appeal.[1] Lord Bingham said that the Secretary of State would be under a duty to provide support under s 55(5)(a) of the Nationality, Immigration and Asylum Act 2002:

> 'when it appears on a fair and objective assessment of all relevant facts and circumstances that an individual applicant faces an imminent prospect of serious suffering caused or materially aggravated by denial of shelter, food or the most basic necessities of life. Many factors may affect that judgment, including age, gender, mental and physical health and condition, any facilities or sources of support available to the applicant, the weather and time of year and the period for which the applicant has already suffered or is likely to continue to suffer privation.
>
> It is not in my opinion possible to formulate any simple test applicable in all cases. But if there were persuasive evidence that a late applicant was obliged to sleep in the street, save perhaps for a short and foreseeably finite period, or was seriously hungry, or unable to satisfy the most basic requirements of hygiene, the threshold would, in the ordinary way, be crossed.'[2]

1 *R (on the application of Limbuela) v Secretary of State for the Home Department* [2005] UKHL 66, [2006] 1 AC 396, [2005] 3 WLR 1014.

2 *R (on the application of Limbuela) v Secretary of State for the Home Department* at para 8f.

INTERIM SUPPORT SCHEME

Exclusions from interim support

Immigration status does not preclude income support

13.137

[In footnote 1, for the reference to the Housing Benefit (General) Regulations 1987, SI 1987/1971, reg 7A(3)(a) substitute the Housing Benefit Regulations 2006, SI 2006/213, reg 10.]

HARD CASES

13.175

[In the text, after the sentence which follows footnote 2 add:]

The IAN 2006[1] has amended[2] Immigration and Asylum Act 1999, s 4 so that the Secretary of State may make regulations to enable a supported person to be provided with specified services or facilities, including vouchers, but not money.

[In the text, replace sub-paragraph (b) with the following:]

(b) he is unable to leave the United Kingdom by reason of a physical impediment to travel or for some other medical reason.[3] This criterion requires that the person is unable to leave the UK, (although it need not be literally impossible to leave); it is not sufficient that the person may have a medical condition making it undesirable in the interests of his or her treatment or prognosis to leave the UK.[4]

[In the text, after the sentence referring to Womba add the following:]

It has been held in the Administrative Court that *Womba* was incorrectly decided.[5] Where a failed asylum seeker makes representations purporting to be a fresh asylum or human rights claim and before the Secretary of State decides whether to accept the representations as such, a NASS caseworker or local authority is entitled to form a view of the merits of the putative claim in order to decide whether the person must be supported in order to avoid a breach of his or her Convention rights. However, 'it is only in the clearest cases that it will be appropriate for the public body concerned to refuse relief on the basis of the manifest inadequacy of the purported fresh grounds'.[6]

1 Section 43(7).
2 With effect from 16th June 2006 – Immigration, Asylum and Nationality Act 2006 (Commencement No 1) Order 2006, SI 2006/1497.
3 Immigration and Asylum (Provision of Accommodation to Failed Asylum-Seekers) Regulations 2005, SI 2005/930.
4 *R (on the application of the Secretary of State for the Home Department) v Asylum Support Adjudicator* [2006] EWHC 1248 (Admin), (2006) Times, 11 July.
5 *R (on the application of AW) v Croydon London Borough Council; R (on the application of A, D and Y) v Hackney London Borough Council* [2005] EWHC 2950 (Admin), [2005] All ER (D) 251 (Dec).
6 Lloyd Jones J in *R (on the application of AW) v Croydon London Borough Council.*

13.176

[Add at end:]

However, if support is withdrawn on the ground that in the Secretary of State's opinion there is a viable route of return to the asylum seeker's country[1] the Asylum Support Adjudicator may consider only whether the Secretary of State held that opinion. The Adjudicator may not determine whether there is in fact a viable route of return because that is a matter of policy and challengeable, if at all, by judicial review.[2]

1 So that Immigration and Asylum (Provision of Accommodation to Failed Asylum Seekers) Regulations 2005, r 3(2)(c) does not, or no longer applies.

2 *R (on the application of Rasul) v Asylum Support Adjudicator* [2006] EWHC 435 (Admin), [2006] All ER (D) 364 (Feb).

COMMUNITY CARE PROVISION FOR THOSE SUBJECT TO IMMIGRATION CONTROL

13.177

[In the text, after the sentence containing footnote 7 add the following:]

Similarly, a failed asylum seeker or other person who is eligible for support under s 21 of the National Assistance Act 1948 would not be eligible for support under s 4 of the Immigration and Asylum Act 1999. That is because the eligibility for s 21 support would exclude the person from the statutory definition of 'destitute' which has to be satisfied in order to qualify for support under s 4.[1]

1 *R (on the application of AW) v Croydon London Borough Council; R (on the application of A, D and Y) v Hackney London Borough Council* [2005] EWHC 2950 (Admin), [2005] All ER (D) 251 (Dec).

13.178

[In the text, after footnote 7 add:]

Schedule 3 to the Nationality, Immigration and Asylum Act 2002 makes various categories of people ineligible for support and assistance, as described in the original text. A person otherwise ineligible may nevertheless be supported if such support is necessary to for the purpose of avoiding a breach of the person's ECHR rights.[1] If a person has made a human rights application to stay in the UK, it may be necessary for a local authority to take a view as to its merits in order to determine whether provision of support whilst the Home Office considers the claim is necessary to avoid a breach of the person's human rights; however, it would only be if the local authority could properly characterise the human rights application as manifestly unfounded that it could withhold support on the basis that it was not necessary to avoid a breach of ECHR rights.[2] Whilst Sch 3 makes a person ineligible for the provision of 'support or assistance' it does not affect a person's eligibility for the provision of a personal adviser and a pathway plan under s 23C of the Children Act 1989 because they are not 'support or assistance'.[3]

1 Nationality, Immigration and Asylum Act 2002, Sch 3, para 3.

2 *R (on the application of B) v London Borough of Southwark* [2006] EWHC 2254 (Admin), applying *R (on the application of Kimani) v Lambeth London Borough Council* [2003] EWCA Civ 1150, [2004] 1 WLR 272, [2003] 3 FCR 222 and *R (on the application of AW) v Croydon London Borough Council; R (on the application of A, D and Y) v Hackney London Borough Council* [2005] EWHC 2950 (Admin), [2005] All ER (D) 251 (Dec).

3 *R (on the application of B) v London Borough of Southwark* (see fn 2 above).

[Footnote 1 – add:]

The Court of Appeal approved Collins J's judgment in *R (on the application of M) v Slough Borough Council* [2006] EWCA Civ 655, (2006) Times, 13 June.

Footnote 11 – add:]

This category includes former asylum seekers present in the UK in breach of the immigration laws: *R (on the application of AW) v Croydon London Borough Council; R (on the application of A, D and Y) v Hackney London Borough Council* [2005] EWHC 2950 (Admin), [2005] All ER (D) 251 (Dec) and *R (on the application of M) v Slough Borough Council* [2006] EWCA Civ 655, (2006) Times, 13 June, [2006] All ER (D) 364 (May).

ACCESS TO HOUSING

13.184

[In the text after footnote 10 insert:]

The Regulations in force since 1 June 2006 are the Allocation of Housing and Homelessness (Eligibility) (England) Regulations 2006, SI 2006/1294[1]. They continue the eligibility for housing, notwithstanding that they are subject to immigration control of three of the four categories described in the original text, ie recognised refugees, persons with exceptional leave to remain and persons with indefinite leave to remain who are habitually resident in the common travel area.[2] The fourth category of persons identified in the original text as eligible for accommodation (nationals of a state which has ratified the European Convention on Social and Medical Assistance or the Council of Europe Social Charter and who are lawfully present and habitually resident) are no longer eligible under the Regulations.

[Replace the text following the four bullet points and up to footnote 15 with the following:]

Persons not subject to immigration control, including nationals of EEA States are ineligible for allocation of housing unless they are habitually resident in the common travel area or if they have a right of residence only as a jobseeker or family member of a jobseeker or they have only an initial three months right of residence.[3] However, the following do not have to be habitually resident in order to be eligible for accommodation: an EEA national who is a worker, self-employed, an accession state worker who is treated as a qualified person under the EEA Regulations or a person with a right to reside permanently under those regulations;[4] a person who left Montserrat after 1 November 1995 because of the effect of the volcanic eruption and a person in the UK owing to deportation or removal from another country.[5]

[Add at end:]

The Court of Appeal has declared s 185(4) of the Housing Act 1996 to be incompatible with Art 14 in conjunction with Art 8 of the ECHR because discriminatory on grounds that included nationality. That is because, for the purpose of determining whether a British citizen is in priority need of accommodation, her non-British child who was subject to immigration control had to be disregarded.[6]

[In footnote 6 for the reference to the Housing Benefit (General) Regulations 1987, SI 1987/1971 substitute the Housing Benefit Regulations 2006, SI 2006/213, reg 10(2).]

[Footnote 14 – add:]

That this was the position was confirmed by the Court of Appeal in *Barnet London Borough Council v Ismail*[7]. Thereafter, the government amended the Homelessness (England) Regulations 2000, SI 2000/701, reg 3 to revoke reg 3(1)(i) which had made those subject to immigration control but receiving income support or jobseeker's allowance eligible for housing assistance. See SI 2006/1093, reg 2(1)(b).

1 Revoking the Homelessness (England) Regulations 2000, SI 2000/701 (referred to in nn 10, 12 and 15 of the original text).
2 The Allocation of Housing and Homelessness (Eligibility) (England) Regulations 2006, SI 2006/1294, reg 3.
3 SI 2006/1294, reg 4(1). The three months right of residence referred to is that conferred by the Immigration (European Economic Area) Regulations 2006, SI 2006/1003, reg 13.
4 SI 2006/1294, reg 4(2).
5 SI 2006/1294, reg 4(2).
6 *R (on the application of Morris) v Westminster City Council; R (on the application of Badhu) v Lambeth London Borough Council* [2005] EWCA Civ 1184, [2006] 1 WLR 505, [2006] HLR 122, Sedley and Auld LLJ, Jonathan Parker LJ dissenting.
7 [2006] EWCA Civ 383, [2006] 1 WLR 2771, (2006) Times, 25 April.

13.186

[Footnote 1 – add:]

The Homelessness (England) Regulations 2000 SI 2000/701 have been revoked by the Allocation of Housing and Homelessness (Eligibility) England Regulations 2006, SI 2006/1294.

[Add at end:]

If accommodation is provided under s 4 of the Immigration and Asylum Act 1999 (to a failed asylum seeker or other person on temporary admission or released from detention) then, as with accommodation provided by NASS under Pt VI of the 1999 Act, the supported person will not benefit from the Protection from Eviction Act 1977,[1] will not have a secure tenancy unless expressly notified by the landlord that he or she does have a secure tenancy,[2] and cannot have an assured tenancy.[3]

1 IAN 2006, s 43(4)(a), amending Protection from Eviction Act 1977, s 3A(7A), with effect from 16 June 2006 – see Immigration, Asylum and Nationality Act 2006 (Commencement No 1) Order 2006, SI 2006/1497.
2 IAN 2006, s 43(4)(d), amending Housing Act 1985, Sch 1, para 4A(1) with effect from 16 June 2006 – SI 2006/1497.

3 IAN 2006, s 43(4)(f), amending Housing Act 1988, Sch 1, para 12A(1) with effect from 16 June 2006 – SI 2006/1497.

13.189

[Replace footnote 1 with the following:]

The Allocation of Housing and Homelessness (Eligibility) (England) Regulations 2006, SI 2006/1294, reg 5(1)(e). SI 2006/1294 revoked the provisions referred to in footnote 1 in the original text.

ACCESS TO EDUCATIONAL PROVISION

Higher education

13.195

[NB:]

The Education (Fees and Awards)(Amendment) Regulations 2006, SI 2006/483 amend the provisions for classifying students for fees purposes.

13.197

[NB:]

The Education (Student Support) Regulations 2005, SI 2005/52 make provision for the support of students by way of grants or loans and in relation to courses in the academic year prior to 1 September 2006. In respect of the academic year beginning 1 September 2006 those Regulations are revoked and replaced by the Education (Student Support) Regulations 2006, SI 2006/119. Under the latter regulations a person is eligible for support[1] if: he or she is settled in the UK and has been ordinarily resident for the three-year period preceding the first day of the first academic year of the course (unless the ordinary residence was wholly or mainly for the purpose of receiving full time education); he or she is settled in the UK as a result of having a right of residence under the EU citizens' directive[2] and has been ordinarily resident for three years (unless the ordinary residence was for the purpose of education); he or she is a recognized refugee or the refugee's spouse, civil partner, child or step-child who is ordinarily resident in the UK on the first day of the first academic year of the course; a person refused asylum but granted leave to enter or remain (or the spouse, civil partner, child or step-child of that person) and who has been ordinarily resident in the UK for three years; an EEA or Swiss worker, self employed person or family member of such a person who has been ordinarily resident in the UK for the three years; the child of an EEA national who is or was a worker in another member state and who has been three years ordinarily resident; a person who is settled in the UK, is ordinarily resident at the start of the course and had been ordinarily resident in the EEA pursuant to the exercise of a right of residence for three years.

1 SI 2006/119, reg 4(1) and Sch 1, Pt 2.

[2] Directive 2004/38/EC of the European Parliament and Council on the right of citizens of the Union and their family members to move and reside freely within the territory of the Member States.

Chapter 14

PENAL AND CARRIER SANCTIONS

INTRODUCTION

14.1

[NB:]

The transformation of immigration officers into an immigration police force is to be given recognition in the Police and Justice Bill 2006, presently going through parliament, clause 46 of which makes provision for the Independent Police Case Commission (IPCC) to exercise its functions by dealing with complaints against immigration officers dealing with their enforcement functions in immigration or asylum investigations.

Arrest with a warrant

14.8

[Footnote 2:]

Section 8 of the Asylum and Immigration Act 1996 is to be replaced by a new offence under s 21 of IAN 2006, not in force as at 1 October 2006: see 14.82A ff below.

Entry and search before arrest

14.9

[Footnote 6:]

Section 8 of the Asylum and Immigration Act 1996 is to be replaced by IAN 2006, s 21, not in force as at 1 October 2006: see 14.82A ff below.

Administrative arrest

14.10

[NB:]

A new category of administrative arrest is added by s 53 of IAN 2006 in deportation cases. The power of arrest with or without a warrant under para 17 of Sch 2 can be exercised in deportation cases when the notice of intention to deport is ready but has not yet been given to the prospective deportee. The purpose of this provision is to enable immigration officers and the police to seek a warrant in such circumstances under para 17(2) to enter named premises in order to give the notice of intention to deport to the prospective deportee and at the same time to arrest him or her.

Fingerprinting and other biometrics

14.21

[NB:]

Under the the Immigration (Provision of Physical Data) Regulations 2006, SI 2006/1743, which came into force on 4 July 2006, the requirement for people to provide information about their physical characteristics has been extended from fingerprints to fingerprints and photos of the person's head. The Regulations are not limited to applicants seeking entry clearance in named posts overseas. They now apply to anyone. Unlike the previous regulations (see fn 5 in the main text), they do not contain any power enabling the Secretary of State to pass on the biometric data to policing and other agencies but this can now be done under general powers to pass on information or to share it with other law enforcement agencies, as for example under powers given by NIAA 2002, s 21 (supply of information by the Secretary of State) or IAN 2006, s 36 (duty to share information), which was not yet in force as at 1 October 2006.

[Footnote 3:]

The Immigration (Provision of Physical Data) Regulations 2003 have been revoked and replaced by the Immigration (Provision of Physical Data) Regulations 2006, SI 2006/1743, which came into force on 4 July 2006.

[Footnote 4:]

The schedule to SI 2003/1875 was further amended in 2005 to include Congo, Holland and Vietnam, but this and all other amendments have been revoked and replaced by the Immigration (Provision of Physical Data) Regulations 2006, SI 2006/1743, which came into force on 4 July 2006.

[Footnote 5:]

SI 2003/1875 has been revoked by the Immigration (Provision of Physical Data) Regulations 2006, SI 2006/1743 which has revoked and replaced all previous regulations.

Passenger information

14.26

[NB:]

The power to demand passenger and crew lists under para 27 of Sch 2 to the Immigration Act 1971 has been extended by s 31 of IAN 2006. This information can now be obtained in advance of the arrival of the ship or aircraft in the United Kingdom and not just on arrival. Secondly, the duty to provide the lists applies to owners and agents of the ship or aircraft as well as the captain.[1] Sections 32 and 33 give the police new and additional powers to obtain from the owners, agents or captains of ships and aircraft details of passengers, crew, flight or voyage and freight. Provision is also made for information sharing between each of the different policing agencies, including immigration officers, in ss 36 to 41 of IAN 2006.[2]

1 As amended by IAN 2006, s 31.

Non-production of passport

14.33

[NB:]

In *R v Navabi; R v Embaye*[1] the Court of Appeal refused to link offences under s 2 of the Asylum and Immigration (Treatment of Claimants etc) Act 2004 with a refugee's rights under Art 31 of the Refugees Convention and rejected the reverse burden of proof submission of the appellant. Kennedy LJ said (para 29):

> 'we see no reason to conclude that the burden of proof should be interpreted as being anything less than a legal burden. An evidential burden would do little to promote the objects of the legislation in circumstances where the prosecution would have very limited means of testing any defence raised.'

However, a very recent decision of the Administrative Court clearly undermines the judgment in Embaye and blunts the ambit of the new offence, created by s 2 of the Asylum and Immigration (Treatment of Claimants etc) Act 2004. In *Thet v DPP*[2], the Court held that a failure to produce a passport or other valid identity document at an immigration interview is not an offence under s 2, if throughout the journey to the UK either a false passport or no passport had been used. The Court held that the correct interpretation of s 2(4)(e) is that an immigration document refers only to a genuine 'in force' passport. If the passenger can prove that he or she travelled to the UK without at any stage having such a document then he or she has an absolute defence. This could mean that that past convictees may now be able to have a remedy, if they apply for leave to appeal the conviction out of time to the Crown Court or, if convicted in the Crown Court, to the Court of Appeal.

1 [2005] EWCA Crim 2865, (2005) Times, 5 December.
2 [2006] EWHC 2701 (Admin), [2006] All ER (D) 09 (Nov).

Refugees

14.38

[NB:]

R v Makuwa[1] the Court of Appeal held that in a prosecution to which s 31 of the Immigration and Asylum Act 1999 applied, the defendant's refugee status was a matter to be determined by proof; but the burden on the defendant was a merely evidential burden and provided he or she adduced sufficient evidence to raise the issue, the burden is then upon the prosecution to prove to the usual standard that the defendant is not a refugee. With regard to the other elements of the defence, the burden remains on the defendant.[2]

In *R v Asfaw*[3] the Court of Appeal's Criminal Division were concerned about cases where an asylum seeker is attempting to leave this country for another place of refuge using false documents and what seemed to be a CPS practice of combining a charge of infringement of the Forgery and Counterfeiting Act 1981, to which s 31 applied, with a charge of attempting to obtain air services by deception, to which it did not. But instead of deciding whether Art 31 of the Refugee Convention had a wider ambit than s 31 of the 1999 Act allowed and whether there had been an abuse of process, as contended by the Appellant, they held that the judge's sentencing remarks, that deterrence was needed against the use of false documents because it undermined the whole system of immigration control, were inappropriate and at odds with the principle reflected in Art 31 and s 31 and gave the appellant an absolute discharge under the Powers of Criminal Courts (Sentencing) Act 2000, s 12, which meant that by virtue of s 14 of that Act, she would not in future be deemed to have had a conviction for any purpose.

Section 31(3) of the 1999 Act has been amended to insert a new para (aa), which adds the false documents offences in s 25(1) and (5) of the Identity Cards Act 2006 to s 31(3) of the Immigration and Asylum Act 1999 giving a specific defence for refugees with false documents refered to s 25(1) or (5).[4]

1 [2006] EWCA Crim 175, [2006] 1 WLR 2755.

2 The Court followed the reasoning used in *R v Navabi; R v Embaye* [2005] EWCA Crim 2865, (2005) Times, 5 December where a reverse burden argument concerning the defences under s 2 of the Asylum and Immigration (Treatment of Claimants etc) Act 2004 was rejected.

3 [2006] EWCA Crim 707, [2006] Crim LR 906 (21 March 2006).

4 Identity Cards Act 2006, s 31(3), not yet in force, s 25 of the same Act will create new criminal offences relating to the possession of false identity documents. Subsections (1) and (2) set out the circumstances in which persons are guilty of an offence if they are in possession of a document which they know or believe to be false or a genuine document that has been improperly obtained or relates to someone else. To be guilty of the offence the person must have the intention that the document be used for identity fraud. Subsection (5) makes it an offence for persons to have in their possession, without reasonable excuse, a false identity document or a genuine document that has been improperly obtained or relates to someone else, or equipment used for making false identity documents. Unless there is a reasonable excuse, these offences apply irrespective of any intent to use the documents or equipment. Subsection (7) prescribes a maximum penalty of two years' imprisonment, a fine or both.

Offences of facilitating unlawful immigration and assisting asylum seekers

14.40

[NB:]

In *R v Javaherifard and Miller*[1], the Court of Appeal held that entry to the UK occurred at the point where someone crossed the border from the Republic into Northern Ireland and not at the point where they first present a passport. The court also held that unlawful presence in the UK is a separate breach of immigration law from illegal entry and facilitating it can form the basis for a separate count. However, in view of the fact that it is possible to facilitate entry by acts which occur close to but after actual entry,[2] and it would be highly undesirable, said the court, if every time the facts involved actions before and immediately after entry, although part and parcel of it, they always had to be the subject matter of a separate count of facilitating 'being' in the UK.

1 [2005] EWCA Crim 3231, [2006] Imm AR 185, CA.
2 *R v Singh and Meeuwsen* [1972] 1 WLR 1600, [1973] 57 Cr App Rep 180, CA.

Breach of conditions and overstaying

14.50

[NB:]

The first sentence of the paragraph which refers to leave being extended by statute until the end of the period allowed for bringing of an appeal and while any appeal is pending is to be limited to in-country appeals, now that s 11 of IAN 2006 is in force.

[Footnote 1:]

The Immigration Act 1971, s 3C has been amended by IAN 2006, s 11, which came into force on 31 August 2006.

EMPLOYER SANCTIONS

14.82 & 14.83

[NB:]

Once ss 15 to 26 of IAN 2006 are brought into force these paragraphs will no longer have effect. As at 1 October only ss 19 and 23, which are powers relating to the making of Codes of Practice, are in force. They came into force on 31 August 2006.

14.82A

[Add new paragraph:]

Employer sanctions are soon to be put on an entirely new statutory footing under ss 15–26 of IAN 2006, the result being that ss 8 and 8A of the Asylum and Immigration Act 1996 will be repealed.[1] The new sanctions have two main prongs: (1) the imposition of the civil penalty by the Home Office, the details of which have still to be worked out; and (2) a new criminal offence where an employer has taken someone on as an employee and that person has not got the right immigration status to take the job. Unlike s 8 of IAA 1999 the new offence is not one of strict liability. In the new offence the prosecution must prove that the employer knew about the immigration status of the employee and knew that he or she was over the age of 16. In the normal case employees should have leave to enter or remain without any conditions attached to their leave restricting or prohibiting employment with that employer. But what about persons who are given temporary admission and are allowed to work? Section 24 of IAN 2006 provides that where such persons have been granted temporary admission,[2] they are to be treated as if they had been granted leave to enter and as if any restriction on employment imposed by the temporary admission was a condition of leave. The practical effect of this is that an employer is not liable to a civil penalty and commits no criminal offence if he or she employs someone who does not have leave to enter or remain, but has been given temporary admission or release from detention without any condition restricting or prohibiting employment.

1 IAN 2006, s 26 and Sch 3.
2 Or release from detention under para 21(1) of Sch 2 to the Immigration Act 1971.

Civil penalty

14.82B

[Add new paragraph:]

Section 15 of IAN 2006 provides that an employer is liable to a civil penalty[1] if he or she employs someone aged 16 or over, who is subject to immigration control and:

(a) has not been granted leave to enter or remain in the UK; or
(b) has a leave which–
  (i) is invalid;
  (ii) has ceased to have effect (by reason of curtailment, revocation, cancellation, passage of time or otherwise); or
  (iii) is subject to a condition preventing him or her from accepting the employment.[2]

Much of the new civil penalty regime will depend upon regulations yet to be made. Under these regulations an employer will have an excuse not to pay the civil penalty if he or she complies with the prescribed requirements to be set out in the regulations. But the excuse will not help the employer if it can be shown that he or she knew that the employment of the employee was unlawful. Section 15 describes the matters to be covered in the penalty notice[4] and sets out the parameters of the regulation making power of the Secretary of State. Section 15(5) makes it clear that he or she can issue a penalty notice without having to investigate whether the employer is likely to have an excuse for the illegal employment. This puts the burden of proving an excuse on the employer. But showing that he or she has complied with any of the prescribed requirements may not be enough, if the Secretary of State can show that the employer knew, at any time during the period of employment, that the employee was being unlawfully employed. The kind of requirements which will give an employer an excuse will be:

(a) requiring the production by the proposed employee of particular documents described in the regulations;
(b) the production of one document of each of a number of specified descriptions;
(c) requiring the employer to take steps to verify, retain, copy or record the contents of documents produced by the proposed employee;
(d) requiring the employer to do certain things before employment begins; or

(e) requiring the employer to do certain things at specified intervals or on specified occasions during the course of employment.[5]

Section 15 is not yet in force and no regulations have been made.

1 IAN 2006, s 15(2). The subsection refers to a prescribed maximum. This remains to be set under an order made under s 20.
2 IAN 2006, s 15(1)(a) and (b).
3 The requirements which may be prescribed are set out in IAN 2006, s 15 (7).
4 The penalty notice must state such things as: (a) why the Secretary of State thinks the employer is liable; (b) must state the amount of the penalty; (c) must specify a date, at least 28 days after the date specified in the notice, by which the penalty must be paid; (d) specify how it must be paid; (e) explain how the employer may object to the penalty; and (f) explain how the Secretary of State may enforce the penalty: IAN 2006, s 15(6).
5 IAN 2006, s 15(7).

14.82C

[Add new paragraph:]

Employers can object to a penalty notice on three grounds:

(a) that they are not liable to the imposition of the penalty;
(b) they have complied with the required prescribed requirements and have an excuse for the employment; or
(c) the penalty is too high.

To make an objection the employer must give a written notice of objection, served within the time period prescribed and giving reasons for the objection.[1] When an objection is received the Secretary of State must consider it and may cancel, reduce, or increase the penalty or take no action. In deciding what to do he or she must have regard to the Code of Practice, issued under s 19, which will set out the criteria to be applied in determining the amount of the civil penalty.[2] The Secretary of State must inform the objector of any decision within a prescribed or agreed period. If the penalty is increased a new notice must be issued. If the penalty is reduced, the Secretary of State must inform the objector of the reduced amount.

1 IAN 2006, s 17(4).
2 IAN 2006, s 17(5).

14.82D

[Add new paragraph:]

Objection is not the only redress open to an aggrieved employer. There is also an appeal to the County Court in England and Wales and Northern Ireland or to the Sheriff Court in Scotland.[1] Employers can appeal on the grounds that they are not liable to the penalty, the amount is too high or they are excused payment because of compliance with the specified requirements.[2] The court can allow the appeal and cancel the penalty, allow the appeal and reduce the penalty, or dismiss the appeal.[3] An appeal is a rehearing of the decision to impose a penalty and the court must have regard to the Code of Practice under s 19 and any other matters the court thinks relevant, including matters of which the Secretary of State was unaware.[4] The appeal must be brought within a 28-day time period which runs:

(1) from the specified date upon which the penalty notice is given;[5]
(2) from the date on which the Secretary of state gives the employer notice that as a result of the objection made, the penalty is reduced; or
(3) the date specified in a notice from the Secretary of State that he or she intends to take no action.[6]

An appeal may be brought by an employer irrespective of whether he or she has made an objection under s 16.[7] Under s 18 a civil penalty imposed by the Secretary of State may be recovered as debt.

1 IAN 2006, s 17(6), which was not yet in force as at 1 October 2006. This applies to all the following fns 2–7.
2 IAN 2006, s 17(1).
3 IAN 2006, s 17(2).
4 IAN 2006, s 17(3).
5 This will include the situation where a new penalty notice is given because the Secretary of State has decided to increase the penalty after consideration of an objection under s 16.
6 IAN 2006, s 17(4).
7 IAN 2006, s 17(5).

Criminal offence

14.83A

[Add new paragraph:]

The second sanction is the creation of a new criminal offence of employing a person knowing that they are an adult subject to immigration control:

(a) who has not been granted leave to enter or remain (unless granted permission to work by the Secretary of State); or
(b) whose leave to remain is–
  (i) invalid;
  (ii) has ceased to have effect (whether by reason of curtailment, revocation, cancellation, passage of time or otherwise); or
  (iii) is subject to a condition preventing him or her from accepting the employment.[1]

On summary conviction, the maximum penalty is six months' imprisonment in England and Wales (12 months once s 154(1) of the Criminal Justice Act 2003 is commenced), six months in Scotland or Northern Ireland, or a fine up to the statutory maximum or both.[2] This new offence will replace the offence under s 8 of the AIA 1996 when s 21 comes into force.

1 IAN 2006, s 21(1), which was not yet in force as at 1 October 2006. This applies to fn 2 below.
2 IAN 2006, s 21(2) and (4)

14.83B

[Add new paragraph:]

The new criminal offence applies not only to individual employers but also to companies and partnerships. Section 22 defines the liability of bodies corporate, their officers and employees, and of members of partnerships in relation to the criminal offence in s 21. Section 22(1) deals with the question of knowledge and enacts that if a person who has responsibility within a body (whether corporate or not) for an aspect of the employment knows relevant facts about an employee, that person's knowledge is imputed to the body. Section 22(2) provides that where an offence under s 21(1) is committed by a body corporate with the consent or connivance of an officer of the body, the officer as well as the body should be treated as having committed the offence. Officers include a director, manager or secretary, a person purporting to act as such and, in the case of bodies managed by its member, a member.[1] Where the offence is committed by a partnership and a partner or a person purporting to act as a partner has consented or connived at the offence that person as well as the partnership is to be treated as having committed the offence.[2] Where an offence under s 21 is being investigated immigration officers have the powers of arrest, entry and search given by ss 28B and 28D, 28E, 28G and 28H of the Immigration Act 1971.[3]

1 IAN 2006, s 21(3), which was not yet in force as at 1 October 2006. This applies to all the following fns 2 and 3 below.
2 IAN 2006, s 22(4).
3 IAN 2006, s 21(3).

14.85

[NB:]

The imposition of new employer sanctions under IAN 2006, ss 15 to 25 carries with it the risk of exacerbating and entrenching racial discrimination in employment, as did section 8 of the 1996 Act. So just as s 8A of the 1996 Act required the Secretary of State to issue a Code of Practice for employers to avoid racial discrimination, so too s 23, which came into force on 31 August 2006, has a similar requirement. The Secretary of state is obliged to issue a Code of Practice to employers specifying how they can avoid contravening the Race Relations Act 1976 or the Race Relations (Northern Ireland) Order 1997 while avoiding liability for a civil penalty under s 15 of IAN 2006 or the commission of a criminal offence under s 21.

14.87

[NB:]

Information provided by an employer, as described, is not admissible in evidence in any criminal proceedings and this will continue to be the case, once s 8 of the 1996 Act is replaced by s 21 of IAN 2006.

CARRIERS' LIABILITY

Liability for inadequately documented passengers

14.94

[NB:]

New offence – IAN 2006, s 34, which was not in force as at 1 October 2006, makes it a summary offence punishable by a fine or imprisonment, if any person fails, without reasonable excuse, to supply information on passengers or crews of ships or aircraft required to be given under s 32(2) or (3) of IAN 2006 or to give freight information required under s 33(2).

[Footnote 6:]

The Immigration (Passenger Transit Visas) Order 2003, SI 2003/1185 has been further amended by SI 2006/493.

Chapter 15

DEPORTATION AND REPATRIATION

DEPORTATION

Introduction

15.1

[NB:]

There has been some fairly frenetic activity in recent months on the issue of deportation, prompted, one suspects, by populist agitation in certain sections of the media over foreign prisoners being released from prison at the end of their sentences without being considered for deportation. At any rate a new Home Secretary acted promptly and we now have an amendment to one of the oldest immigration rules on deportation, which dates back to the first published rules in the 1970's. The full legal implications of the position of foreign prisoners in UK jails is beyond the scope of this work (for example, their re-categorisation under prison law), but full details of these matters can be found by going on line to http://groups.yahoo.com/group/ForeignNationalPrisoners/

Beyond these seismic events, there are few amendments to this chapter and we have an update on the IDI as at August 2006 with interesting instructions on spent convictions and rehabilitated offenders.

Grounds for deportation

15.11

[NB:]

The Home Office announced a Statement of Changes in Immigration Rules to amend paragraph 364 to 'make it clear that where a person is liable to deportation then the presumption shall be that the public interest requires deportation and that it will only be in exceptional circumstances that the public interest in deportation will be outweighed in a case where it would not be contrary to the European Convention on Human Rights and the Refugee Convention to deport.' For more details, see 15.30 of this supplement below.

Criminal conviction

15.13

[NB:]

The reference to Directive 64/221 (EEC) should now be a reference to Directive 2004/38/EC (The Citizens' Directive), Chapter VI.

Criminal conviction – some conclusions

15.16

[NB:]

The reference to Directive 64/221 (EEC) should now be a reference to Directive 2004/38/EC (The Citizens' Directive), Chapter VI.

Deportation of family members

15.21

[NB:]

Section 5(4) of the Immigration Act 1971 now provides that the civil partner of a man or woman, who is or has been ordered to be deported, can be a member of that person's family for the purposes of deportation.[1]

[1] Immigration Act 1971, s 5 (4), as amended by Civil Partnership Act 2004, s 261(1) and Sch 27, para 37(a), which came into force on 5 December 2005.

The decision to deport: consideration of the merits

15.30

[NB:]

The current rules for deciding on the merits of a decision to deport were amended by the changes contained in HC 1337, which took effect on 20 July 2006. Old para 364 goes and in its place there is substituted the following paragraph:

> '**364.** Subject to paragraph 380, while each case will be considered on its merits, where a person is liable to deportation the presumption shall be that the public interest requires deportation. The Secretary of State will consider all relevant factors in considering whether the presumption is outweighed in any particular case, although it will only be in exceptional circumstances that the public interest in deportation will be outweighed in a case where it would not be contrary to the Human Rights Convention and the Convention and Protocol relating to the Status of Refugees to deport. The aim is an exercise of the power of deportation which is consistent and fair as between one person and another, although one case will rarely be identical with another in all material respects. In the cases detailed in paragraph 363A deportation will normally be the proper course where a person has failed to comply with or has contravened a condition or has remained without authority'.

15.30A

[Add new paragraph:]

There a number of points arising out of these changes. First, the list of relevant factors spelt out in the old paragraph 364 have been omitted. Now relevant factors are at large and not confined to a list (see 15.32 of the main text).

Secondly, the presumption that the public interest requires deportation is not a new concept in this area, but it is the first time it has been spelt out. Thirdly, it is not a new concept that the Secretary of State should consider whether the publc interest is outweighed by the relevant circumstances of the particular case. If anything the new wording is an improvement on the old, by which the public interest was to be balanced against the compassionate circumstances of the case and the reader was left wondering how exactly all the other relevant factors fitted in. Fourthly, it is implied that the public interest is outweighed if deportation would be contrary to to either the obligations under the Human Rights Convention or the Refugee Convention and Protocol. If it is not, the decision to deport will only be outweighed in exceptional circumstances. Fifthly, there will be many deportation cases where neither Convention applies, for example, single men or women without long standing residence or entrenched family or private lives in the UK, who have been convicted of criminal offence.

15.30B

[Add new paragraph:]

What is not clear is how the Secretary of State is expected to make the leap from (i) liability to be deported to (ii) the presumption that it is in the public interest to deport that person and then (iii) to the exercise spelt out in the new para 364. These are largely operational matters, but the guidance in new para 364 is not altogether clear. The main focus of the new rule is on persons who have been convicted of crime and are coming to the end of a sentence of imprisonment or other form of custody. Fixing where the public interest lies depends, first, upon certain broad generalities of policy, which can be narrow or wide, such as the prevention and punishment of crime and the interests of public safety, but, secondly, on very fact-specific factors relating to the particular case, like the nature of the criminal offending and the risk posed by the particular offender. The relevant factors are not simply balancing factors to set against some rigid concept of the public interest, but are of themselves part of what gives weight to the public interest, whether as mitigating factors or as aggravating ones. That is why it will be very difficult to guage two of the key elements in the new paragraph – what is the weight of the public interest and what makes for exceptionality.

15.30C

[Add new paragraph:]

Some idea of the Secretary of State's thinking on the operation of the new rule as regards foreign prisoners is contained in his Written Ministerial Statements of 23 May 2006.[1] First he spoke very clearly of the balance between the interests of the offender and public safety, saying: 'It is not right that the system should tilt the exercise of discretion in favour of the criminal rather than public safety'. This suggests that the public interest in para 364 is rather sensibly confined to the issue of public safety. If right, that would put a premium on deporting prisoners who pose a risk to public safety, but not those who pose little or none. Our description of past decisions shows that the courts go much wider than this, particularly, when dealing with the vexed issue of the risk of re-offending.

1 Home Secretary's written ministerial statement of the 23 May (Official Report, Column 80WS).

15.30D

[Add new paragraph:]

Secondly, the Secretary of State gave some idea of IND priorities, when he said that he wanted to change the criteria for considering offenders for deportation on conducive grounds. Instead of considering for deportation those with three convictions regardless of seriousness or risk, they ought to look at people who have had two custodial sentences of under a year for, say, actual bodily harm.[1] His words are now reflected in the August 2006 IDI. They indicate that the Home Office have set a starting threshold of 12 months' imprisonment (which may be an aggregate of more than one offence in the previous five years[2]) for non-EEA nationals and a two-year threshold for EEA nationals.[3] Where a person has valid leave, including indefinite leave to enter or remain or is entitled to reside in the United Kingdom under the Immigration (European Economic Area) Regulations 2006 and a borderline decision has been taken not to deport, the IDI suggest that it may be appropriate to send the person a warning letter. This indicates that any further criminal conviction will lead to their immigration status being reviewed and may result in their deportation.[4] For a recent decision on deportation of an EEA citizen see *Machado v Secretary of State for the Home Department* [2005] EWCA Civ 597, [2005] All ER (D) 289 (May).

1 Home Secretary's written ministerial statement of the 23 May (Official Report, Column 80WS).
2 Clearly the five-year period has been chosen so as to avoid the risk of falling foul of the Rehabilitation of Offenders Act 1974 by relying on a spent conviction: see further IDI, ch 13, s 4, para 3.
3 IDI, ch 13, s 4, para 2 contains instructions that conviction referrals to IND from the Prison Service, the Courts and the police are to be forwarded to IND's Criminal Casework Directorate to consider if there has been (i) a court recommendation for deportation, (ii) in the case of non-EEA nationals, a custodial sentence of 12 months or more either in one sentence, or as an aggregate of two or three sentences over a period of five years, or (iii) in the case of EEA nationals, a custodial sentence of 24 months or more.
4 IDI, ch 13, s 4, para 2.

Family deportations

15.37

[NB:]

The amendments to para 367 mean that the rule no longer contains a long list of relevant factors, common to every kind of deportation, as before, but this does not exclude consideration of such factors should they arise in the particular case. On the other hand the rule retains the list of factors which are very specific to this type of deportation. These are set out in the main text.

Procedure and appeals

Political cases

15.43

[NB:]

Section 7 of IAN 2006, which came into force on 31 August 2008, inserts a new s 97A into the NIAA 2002. The section requires that an appeal against a decision to make a deportation order, which has been certified as having been made on national security grounds, should normally only be able to be brought from outside the United Kingdom, unless the appellant makes a human rights claim. Then he or she is allowed to bring the appeal in-country unless the Secretary of State certifies that removal would not breach the UK's obligations under the European Convention on Human Rights (ECHR). The section also provides for an in-country appeal against this certificate to the Special Immigration Appeals Commission (SIAC).

Deportation of EEA nationals

15.44

[NB:]

The references to Directive 64/221 (EEC) should now be a reference to Directive 2004/38/EC (The Citizens' Directive), Chapter VI. These provisions have also been transposed into domestic law by the Immigration (European Economic Area) Regulations 2006. They provide that those EEA nationals and their family members (who may not be EEA nationals themselves), who would otherwise be entitled to reside in the United Kingdom under the 2006 Regulations may only be removed on grounds of public policy, public security or public health in accordance with reg 19(3)(b) of the 2006 Regulations. Regulation 24(3) further provides that such persons are to be treated as if they are persons to whom s 3(5)(a) of the Immigration Act 1971 Act applies. For a recent decision on deportation of an EEA citizen see *Machado v Secretary of State for the Home Department* [2005] EWCA Civ 597, [2005] All ER (D) 289 (May).

Removal of deportees

15.49

[NB:]

A person who is already the subject of a deportation order but who subsequently leaves the United Kingdom of his or her own volition is regarded as having 'deported' him or herself irrespective of whether the persons were aware of the signing of a deportation order against them.[1] This guidance must be of dubious legality, especially in light of the House of Lords ruling in *R (on the application of Anufrijeva) v Secretary of State for the Home Department* [2003] UKHL 36, [2004] 1 AC 604, [2003] 3 All ER 827. See further 15.39 of the main text.

1 IDI, ch 13, s 1, para 10.

[Footnote 3:]

Remove reference to IDI. The current IDI (Aug/2006 makes no reference to this).

Revocation of deportation orders

15.51

[NB:]

The provisions of the Rehabilitation of Offenders Act 1974 Act should be taken into account in reviewing Deportation Orders where the person's criminal record was a significant factor in the decision to deport.[1] Pill LJ in the Court of Appeal in *N v Secretary of State for the Home Department*[2], a case originating from SIAC, observed that para 390 of the Immigration Rules requires consideration of 'all the circumstances' and these are expressly stated to include 'the grounds of which the order was made', with the consequence that the analysis of an alleged change of circumstances inevitably involves a consideration of the grounds on which the order was made.

1 IDI, ch 13, s 4, para 5.5 (Aug/2006).
2 [2006] EWCA Civ 299 (28 March 2006).

REPATRIATION

Prison Repatriation

15.55

[NB:]

Clause 49 of the Police and Justice Bill 2006, introduced by the government in the House of Lords, would amend s 1 of the Repatriation of Prisoners Act 1984 to enable transfers of serving foreign prisoners to take place without their consent except in those cases where the Prisoner Transfer Agreement (PTA) makes consent obligatory.

When a decision is taken to repatriate a prisoner to serve his or her sentence in his home country, IND will be informed of this decision and asked to serve a deportation order prohibiting that person's return to the United Kingdom.[1]

Because of the overcrowding crisis in British prisons, the Home Secretary has set up a scheme to encourage foreign prisoners to volunteer for a transfer to their home country under a Prisoner Transfer Agreement (PTA) to serve the rest of their sentence there. Under the scheme they will be provided with 'reintegration assistance' in their home country.[2]

[1] IDI, ch 13, s 1, para 4.
[2] Letter Home Office to Prison Reform Trust (9 October 2006).

Chapter 16

REMOVAL AND OTHER EXPULSION

Nationals of EEA and Association Agreement States

16.27

[NB:]

The references to the Immigration (European Economic Area) Regulations 2000 should now be a reference to the Immigration (European Economic Area) Regulations 2006, SI 2006/1003.

The references to Directive 64/221 (EEC) should now be a reference to Directive 2004/38/EC ('The Citizens' Directive'), Chapter VI.

[Footnote 1 should read:]

SI 2006/1003.

[Footnote 2 should read:]

SI 2006/1003, reg 11.

[Footnote 3 should read:]

SI 2006/1003, reg 21.

OVERSTAYERS AND OTHERS

16.33

[NB:]

Section 48 of IAN 2006 amends s 10(8) of the Immigration and Asylum Act 1999, so that notification of a decision to remove in accordance with that section invalidates any leave to enter or remain in the United Kingdom which was previously given to the person. Prior to this amendment leave was invalidated only at the point at which removal directions were given under s 10. Invalidation of the person's leave has the effect of stopping access to any benefits, financial or otherwise, which may have been conditional on the leave.

Overstaying and breach of conditions

16.38

[NB:]

Section 3C of the Immigration Act 1971 has been amended so that a leave is only extended during an appeal period if the person has a right to an in-country appeal (IAN 2006, s 11, which came into force on 31 August 2006).

Use of deception in seeking leave to remain

16.42

[Add at end:]

Removal for practicing deception only applies to persons who have practiced deception from 1 October 1996.[6] If it appears that leave to remain was obtained by deception prior to that date this does not stop the case being referred for possible deportation action on non-conducive grounds under s 3(5)(a) of the Immigration Act 1971.[7] Leave obtained by deception is now invalidated when notice of removal is given, not when removal directions are given.[8]

6 IDI, Ch 13, s 2, para 2.1.2.
7 See n 6 above.
8 Immigration and Asylum Act 1999, s 10(8), amended by IAN 2006, s 48, which came into force on 16 June 2006.

Family members

16.44

[Add at end:]

Section 5(4) of the Immigration Act 1971 now provides that the civil partner of a man or woman, who is or has been ordered to be deported, can be a member of that person's family for the purposes of deportation.[2] Family members are the non-settled spouse or civil partner, or children under the age of 18 belonging to the family of a person in respect of whom removal directions have been given under s 10.[3]

2 Immigration Act 1971, s 5 (4), as amended by Civil Partnership Act 2004, s 261(1) and Sch 27, para 37(a), which came into force on 5 December 2005.
3 IDI, Ch 13, s 2, para 2.4.

USE OF DISCRETION IN REMOVAL CASES

16.46

[NB:]

Although HC 1337 has altered the wording of HC 395C by an express incorporation into the rule of the list of relevant factors to be taken into account (it was previously written out in para 364), in fact the change is purely cosmetic.

The long residence rule

16.47 & 16.48

[NB:]

In *OS (10 years' lawful residence) Hong Kong*[1] the Tribunal noted that the 'long residence' concession had not been withdrawn when the rules relating to long residence were introduced. The Tribunal ruled that paras 276A–D of the Immigration Rules (HC 395) stand alongside the published concession in long residence cases. The rules mean what they say and a person who does not meet the requirements of the rules may still get the benefit of the Secretary of State's exercise of discretion in his favour under the concession. Under the concession, there is no absolute requirement that every day of residence during the ten years be a day of lawful residence.

1 [2006] UKAIT 00031 (20 March 2006).

CHALLENGING DECISIONS TO REMOVE

Appeal rights

16.60

[NB:]

Section 2 of IAN 2006, which came into force on 31 August 2006, has made an important amendment to appeal rights against a decision to remove. It amends s 82(2)(g) of NIAA 2002 to provide a right of appeal against a decision to remove under s 10(1)(ba) of the 1999 Act, which provides for the removal from the UK of those whose leave has been revoked under s 76(3) of the 2002 Act, because that person or a dependent has ceased to be a refugee. The amendment gives the person a separate right of appeal at each of the two decision stages: the first at the revocation stage and the second at the stage the decision to remove is taken. This separation of appeal rights is seen as necessary in the light of the importance of refugee status. No decision to remove will be taken whilst an appeal of revocation is ending in the UK.

EXTRADITION

16.73

[Add at end:]

In extradition proceedings in relation to whether an individual convicted in his absence would receive a retrial that accorded with the European Convention on Human Rights 1950, Protocol 1 Art 6 if extradited, it was unnecessary to examine what a requesting state did in practice provided that the Convention was unequivocally incorporated into its body of laws and that the terms of the Convention would prevail if any conflict arose between it and those laws.[6]

Occasionally a deportation case will also be subject to extradition or repatriation proceedings. These proceedings will make no difference to the consideration of whether deportation should go ahead. Deportation consideration and extradition / repatriation proceedings should continue simultaneously.[7]

6 *Chen v Romania* [2006] EWHC 1752 (Admin), [2006] All ER (D) 265 (June).
7 IDI, Ch 13, s 1, para 4.

Chapter 17

DETENTION AND BAIL

IMMIGRATION OFFICERS' POWERS TO DETAIN

17.9

[Immediately after the numbered sub-paragraphs add:]

In addition, an immigration officer's powers to detain under para 16 of Sch 2 to the Immigration Act 1971 are applicable to the following:

(viii) a person claiming a right of admission as the family member of an EEA national or as a family member who has retained a right of residence or as a person with a permanent right of residence under the EEA Regulations whilst the person's claim is being examined;[1]

(ix) a person claiming a right of admission as an EEA national where there is reason to believe that he or she may be excluded from the UK on grounds of public policy, public security or public health pending examination of the claim;[2]

(x) a person refused admission to the UK because he or she does not qualify under the EEA Regulations, pending his or her removal from the UK;[3]

(xi) a person whose EEA residence card or family permit has been revoked on arrival by an immigration on the grounds that he or she is not a family member of a qualified person or of an EEA national with a right of residence or does not possess a right of residence him or herself or if the revocation is justified on public policy, public security or public health grounds pending removal from the UK;[4]

(xii) a person refused admission as a family member of an EEA national, a family member who has retained a right of residence or other person with a right of residence under the EEA Regulations on grounds of public policy, public security or public health pending removal from the UK;[5]

(xiii) a person who does not have or ceases to have a right to reside under the EEA Regulations pending his or her removal;[6]

(xiv) a person who enters or seeks to enter in breach of a deportation order.[7]

[At the end of the paragraph, add:]

When the IAN 2006, s 47 comes into force the Secretary of State will be able to make a decision that a person with statutory leave[8] is to be removed from the UK by way of directions to be given by an immigration officer. The administrative provisions of Immigration Act 1971, Sch 2, including the power to detain under para 16 will apply in relation to directions given by an immigration officer under s 47[9]. However, this will not mean that an immigration officer will be able to detain a person as soon as a s 47 decision is made against him or her, a decision which may be made at the same time as, eg a decision refusing to extend the person's leave to remain. That is because an immigration officer will only be able to detain if there are 'reasonable grounds for suspecting that a person is someone in respect of whom' removal directions may be given.[10] The immigration officer will only be able to give removal directions 'if and when' the statutory leave ends;[11] whilst an appeal might be brought or an appeal is pending, the immigration officer has no power to give removal directions and so will be unable to have reasonable grounds for suspecting that removal directions may be given.[12]

1 Immigration (European Economic Area) Regulations 2006, reg 22(1)(a).
2 Immigration (European Economic Area) Regulations 2006, reg 22(1)(b).
3 Immigration (European Economic Area) Regulations 2006, reg 23(1)(a).
4 Immigration (European Economic Area) Regulations 2006, reg 23(1)(a).
5 Immigration (European Economic Area) Regulations 2006, reg 23(1)(b).
6 Immigration (European Economic Area) Regulations 2006, reg 24(2).
7 Immigration (European Economic Area) Regulations 2006, reg 24(3).
8 Ie leave under Immigration Act 1971, s 3C(2)(b) (as amended) or s 3D(2)(a) (as inserted by IAN 2006, s 11) – which is leave extended following a refusal to vary leave, a variation or a revocation of leave whilst an appeal may be brought and whilst any appeal is pending.
9 IAN 2006, s 47(3).
10 Immigration Act 1971, Sch 2, para 16(2).
11 IAN 2006, s 47(1).
12 Moreover, the Minister (Tony McNulty) gave an assurance in Parliament that s 47 did not create any new power to impose restrictions on a person, eg to detain him or her, whilst the person has statutory leave: *Hansard*, 29.3.06, col 906.

17.10

[In the text after footnote 2 add:]

The European Court of Human Rights agreed with the House of Lords (by a majority of 4:3) that detention of an asylum seeker, who presented no risk of absconding and was only detained for reasons of administrative convenience, did not breach Art 5(1)(f).[1]

1 *Saadi v United Kingdom (Application No 13229/03)* (2006) Times, 3 August, [2006] All ER (D) 125 (Jul), ECtHR. See further chapter 8.

Temporary admission

17.11

[In the text after footnote 2 add:]

There is no power to grant temporary admission instead of granting leave to enter (eg in circumstances where the Secretary of State accepts that a person cannot be removed because removal would breach his or her human rights but considers it 'inappropriate' to grant discretionary leave); temporary admission may only be granted whilst an application for leave to enter is being considered or pending removal from the UK[1].

1 *R (on the application of GG) v Secretary of State for the Home Department* [2006] EWHC 1111 (Admin), (2006) Times, 14 June, [2006] All ER (D) 143 (May); *affd sub nom S v Secretary of State for the Home Department (sub nom R (on the application of GG) v Secretary of State for the Home Department)* [2006] EWCA Civ 1157, [2006] All ER (D) 30 (Aug), upheld in *S v Secretary of State for the Home Department (sub nom R (on the application of GG) v Secretary of State for the Home Department)* [2006] EWCA Civ 1157, [2006] All ER (D) 30 (Aug).

17.13

[Add at end:]

In *Ex p Khadir* the House of Lords[1] decided that both Crane J and the Court of Appeal were wrong to have held that removal was not 'pending' for the purpose of Immigration Act 1971, Sch 2, para 16, if it was not possible to effect removal within a reasonable or tolerable time. A person's removal would be 'pending' for as long as an immigration officer or the Secretary of State intended to remove the person and there was some prospect of achieving the person's removal. The person would remain liable to be detained until one or both of the intention to remove and the prospect of removal ceased. The line of cases following *Ex p Singh*[2] and holding that the power to detain was implicitly limited to the period reasonably necessary for the purpose of effecting removal were concerned with the exercise but not the existence of the power to detain.[3] Accordingly, it was unnecessary to have enacted Nationality, Immigration and Asylum Act 2002, s 67.[4]

1 *R (on the application of Khadir) v Secretary of State for the Home Department* [2005] UKHL 39, [2006] 1 AC 207, [2005] 4 All ER 114, [2005] 3 WLR 1.
2 *R v Governor of Durham Prison, ex p Singh* [1984] 1 All ER 983, [1984] 1 WLR 704, [1983] Imm AR 198, QBD. See further para 17.42 of the main text.
3 See fn 1 above.
4 See fn 1 above.

SECRETARY OF STATE'S POWERS TO DETAIN

17.14

[In the text, add the following to the end of sub-para (ii) that begins ***Decision to deport****:]*

IAN 2006, s 53 came into force on 31 August 2006[1] with the effect that a person will be liable to detention not only (as the law previously stood) when he or she has been given notice of a decision to make a deportation order but also when there is such a notice ready to be given to the person. A police or immigration officer will have the power to arrest the person once notice of a decision to make a deportation order is ready to be given.

[At the end of the paragraph add the following:]

A person admitted to or residing in the UK under the EEA Regulations may be detained under the powers contained in Immigration Act 1971, Sch 3 if a decision is taken to remove the person on the grounds that he or she does not have or no longer has a right of admission or residence under the Regulations or the person's removal is justified on public policy, public security or public health grounds.[2]

1 SI 2006/2226.
2 Immigration (European Economic Area) Regulations 2006, SI 2006/1003, reg 24(3).

Prisoners recommended for deportation

17.17

[Add at end:]

The principle that there is no presumption in favour of detaining a person who is subject to a decision to make a deportation order applies with particular force if the Court could have but did not recommend deportation.[1]

1 *R (on the application of Faulkner) v Secretary of State for the Home Department* [2005] EWHC 2567 (Admin), [2005] All ER (D) 03 (Nov).

WHY, WHERE AND HOW DETAINED

Conditions of detention

17.24

[NB:]

The Chief Inspector of Prisons (HMCIP) has at present a voluntary right to inspect Immigration Short Term Holding Facilities (STHFs) and escort arrangements. Section 46 of IAN 2006 amends s 5A(5A) of the Prison Act 1952 to put these powers on a statutory footing. It now means that inspection of STHFs and escort arrangements are in line with the position on immigration removal centres, which were made subject to statutory inspection by s 152(5) of the IAA 1999.

Reasons for detention

17.26

[Add at end:]

In *Faulkner* it was held that there was an obligation to inform a person of the essential factual and legal grounds for his or her detention and that failure to give reasons for detention made the detention unlawful.[1] In *Saadi v United Kingdom* the European Court of Human Rights held that there was a breach of the obligation under Art 5(2) of the Convention to inform a person 'promptly' of the reasons for his arrest in circumstances where an asylum seeker was not told for 76 hours why he was being detained at Oakington Detention Centre.[2]

1 *R (on the application of Faulkner) v Secretary of State for the Home Department* [2005] EWHC 2567 (Admin), [2005] All ER (D) 03 (Nov).

2 *Saadi v United Kingdom (Application No 13229/03)* (2006) Times, 3 August, [2006] All ER (D) 125 (Jul), ECtHR.

POLICY AND CRITERIA FOR DETENTION

17.27

[Amend footnote 3 to read:]

Chapter 38 of the Operational Enforcement Manual, updated (but also undated), is now available on the IND website. In section 38.3 it sets out the same factors relevant to decisions on detention as listed in this paragraph in the original text save that (xi) is not amongst them.

Special categories of detainee

17.30

[In place of the text in the first sub-para (i) substitute:]

(i) *Women*: are no longer treated as special cases. It is now only pregnant women who are treated as a special case to the extent that pregnant women should not normally be detained unless removal is imminent or, if less than 24 weeks pregnant, are considered suitable for the fast-track.[1]

[In the first sub-para (ii) add:]

detention should not be considered in the case of the spouse of an EEA national unless there is strong evidence that the spouse is no longer exercising treaty rights or the marriage was one of convenience and the parties had no intention of living together from the outset.[2]

[The second sub-para (ii) should be amended so as to say that:]

pregnant women should be detained only in very exceptional circumstances unless there is a clear prospect of early removal or, in the early stages of pregnancy and they are suitable for the fast-track.[3]

[Footnote 6 – add:]

The case *R (on the application of I) v Secretary of State for the Home Department* has now been decided. Owen J held that the continued detention of the applicants was irrational once their claims to be minors were supported by age assessments by a consultant paediatrician.[4]

1 Operational Enforcement Manual, chapter 38.9.1.
2 Operational Enforcement Manual, chapter 38.9.2.
3 Operational Enforcement Manual, chapter 38.10.
4 *R (on the application of I) v Secretary of State for the Home Department* [2005] EWHC 1025 (Admin), (2005) Times, 10 June, [2005] All ER (D) 440 (May).

Oakington and Harmondsworth – fast track detention

17.34

[Add at end:]

Chapter 38 of the Operational Enforcement Manual as revised[1] sets out the same categories of persons identified as unsuitable for the detained fast track as in the original text of this chapter save for the last category listed – any case where a quick decision appears unlikely – and with the additions of: violent or uncooperative 'cases'; those with criminal convictions except where specifically authorised; those where detention would be contrary to published criteria. In addition, the policy with respect to disputed minors has been altered in favour of exclusion unless there is clear documentary evidence that the person is over 18; a full 'Merton-compliant' age assessment by social services states that the person is over 18 or the person's appearance or demeanour 'very strongly indicates' that the person is 'significantly' over 18 and no other credible evidence exists to the contrary.[2]

1 In its current version, available on the IND website.
2 Operational Enforcement Manual, Chapter 38.4.

17.35

[Add before the sentence containing footnote 1:]

The Detention Centre Rules provide for new arrivals to a detention centre to be medically examined within 24 hours of arrival and for the medical practitioner conducting the examination to report any concern that the detainee may have been the victim of torture to the Secretary of State.[1] The objective is in part to ensure that victims of torture are identified and so not subject to the fast-track procedure and to being detained in breach of the policy not to detain victims of torture. However, deliberately and in breach of the statutory obligation under the Detention Centre Rules, medical examinations at Oakington detention centre were routinely delayed beyond 24 hours. Continued detention beyond the point at which a person should have been identified, by a timely medical examination, as a victim of torture and so released in accordance with the detention and fast-track policies was held to be unlawful.[2]

1 2001, SI 2001/238, rr 34 and 35.
2 *R (on the application of D) v Secretary of State for the Home Department; R (on the application of K) v same* [2006] EWHC 980 (Admin), 150 Sol Jo LB 743, [2006] All ER (D) 300 (May).

The purpose and length of detention

17.42

[Add at end:]

In *R (on the application of H) v Secretary of State for the Home Department*[1] the claimant's detention was held to be unlawful because in excess of a period reasonably necessary for the purpose of effecting removal. The Court is not limited to making an assessment on *Wednesbury* grounds of the Secretary of State's view that detention was for a reasonable period; the question of the reasonableness of the period of detention is for the Court as primary decision maker.[2] The Court has identified a practice on the part of the Home Office of detaining claimants and then serving a refusal of any outstanding claim with a view to removal within a day or two, thereby preventing or impeding the claimant's access to legal advice.[3] Munby J held such detention to be unlawful because for the improper purpose of 'spiriting away of the claimants from the jurisdiction before there was likely to be time for them to act upon legal advice or apply to the court', revealing 'at best an unacceptable disregard by the Home Office of the rule of law, at worst an unacceptable disdain by the Home Office for the rule of law'.[4]

1 [2005] EWHC 1702 (Admin), [2005] All ER (D) 95 (Jul).
2 *Youssef v The Home Office* [2004] EWHC 1884 (QB), [2004] NLJR 1452 applied in *R (on the application of Karas and another) v Secretary of State for the Home Department* [2006] EWHC 747 (Admin), [2006] All ER (D) 107 (Apr).
3 *R (on the application of Collaku) v Secretary of State for the Home Department* [2005] EWHC 2855 (Admin), [2005] All ER (D) 124 (Nov) and *R (on the application of Karas and another) v Secretary of State for the Home Department.*
4 *R (on the application of Karas and another) v Secretary of State for the Home Department* (fn 2 above).

PROVISIONS FOR RELEASE OR BAIL

New arrivals and those detained for removal: bail under the Immigration Act 1971

17.56

[Add at end:]

A person may be released on bail pending examination or pending removal subject to a requirement to appear before an immigration officer at a particular time and place.[1] An immigration officer may vary that requirement by notice in writing[2] so as to require an earlier appearance before an immigration officer than that directed by the tribunal. However, the power to do so is subject to implied limitation; an immigration officer could not merely rely on reasserting the underlying power to detain because that would undermine the basis upon which the tribunal had granted bail. There would need to be a material change of circumstances since the tribunal granted bail.[3]

1 Immigration Act 1971, Sch 2, para 22(1).
2 Immigration Act 1971, Sch 2, para 22(1A).
3 *Re Mahmood* [2006] EWHC 228 (Admin), [2006] All ER (D) 303 (Feb).

Detained persons: national minimum wage

17.66

[Add new paragraph:]

IAN 2006, s 59 disqualifies detainees in removal centres from entitlement to the national minimum wage.

Chapter 18

IMMIGRATION APPEALS

RIGHTS OF APPEAL

18.14

[NB:]

The Immigration, Asylum and Nationality Act 2006 (IAN 2006) adds a fifth situation in which a person will have a right of appeal.[1] That is where the person had limited leave to enter or remain as a refugee;[2] a subsequent decision (in response to an application for further leave as a refugee or an 'active review'[3]) is made that the person is not a refugee and following the decision he or she has limited leave to enter or remain but not as a refugee (eg discretionary leave). The intention of that provision[4] is to introduce a new right of appeal enabling the issue of entitlement to refugee status to be litigated by people who are no longer recognized as refugees but who are permitted to stay in the UK on another basis. The appeal may only be brought on the ground that removal of the appellant from the UK would breach the UK's obligations under the Refugee Convention.[5] The appeal may be brought 'against the decision to curtail or to refuse to extend his limited leave'.[6]

1 IAN 2006 (IAN 2006), s 1 inserting s 83A into the Nationality, Immigration and Asylum Act 2002, brought into force on 31 August 2006 by SI 2006/2226.
2 Following recognition as a refugee on or after 30th August 2005 when the Home Office policy became to grant limited (five years) leave to enter or remain instead of indefinite leave to enter or remain.
3 See chapter 12.
4 See for example, IAN 2006, Explanatory Notes, para 14.
5 IAN 2006, s 3 introducing a new s 84(4) into the Nationality, Immigration and Asylum Act 2002, brought into force on 31 August 2006 by SI 2006/2226.
6 The new Nationality, Immigration and Asylum Act 2002, s 83A(2)

[Footnote 7 – delete and replace:]

The Immigration (European Economic Area) Regulations 2006, SI 2006/1003, reg 2(1).

Immigration decisions

18.15

[NB:]

The IAN 2006 adds three new decisions to the list of 'immigration decisions' in Nationality, Immigration and Asylum Act 2002, s 82(2) against which an appeal to the tribunal may be brought. The first (now in force) is a decision to give directions for the removal of a person whose indefinite leave to enter or remain as a refugee or dependant of a refugee was revoked because the refugee availed himself or herself of the protection of another country.[1] Such a person would already have had a right of appeal against the decision to revoke his or her leave to enter or remain[2]. The Act creates a further right of appeal against the subsequent decision to remove and it does so in recognition of the importance of refugee status[3]. The second new 'immigration decision'[4] is a decision that a person is to be removed by way of directions under IAN 2006, s 47 which is a new power to make a decision to give removal directions to a person whose leave to enter or remain has been extended by statute pending an appeal[5] and which is considered elsewhere in this supplement. The third new immigration decision[6] against which an appeal may be brought is a decision of the Secretary of State to make an order removing a person's right of abode on the ground that the person's removal or exclusion from the UK would be conducive to the public good.[7] These provisions came into force on 16 June 2006.

1 IAN 2006, s 2, brought into force on 31 August 2006 by SI 2006/2226. Section 2 amends the Nationality, Immigration and Asylum Act 2002, s 82(2)(g) to include a decision that a person is to be removed by way of directions under Immigration and Asylum Act 1999, s 10(1)(ba) which is a decision to give directions for the removal of a person whose indefinite leave has been revoked under Nationality, Immigration and Asylum Act 2002, s 76(3).
2 Nationality, Immigration and Asylum Act 2002, s 82(2)(g).
3 IAN 2006, Explanatory Notes, para 16.
4 To be inserted as Nationality, Immigration and Asylum Act 2002, s 82(2)(ha), not yet in force.
5 By Immigration Act 1971, s 3C(2)(b), as amended by IAN 2006, ss 11(2) or 3D(2)(a), as inserted by IAN 2006, s 11(5).
6 The Nationality, Immigration and Asylum Act 2002, s 82(2)(ib), as inserted by IAN 2006, s 57(2) with effect from 16 June 2006 (Immigration, Asylum and Nationality Act 2006 (Commencement No 1) Order 2006, SI 2006/1497).
7 IAN 2006, s 57(1), inserting a new s 2A into Immigration Act 1971 and which came into force on 16 June 2006 (Immigration, Asylum and Nationality Act 2006 (Commencement No 1) Order 2006, SI 2006/1497).

Refusal of asylum

18.16

[NB:]

This section in the original work should be read in the light of para 18.14 of this supplement, s 1 of the IAN 2006 having come into force.

EEA decisions

18.17

[NB:]

The Immigration (European Economic Area) Regulations 2006, SI 2006/1003 have replaced the 2000 Regulations but to broadly similar effect with relation to appeals. Consequently, the references in the footnotes to the original text need to be substituted with the following references to the 2006 Regulations:

1 As defined in reg 7.
2 Regulation 26.

3 Regulation 2(1) – the definition of an EEA decision is broadly similar to the previous Regulations.
4 Regulation 26(2).
5 Regulation 26(3).

Human rights and race discrimination

18.19

[Footnote 4 – delete and replace:]

The Immigration (European Economic Area) Regulations 2006, SI 2006/1003, reg 26(7) and Sch 1.

Venue

18.20

[NB:]

The references to appeals against EEA decisions need to be amended to refer to the Immigration (European Economic Area) Regulations 2006, SI 2006/1003 instead of the 2000 Regulations which they replaced as follows:

1 Regulation 26(6).
2 Regulation 28.
3 Regulation 28.
4 Regulation 28.
5 Regulation 28.

Exclusion of the right of appeal

18.21

[NB:]

Section 5 of the IAN 2006[1] creates a new basis upon which a person will be ineligible to appeal (save on race discrimination, human rights and asylum grounds) which is that the decision was taken on the ground that the person failed to supply a medical report or medical certificate in accordance with a requirement of the Immigration Rules.[2] Sections 4[3] and 6[4] of the IAN 2006 will replace the restrictions on the rights of appeal described at para 18.21(2)–(4) of the original work with the much more draconian restrictions described below.

1 Brought into force on 31 August 2006 by SI 2006/2226, adding a new s 88(2)(ba) to the Nationality, Immigration and Asylum Act 2002.
2 The current intention is that the requirement would relate to medical reports or certificates concerning TB and that the requirement would be piloted in a number of countries characterised as high risk for TB and from which significant numbers seek entry to the UK. The Home Office Race Equality Impact Assessment (13 October 2005) acknowledged that the application of the measure could amount to discrimination towards nationals of the countries to which it would apply.
3 Yet to come into force at time of writing (October 2006).
4 Brought into force on 31 August 2006.

Exclusion of rights of appeal against refusal of entry clearance

18.21A

[Add new paragraph:]

Section 4(1) of the IAN 2006[1], when it comes into force, will prevent anyone from appealing against a refusal of entry clearance unless (a) the application was made for the purpose of visiting a person of a class or description to be specified in regulations;[2] (b) the application was made for the purpose of entering as the dependant of a person in circumstances prescribed in regulations[3]; or (c) an appeal is brought against the refusal of entry clearance on race discrimination or human rights grounds.[4] Consequently, a person refused entry clearance for any other purpose, eg to study, work or conduct business in the UK will have no right of appeal against the refusal save on race discrimination or human rights grounds. One can envisage substantial numbers of appeals being brought on such grounds by unsuccessful applicants for entry clearance as the only means by which to appeal a wrongful refusal of entry clearance. The regulations referred to in (a) and (b) may make provision about: the requisite family relationship between the visitor and the person visited; the determination of whether one person is dependant upon another; the circumstances of the applicant and of the person to be visited or joined including the person's immigration status and the duration of two individuals' residence together and about the applicant's purpose in seeking entry as a dependant.[5] The Secretary of State will be required to appoint a person to monitor refusals of entry clearance where there is no right of appeal[6] and within three years of these new restrictions on entry clearance appeals commencing, the Secretary of State will be required to report on their operation to Parliament.[7]

1 By substituting for Nationality, Immigration and Asylum Act 2002, ss 88A, 90 and 91 a new s 88A.
2 Nationality, Immigration and Asylum Act 2002, s 88A(1)(a), as substituted by IAN 2006, s 4(1).
3 Nationality, Immigration and Asylum Act 2002, s 88A(1)(b), as substituted.
4 Nationality, Immigration and Asylum Act 2002, s 88A(3), as substituted.
5 Nationality, Immigration and Asylum Act 2002, s 88A(2), as substituted. With regard to regulations making provision about an applicant's purpose in seeking entry as a dependant, 'the measure is not intended to do any of the things that the primary purpose rule did' (Baroness Ashton of Upholland, Lords Grand Committee, 11 January 2006, col GC73).
6 IAN 2006, s 4(2), substituting a new Immigration and Asylum Act 1999, s 23(1).
7 IAN 2006, s 4(3).

Exclusion of rights of appeal against refusal of leave to enter

18.21B

[Add new paragraph:]

IAN 2006, s 6 has the effect that a person cannot appeal against refusal of leave to enter *at all* unless (a) the person had entry clearance on arrival in the UK and he or she sought leave to enter for the same purpose as that specified in the entry clearance[1]; or (b) an appeal is brought on race discrimination, human rights or Refugee Convention grounds.[2] The existing provisions deny a right of appeal against refusal of leave to enter only to visitors, short-term students and prospective students and their dependants without entry clearance[3] or those who are ineligible to appeal because refused on the ground that they do not satisfy a requirement of the rules as to age, nationality or citizenship or do not possess a requisite document or are seeking entry for a period greater or a purpose other than provided by the rules.[4] One can foresee disputes arising as to what was said by a person on arrival in the UK; did he or she apply for entry for a purpose other than that specified in the entry clearance (as the immigration officer may allege and with the consequence that there is no right of appeal against refusal of leave to enter) or did the person apply for the same purpose as specified in the entry clearance? The tribunal will need to establish a procedure for resolving such disputes because their resolution may be determinative of whether a person has a right of appeal against being refused leave to enter.

1 Nationality, Immigration and Asylum Act 2002, s 89(1), as substituted by IAN 2006, s 6. Note that a returning resident or a person returning to the UK with non-lapsing leave will not necessarily have entry clearance upon return but in seeking entry may rely on the previously granted leave. The want of entry clearance will not by itself prevent such a person appealing once the new s 89(1)(a) comes into effect. On return to the UK an immigration officer may cancel the person's leave and if that happens, he or she is to be treated for the purpose of the appeals provisions as if refused leave to enter at a time when the person had current entry clearance. See Immigration Act 1971, Sch 2, para 2A(9).
2 Nationality, Immigration and Asylum Act 2002, s 89(2), as substituted by IAN 2006, s 6.
3 Nationality, Immigration and Asylum Act 2002, s 89.
4 Nationality, Immigration and Asylum Act 2002, s 88.

Presence of appellants in the UK

18.23

[The text in sub-para (8) is to be replaced, after footnote 20, with the following:]

or to remove the person from the UK after entering or seeking entry in breach of a deportation order[1] unless (a) the person held an EEA family permit, registration certificate, residence card, a document certifying permanent residence or a permanent residence card on arrival in the UK or can otherwise prove permanent residence in the UK;[2] (b) the person has been in the UK in detention or on temporary admission for at least 3 months although not 'admitted' within the meaning of the regulations[3]; or (c) the person is in the UK and a ground of appeal is that the decision breaches the Human Rights Convention or the Refugee Convention and the Secretary of State has not certified the ground as clearly unfounded.[4]

[Add new sub-para (11):]

(11) The effect of s 7 of the Immigration, Asylum and Nationality Act 2006[5] is that a person is not able to appeal from within the UK against a decision to make a deportation order against him or her if the Secretary of State certifies that the decision was taken on the grounds that the person's removal from the UK would be in the interests of national security.[6] The person may appeal against the decision to make the deportation order from within the UK if he or she makes a human

rights claim unless the Secretary of State certifies that the person's removal would not breach the UK's obligations under the ECHR.[7] If such a certificate is made, the person may appeal against the certificate to the Special Immigration Appeals Commission and that appeal may be brought whilst in the UK.[8] There is no provision for an in-country appeal on Refugee Convention grounds against a certified decision to make a deportation order.

1 The Immigration (European Economic Area) Regulations 2006, SI 2006/1003, reg 27(1).
2 Regulation 27(2)(a).
3 Regulation 27(2)(b).
4 Regulation 27(2)(c).
5 Brought into force on 31 August 2006, inserting s 97A into Nationality, Immigration and Asylum Act 2002.
6 The new s 97A prevents the appeal from being brought in-country by disapplying Nationality, Immigration and Asylum Act 2002, s 92(2) (which otherwise applies to decisions to make deportation orders so that appeals against such decisions are 'in-country') and by disapplying s 92(4)(a) in respect of an asylum claim, the making of which would otherwise have the effect of permitting the appeal to be brought 'in-country'. In response to arguments that denial of an in-country right of appeal against deportation was unfair the government said (with breath-taking candour as to the value of an appellant's right to be heard by SIAC): 'I do not think that appellants are disadvantaged by conducting the appeal from overseas. In the great majority of cases, much of the evidence is closed; that is, the detail is not disclosed to the appellant. The noble Lord, Lord Avebury, referred to the role of the special advocate. The appellant of course will be able to have a solicitor to represent him or her and to deal with open evidence' (The Baroness of Ashton of Upholland, 7 February 2006, *Hansard* col 549).
7 New Nationality, Immigration and Asylum Act 2002, s 97A(2)(c)(iii).
8 New Nationality, Immigration and Asylum Act 2002, s 97A(3).

18.23A

[Add new paragraph:]

An appeal against a decision to give removal directions under IAN 2006, s 47 may be brought from within the UK[1] unless an asylum or human rights claim has been made and certified as clearly unfounded.[2]

1 IAN 2006, s 47(7).
2 IAN 2006, s 47(8).

Suspensory effect of an appeal

18.24

[In the text, after footnote 3 add:]

A deportation order may not be made whilst an appeal against the decision to make a deportation order could be brought or is pending.[1] However, under IAN 2006, s 7 comes into effect, if the Secretary of State certifies that the decision to make a deportation order was made on national security grounds then the possibility of an appeal being brought does not prevent the making of a deportation order.[2]

[In the text, after footnote 5 add:]

An appeal is 'pending' even if the tribunal makes a decision[3] that the notice of appeal was given out of time if the evidence clearly shows that the notice of appeal was given in time[4].

[Footnote 8 – add:]

In *YD (Turkey) v Secretary of State for the Home Department* [2006] EWCA Civ 52, [2006] 1 WLR 1646, (2006) Times, 28 February the Court of Appeal said that there could be no doubt that once permission to appeal on an out of time application had been granted an appeal would be pending under s 103B and s 78 would prevent the appellant's removal.

1 Nationality, Immigration and Asylum Act 2002, s 79.
2 Nationality, Immigration and Asylum Act 2002, s 97A(2)(a), to be inserted by IAN 2006, s 7, disapplying s 79 of the Nationality, Immigration and Asylum Act 2002.
3 Asylum and Immigration Tribunal (Procedure) Rules 2005, r 10(6).
4 *EA (Ghana)* [2006] UKAIT 00036.

18.27A

[Add new paragraph:]

Section 47 of the IAN 2006 (when it comes into force) will create a new power to make a decision to give directions for a person's removal. Such a decision to give removal directions can be given during the period when the person may bring an appeal against a variation decision or a revocation of leave. During that period, the person will have statutorily extended leave to enter or remain[1]. However, whilst a decision to give removal directions can be made whilst the person has statutorily extended leave, actual removal directions cannot be given until the leave ends[2].

1 Ie by Immigration Act 1971, ss 3C(2)(b) or 3D(2)(a), inserted by IAN 2006, s 11 with effect from 31 August 2006 – whilst an appeal could be brought against the variation decision or revocation of leave.
2 IAN 2006, s 47(1).

Entry clearance appeals

18.30

[NB:]

The paragraph in the original text should be read with para 18.21A of this supplement.

Refusal of leave to enter

18.31

[NB:]

IAN 2006, s 6 having come into force the main issue in relation to refusal of leave to enter will no longer be whether the appeal is in country or out of country. The main issue will be whether there is a right of appeal at all. In general, appeals against refusal of leave to enter may be in-country because possession of an entry clearance which is a precondition for having an appeal against refusal of leave to enter[1] is also a qualification for bringing an appeal in country.[2] The making of an asylum or human rights claim also enables an appeal against refusal of leave to enter to be brought[3] and to be brought in-country[4] unless the claim is certified as clearly unfounded.[5] Whilst a person who does not otherwise qualify to appeal against refusal of leave to enter can bring an appeal on race discrimination grounds,[6] such an appeal may not be brought whilst the person is in the UK.[7] In short, an appeal against refusal of leave to enter may be brought in country unless the person made an asylum or human rights claim which has been certified as clearly unfounded or the person is only able to appeal against the refusal of leave to enter by virtue of having race discrimination grounds of appeal. Prior to IAN 2006, s 6 being brought into force the holder of a work permit who is a British Overseas territories citizen, a British Overseas citizen, a British National (Overseas), a British protected person or a British subject could appeal in country against refusal of leave to enter.[8] The effect of s 6 is that such a person cannot appeal against refusal of leave to enter at all (unless one of the other criteria for having a right of appeal is satisfied).

1 IAN 2006, s 6 (creating new Nationality, Immigration and Asylum Act 2002, s 89(1)(a)).
2 Nationality, Immigration and Asylum Act 2002, s 92(3).
3 IAN 2006, s 6 (creating new Nationality, Immigration and Asylum Act 2002, s 89(2)).
4 Nationality, Immigration and Asylum Act 2002, s 92(4)(a).
5 Nationality, Immigration and Asylum Act 2002, s 94(2).
6 IAN 2006, s 6 (creating new Nationality, Immigration and Asylum Act 2002, s 89(2)).
7 Because Nationality, Immigration and Asylum Act 2002, s 92 does not apply to such an appeal.
8 Nationality, Immigration and Asylum Act 2002, s 92(3D).

Appeals by EEA nationals: refusal to issue or to renew, or revocation of residence documents

18.34

[NB:]

The references in the text and footnotes to the Immigration (European Economic Area) Regulations 2000 need to be substituted with the following references to the Immigration (European Economic Area) Regulations 2006, SI 2006/1003:

1 Regulation 20.
2 Regulation 20.
3 Regulation 20.
4 Regulation 20.

Deportation appeals

18.35

[Footnote 10:]

Delete 'The Immigration (European Economic Area) Regulations 2000, as amended' and substitute 'The Immigration (European Economic Area) Regulations 2006, SI 2006/1003, reg 28'.

18.36

[NB:]

The references in the footnotes to 'The Immigration (European Economic Area) Regulations 2000, as amended' need to be substituted with the following references to 'The Immigration (European Economic Area) Regulations 2006, SI 2006/1003':

1 Regulation 19(3)(b).
2 Regulation 24(3).
3 Regulation 28.
4 Regulation 26(6).
5 Regulation 29(6).
6 Regulation 27(1)(b).

EEA decisions to remove on grounds of non-qualification

18.38

[NB:]

Delete references in the footnotes to the 'Immigration (European Economic Area) Regulations 2000, as amended' and substitute with the following references to the 'Immigration (European Economic Area) Regulations 2006, SI 2006/1003':

1 Regulation 19(3)(a).
2 Regulation 24(2).
3 Regulation 26(2).
4 Regulation 26(3).
5 Regulation 26(7) and Sch 1.

One-stop appeals

18.40

[NB:]

As matters currently stand, a removal decision cannot be made at the same time as a variation decision because the recipient of an adverse variation decision will have his or her leave extended by Immigration Act 1971, s 3C. There is no power to make a removal decision against a person with statutorily extended leave. A removal decision (under the Immigration and Asylum Act 1999, s 10) can only be made once any appeal against the variation decision has been disposed of. Moreover, the removal decision gives rise to a new right of appeal. This state of affairs was perceived by the government as inimical to a one stop appeal, enabling a person to pursue sequential appeals, thereby delaying removal. The intention behind the IAN 2006, s 47 is to further the objective of a 'one-stop appeal'. It will enable a decision to give removal directions to be made as soon as a variation decision (either refusing to vary leave or varying leave so that the person has no leave) is made. The tribunal will hear appeals against the variation decision and the removal decision at the same time. If those appeals are dismissed, an immigration officer will be able to give removal directions against the person without the need for a further appealable immigration decision to be made.

18.43

[Footnote 5 – delete existing text and substitute:]

The Immigration (European Economic Area) Regulations 2006, SI 2006/1003, Sch 2, para 4(7) and (8).

POWERS OF THE TRIBUNAL

18.47

[In the text, after footnote 7 add:]

Even if an appellant is only able to appeal in country by virtue of having made a human rights claim,[1] he or she is not limited to pursuing human rights grounds of appeal but may rely on all of the statutory grounds.[2]

[Footnote 8 – add:]

So that an adjudicator had no jurisdiction to allow a s 83 appeal on the ground that the decision was 'not in accordance with the law' – *SS (Somalia)* [2005] UKAIT 00167. However, it is difficult to reconcile that limitation of the grounds of appeal to the issue of refugee status with the obligation imposed on the tribunal by s 86(3)(a) to allow an appeal under s 83 if the decision 'was not in accordance with the law'.

1 Nationality, Immigration and Asylum Act 2002, s 92(4).
2 *SA (Bangladesh)* [2005] UKAIT 00178.

'Including immigration rules'

18.56

[In the text, after footnote 2 add:]

The tribunal has held that in an entry clearance appeal, the rules to be considered by the tribunal are those in force at the time of the decision, not those applicable at the time of the application.[1]

[In the text, after footnote 9 add:]

However, if the facts known to the decision maker could support a ground for refusal that is not cited in the notice of decision, the tribunal is entitled to assume that that potential ground is not in issue.[2]

[At the end of the text add a new sub-para (8):]

(8) Given the obligation on the tribunal to consider circumstances in existence at the date of the hearing[3] (other than in entry clearance appeals and appeals against refusal of a certificate of entitlement), an appellant able to show that he or she meets the requirements of the rules at the time of the hearing is entitled to succeed on the ground that the decision was not in accordance with the rules even if he or she did not qualify at the time of the decision.[4]

[Footnote 8 – add:]

CP (Dominica) [2006] UKAIT 00040.

1 *PP and SP (India)* [2005] UKAIT 00141.
2 *RM (India)* [2006] UKAIT 00039.
3 Nationality, Immigration and Asylum Act 2002, s 85(4).
4 *LS (Gambia)* [2005] UKAIT 00085.

Reviewing questions of fact

18.63

[In the text, after footnote 7 add:]

The tribunal can hear of facts that were unknown to the original decision maker in an appeal against a refusal of entry clearance where the tribunal is limited to considering circumstances appertaining at the time of the decision.[1]

[In the text, immediately before footnote 9 and within the parentheses add:]

or 'is' not in accordance with the rules.[2]

[Footnote 3 – add:]

Hence in *SA (Pakistan)* [2006] UKAIT 00018 it was an error of law for an adjudicator to allow an appeal against refusal of entry clearance on Art 8 grounds by reference to the fact of a child born more than a year after the decision appealed against.

1 *DM (Zimbabwe)* [2005] UKAIT 00130.
2 *LS (Gambia)* [2005] UKAIT 00085.

The appellate jurisdiction in asylum and human rights appeals

18.66

[In the text, after footnote 4 add:]

The tribunal has held, in a starred decision[1] that human rights issues can only be raised in an appeal against a removal decision and not in an appeal against a variation decision. In reaching that conclusion, the only statutory ground of appeal that the tribunal considered was that 'removal of the appellant ... would be ... incompatible with the appellant's Convention rights'.[2] It did not consider whether a variation appeal might succeed on the broader human rights ground that the decision (as opposed to removal) might be 'unlawful ... as being incompatible with the appellant's human rights'.[3] Such unlawfulness might consist in rendering the presence of a person with a human rights claim to stay in the UK unlawful and indeed criminal[4] or it might consist in breaching the person's right to respect for his or her Art 8 rights by withholding lawful immigration status.[5] The Court of Appeal has now held that the tribunal was wrong to find that human rights issues could not be litigated where there was no decision to remove but its written judgment is still awaited.

Human rights issues can arise in relation to the method, route or destination of removal consequent on an immigration decision, but only if the appellant is able to discharge the burden of showing what the method, route or destination will be. It may be possible to do that if an immigration decision is accompanied by removal directions or, in the absence of removal directions if there is an applicable policy, statement or undertaking in relation to removal. Otherwise the only human rights issues that can be litigated will be the consequences of removal from the UK and of presence in the destination country.[6] The absence of removal directions did not prevent the tribunal from determining whether, if and when the appellant was eventually removed, he would be refused entry to his country of habitual residence and where such refusal would amount to persecution; the relevant ground for appeal ('removal in consequence of the immigration decision would breach the Refugee Convention'[7]) required a hypothetical question to be addressed and did not require the existence of removal directions[8].

1. *JM (Liberia)* [2006] UKAIT 00009
2. Nationality, Immigration and Asylum Act 2002, s 84(1)(g).
3. Nationality, Immigration and Asylum Act 2002, s 84(1)(c).
4. Immigration Act 1971, s 24(1)(b) making it a criminal offence to overstay a limited leave. On the tribunal's reasoning in JM a person would have to commit that offence before they would be subject to a removal decision attracting a meaningful appeal on human rights grounds.
5. Eg *Sisojeva v Latvia* (2005) ECtHR App. 60654/00 – Art 8 may entail not merely a negative obligation to refrain from removing but a positive obligation to confer such status as may be necessary to enable the individual to exercise the protected right; see also *R (on the application of S) v Secretary of State for the Home Department* (2006) Sullivan J, Admin (10 May 2006) (judicial review of the withholding of discretionary leave from successful appellants).
6. *GH v Secretary of State for the Home Department* [2005] EWCA Civ 1182, [2005] 42 LS Gaz R 25, [2005] All ER (D) 113 (Oct), upheld in the Court of Appeal which said 'the Home Department statutory scheme of immigration control postulated that someone who successfully maintained that their removal would constitute a violation of their ECHR rights should be entitled to leave to enter' – *S v Secretary of State for the Home Department (sub nom R (on the application of GG) v Secretary of State for the Home Department)* [2006] EWCA Civ 1157, [2006] All ER (D) 30 (Aug).
7. Nationality, Immigration and Asylum Act 2002, s 84(1)(g).
8. *AK v Secretary of State for the Home Department* [2006] EWCA Civ 1117, [2006] All ER (D) 470 (Jul).

[At the end of the sentence containing footnotes 9 and 10 add a new footnote 10A:]

[10A] *SA(Bangladesh)* [2005] UKAIT 00178.

Giving directions where an appeal is allowed

18.69

[In the text, after footnote 7 add:]

It would be an error of law for the tribunal, upon allowing an appeal, to direct the grant of entry clearance in cases where entry in a temporary capacity was being sought[1].

[At the end of the text add:]

Home Office policy is to give effect to a decision allowing an appeal, usually by granting leave[2] or asylum.[3] However, if an appellant wins an asylum appeal where nationality has been disputed by the Secretary of State his policy is, in certain circumstances, to make a new immigration decision, specifying an alternative country of destination instead of granting asylum. Those circumstances are that the Secretary of State has 'very strong grounds' such as 'reliable documentary evidence' to believe the person is entitled to reside in that alternative country and that he or she would not be at risk there. Otherwise, asylum would be granted.[4] Once an appeal against refusal of leave to enter has been allowed and there is no further appeal there is a clear duty on the Secretary of State to give effect to the immigration judge's decision; 'it would strike at the heart of the independent appeal system … if the Secretary of State felt free to deliberately circumvent an adverse decision by the Tribunal simply because he disagreed with the outcome on the merits'.[5]

1 *EA (Ghana)* [2005] UKIAT 00108; and *EB (Ghana)* [2005] UKAIT 00131.
2 Immigration Directorate Instruction, ch 12, s 4, para 6.3 'Handling Appeals'.
3 Asylum Directorate Instruction, 'Handling Appeals'.
4 Asylum Directorate Instruction 'Disputed Nationality: Allowed Appeals'.
5 *R (on the application of GG) v Secretary of State for the Home Department* [2006] EWHC 1111 (Admin), (2006) Times, 14 June, [2006] All ER (D) 143 (May); *affd sub nom S v Secretary of State for the Home Department (sub nom R (on the application of GG) v Secretary of State for the Home Department)* [2006] EWCA Civ 1157, [2006] All ER (D) 30 (Aug), upheld in *S v Secretary of State for the Home Department (sub nom R (on the application of GG) v Secretary of State for the Home Department)* [2006] EWCA Civ 1157, [2006] All ER (D) 30 (Aug).

[Footnote 9 – add:]

In *R (on the application of Rahman) v Entry Clearance Officer* [2006] EWHC 1755 (Admin), [2006] All ER (D) 143 (Jun), Newman J upheld the principle that following a successful appeal against refusal of entry clearance the Entry Clearance Officer could not embark on further enquiries intended to circumvent the decision on the appeal. The ECO was nevertheless obliged to determine whether, on the facts before him or her, including those that might establish earlier deception or mistake of fact, entry clearance should be granted.

Notices of action or decision

18.83

[Add at end:]

The Immigration (Notices) Regulations 2003 have been amended to enable the decision maker to specify more than one destination country if it appears to the decision maker that the person may be removable to more than one country[1].

1 The Immigration (Notices) (Amendment) Regulations 2006, SI 2006/2168, substituting a new reg 5(1) into the Notices Regulations.

Service of notice of decision

18.85

[In the text, after footnote 12 add:]

If a notice is sent other than by one of the methods required by the Notice Regulations[1] (eg by mail but not recorded delivery) then it will not be treated as lawfully served and time for appealing will not start to run against the recipient.[2]

1 Immigration (Notices) Regulations 2003, SI 2003/658, reg 7.
2 *OI (Nigeria)* [2006] UKAIT 00042.

Time limits for appealing

18.92

[In the text, after footnote 7 add:]

If the notice of decision is undated, it is likely that the only evidence as to the date on which it was served will be the appellant's and the tribunal will generally have to accept that.[1]

1 *OI (Nigeria)* [2006] UKAIT 00042.

Late notice of appeal

18.94

[Add at end:]

If the tribunal decides to treat a notice of appeal as being out of time but evidence clearly shows that it was given in time, the tribunal can ignore the previous decision and treat the appeal as pending.[1]

1 *EA (Ghana)* [2006] UKAIT 00036.

18.95

[Add at end:]

The tribunal has given the following guidance as to how decisions whether to extend time will be made:[1] the starting point will be the explanation for the lateness of the notice of appeal. The explanation would need to be supported by such evidence as is available. Admitted delay by the appellant's representative might be a satisfactory explanation. An extension of time could be granted no matter how long the delay, provided it was satisfactorily explained. Time would only be extended in the absence of a satisfactory explanation if there were exceptional reasons for doing so. Other factors to be considered include the merits of the grounds of appeal and the consequences for the appellant of the decision. Mistakes, breaches of rules of procedure or very long delays on the part of the respondent might make it unjust or disproportionate not to extend time for appealing.

1 *BO (Nigeria)* [2006] UKAIT 00035.

Respondent's duty to file appeal papers

18.100

[Add at end:]

The tribunal's policy of allowing entry clearance officers 19 weeks in which to file documents with the tribunal in appeals against refusal of settlement applications was held to be rational and lawful[1]. The tribunal operates a system to expedite appeals in cases where there are compelling compassionate circumstances; requests for expedition under the scheme are made to the Duty Immigration Judge at the AIT's Operational Support Centre in Loughborough[2].

1 *R (on the application of Uddin) v Asylum and Immigration Tribunal; R (on the application of Ali) v Asylum and Immigration Tribunal* [2006] EWHC 2127 (Admin), [2006] All ER (D) 36 (Aug).
2 See fn 1 above.

Abandonment of appeal

18.106

[NB:]

Section 9 of the IAN 2006 (when brought into force) will introduce welcome changes to the provisions for statutory abandonment. First of all, if an appellant is granted leave to enter or remain for a period exceeding 12 months he or she will be able to continue with the appeal on Refugee Convention grounds as long as the person gives notice in accordance with (yet to be drafted) Procedure Rules.[1] Secondly, a grant of leave to enter or remain in the UK will not prevent an appeal from being continued on race discrimination grounds so long as similar notice of the intention to continue with the appeal is given.[2] The effect of the current abandonment provisions is that a race discrimination ground of appeal cannot be pursued in the tribunal if leave to enter or remain is granted. In such circumstances, civil proceedings could then be brought under Race Relations Act 1976, s 57(1). However, civil proceedings cannot be brought if in the immigration proceedings the race discrimination ground has failed[3] and the immigration appeal is treated as abandoned before the decision on the race discrimination grounds can be overturned.[4] That possibility and the obvious unfairness to which it gives rise will be avoided by the amendment to the abandonment provisions.

[For the text in brackets immediately prior to footnote 5 in the original text substitute the following:]

(or, in an EEA appeal, a registration certificate, residence card, a document certifying permanent residence or a permanent residence card under the Immigration (European Economic Area) Regulations 2006 or a registration certificate under the Accession (Immigration and Worker Registration) Regulations 2004)[5].

1 Nationality, Immigration and Asylum Act 2002, s 104(4B) as to be substituted by IAN 2006, s 9.
2 Nationality, Immigration and Asylum Act 2002, s 104(4C) as to be substituted by IAN 2006, s 9.
3 Race Relations Act 1976, s 57A(1)(b).
4 *Emunefe v Secretary of State for the Home Department* [2005] EWCA Civ 1002.
5 Immigration (European Economic Area) Regulations 2006, SI 2006/1003, Sch 2, para 4(2).

TRIBUNAL HEARINGS

Adjournments

18.126

[Add to the text after footnote 3:]

It was an error of law for the tribunal to refuse an adjournment to obtain further evidence on a material issue in circumstances where the reliability of the existing evidence on that issue had not been questioned prior to the hearing.[1]

1 *Shkembi v Secretary of State for the Home Department* [2005] EWCA Civ 1592, [2005] All ER (D) 323 (Nov).

Procedure at the hearing

18.130

[Footnote 5 – add:]

XS (Serbia and Montenegro) [2005] UKIAT 00093.

Evidence

18.133

[NB:]

Evidence obtained by means of torture, whether in the UK or abroad and by whoever obtained is inadmissible in SIAC or in any other proceedings. In SIAC proceedings, if an appellant raises a plausible reason for believing that evidence relied on against him or her was obtained by torture, the Commission was bound to initiate relevant inquiries and to exclude the evidence if satisfied on a balance of probabilities that it was so obtained.[1]

1 *A v Secretary of State for the Home Department (No 2)* [2005] UKHL 71, [2006] 2 AC 221, [2006] 1 All ER 575.

18.134

[After footnote 14 add:]

In an asylum appeal an adjudicator was bound to take account of the grant of refugee status to the witness called to support the appellant's claim although the reliability and relevance of the witness' evidence was a matter for the adjudicator.[14A]

14A *AC (Somalia)* [2005] UKAIT 00124.

Credibility of witnesses

18.135

[After footnote 8 add:]

Where an allegation is made against a previous representative in order to explain a procedural failing or an earlier deficiency in the evidence, it will be difficult to establish the credibility of the allegation if evidence is not produced to show that it was put to the previous representative together with evidence of the reply or want of reply.[1]

1 *MM (Burundi)* [2004] UKIAT 00182*; *SV (Iran)* [2005] UKAIT 00160.

[After footnote 28 add:]

The Court of Appeal has warned that reliance by a decision maker on the 'inherent probability' of an account 'can be a dangerous, even a wholly inappropriate, factor to rely on in some asylum cases. Much of the evidence will be referable to societies with customs and circumstances which are very different from those of which the members of the fact-finding tribunal have any (even second hand) experience. Indeed, it is likely that the country which an asylum-seeker has left will be suffering from the sort of problems and dislocations with which the overwhelming majority of residents of this country will be wholly unfamiliar. The point is well made in *Hathaway on the Law of Refugee Status* (1991) at p 81: 'In assessing the general human rights information, decision-makers must constantly be on guard to avoid implicitly recharacterizing the nature of the risk based on the own perceptions of reasonability'.[1]

1 *HK v Secretary of State for the Home Department* [2006] EWCA Civ 1037, [2006] All ER (D) 281 (Jul). See also *Y v Secretary of State for the Home Department* [2006] EWCA Civ 1223.

[After footnote 30 add:]

It would be an error of law for the tribunal to reach an adverse view of an appellant's credibility without first having regard to the context provided by expert evidence (including medical and country evidence) and making the assessment of credibility in that context.[1] An immigration judge may rely on discrepancies in an appellant's testimony to put his or her veracity in question but they must also be evaluated in the context of the evidence as a whole; in some cases it is sufficient for the judge to identify the discrepancy and state his or her conclusion on the appellant's veracity. In other cases, the nature of the discrepancy may require further explanation of why it does or does not undermine the veracity of the testimony.[2]

1 *Mibanga v Secretary of State for the Home Department* [2005] EWCA Civ 367, [2005] All ER (D) 307 (Mar); and *SA v Secretary of State for the Home Department* [2006] EWCA Civ 1302, [2006] All ER (D) 103 (Oct), confirming the principle in *Mibanga*. See also *S v Secretary of State for the Home Department* [2006] EWCA Civ 1153.
2 *AK v Secretary of State for the Home Department* [2006] EWCA Civ 1182.

[Footnote 8 – add:]

C v Secretary of State for the Home Department [2006] EWCA Civ 151, [2006] All ER (D) 122 (Feb).

[Footnote 30 – add:]

Diaby v Secretary of State for the Home Department [2005] EWCA Civ 651, [2005] All ER (D) 32 (Jul).

18.135A

[Add new paragraph:]

Section 8 of the Asylum and Immigration (Treatment of Claimants etc) Act 2004 identifies various matters which the tribunal is obliged to consider as damaging the credibility of an asylum seeker or human rights claimant.[1] The obligation arises even if the matter predates the coming into force of s 8.[2] However, the assessment of credibility remains a matter for the tribunal considering the evidence as a whole and attaching such weight to individual features of the evidence as the tribunal considers appropriate.[3]

1 See 12.166 ff.
2 *MM (Iran)* [2005] UKAIT 00115.
3 *SM (Iran)* [2005] UKAIT 00116. See also Carnwath LJ's judgment in *Y v Secretary of State for the Home Department* [2006] EWCA Civ 1223.

18.137

[Add at end:]

An immigration judge should not reject an appellant's account of being tortured on the ground that there were no visible marks on the appellant's body unless medical evidence or the judge's own, explicitly disclosed expertise established that such marks would be present.[1] A GP's report is capable of constituting independent evidence of torture.[2] A medical report that merely documents scars or injuries without stating the doctor's opinion as to their consistency with the appellant's account will have little or no corroborative weight.[3] Those preparing medical reports intended as corroborative evidence would be well advised to have regard to the Istanbul Protocol,[4] paras 186–187 on 'Examination and Evaluation following specific forms of torture'.[5]

1 *Reka v Secretary of State for the Home Department* [2006] EWCA Civ 552, [2006] All ER (D) 224 (May).
2 *R (on the application of D) v Secretary of State for the Home Department; R (on the application of K) v same* [2006] EWHC 980 (Admin), 150 Sol Jo LB 743, [2006] All ER (D) 300 (May).
3 *SA v Secretary of State for the Home Department* [2006] EWCA Civ 1302, [2006] All ER (D) 103 (Oct).
4 *Manual on the Effective Investigation and Documentation of Torture and Other Cruel, Inhuman or Degrading Treatment of Punishment* (Submitted to the United Nations High Commissioner for Human Rights – 9 August 1999).
5 See fn 3 above.

[Footnote 2 – add:]

Diaby v Secretary of State for the Home Department [2005] EWCA Civ 651, [2005] All ER (D) 32 (Jul).

[Footnote 5 – add:]

KK v Secretary of State for the Home Department [2005] EWCA Civ 1082, [2005] All ER (D) 214 (Jul).

18.138

[In the text, after footnote 3 add:]

Instead of simply rejecting a claim to fear being persecuted because of a young appellant's inability to explain why she should be at risk, particular reliance should be placed on the background material to see whether it affords an explanation.[1]

1 *De Sousa v Secretary of State for the Home Department* [2006] EWCA Civ 183, [2006] All ER (D) 60 (Feb).

Evidence of post decision facts

18.139

[In the text, after footnote 11 add:]

An appeal against refusal of leave to remain had to be allowed because, although at the time of the decision the appellant could not qualify under the applicable immigration rule, by the time of the hearing she had become over 65 and so satisfied the requirements of another immigration rule.[1]

[1] *YZ and LK (China)* [2005] UKAIT 00157.

[Footnote 15 – add:]

AH (Bangladesh) [2006] UKAIT 00028 – nor would the reconsideration and upholding of the original decision in the explanatory statement amount to a new, appealable immigration decision.

EVIDENCE OF LIKE FACTS IN OTHER APPEALS

18.141

[Replace the text from footnote 2 to footnote 3 with the following:]

The AIT Practice Direction[1] provides that unreported determinations of the Tribunal may not be cited unless the appellant or a member of his family was a party to the proceedings in which the previous determination was issued or the tribunal gives permission. Such permission will be given 'only in exceptional cases' and an application for permission must include a full transcript of the determination; identify the proposition for which the determination is to be cited; certify that the proposition is not found in any reported determination of the AIT or IAT and has not been superseded by higher authority and be accompanied by an analysis of tribunal and decisions of higher authority on the same issue over the previous six months. The tribunal would not have regard to an unreported authority cited without compliance with the Practice Direction.[2]

[1] 4 April 2005, para 17.
[2] *KK (Sudan)* [2006] UKAIT 00008.

COUNTRY GUIDELINE DETERMINATIONS

18.142

[In the text, after footnote 10 add:]

Nevertheless, the AIT Practice Direction[1] provides that a country guidance decision is to be treated as binding authority on the country guidance issue identified in the determination insofar as the appeal relies on the same or similar evidence. The tribunal has refused to permit argument intended to challenge a country guidance decision unless supported by fresh evidence,[2] an approach that has been approved by the Court of Appeal.[3] On the other hand, the Court of Appeal has been willing to subject the tribunal's factual assessments in the making of country guidance decisions to the most detailed scrutiny.[4] Moreover, whilst the House of Lords has endorsed the principle that country guidance decisions should be followed by immigration judges, it added the qualification that 'in the end of the day each case, whether or not such guidance is available, must depend on an objective and fair assessment of its own facts'.[5]

[1] 4 April 2005, para 18.

2 *MY (Eritrea)* UKIAT 00158.
3 *Ariaya v Secretary of State for the Home Department* [2006] EWCA Civ 48, (2006) Times, 20 February, [2006] All ER (D) 93 (Feb).
4 Eg *S v Secretary of State for the Home Department* [2002] EWCA Civ 539, [2002] All ER (D) 212 (Apr); and *AA v Secretary of State for the Home Department; LK v Secretary of State for the Home Department* [2006] EWCA Civ 401, [2006] NLJR 681, (2006) Times, 17 April.
5 *Januzi v Secretary of State for the Home Department; Hamid v Same; Gaafar v Same; Mohammed v Same* [2006] UKHL 5, [2006] 3 All ER 305, [2006] 2 WLR 397 per Lord Hope, para 50.

Evidence of facts found in appeals by family members

18.144

[Add at end:]

Devaseelan principles apply to the approach that a tribunal should take to the findings of fact by another tribunal about a family member giving evidence in support of an appeal and those findings of fact could be displaced by evidence that had not been before the original tribunal.[1]

1 *Ocampo v Secretary of State for the Home Department* [2006] EWCA Civ 1276, [2006] All ER (D) 59 (Oct).

Previous findings of fact in respect of the same person

18.145

[At the end of the original text, add the following:]

It would be an error of law for an immigration judge to have regard to findings of fact made in an earlier determination if that determination was properly to be regarded as a nullity because it related to an appeal that had been abandoned.[1] However, even if all of the findings of fact in an earlier determination are vitiated owing to an error of law, the tribunal reconsidering the appeal should receive and be entitled to consider the original determination; only in special circumstances would the interests of justice require the reconsidering tribunal not to see the original determination.[2]

1 *N (Cameroon)* [2005] UKAIT 00146.
2 *Swash v Secretary of State for the Home Department* [2006] EWCA Civ 1093, (2006) Times, 14 August, [2006] All ER (D) 390 (Jul).

Burden and standard of proof

18.146

[At the end of sub-para (6) add:]

Internal flight is not a legitimate issue unless proper notice has been given by the Secretary of State that it is to be raised.[1]

1 *Daoud v Secretary of State for the Home Department* [2005] EWCA Civ 755, [2005] All ER (D) 259 (May).

18.147

[Add at end:]

Although proceedings in the AIT are predominantly adversarial, in a human rights case the Secretary of State has a public responsibility to assist the AIT to decide the real issues in the case including by the production of documents in his possession that may be of assistance to an appellant. The AIT also has an obligation to ascertain enough to make an informed decision on the critical issues.[1]

1 *Rahman v Secretary of State for the Home Department* [2005] EWCA Civ 1826, [2005] All ER (D) 267 (Dec). See also *Mukarkar v Secretary of State for the Home Department* [2006] EWCA Civ 1045, (2006) Times, 16 August, [2006] All ER (D) 367 (Jul); and *CS (Jamaica)* [2006] UKAIT 00004.

Making a determination

18.158

[Add at end:]

There is a statutory obligation on the tribunal to determine 'any matter raised as a ground of appeal'.[1] The tribunal may not, because it decides to allow an appeal on one ground, decline to determine the other grounds of appeal.

1 Nationality, Immigration and Asylum Act 2002, s 86(2)(a); *Emunefe v Secretary of State for the Home Department* [2005] EWCA Civ 1002; *CS (Jamaica)* [2006] UKAIT 00004.

ONWARD APPEALS AND REVIEW

Error of law

18.166

[NB:]

The Court of Appeal has recently given much consideration to the question of what is an error of law in the various statutory contexts relating to immigration appeals where that issue arises or arose.[1] In *R v Secretary of State for the Home Department*[2] the court gave guidance on the points of law most frequently encountered in practice and categorised them as follows:

'(i) making perverse or irrational findings on a matter or matters that were material to the outcome ("material matters");
(ii) failing to give reasons or any adequate reasons for findings on material matters;
(iii) failing to take into account and/or resolve conflicts of fact or opinion on material matters;
(iv) giving weight to immaterial matters;
(v) making a material misdirection of law on any material matter;
(vi) committing or permitting a procedural or other irregularity capable of making a material difference to the outcome or the fairness of proceedings;
(vii) making a mistake as to a material fact which could be established by objective and uncontentious evidence, where the appellant and/or his

> advisers were not responsible for the mistake, and where unfairness resulted from the fact that a mistake was made'.

Further consideration is given to these errors of law in the following paragraphs.

1 Nationality, Immigration and Asylum Act 2002, s 101 (repealed on 4 April 2005) which limited the right of appeal to the tribunal to 'a point of law' and now s 103A where an order for reconsideration may be made of the Tribunal 'may have made an error of law' and the Asylum and Immigration Tribunal (Procedure) Rules 2005, r 31(2)(a) where, on reconsideration, the tribunal is required to determine whether there was a 'material error of law'.

2 [2005] EWCA Civ 982, (2005) Times, 19 August, [2005] All ER (D) 384 (Jul).

Perversity

18.166A

[Add new paragraph:]

Perversity amounting to an error of law can be established if the 'decision is one to which no reasonable decision maker, properly instructing himself on the law could have come on the evidence before him',[1] it does not require 'wilful or conscious departure from the rational. A finding of fact which is wholly unsupported by the evidence is capable of amounting to an error of law by this analysis'[2] as is a finding of fact that is unfounded or erroneous.[3]

1 Keene LJ in *Miftari v Secretary of State for the Home Department* [2005] EWCA Civ 481, [2005] All ER (D) 279 (May).

2 Maurice Kay LJ in *Miftari*.

3 *Krasniqi v Secretary of State for the Home Department* [2006] EWCA Civ 391, (2006) Times, 20 April.

Failure to give adequate reasons

18.166B

[Add new paragraph:]

Failure to give adequate reasons would be an error of law.[1] However, an immigration judge is not required to give reasons for findings on matters of peripheral importance and an appellate court would be anxious to avoid overturning a first instance decision for want of reasoning 'unless it really cannot understand the original judge's thought processes when he/she was making material findings'.[2] If one or some of the reasons given by the tribunal for its decision are found to be unsustainable, the question then to be determined is whether it would nevertheless be just to let the tribunal's decision stand; answering that question depends upon whether the tribunal's decision would have been the same on the basis of the reasons which have survived scrutiny.[3] Reasons should be given for rejecting the opinion of an expert.[4] The Court of Appeal does not have power to invite the tribunal to supplement its reasoning as an alternative to determining whether the tribunal had erred in law by failing to give adequate reasons.[5]

1 *R v Secretary of State for the Home Department* [2005] EWCA Civ 982, (2005) Times, 19 August, [2005] All ER (D) 384 (Jul).

2 *R v Secretary of State for the Home Department* having cited with approval *Eagil Trust Co Ltd v Pigott Brown* [1985] 3 All ER 119, CA and *English v Emery Reimbold & Strick Ltd* [2002] EWCA Civ 605, [2002] 3 All ER 385, [2002] 1 WLR 2409. The Court of Appeal in *Barikzai v Secretary of State for the Home Department* [2006] EWCA Civ 922, 150 Sol Jo LB 705, [2006] All ER (D) 302 (May) suggested that the giving of inadequate reasons did not by itself establish an error of law and that it would be necessary to show, in addition, that the tribunal's decision was perverse. This would seem to be a radical departure from the well established principle that the tribunal has an obligation to give adequate reasons for its decisions, failing in which is an error of law, as acknowledged in *R (Iran)* [2005] EWCA Civ 982 and recently applied without the additional perversity requirement in, for example, *DK v Secretary of State for the Home Department* [2006] EWCA Civ 682 (failure by the tribunal to explain why it was 'not greatly assisted' by relevant country expert evidence); *EK v Secretary of State for the Home Department* [2006] EWCA Civ 926 (failure by adjudicator to give adequate reasons for the conclusion that the appellant was living alone); *Hussein v Secretary of State for the Home Department* [2006] EWCA Civ 953, [2006] All ER (D) 221 (Jun) (failure by the tribunal to give reasons for rejecting the evidence in the appellant's witness statement); *Malaba v Secretary of State for the Home Department* [2006] EWCA Civ 820, [2006] All ER (D) 225 (Jun) (failure by the adjudicator to give adequate reasons for her finding that discrepancies in the appellant's evidence did not undermine the core of her account. In that case, Pill LJ said: 'In assessing the adequacy of a fact-finding exercise, an appellate tribunal not only tells the losing party why he has lost but may also be able to demonstrate that it has adequately and conscientiously addressed the issue of fact which has arisen. That is particularly important when it is the credibility of an applicant which is in issue. A lack of reasoning may demonstrate a failure adequately to address the fundamental question: "Is the applicant telling the truth?" ').

3 *HK v Secretary of State for the Home Department* [2006] EWCA Civ 1037, [2006] All ER (D) 281 (Jul).

4 *Mibanga v Secretary of State for the Home Department* [2005] EWCA Civ 367, [2005] All ER (D) 307 (Mar).

5 *Hatungimana v Secretary of State for the Home Department* [2006] EWCA Civ 231, (2006) Times, 2 March, [2006] All ER (D) 281 (Feb).

Proportionality

18.166C

[Add new paragraph:]

In relation to a judgment on proportionality under Art 8 ECHR so long as the immigration judge 'correctly directed himself as to his duty under the law, and clearly adopted the approach prescribed in *Razgar*[1] and *Huang*,[2] then an error of law could be found only on 'traditional public law' grounds.[3] However, although a finding as to whether a case is 'truly exceptional' (made for the purpose of determining whether an interference with a right protected by Art 8 is disproportionate) is a question of fact, it is a question of 'secondary fact dictated by law and therefore ... susceptible to closer scrutiny than findings of primary fact'.[4] If a tribunal allows an appeal on Art 8 grounds by taking 'what may seem an unusually generous view of the facts of a particular case' that 'does not mean that it has made an error of law'.[5]

1 *R (on the application of Razgar) v Secretary of State for the Home Department* [2004] UKHL 27, [2004] 2 AC 368, [2004] 3 All ER 821, [2004] 3 WLR 58.

2 *Huang v Secretary of State for the Home Department* [2005] EWCA Civ 105, [2006] QB 1.

[3] *R v Secretary of State for the Home Department* [2005] EWCA Civ 982, (2005) Times, 19 August, [2005] All ER (D) 384 (Jul). See *Boran v Secretary of State for the Home Department* [2005] EWCA Civ 1141, [2005] All ER (D) 198 (Oct) as an example of a failure by the immigration judge to direct himself properly as to the need for 'exceptionality' to find a breach of Art 8 amounting to an error of law. See also *Jasarevic v Secretary of State for the Home Department* [2005] EWCA Civ 1784, [2005] All ER (D) 87 (Dec).

[4] *Krasniqi v Secretary of State for the Home Department* [2006] EWCA Civ 391, (2006) Times, 20 April per Sedley LJ.

[5] *Mukarkar v Secretary of State for the Home Department* [2006] EWCA Civ 1045, (2006) Times, 16 August, [2006] All ER (D) 367 (Jul).

Failure to follow a relevant country guidance decision

18.166D

[Add new paragraph:]

'Failure to apply a country guidance decision unless there was good reason, explicitly stated, for not doing so would constitute an error of law in that a material consideration had been ignored or legally inadequate reasons for the decision had been given'.[1] It would be an error of law for the tribunal to determine an appeal inconsistently with relevant country guidance, even in circumstances where the country guidance was not placed before the tribunal and even if the factual assessment made by the tribunal was based upon a concession (inconsistent with the country guidance) made by the appellant's representative.[2] However, an error of law could not be established by reference to failure to follow a country guidance decision that post-dated the decision under challenge.[3]

[1] *R v Secretary of State for the Home Department* [2005] EWCA Civ 982, (2005) Times, 19 August, [2005] All ER (D) 384 (Jul), approving Ouseley J's analysis of tribunal country guidance in *NM (Somalia) CG* [2005] UKIAT 00076 and the AIT *Practice Direction* (4 April 2005).

[2] *Bozkurt v Secretary of State for the Home Department* [2006] EWCA Civ 289, [2006] All ER (D) 188 (Feb).

[3] *AK v Secretary of State for the Home Department* [2006] EWCA Civ 1117, [2006] All ER (D) 470 (Jul).

Failure to have regard to relevant considerations/taking account of irrelevant considerations

18.166E

[Add new paragraph:]

Misunderstanding of evidence by an immigration judge would be an error of fact rather than an error of law. However, were the judge then to rely upon the evidence as misunderstood that would be to make a decision on the basis of no evidence which would amount to an error of law.[1]

[1] Buxton LJ in *Miftari v Secretary of State for the Home Department* [2005] EWCA Civ 481, [2005] All ER (D) 279 (May).

Unfairness resulting from a mistake of fact

18.166F

[Add new paragraph:]

Unfairness resulting from a mistake of fact and amounting to an error of law ordinarily required the following to be established:

> '(i) there must have been a mistake as to an existing fact, including a mistake as to the availability of evidence on a particular matter;
> (ii) it must be possible to categorise the relevant fact or evidence as "established" in the sense that it was uncontentious and objectively verifiable;
> (iii) the appellant (or his advsers) must not have been responsible for the mistake;
> (iv) the mistake must have played a material (not necessarily decisive) part in the tribunal's reasoning'.[1]

New evidence to establish the existence of such a mistake could be admitted if the '*Ladd v Marshall* principles'[2] could be satisfied, although they might be departed from in exceptional circumstances where the interests of justice required.[3] Those principles are that:

(a) the new evidence could not with reasonable diligence have been obtained for use at the trial (or hearing);
(b) the new evidence must be such that, if given, it would probably have had an important influence on the result of the case (though it need not be decisive); and
(c) the new evidence was apparently credible although it need not be incontrovertible.

The Court of Appeal[4] and the tribunal[5] have held that in certain circumstances new evidence undermining the credibility of a successful appellant may be relied on to establish an error of fact amounting to an error of law. However, the Court of Appeal has subsequently indicated that the issue of whether and in what circumstances such an approach may be adopted needs to be revisited.[6]

1 *R v Secretary of State for the Home Department* [2005] EWCA Civ 982, (2005) Times, 19 August, [2005] All ER (D) 384 (Jul), citing *E v Secretary of State for the Home Department* [2004] EWCA Civ 49, [2004] QB 1044, [2004] 2 WLR 1351.
2 A reference to *Ladd v Marshall* [1954] 3 All ER 745, [1954] 1 WLR 1489, 98 Sol Jo 870, CA.
3 *R v Secretary of State for the Home Department* [2005] EWCA Civ 982, (2005) Times, 19 August, [2005] All ER (D) 384 (Jul).
4 *Verde v Secretary of State for the Home Department* [2004] EWCA Civ 1726, [2004] All ER (D) 75 (Dec).
5 *EA (Ghana)* [2005] UKAIT 00108.
6 *Shaheen v Secretary of State for the Home Department* [2005] EWCA Civ 1294, [2005] All ER (D) 31 (Nov).

Application for reconsideration

18.167

[Footnote 16 – add at beginning:]

BO (Nigeria) [2006] UKAIT 00035 confirming that a decision not to extend time for appealing is not susceptible to reconsideration under Nationality, Immigration and Asylum Act 2002, s 103A.

Grounds of appeal

18.167A

[Add new paragraph:]

There has been much litigation about whether, on an appeal from an adjudicator to the Immigration Appeal Tribunal on a point of law,[1] the Tribunal was restricted to consideration of what was contained in the grounds of appeal or whether it could consider other apparent errors of law in the adjudicator's determination. These cases remain of relevance, notwithstanding abolition of the Immigration Appeal Tribunal, in relation to the development of principles concerning the jurisdiction of the Asylum and Immigration Tribunal on reconsideration of an appeal.[2] In the context of an appeal from an adjudicator to the Immigration Appeal Tribunal on a point of law it was clearly established that the Tribunal only had jurisdiction to consider what was legitimately to be found in the grounds of appeal as originally propounded or amended.[3] Even if it was clear that the adjudicator had made an error of law, the tribunal did not have jurisdiction to allow an appeal if the grounds of appeal (as originally propounded or amended) had not identified that error.[4] The Court would look at the grounds in a 'fair and reasonable fashion', not pedantically[5] or in a narrow and formalistic way[6] in order to discern whether a point of law could be found in them and an appeal would not fail simply on a point of language.[7] The Court of Appeal has held that perversity had to be expressly pleaded and grounds that merely articulated a factual disagreement would not establish jurisdiction to consider perversity[8] but that strict approach has not been maintained.[9] An exception to the principle that inclusion of a point within the grounds of appeal was necessary to establish jurisdiction[10] was the obligation on the tribunal to consider an obvious point of refugee Convention law that might avail an appellant, even if not pleaded in the grounds[11]. That obligation was a 'one way street'[12] save for the 'modest extension'[13] on behalf of the Secretary of State that was necessary to avoid a possible breach of the Refugee Convention that would result from recognising a person as a refugee in breach of one of the exclusion clauses[14]. The Secretary of State has conceded that the *Robinson* principle also applies on an application for reconsideration even if, by virtue of transitional provisions[15] the reconsideration is limited to the grounds upon which the Immigration Appeal Tribunal had granted permission to appeal.[16]

1 Under the now repealed Nationality, Immigration and Asylum Act 2002, s 101.
2 Nationality, Immigration and Asylum Act 2002, s 103A and the Asylum and Immigration Tribunal (Procedure) Rules 2005, r 31(2)(a).

[3] *Miftari v Secretary of State for the Home Department* [2005] EWCA Civ 481, [2005] All ER (D) 279 (May). See also *B v Secretary of State for the Home Department* [2005] EWCA Civ 61, [2005] All ER (D) 15 (Feb).
[4] As in *Miftari* and also *H v Secretary of State for the Home Department* [2005] EWCA Civ 1603, [2005] All ER (D) 306 (Dec).
[5] *Jasarevic v Secretary of State for the Home Department* [2005] EWCA Civ 1784, [2005] All ER (D) 87 (Dec).
[6] *R (on the application of Rodriguez-Torres) v Secretary of State for the Home Department* [2005] EWCA Civ 1328, (2005) Times, 6 December.
[7] *K v Secretary of State for the Home Department* [2005] EWCA Civ 1655, 149 Sol Jo LB 1455, [2005] All ER (D) 318 (Nov).
[8] Abbas v Secretary of State for the Home Department [2005] EWCA Civ 992, [2005] All ER (D) 34 (Jul).
[9] *IO (Congo) v Secretary of State for the Home Department* [2006] EWCA Civ 796.
[10] *Miftari v Secretary of State for the Home Department* [2005] EWCA Civ 481, [2005] All ER (D) 279 (May).
[11] *R v Secretary of State for the Home Department, ex p Robinson* [1998] QB 929, [1997] 4 All ER 210, [1997] 3 WLR 1162, [1997] NLJR 1345, CA.
[12] *Miftari v Secretary of State for the Home Department* [2005] EWCA Civ 481, [2005] All ER (D) 279 (May) per Maurice Kay LJ.
[13] *H v Secretary of State for the Home Department* [2005] EWCA Civ 1603, [2005] All ER (D) 306 (Dec).
[14] *A (Iraq) v Secretary of State for the Home Department* [2005] EWCA Civ 1438, 149 Sol Jo LB 1492, [2005] All ER (D) 22 (Dec) – withholding from the Secretary of State the benefit of the Robinson principle and thereby preventing the Refugee Convention exclusion clause from being raised for the first time in the tribunal might have led to a person being recognised as a refugee in breach of the obligation to exclude. In *GH (Afghanistan)* the Court of Appeal indicated that it would be reluctant to extend the principle further to the benefit of the Secretary of State, 'not least because the inequality of resources between the government and the average asylum seeker makes it unattractive for the Secretary of State to appeal to a forensic indulgence originally formulated in favour of the asylum-seeker'.
[15] The Asylum and Immigration Tribunal (Procedure) Rules 2005, r 62(7), applicable to appeals pending before the Immigration Appeal Tribunal prior to 4 April 2005 where, by virtue of a transitional provisions order, the grant of permission to appeal is treated as an order for the Tribunal to reconsider the adjudicator's determination. In such a case, the tribunal has held, the reconsideration is limited to the grounds upon which permission to appeal to the tribunal was granted and that the tribunal cannot permit the grounds to be amended: *JM(Liberia)** [2006] UKAIT 00009.
[16] *A v Secretary of State for the Home Department* [2006] EWCA Civ 149, [2006] All ER (D) 95 (Feb).

Grounds for reconsideration

18.167B

[Add new paragraph:]

The jurisdiction of the Asylum and Immigration Tribunal upon reconsidering an appeal is not so confined and its jurisdiction is not limited to consideration of what can be found in the grounds.[1] When an Immigration Judge makes an order that the tribunal is to reconsider its decision on the appeal[2] he or she must 'state the grounds on which the Tribunal is ordered to reconsider its decision on the appeal'.[3] The tribunal has held, however, that that statement of grounds does not have the effect of defining or limiting the issues before the tribunal when it determines the issue of whether the original tribunal made a material error of law[4] or (if it finds such an error) when it makes its own decision on the appeal.[5] The statement of grounds merely explains why the judge ordered that reconsideration take place. Nevertheless, the tribunal should be rigorous in ensuring that a new decision is made on an appeal (ie that it should go to 'second stage reconsideration') only if there is an issue of law[6]. The tribunal's jurisdiction is limited (so the tribunal has held) not by the grounds upon which the application for reconsideration was made, but only by the grounds upon which the appeal against the immigration decision was originally brought[7]. The Court of Appeal has also held that the grounds on which reconsideration was sought do not conclusively determine the scope of the tribunal's jurisdiction, but has been more circumspect than the tribunal saying that on a reconsideration '*depending on the terms on which it was ordered*, the AIT may review the whole case'[8] [emphasis added].

1 *AA v Secretary of State for the Home Department; LK v Secretary of State for the Home Department* [2006] EWCA Civ 401, [2006] NLJR 681, (2006) Times, 17 April. Accordingly, the Court of Appeal permitted the Secretary of State to raise an issue in the Court of Appeal that had not been raised in the tribunal. See also *Hussain v Secretary of State for the Home Department* [2006] EWCA Civ 382 'by virtue of section 103A the AIT has jurisdiction if there is an error of law. The section does not require the error to be pleaded in the grounds'.
2 Under Nationality, Immigration and Asylum Act 2002, s 103A(1).
3 Asylum and Immigration Tribunal (Procedure) Rules 2005, r 27(2)(a).
4 Asylum and Immigration Tribunal (Procedure) Rules 2005, r 31(2)(a).
5 Asylum and Immigration Tribunal (Procedure) Rules 2005, r 31(3).
6 *Krasniqi v Secretary of State for the Home Department* [2006] EWCA Civ 391, (2006) Times, 20 April.
7 *AH (Sudan)* [2006] UKAIT 00038.
8 *AA v Secretary of State for the Home Department* (n 1 above), para 82: 'On such a reconsideration, depending on the terms on which it was ordered, the AIT may review the whole case. It is not exercising the confined jurisdiction of the IAT under s 101(1) of the 2002 Act. Accordingly the restricted approach required by *Miftari* and later cases does not apply. That is not to authorise a free for all in this court. All applicable procedural requirements must be respected, and if an appellant seeks to raise a new point here the court will be alert to see that the other side suffers no prejudice. So much is in truth elementary. That said, the court will entertain a new point if it thinks it just and right to do so; that is no less elementary'.

The reconsideration hearing

18.174

[In the text, after footnote 8 add as follows:]

If the tribunal purports to find an error of law it must be properly identified and explained in its determination.[1] The Immigration Judge who orders reconsideration of an appeal is obliged to state the grounds upon which the tribunal is to reconsider its decision.[2] However, when deciding whether the original tribunal made a material error of law[3] the tribunal is not limited to considering the grounds stated by the Immigration Judge who ordered reconsideration[4] nor is it limited to considering the grounds upon which the order for reconsideration was sought.[5] If an error of law is found, the tribunal may carry on to substitute its own decision on the appeal or it may adjourn the hearing for further reconsideration, possibly by a different judge or panel of judges. If the reconsideration is adjourned following the finding of an error of law, the tribunal that made that finding should set out its reasons for that finding in writing and its written reasons should be made available to the parties appearing at the further reconsideration hearing[6]. In 'very exceptional cases' the parties should be able to argue at the further reconsideration hearing either that the tribunal was wrong to have found an error of law in the original decision or that it should have found additional or alternative errors of law.[7] It would normally be an abuse of process to apply for judicial review of a tribunal's decision that there is a material error of law in the original determination, given the availability of an appeal to the Court of Appeal once the reconsideration is concluded.[8] The reconsidering tribunal would normally be in possession of the original determination and would be entitled to consider it, even where the findings of fact made were vitiated by error of law.[9]

1 *Abdulrahman v Secretary of State for the Home Department* [2005] EWCA Civ 1620, 149 Sol Jo LB 1451, [2005] All ER (D) 263 (Nov).
2 Asylum and Immigration Tribunal (Procedure) Rules 2005, r 27(2)(a).
3 Asylum and Immigration Tribunal (Procedure) Rules 2005, r 31(2)(a).
4 *R (on the application of Wani) v Secretary of State for the Home Department* [2005] EWHC 2815 (Admin), [2005] All ER (D) 279 (Dec). However, as the law currently stands, in 'transitional cases' (i e where leave to appeal was granted by the Immigration Appeal Tribunal before 4 April 2005 and the appeal is then treated as a reconsideration) to which the Asylum and Immigration Tribunal (Procedure) Rules 2005, r 62(7) applies, the reconsideration is limited to the grounds upon which the Immigration Appeal Tribunal granted leave to appeal. Whether this is correct is soon to be decided by the Court of Appeal.
5 *AH (Sudan)* [2006] UKAIT 00038.
6 *R (Wani)*: see fn 4 above.
7 *R (Wani)*: see fn 4 above.
8 *R (Wani)*: see fn 4 above.
9 *Swash v Secretary of State for the Home Department* [2006] EWCA Civ 1093, (2006) Times, 14 August, [2006] All ER (D) 390 (Jul).

Appeal to the Court of Appeal or Court of Session

18.178

[Add at end:]

If the tribunal upon reconsideration of the appeal upheld the original decision of the adjudicator or tribunal then it would not be enough to show an error of law in the decision on the reconsideration; it would also be necessary to identify an error of law in the original tribunal's decision which was uncorrected by the reconsideration.[1]

1 *Amare v Secretary of State for the Home Department* [2005] EWCA Civ 1600, [2005] All ER (D) 300 (Dec); and *Reka v Secretary of State for the Home Department* [2006] EWCA Civ 552, [2006] All ER (D) 224 (May).

18.179

[In the text, after the sentence which follows footnote 9 add:]

If the time limit for applying to the tribunal for permission to appeal to the Court of Appeal has passed, then notwithstanding that the tribunal may not extend time for the making of such an application[1] an application to the tribunal must be made before the Court of Appeal can entertain an application for permission. The Court of Appeal will treat the tribunal's refusal to accept the out of time application because it has no jurisdiction to do so as being the refusal of permission by the tribunal that is required to establish the Court's jurisdiction.[2] Whilst the Court of Appeal considers the out of time application for permission to appeal it has an inherent jurisdiction to order a stay on removal.[3]

1 The Asylum and Immigration Tribunal (Procedure) Rules 2005, r 35(2).
2 Nationality, Immigration and Asylum Act 2002, ss 103B(3)(b) and 103E(3)(b). See *Yacoubou v Secretary of State for the Home Department* [2005] EWCA Civ 1051 holding that *Ozdemir v Secretary of State for the Home Department* [2003] EWCA Civ 167 applies to appeals under ss 103B and 103E.
3 *YD (Turkey) v Secretary of State for the Home Department* [2006] EWCA Civ 52, [2006] 1 WLR 1646, (2006) Times, 28 February.

Appendix

LEGISLATION AND MATERIALS

CONTENTS

European legislation

UK IMMIGRATION STATUTES

IMMIGRATION, ASYLUM AND NATIONALITY ACT 2006

2006 CHAPTER 13

An Act to make provision about immigration, asylum and nationality; and for connected purposes.

[30th March 2006]

Be it enacted by the Queen's most Excellent Majesty, by and with the advice and consent of the Lords Spiritual and Temporal, and Commons, in this present Parliament assembled, and by the authority of the same, as follows:—

APPEALS

1 Variation of leave to enter or remain

After section 83 of the Nationality, Immigration and Asylum Act 2002 (c 41) (right of appeal: asylum claim) insert—

"83A Appeal: variation of limited leave

(1) This section applies where—

(a) a person has made an asylum claim,
(b) he was granted limited leave to enter or remain in the United Kingdom as a refugee within the meaning of the Refugee Convention,
(c) a decision is made that he is not a refugee, and
(d) following the decision specified in paragraph (c) he has limited leave to enter or remain in the United Kingdom otherwise than as a refugee.

(2) The person may appeal to the Tribunal against the decision to curtail or to refuse to extend his limited leave."

Appointment
31 August 2006: see SI 2006/2226, art 3, Sch 1; for transitional provisions see art 4(1) thereof.

2 Removal

In section 82(2)(g) of the Nationality, Immigration and Asylum Act 2002 (c 41) (right of appeal: removal) for "section 10(1)(a), (b) or (c)" substitute "section 10(1)(a), (b), (ba) or (c)".

Appointment
31 August 2006: see SI 2006/2226, art 3, Sch 1; for transitional provisions see art 4(1) thereof.

3 Grounds of appeal

After section 84(3) of the Nationality, Immigration and Asylum Act 2002 (c 41) (grounds of appeal) add—

"(4) An appeal under section 83A must be brought on the grounds that removal of the appellant from the United Kingdom would breach the United Kingdom's obligations under the Refugee Convention."

Appointment
31 August 2006: see SI 2006/2226, art 3, Sch 1; for transitional provisions see art 4(1) thereof.

4 Entry clearance

(1) For sections 88A, 90 and 91 of the Nationality, Immigration and Asylum Act 2002 (restricted right of appeal in relation to refusal of entry clearance for visitor or student) substitute—

"88A Entry clearance

(1) A person may not appeal under section 82(1) against refusal of an application for entry clearance unless the application was made for the purpose of—

- (a) visiting a person of a class or description prescribed by regulations for the purpose of this subsection, or
- (b) entering as the dependant of a person in circumstances prescribed by regulations for the purpose of this subsection.

(2) Regulations under subsection (1) may, in particular—

- (a) make provision by reference to whether the applicant is a member of the family (within such meaning as the regulations may assign) of the person he seeks to visit;
- (b) provide for the determination of whether one person is dependent on another;
- (c) make provision by reference to the circumstances of the applicant, of the person whom the applicant seeks to visit or on whom he depends, or of both (and the regulations may, in particular, include provision by reference to—
  - (i) whether or not a person is lawfully settled in the United Kingdom within such meaning as the regulations may assign;
  - (ii) the duration of two individuals' residence together);
- (d) make provision by reference to an applicant's purpose in entering as a dependant;
- (e) make provision by reference to immigration rules;
- (f) confer a discretion.

(3) Subsection (1)—

- (a) does not prevent the bringing of an appeal on either or both of the grounds referred to in section 84(1)(b) and (c), and
- (b) is without prejudice to the effect of section 88 in relation to an appeal under section 82(1) against refusal of entry clearance."

(2) For section 23(1) of the Immigration and Asylum Act 1999 (c 33) (monitoring refusals of entry clearance) substitute—

"(1) The Secretary of State must appoint a person to monitor, in such manner as the Secretary of State may determine, refusals of entry clearance in cases where, as a result of section 88A of the Nationality, Immigration and Asylum Act 2002 (c 41) (entry clearance: non-family visitors and students), an appeal under section 82(1) of that Act may be brought only on the grounds referred to in section 84(1)(b) and (c) of that Act (racial discrimination and human rights)."

(3) Within the period of three years beginning with the commencement (for any purpose) of subsection (1), the Secretary of State shall lay before Parliament a report about the effect of that subsection; and the report—

- (a) must specify the number of applications for entry clearance made during that period,
- (b) must specify the number of those applications refused,
- (c) must specify the number of those applications granted, after an initial indication to the applicant of intention to refuse the application, as a result of further consideration in accordance with arrangements established by the Secretary of State,

(d) must describe those arrangements,
(e) must describe the effect of regulations made under section 88A(1)(a) or (b) as substituted by subsection (1) above,
(f) may include other information about the process and criteria used to determine applications for entry clearance, and
(g) may record opinions.

Appointment
To be appointed: see s 62(1).

5 Failure to provide documents

After section 88(2)(b) of the Nationality, Immigration and Asylum Act 2002 (c 41) (appeal: ineligibility) insert—

"(ba)has failed to supply a medical report or a medical certificate in accordance with a requirement of immigration rules,".

Appointment
31 August 2006: see SI 2006/2226, art 3, Sch 1; for transitional provisions see art 4(1) thereof.

6 Refusal of leave to enter

For section 89 of the Nationality, Immigration and Asylum Act 2002 (appeal against refusal of leave to enter: visitor or student without entry clearance) substitute—

"89 Refusal of leave to enter

(1) A person may not appeal under section 82(1) against refusal of leave to enter the United Kingdom unless—

(a) on his arrival in the United Kingdom he had entry clearance, and
(b) the purpose of entry specified in the entry clearance is the same as that specified in his application for leave to enter.

(2) Subsection (1) does not prevent the bringing of an appeal on any or all of the grounds referred to in section 84(1)(b), (c) and (g)."

Appointment
31 August 2006: see SI 2006/2226, art 3, Sch 1; for transitional provisions see art 4(1) thereof.

7 Deportation

(1) After section 97 of the Nationality, Immigration and Asylum Act 2002 (c 41) (appeals: national security) insert—

"97A National security: deportation

(1) This section applies where the Secretary of State certifies that the decision to make a deportation order in respect of a person was taken on the grounds that his removal from the United Kingdom would be in the interests of national security.

(2) Where this section applies—

(a) section 79 shall not apply,
(b) the Secretary of State shall be taken to have certified the decision to make the deportation order under section 97, and
(c) for the purposes of section 2(5) of the Special Immigration Appeals Commission Act 1997 (c 68) (appeals from within United Kingdom) it shall be assumed that section 92 of this Act—

(i) would not apply to an appeal against the decision to make the deportation order by virtue of section 92(2) to (3D),
(ii) would not apply to an appeal against that decision by virtue of section 92(4)(a) in respect of an asylum claim, and
(iii) would be capable of applying to an appeal against that decision by virtue of section 92(4)(a) in respect of a human rights claim unless the Secretary of State certifies that the removal of the person from the United Kingdom would not breach the United Kingdom's obligations under the Human Rights Convention.

(3) A person in respect of whom a certificate is issued under subsection (2)(c)(iii) may appeal to the Special Immigration Appeals Commission against the issue of the certificate; and for that purpose the Special Immigration Appeals Commission Act 1997 shall apply as to an appeal against an immigration decision to which section 92 of this Act applies.

(4) The Secretary of State may repeal this section by order."

(2) In section 112 of that Act (regulations, &c) after subsection (5A) insert—

"(5B) An order under section 97A(4)—

(a) must be made by statutory instrument,
(b) shall be subject to annulment in pursuance of a resolution of either House of Parliament, and
(c) may include transitional provision."

Appointment
31 August 2006: see SI 2006/2226, art 3, Sch 1.

8 Legal aid

(1) Section 103D of the Nationality, Immigration and Asylum Act 2002 (c 41) (reconsideration: legal aid) shall be amended as follows.

(2) In subsection (2) for the words "where the Tribunal has decided an appeal following reconsideration pursuant to an order made" substitute "where an order for reconsideration is made".

(3) For subsection (3) substitute—

"(3) The Tribunal may order payment out of that Fund of the appellant's costs—

(a) in respect of the application for reconsideration;
(b) in respect of preparation for reconsideration;
(c) in respect of the reconsideration."

Appointment
To be appointed: see s 62(1).

9 Abandonment of appeal

For section 104(4) of the Nationality, Immigration and Asylum Act 2002 (c 41) (pending appeal: deemed abandonment) substitute—

"(4) An appeal under section 82(1) brought by a person while he is in the United Kingdom shall be treated as abandoned if the appellant leaves the United Kingdom.

(4A) An appeal under section 82(1) brought by a person while he is in the United Kingdom shall be treated as abandoned if the appellant is granted leave to enter or remain in the United Kingdom (subject to subsections (4B) and (4C)).

(4B) Subsection (4A) shall not apply to an appeal in so far as it is brought on the ground relating to the Refugee Convention specified in section 84(1)(g) where the appellant—

(a) is granted leave to enter or remain in the United Kingdom for a period exceeding 12 months, and
(b) gives notice, in accordance with any relevant procedural rules (which may include provision about timing), that he wishes to pursue the appeal in so far as it is brought on that ground.

(4C) Subsection (4A) shall not apply to an appeal in so far as it is brought on the ground specified in section 84(1)(b) where the appellant gives notice, in accordance with any relevant procedural rules (which may include provision about timing), that he wishes to pursue the appeal in so far as it is brought on that ground."

Appointment
To be appointed: see s 62(1).

10 Grants

Section 110 (grants to advisory organisations) of the Nationality, Immigration and Asylum Act 2002 shall cease to have effect.

Appointment
16 June 2006: see SI 2006/1497, art 3, Schedule.

11 Continuation of leave

(1) Section 3C of the Immigration Act 1971 (c 77) (continuation of leave to enter or remain pending variation decision) shall be amended as follows.

(2) In subsection (2)(b) (continuation pending possible appeal) after "could be brought" insert ", while the appellant is in the United Kingdom".

(3) In subsection (2)(c) (continuation pending actual appeal) after "against that decision" insert ", brought while the appellant is in the United Kingdom,".

(4) For subsection (6) (decision) substitute—

"(6) The Secretary of State may make regulations determining when an application is decided for the purposes of this section; and the regulations—

(a) may make provision by reference to receipt of a notice,
(b) may provide for a notice to be treated as having been received in specified circumstances,
(c) may make different provision for different purposes or circumstances,
(d) shall be made by statutory instrument, and
(e) shall be subject to annulment in pursuance of a resolution of either House of Parliament."

(5) After section 3C insert—

"3D Continuation of leave following revocation

(1) This section applies if a person's leave to enter or remain in the United Kingdom—

(a) is varied with the result that he has no leave to enter or remain in the United Kingdom, or
(b) is revoked.

(2) The person's leave is extended by virtue of this section during any period when—

(a) an appeal under section 82(1) of the Nationality, Immigration and Asylum Act 2002 could be brought, while the person is in the United Kingdom, against the variation or revocation (ignoring any possibility of an appeal out of time with permission), or
(b) an appeal under that section against the variation or revocation, brought while the appellant is in the United Kingdom, is pending (within the meaning of section 104 of that Act).

(3) A person's leave as extended by virtue of this section shall lapse if he leaves the United Kingdom.

(4) A person may not make an application for variation of his leave to enter or remain in the United Kingdom while that leave is extended by virtue of this section."

(6) Section 82(3) of the Nationality, Immigration and Asylum Act 2002 (c 41) (variation and revocation: extension of leave pending appeal) shall cease to have effect.

Appointment
31 August 2006: see SI 2006/2226, art 3, Sch 1; for transitional provisions see art 4(3)–(5) thereof.

12 Asylum and human rights claims: definition

(1) Section 113(1) of the Nationality, Immigration and Asylum Act 2002 (c 41) (appeals: interpretation) shall be amended as follows.

(2) For the definition of "asylum claim" substitute—

""asylum claim"—
(a) means a claim made by a person that to remove him from or require him to leave the United Kingdom would breach the United Kingdom's obligations under the Refugee Convention, but
(b) does not include a claim which, having regard to a former claim, falls to be disregarded for the purposes of this Part in accordance with immigration rules,".

(3) For the definition of "human rights claim" substitute—

""human rights claim"—
(a) means a claim made by a person that to remove him from or require him to leave the United Kingdom would be unlawful under section 6 of the Human Rights Act 1998 (c 42) (public authority not to act contrary to Convention) as being incompatible with his Convention rights, but
(b) does not include a claim which, having regard to a former claim, falls to be disregarded for the purposes of this Part in accordance with immigration rules,".

Appointment
To be appointed: see s 62(1).

13 Appeal from within United Kingdom: certification of unfounded claim

After section 94(6A) of the Nationality, Immigration and Asylum Act 2002 (c 41) (appeal from within United Kingdom: unfounded human rights or asylum claim) insert—

"(6B) A certificate under subsection (1A) or (2) may not be issued (and subsection (3) shall not apply) in relation to an appeal under section 82(2)(d) or (e) against a decision relating to leave to enter or remain in the United Kingdom, where the leave was given in circumstances specified for the purposes of this subsection by order of the Secretary of State."

Appointment
To be appointed: see s 62(1).

14 Consequential amendments

Schedule 1 (which makes amendments consequential on the preceding provisions of this Act) shall have effect.

Appointment
Appointment (for certain purposes): 31 August 2006: see SI 2006/2226, art 3, Sch 1.

EMPLOYMENT

15 Penalty

(1) It is contrary to this section to employ an adult subject to immigration control if—

- (a) he has not been granted leave to enter or remain in the United Kingdom, or
- (b) his leave to enter or remain in the United Kingdom—
  - (i) is invalid,
  - (ii) has ceased to have effect (whether by reason of curtailment, revocation, cancellation, passage of time or otherwise), or
  - (iii) is subject to a condition preventing him from accepting the employment.

(2) The Secretary of State may give an employer who acts contrary to this section a notice requiring him to pay a penalty of a specified amount not exceeding the prescribed maximum.

(3) An employer is excused from paying a penalty if he shows that he complied with any prescribed requirements in relation to the employment.

(4) But the excuse in subsection (3) shall not apply to an employer who knew, at any time during the period of the employment, that it was contrary to this section.

(5) The Secretary of State may give a penalty notice without having established whether subsection (3) applies.

(6) A penalty notice must—

- (a) state why the Secretary of State thinks the employer is liable to the penalty,
- (b) state the amount of the penalty,
- (c) specify a date, at least 28 days after the date specified in the notice as the date on which it is given, before which the penalty must be paid,
- (d) specify how the penalty must be paid,
- (e) explain how the employer may object to the penalty, and
- (f) explain how the Secretary of State may enforce the penalty.

(7) An order prescribing requirements for the purposes of subsection (3) may, in particular—

- (a) require the production to an employer of a document of a specified description;
- (b) require the production to an employer of one document of each of a number of specified descriptions;
- (c) require an employer to take specified steps to verify, retain, copy or record the content of a document produced to him in accordance with the order;
- (d) require action to be taken before employment begins;
- (e) require action to be taken at specified intervals or on specified occasions during the course of employment.

Appointment
To be appointed: see s 62(1).

16 Objection

(1) This section applies where an employer to whom a penalty notice is given objects on the ground that—

(a) he is not liable to the imposition of a penalty,
(b) he is excused payment by virtue of section 15(3), or
(c) the amount of the penalty is too high.

(2) The employer may give a notice of objection to the Secretary of State.

(3) A notice of objection must—

(a) be in writing,
(b) give the objector's reasons,
(c) be given in the prescribed manner, and
(d) be given before the end of the prescribed period.

(4) Where the Secretary of State receives a notice of objection to a penalty he shall consider it and—

(a) cancel the penalty,
(b) reduce the penalty,
(c) increase the penalty, or
(d) determine to take no action.

(5) Where the Secretary of State considers a notice of objection he shall—

(a) have regard to the code of practice under section 19 (in so far as the objection relates to the amount of the penalty),
(b) inform the objector of his decision before the end of the prescribed period or such longer period as he may agree with the objector,
(c) if he increases the penalty, issue a new penalty notice under section 15, and
(d) if he reduces the penalty, notify the objector of the reduced amount.

Appointment
To be appointed: see s 62(1).

17 Appeal

(1) An employer to whom a penalty notice is given may appeal to the court on the ground that—

(a) he is not liable to the imposition of a penalty,
(b) he is excused payment by virtue of section 15(3), or
(c) the amount of the penalty is too high.

(2) The court may—

(a) allow the appeal and cancel the penalty,
(b) allow the appeal and reduce the penalty, or
(c) dismiss the appeal.

(3) An appeal shall be a re-hearing of the Secretary of State's decision to impose a penalty and shall be determined having regard to—

(a) the code of practice under section 19 that has effect at the time of the appeal (in so far as the appeal relates to the amount of the penalty), and
(b) any other matters which the court thinks relevant (which may include matters of which the Secretary of State was unaware);

and this subsection has effect despite any provision of rules of court.

(4) An appeal must be brought within the period of 28 days beginning with—

- (a) the date specified in the penalty notice as the date upon which it is given, or
- (b) if the employer gives a notice of objection and the Secretary of State reduces the penalty, the date specified in the notice of reduction as the date upon which it is given, or
- (c) if the employer gives a notice of objection and the Secretary of State determines to take no action, the date specified in the notice of that determination as the date upon which it is given.

(5) An appeal may be brought by an employer whether or not—

- (a) he has given a notice of objection under section 16;
- (b) the penalty has been increased or reduced under that section.

(6) In this section "the court" means—

- (a) where the employer has his principal place of business in England and Wales, a county court,
- (b) where the employer has his principal place of business in Scotland, the sheriff, and
- (c) where the employer has his principal place of business in Northern Ireland, a county court.

Appointment
To be appointed: see s 62(1).

18 Enforcement

(1) A sum payable to the Secretary of State as a penalty under section 15 may be recovered by the Secretary of State as a debt due to him.

(2) In proceedings for the enforcement of a penalty no question may be raised as to—

- (a) liability to the imposition of the penalty,
- (b) the application of the excuse in section 15(3), or
- (c) the amount of the penalty.

(3) Money paid to the Secretary of State by way of penalty shall be paid into the Consolidated Fund.

Appointment
To be appointed: see s 62(1).

19 Code of practice

(1) The Secretary of State shall issue a code of practice specifying factors to be considered by him in determining the amount of a penalty imposed under section 15.

(2) The code—

- (a) shall not be issued unless a draft has been laid before Parliament, and
- (b) shall come into force in accordance with provision made by order of the Secretary of State.

(3) The Secretary of State shall from time to time review the code and may revise and re-issue it following a review; and a reference in this section to the code includes a reference to the code as revised.

Appointment
31 August 2006: see SI 2006/2226, art 3, Sch 1.

20 Orders

(1) An order of the Secretary of State under section 15, 16 or 19—

- (a) may make provision which applies generally or only in specified circumstances,
- (b) may make different provision for different circumstances,
- (c) may include transitional or incidental provision, and
- (d) shall be made by statutory instrument.

(2) An order under section 15(2) may not be made unless a draft has been laid before and approved by resolution of each House of Parliament.

(3) Any other order shall be subject to annulment in pursuance of a resolution of either House of Parliament.

Appointment
To be appointed: see s 62(1).

21 Offence

(1) A person commits an offence if he employs another ("the employee") knowing that the employee is an adult subject to immigration control and that—

- (a) he has not been granted leave to enter or remain in the United Kingdom, or
- (b) his leave to enter or remain in the United Kingdom—
  - (i) is invalid,
  - (ii) has ceased to have effect (whether by reason of curtailment, revocation, cancellation, passage of time or otherwise), or
  - (iii) is subject to a condition preventing him from accepting the employment.

(2) A person guilty of an offence under this section shall be liable—

- (a) on conviction on indictment—
  - (i) to imprisonment for a term not exceeding two years,
  - (ii) to a fine, or
  - (iii) to both, or
- (b) on summary conviction—
  - (i) to imprisonment for a term not exceeding 12 months in England and Wales or 6 months in Scotland or Northern Ireland,
  - (ii) to a fine not exceeding the statutory maximum, or
  - (iii) to both.

(3) An offence under this section shall be treated as—

- (a) a relevant offence for the purpose of sections 28B and 28D of the Immigration Act 1971 (c 77) (search, entry and arrest), and
- (b) an offence under Part III of that Act (criminal proceedings) for the purposes of sections 28E, 28G and 28H (search after arrest).

(4) In relation to a conviction occurring before the commencement of section 154(1) of the Criminal Justice Act 2003 (c 44) (general limit on magistrates' powers to imprison) the reference to 12 months in subsection (2)(b)(i) shall be taken as a reference to 6 months.

Appointment
To be appointed: see s 62(1).

22 Offence: bodies corporate, &c

(1) For the purposes of section 21(1) a body (whether corporate or not) shall be treated as knowing a fact about an employee if a person who has responsibility within the body for an aspect of the employment knows the fact.

(2) If an offence under section 21(1) is committed by a body corporate with the consent or connivance of an officer of the body, the officer, as well as the body, shall be treated as having committed the offence.

(3) In subsection (2) a reference to an officer of a body includes a reference to—

- (a) a director, manager or secretary,
- (b) a person purporting to act as a director, manager or secretary, and
- (c) if the affairs of the body are managed by its members, a member.

(4) Where an offence under section 21(1) is committed by a partnership (whether or not a limited partnership) subsection (2) above shall have effect, but as if a reference to an officer of the body were a reference to—

- (a) a partner, and
- (b) a person purporting to act as a partner.

Appointment
To be appointed: see s 62(1).

23 Discrimination: code of practice

(1) The Secretary of State shall issue a code of practice specifying what an employer should or should not do in order to ensure that, while avoiding liability to a penalty under section 15 and while avoiding the commission of an offence under section 21, he also avoids contravening—

- (a) the Race Relations Act 1976 (c 74), or
- (b) the Race Relations (Northern Ireland) Order 1997 (SI 869 (NI 6)).

(2) Before issuing the code the Secretary of State shall—

- (a) consult—
  - (i) the Commission for Equality and Human Rights,
  - (ii) the Equality Commission for Northern Ireland,
  - (iii) such bodies representing employers as he thinks appropriate, and
  - (iv) such bodies representing workers as he thinks appropriate,
- (b) publish a draft code (after that consultation),
- (c) consider any representations made about the published draft, and
- (d) lay a draft code before Parliament (after considering representations under paragraph (c) and with or without modifications to reflect the representations).

(3) The code shall come into force in accordance with provision made by order of the Secretary of State; and an order—

- (a) may include transitional provision,
- (b) shall be made by statutory instrument, and
- (c) shall be subject to annulment in pursuance of a resolution of either House of Parliament.

(4) A breach of the code—

- (a) shall not make a person liable to civil or criminal proceedings, but
- (b) may be taken into account by a court or tribunal.

(5) The Secretary of State shall from time to time review the code and may revise and re-issue it following a review; and a reference in this section to the code includes a reference to the code as revised.

(6) Until the dissolution of the Commission for Racial Equality, the reference in subsection (2)(a)(i) to the Commission for Equality and Human Rights shall be treated as a reference to the Commission for Racial Equality.

Appointment
31 August 2006: see SI 2006/2226, art 3, Sch 1.

24 Temporary admission, &c

Where a person is at large in the United Kingdom by virtue of paragraph 21(1) of Schedule 2 to the Immigration Act 1971 (c 77) (temporary admission or release from detention)—

(a) he shall be treated for the purposes of sections 15(1) and 21(1) as if he had been granted leave to enter the United Kingdom, and
(b) any restriction as to employment imposed under paragraph 21(2) shall be treated for those purposes as a condition of leave.

Appointment
To be appointed: see s 62(1).

25 Interpretation

In sections 15 to 24—

(a) "adult" means a person who has attained the age of 16,
(b) a reference to employment is to employment under a contract of service or apprenticeship, whether express or implied and whether oral or written,
(c) a person is subject to immigration control if under the Immigration Act 1971 he requires leave to enter or remain in the United Kingdom, and
(d) "prescribed" means prescribed by order of the Secretary of State.

Appointment
To be appointed: see s 62(1).

26 Repeal

Sections 8 and 8A of the Asylum and Immigration Act 1996 (c 49) (restrictions on employment) shall cease to have effect.

Appointment
To be appointed: see s 62(1).

INFORMATION

27 Documents produced or found

(1) For paragraph 4(4) of Schedule 2 to the Immigration Act 1971 (c 77) (control on entry: documents) substitute—

"(4) Where a passport or other document is produced or found in accordance with this paragraph an immigration officer may examine it and detain it—

(a) for the purpose of examining it, for a period not exceeding 7 days;
(b) for any purpose, until the person to whom the document relates is given leave to enter the United Kingdom or is about to depart or be removed following refusal of leave or until it is decided that the person does not require leave to enter;
(c) after a time described in paragraph (b), while the immigration officer thinks that the document may be required in connection with proceedings in respect of an appeal under the Immigration Acts or in respect of an offence.

(5) For the purpose of ascertaining that a passport or other document produced or found in accordance with this paragraph relates to a person examined under paragraph 2, 2A or 3 above, the person carrying out the examination may require the

person being examined to provide information (whether or not by submitting to a process by means of which information is obtained or recorded) about his external physical characteristics (which may include, in particular, fingerprints or features of the iris or any other part of the eye)."

(2) Paragraph 4(2A) of that Schedule shall cease to have effect.

Appointment
31 August 2006: see SI 2006/2226, art 3, Sch 1; for transitional provisions see art 4(6), (7) thereof.

28 Fingerprinting

(1) Section 141 of the Immigration and Asylum Act 1999 (c 33) (fingerprinting) shall be amended as follows.

(2) In subsection (7)(d) for "arrested under paragraph 17 of Schedule 2 to the 1971 Act;" substitute "detained under paragraph 16 of Schedule 2 to the 1971 Act or arrested under paragraph 17 of that Schedule;".

(3) In subsection (8)(d) for "arrest;" substitute "detention or arrest;".

(4) At the end add—

"(17) Section 157(1) applies to this section (in so far as it relates to removal centres by virtue of subsection (5)(e)) as it applies to Part VIII."

Appointment
31 August 2006: see SI 2006/2226, art 3, Sch 1.

29 Attendance for fingerprinting

For section 142(2) of the Immigration and Asylum Act 1999 (c 33) (attendance for fingerprinting: timing) substitute—

"(2) In the case of a notice given to a person of a kind specified in section 141(7)(a) to (d) or (f) (in so far as it applies to a dependant of a person of a kind specified in section 141(7)(a) to (d)), the notice—

(a) must require him to attend during a specified period of at least seven days beginning with a day not less than seven days after the date given in the notice as its date of issue, and
(b) may require him to attend at a specified time of day or during specified hours.

(2A) In the case of a notice given to a person of a kind specified in section 141(7)(e) or (f) (in so far as it applies to a dependant of a person of a kind specified in section 141(7)(e)), the notice—

(a) may require him to attend during a specified period beginning with a day not less than three days after the date given in the notice as its date of issue,
(b) may require him to attend on a specified day not less than three days after the date given in the notice as its date of issue, and
(c) may require him to attend at a specified time of day or during specified hours."

Appointment
31 August 2006: see SI 2006/2226, art 3, Sch 1.

30 Proof of right of abode

For section 3(9) of the Immigration Act 1971 (c 77) (proof of right of abode) substitute—

"(9) A person seeking to enter the United Kingdom and claiming to have the right of abode there shall prove it by means of—

(a) a United Kingdom passport describing him as a British citizen,
(b) a United Kingdom passport describing him as a British subject with the right of abode in the United Kingdom,
(c) an ID card issued under the Identity Cards Act 2006 describing him as a British citizen,
(d) an ID card issued under that Act describing him as a British subject with the right of abode in the United Kingdom, or
(e) a certificate of entitlement."

Appointment
16 June 2006: see SI 2006/1497, art 3, Schedule.

31 Provision of information to immigration officers

(1) Schedule 2 to the Immigration Act 1971 (controls on entry: administration) shall be amended as follows.

(2) In paragraph 27 (provision of passenger lists, &c) for sub-paragraph (2) substitute—

"(2) The Secretary of State may by order require, or enable an immigration officer to require, a responsible person in respect of a ship or aircraft to supply—

(a) a passenger list showing the names and nationality or citizenship of passengers arriving or leaving on board the ship or aircraft;
(b) particulars of members of the crew of the ship or aircraft.

(3) An order under sub-paragraph (2) may relate—

(a) to all ships or aircraft arriving or expected to arrive in the United Kingdom;
(b) to all ships or aircraft leaving or expected to leave the United Kingdom;
(c) to ships or aircraft arriving or expected to arrive in the United Kingdom from or by way of a specified country;
(d) to ships or aircraft leaving or expected to leave the United Kingdom to travel to or by way of a specified country;
(e) to specified ships or specified aircraft.

(4) For the purposes of sub-paragraph (2) the following are responsible persons in respect of a ship or aircraft—

(a) the owner or agent, and
(b) the captain.

(5) An order under sub-paragraph (2)—

(a) may specify the time at which or period during which information is to be provided,
(b) may specify the form and manner in which information is to be provided,
(c) shall be made by statutory instrument, and
(d) shall be subject to annulment in pursuance of a resolution of either House of Parliament."

(3) In paragraph 27B (passenger information)—

(a) in each place after "passenger information" insert "or service information", and
(b) after sub-paragraph (9) insert—

"(9A) "Service information" means such information relating to the voyage or flight undertaken by the ship or aircraft as may be specified."

(4) In section 27 of the Immigration Act 1971 (c 77) (offences)—

(a) in paragraph (b)(iv) for "the requirements of paragraph 27B or 27C of Schedule 2" substitute "a requirement imposed by or under Schedule 2", and
(b) in paragraph (c) omit "as owner or agent of a ship or aircraft or".

Appointment
To be appointed: see s 62(1).

32 Passenger and crew information: police powers

(1) This section applies to ships and aircraft which are—

(a) arriving, or expected to arrive, in the United Kingdom, or
(b) leaving, or expected to leave, the United Kingdom.

(2) The owner or agent of a ship or aircraft shall comply with any requirement imposed by a constable of the rank of superintendent or above to provide passenger or service information.

(3) A passenger or member of crew shall provide to the owner or agent of a ship or aircraft any information that he requires for the purpose of complying with a requirement imposed by virtue of subsection (2).

(4) A constable may impose a requirement under subsection (2) only if he thinks it necessary—

(a) in the case of a constable in England, Wales or Northern Ireland, for police purposes, or
(b) in the case of a constable in Scotland, for police purposes which are or relate to reserved matters.

(5) In this section—

(a) "passenger or service information" means information which is of a kind specified by order of the Secretary of State and which relates to—
  (i) passengers,
  (ii) members of crew, or
  (iii) a voyage or flight,
(b) "police purposes" has the meaning given by section 21(3) of the Immigration and Asylum Act 1999 (c 33) (disclosure by Secretary of State), and
(c) "reserved matters" has the same meaning as in the Scotland Act 1998 (c 46).

(6) A requirement imposed under subsection (2)—

(a) must be in writing,
(b) may apply generally or only to one or more specified ships or aircraft,
(c) must specify a period, not exceeding six months and beginning with the date on which it is imposed, during which it has effect,
(d) must state—
  (i) the information required, and
  (ii) the date or time by which it is to be provided.

(7) The Secretary of State may make an order specifying a kind of information under subsection (5)(a) only if satisfied that the nature of the information is such that there are likely to be circumstances in which it can be required under subsection (2) without breaching Convention rights (within the meaning of the Human Rights Act 1998 (c 42)).

(8) An order under subsection (5)(a)—

(a) may apply generally or only to specified cases or circumstances,
(b) may make different provision for different cases or circumstances,

(c) may specify the form and manner in which information is to be provided,
(d) shall be made by statutory instrument, and
(e) shall be subject to annulment in pursuance of a resolution of either House of Parliament.

Appointment
To be appointed: see s 62(1).

33 Freight information: police powers

(1) This section applies to ships, aircraft and vehicles which are—

(a) arriving, or expected to arrive, in the United Kingdom, or
(b) leaving, or expected to leave, the United Kingdom.

(2) If a constable of the rank of superintendent or above requires a person specified in subsection (3) to provide freight information he shall comply with the requirement.

(3) The persons referred to in subsection (2) are—

(a) in the case of a ship or aircraft, the owner or agent,
(b) in the case of a vehicle, the owner or hirer, and
(c) in any case, persons responsible for the import or export of the freight into or from the United Kingdom.

(4) A constable may impose a requirement under subsection (2) only if he thinks it necessary—

(a) in the case of a constable in England, Wales or Northern Ireland, for police purposes, or
(b) in the case of a constable in Scotland, for police purposes which are or relate to reserved matters.

(5) In this section—

(a) "freight information" means information which is of a kind specified by order of the Secretary of State and which relates to freight carried,
(b) "police purposes" has the meaning given by section 21(3) of the Immigration and Asylum Act 1999 (c 33) (disclosure by Secretary of State), and
(c) "reserved matters" has the same meaning as in the Scotland Act 1998 (c 46).

(6) A requirement imposed under subsection (2)—

(a) must be in writing,
(b) may apply generally or only to one or more specified ships, aircraft or vehicles,
(c) must specify a period, not exceeding six months and beginning with the date on which it is imposed, during which it has effect, and
(d) must state—
 (i) the information required, and
 (ii) the date or time by which it is to be provided.

(7) The Secretary of State may make an order specifying a kind of information under subsection (5)(a) only if satisfied that the nature of the information is such that there are likely to be circumstances in which it can be required under subsection (2) without breaching Convention rights (within the meaning of the Human Rights Act 1998 (c 42)).

(8) An order under subsection (5)(a)—

(a) may apply generally or only to specified cases or circumstances,
(b) may make different provision for different cases or circumstances,
(c) may specify the form and manner in which the information is to be provided,

(d) shall be made by statutory instrument, and
(e) shall be subject to annulment in pursuance of a resolution of either House of Parliament.

Appointment
To be appointed: see s 62(1).

34 Offence

(1) A person commits an offence if without reasonable excuse he fails to comply with a requirement imposed under section 32(2) or (3) or 33(2).

(2) But—

(a) a person who fails without reasonable excuse to comply with a requirement imposed under section 32(2) or 33(2) by a constable in England and Wales or Northern Ireland otherwise than in relation to a reserved matter (within the meaning of the Scotland Act 1998 (c 46)) shall not be treated as having committed the offence in Scotland (but has committed the offence in England and Wales or Northern Ireland), and
(b) a person who fails without reasonable excuse to comply with a requirement which is imposed under section 32(3) for the purpose of complying with a requirement to which paragraph (a) applies—
  (i) shall not be treated as having committed the offence in Scotland, but
  (ii) shall be treated as having committed the offence in England and Wales or Northern Ireland.

(3) A person who is guilty of an offence under subsection (1) shall be liable on summary conviction to—

(a) imprisonment for a term not exceeding 51 weeks in England and Wales or 6 months in Scotland or Northern Ireland,
(b) a fine not exceeding level 4 on the standard scale, or
(c) both.

(4) In relation to a conviction occurring before the commencement of section 281(5) of the Criminal Justice Act 2003 (c 44) (51 week maximum term of sentences) the reference to 51 weeks in subsection (2)(a) shall be taken as a reference to three months.

Appointment
To be appointed: see s 62(1).

35 Power of Revenue and Customs to obtain information

In section 35(2) and (3) of the Customs and Excise Management Act 1979 (c 2) (arrivals in the United Kingdom) after "arriving" insert ", or expected to arrive,".

Appointment
To be appointed: see s 62(1).

36 Duty to share information

(1) This section applies to—

(a) the Secretary of State in so far as he has functions under the Immigration Acts,
(b) a chief officer of police, and
(c) Her Majesty's Revenue and Customs.

(2) The persons specified in subsection (1) shall share information to which subsection (4) applies and which is obtained or held by them in the course of their functions to the extent that the information is likely to be of use for—

(a) immigration purposes,
(b) police purposes, or
(c) Revenue and Customs purposes.

(3) But a chief officer of police in Scotland shall share information under subsection (2) only to the extent that it is likely to be of use for—

(a) immigration purposes,
(b) police purposes, in so far as they are or relate to reserved matters within the meaning of the Scotland Act 1998, or
(c) Revenue and Customs purposes other than the prosecution of crime.

(4) This subsection applies to information which—

(a) is obtained or held in the exercise of a power specified by the Secretary of State and the Treasury jointly by order and relates to—
(i) passengers on a ship or aircraft,
(ii) crew of a ship or aircraft,
(iii) freight on a ship or aircraft, or
(iv) flights or voyages, or
(b) relates to such other matters in respect of travel or freight as the Secretary of State and the Treasury may jointly specify by order.

(5) The Secretary of State and the Treasury may make an order under subsection (4) which has the effect of requiring information to be shared only if satisfied that—

(a) the sharing is likely to be of use for—
(i) immigration purposes,
(ii) police purposes, or
(iii) Revenue and Customs purposes, and
(b) the nature of the information is such that there are likely to be circumstances in which it can be shared under subsection (2) without breaching Convention rights (within the meaning of the Human Rights Act 1998 (c 42)).

(6) Information shared in accordance with subsection (2)—

(a) shall be made available to each of the persons specified in subsection (1), and
(b) may be used for immigration purposes, police purposes or Revenue and Customs purposes (regardless of its source).

(7) An order under subsection (4) may not specify—

(a) a power of Her Majesty's Revenue and Customs if or in so far as it relates to a matter to which section 7 of the Commissioners for Revenue and Customs Act 2005 (c 11) (former Inland Revenue matters) applies, or
(b) a matter to which that section applies.

(8) An order under subsection (4)—

(a) shall be made by statutory instrument, and
(b) may not be made unless a draft has been laid before and approved by resolution of each House of Parliament.

(9) In this section—

"chief officer of police" means—
(a) in England and Wales, the chief officer of police for a police area specified in section 1 of the Police Act 1996 (c 16),
(b) in Scotland, the chief constable of a police force maintained under the Police (Scotland) Act 1967 (c 77), and
(c) in Northern Ireland, the chief constable of the Police Service of Northern Ireland,

"immigration purposes" has the meaning given by section 20(3) of the Immigration and Asylum Act 1999 (c 33) (disclosure to Secretary of State),
"police purposes" has the meaning given by section 21(3) of that Act (disclosure by Secretary of State), and
"Revenue and Customs purposes" means those functions of Her Majesty's Revenue and Customs specified in section 21(6) of that Act.

(10) This section has effect despite any restriction on the purposes for which information may be disclosed or used.

Appointment
To be appointed: see s 62(1).

37 Information sharing: code of practice

(1) The Secretary of State and the Treasury shall jointly issue one or more codes of practice about—

(a) the use of information shared in accordance with section 36(2), and
(b) the extent to which, or form or manner in which, shared information is to be made available in accordance with section 36(6).

(2) A code—

(a) shall not be issued unless a draft has been laid before Parliament, and
(b) shall come into force in accordance with provision made by order of the Secretary of State and the Treasury jointly.

(3) The Secretary of State and the Treasury shall jointly from time to time review a code and may revise and re-issue it following a review; and subsection (2) shall apply to a revised code.

(4) An order under subsection (2)—

(a) shall be made by statutory instrument, and
(b) shall be subject to annulment in pursuance of a resolution of either House of Parliament.

Appointment
To be appointed: see s 62(1).

38 Disclosure of information for security purposes

(1) A person specified in subsection (2) may disclose information obtained or held in the course of his functions to a person specified in subsection (3) if he thinks that the information is likely to be of use for a purpose specified in—

(a) section 1 of the Security Service Act 1989 (c 5), or
(b) section 1 or 3 of the Intelligence Services Act 1994 (c 13).

(2) The persons who may disclose information in accordance with subsection (1) are—

(a) the Secretary of State in so far as he has functions under the Immigration Acts,
(b) a chief officer of police, and
(c) Her Majesty's Revenue and Customs.

(3) The persons to whom information may be disclosed in accordance with subsection (1) are—

(a) the Director-General of the Security Service,
(b) the Chief of the Secret Intelligence Service, and
(c) the Director of the Government Communications Headquarters.

(4) The information referred to in subsection (1) is information—

(a) which is obtained or held in the exercise of a power specified by the Secretary of State and the Treasury jointly by order and relates to—
(i) passengers on a ship or aircraft,
(ii) crew of a ship or aircraft,
(iii) freight on a ship or aircraft, or
(iv) flights or voyages, or
(b) which relates to such other matters in respect of travel or freight as the Secretary of State and the Treasury may jointly specify by order.

(5) In subsection (2) "chief officer of police" means—

(a) in England and Wales, the chief officer of police for a police area specified in section 1 of the Police Act 1996 (c 16),
(b) in Scotland, the chief constable of a police force maintained under the Police (Scotland) Act 1967 (c 77), and
(c) in Northern Ireland, the chief constable of the Police Service of Northern Ireland.

(6) An order under subsection (4) may not specify—

(a) a power of Her Majesty's Revenue and Customs if or in so far as it relates to a matter to which section 7 of the Commissioners for Revenue and Customs Act 2005 (c 11) (former Inland Revenue matters) applies, or
(b) a matter to which that section applies.

(7) An order under this section—

(a) shall be made by statutory instrument, and
(b) may not be made unless a draft has been laid before and approved by resolution of each House of Parliament.

(8) This section has effect despite any restriction on the purposes for which information may be disclosed or used.

Appointment
To be appointed: see s 62(1).

39 Disclosure to law enforcement agencies

(1) A chief officer of police may disclose information obtained in accordance with section 32 or 33 to—

(a) the States of Jersey police force;
(b) the salaried police force of the Island of Guernsey;
(c) the Isle of Man constabulary;
(d) any other foreign law enforcement agency.

(2) In subsection (1) "foreign law enforcement agency" means a person outside the United Kingdom with functions similar to functions of—

(a) a police force in the United Kingdom, or
(b) the Serious Organised Crime Agency.

(3) In subsection (1) "chief officer of police" means—

(a) in England and Wales, the chief officer of police for a police area specified in section 1 of the Police Act 1996,
(b) in Scotland, the chief constable of a police force maintained under the Police (Scotland) Act 1967, and
(c) in Northern Ireland, the chief constable of the Police Service of Northern Ireland.

Appointment
To be appointed: see s 62(1).

40 Searches: contracting out

(1) An authorised person may, in accordance with arrangements made under this section, search a searchable ship, aircraft, vehicle or other thing for the purpose of satisfying himself whether there are individuals whom an immigration officer might wish to examine under paragraph 2 of Schedule 2 to the Immigration Act 1971 (c 77) (control of entry: administrative provisions).

(2) For the purposes of subsection (1)—

- (a) "authorised" means authorised for the purpose of this section by the Secretary of State, and
- (b) a ship, aircraft, vehicle or other thing is "searchable" if an immigration officer could search it under paragraph 1(5) of that Schedule.

(3) The Secretary of State may authorise a specified class of constable for the purpose of this section.

(4) The Secretary of State may, with the consent of the Commissioners for Her Majesty's Revenue and Customs, authorise a specified class of officers of Revenue and Customs for the purpose of this section.

(5) The Secretary of State may authorise a person other than a constable or officer of Revenue and Customs for the purpose of this section only if—

- (a) the person applies to be authorised, and
- (b) the Secretary of State thinks that the person is—
  - (i) fit and proper for the purpose, and
  - (ii) suitably trained.

(6) The Secretary of State—

- (a) may make arrangements for the exercise by authorised constables of the powers under subsection (1),
- (b) may make arrangements with the Commissioners for Her Majesty's Revenue and Customs for the exercise by authorised officers of Revenue and Customs of the powers under subsection (1), and
- (c) may make arrangements with one or more persons for the exercise by authorised persons other than constables and officers of Revenue and Customs of the power under subsection (1).

(7) Where in the course of a search under this section an authorised person discovers an individual whom he thinks an immigration officer might wish to examine under paragraph 2 of that Schedule, the authorised person may—

- (a) search the individual for the purpose of discovering whether he has with him anything of a kind that might be used—
  - (i) by him to cause physical harm to himself or another,
  - (ii) by him to assist his escape from detention, or
  - (iii) to establish information about his identity, nationality or citizenship or about his journey;
- (b) retain, and as soon as is reasonably practicable deliver to an immigration officer, anything of a kind described in paragraph (a) found on a search under that paragraph;
- (c) detain the individual, for a period which is as short as is reasonably necessary and which does not exceed three hours, pending the arrival of an immigration officer to whom the individual is to be delivered;

(d) take the individual, as speedily as is reasonably practicable, to a place for the purpose of delivering him to an immigration officer there;
(e) use reasonable force for the purpose of doing anything under paragraphs (a) to (d).

(8) Despite the generality of subsection (7)—

(a) an individual searched under that subsection may not be required to remove clothing other than an outer coat, a jacket or a glove (but he may be required to open his mouth), and
(b) an item may not be retained under subsection (7)(b) if it is subject to legal privilege—
 (i) in relation to a search carried out in England and Wales, within the meaning of the Police and Criminal Evidence Act 1984 (c 60),
 (ii) in relation to a search carried out in Scotland, within the meaning of section 412 of the Proceeds of Crime Act 2002 (c 29), and
 (iii) in relation to a search carried out in Northern Ireland, within the meaning of the Police and Criminal Evidence (Northern Ireland) Order 1989 (SI 1989/1341 (NI 12)).

Appointment
31 August 2006: see SI 2006/2226, art 3, Sch 1.

41 Section 40: supplemental

(1) Arrangements under section 40(6)(c) must include provision for the appointment of a Crown servant to—

(a) monitor the exercise of powers under that section by authorised persons (other than constables or officers of Revenue and Customs),
(b) inspect from time to time the way in which the powers are being exercised by authorised persons (other than constables or officers of Revenue and Customs), and
(c) investigate and report to the Secretary of State about any allegation made against an authorised person (other than a constable or officer of Revenue and Customs) in respect of anything done or not done in the purported exercise of a power under that section.

(2) The authorisation for the purpose of section 40 of a constable or officer of Revenue and Customs or of a class of constable or officer of Revenue and Customs—

(a) may be revoked, and
(b) shall have effect, unless revoked, for such period as shall be specified (whether by reference to dates or otherwise) in the authorisation.

(3) The authorisation of a person other than a constable or officer of Revenue and Customs for the purpose of section 40—

(a) may be subject to conditions,
(b) may be suspended or revoked by the Secretary of State by notice in writing to the authorised person, and
(c) shall have effect, unless suspended or revoked, for such period as shall be specified (whether by reference to dates or otherwise) in the authorisation.

(4) A class may be specified for the purposes of section 40(3) or (4) by reference to—

(a) named individuals,
(b) the functions being exercised by a person,
(c) the location or circumstances in which a person is exercising functions, or
(d) any other matter.

(5) An individual or article delivered to an immigration officer under section 40 shall be treated as if discovered by the immigration officer on a search under Schedule 2 to the Immigration Act 1971 (c 77).

(6) A person commits an offence if he—

(a) absconds from detention under section 40(7)(c),
(b) absconds while being taken to a place under section 40(7)(d) or having been taken to a place in accordance with that paragraph but before being delivered to an immigration officer,
(c) obstructs an authorised person in the exercise of a power under section 40, or
(d) assaults an authorised person who is exercising a power under section 40.

(7) But a person does not commit an offence under subsection (6) by doing or failing to do anything in respect of an authorised person who is not readily identifiable—

(a) as a constable or officer of Revenue and Customs, or
(b) as an authorised person (whether by means of a uniform or badge or otherwise).

(8) A person guilty of an offence under subsection (6) shall be liable on summary conviction to—

(a) imprisonment for a term not exceeding 51 weeks, in the case of a conviction in England and Wales, or six months, in the case of a conviction in Scotland or Northern Ireland,
(b) a fine not exceeding level 5 on the standard scale, or
(c) both.

(9) In relation to a conviction occurring before the commencement of section 281(5) of the Criminal Justice Act 2003 (c 44) (51 week maximum term of sentences) the reference in subsection (8)(a) to 51 weeks shall be treated as a reference to six months.

Appointment
31 August 2006: see SI 2006/2226, art 3, Sch 1.

42 Information: embarking passengers

(1) Schedule 2 to the Immigration Act 1971 (c 77) (control on entry, &c) shall be amended as follows.

(2) In paragraph 3(1) for the words from "and if he is not" to the end substitute—

"and, if he is not a British citizen, for the purpose of establishing—

(a) his identity;
(b) whether he entered the United Kingdom lawfully;
(c) whether he has complied with any conditions of leave to enter or remain in the United Kingdom;
(d) whether his return to the United Kingdom is prohibited or restricted.

(1A) An immigration officer who examines a person under sub-paragraph (1) may require him, by notice in writing, to submit to further examination for a purpose specified in that sub-paragraph."

(3) After paragraph 16(1A) insert—

"(1B) A person who has been required to submit to further examination under paragraph 3(1A) may be detained under the authority of an immigration officer, for a period not exceeding 12 hours, pending the completion of the examination."

(4) In paragraph 21(1) after "16" insert " (1), (1A) or (2)".

Appointment
31 August 2006: see SI 2006/2226, art 3, Sch 1.

CLAIMANTS AND APPLICANTS

43 Accommodation

(1) In section 99(1) of the Immigration and Asylum Act 1999 (c 33) (provision of support by local authorities)—

(a) for "asylum-seekers and their dependants (if any)" substitute "persons", and
(b) after "section" insert "4,".

(2) In section 99(4) (expenditure) after "section" insert "4,".

(3) In section 118(1)(b) (housing authority accommodation) for "95" substitute "4, 95 or 98".

(4) In the following provisions for "under Part VI of the Immigration and Asylum Act 1999" substitute "under section 4 or Part VI of the Immigration and Asylum Act 1999"—

(a) section 3A(7A) of the Protection from Eviction Act 1977 (c 43) (excluded tenancies and licences),
(b) paragraph 3A(1) of Schedule 2 to the Housing (Northern Ireland) Order 1983 (SI 1983/1118 (NI 15)) (non-secure tenancies),
(c) section 23A(5A) of the Rent (Scotland) Act 1984 (c 58) (excluded tenancies and occupancy rights),
(d) paragraph 4A(1) of Schedule 1 to the Housing Act 1985 (c 68) (non-secure tenancies),
(e) paragraph 11B of Schedule 4 to the Housing (Scotland) Act 1988 (c 43) (non-assured tenancies), and
(f) paragraph 12A(1) of Schedule 1 to the Housing Act 1988 (c 50) (non-assured tenancies).

(5) A tenancy is not a Scottish secure tenancy (within the meaning of the Housing (Scotland) Act 2001 (asp 10)) if it is granted in order to provide accommodation under section 4 of the Immigration and Asylum Act 1999 (accommodation).

(6) A tenancy which would be a Scottish secure tenancy but for subsection (4) becomes a Scottish secure tenancy if the landlord notifies the tenant that it is to be regarded as such.

(7) At the end of section 4 of the Immigration and Asylum Act 1999 (c 33) (accommodation) add—

"(10) The Secretary of State may make regulations permitting a person who is provided with accommodation under this section to be supplied also with services or facilities of a specified kind.

(11) Regulations under subsection (10)—

(a) may, in particular, permit a person to be supplied with a voucher which may be exchanged for goods or services,
(b) may not permit a person to be supplied with money,
(c) may restrict the extent or value of services or facilities to be provided, and
(d) may confer a discretion."

Appointment
16 June 2006: see SI 2006/1497, art 3, Schedule.

44 Failed asylum-seekers: withdrawal of support

(1) The Secretary of State may by order provide for paragraph 7A of Schedule 3 to the Nationality, Immigration and Asylum Act 2002 (c 41) (failed asylum-seeker with family: withdrawal of support) to cease to have effect.

(2) An order under subsection (1) shall also provide for the following to cease to have effect—

(a) section 9(1), (2) and (4) of the Asylum and Immigration (Treatment of Claimants, etc) Act 2004 (c 19) (which insert paragraph 7A of Schedule 3 and make consequential provision), and
(b) in section 9(3)(a) and (b) of that Act, the words "other than paragraph 7A."

(3) An order under subsection (1)—

(a) may include transitional provision,
(b) shall be made by statutory instrument, and
(c) shall be subject to annulment in pursuance of a resolution of either House of Parliament.

Appointment
To be appointed: see s 62(1).

45 Integration loans

(1) Section 13 of the Asylum and Immigration (Treatment of Claimants, etc) Act 2004 (c 19) (integration loan for refugees) shall be amended as follows.

(2) In subsection (1) for "to refugees." substitute "—

(a) to refugees, and
(b) to such other classes of person, or to persons other than refugees in such circumstances, as the regulations may prescribe.".

(3) In subsection (2)(b) for "granted him indefinite leave to enter or remain" substitute "granted him leave to enter or remain".

(4) In subsection (3)(a)(iii) after "as a refugee" insert "or since some other event)".

(5) In subsection (3)(h) for "refugee" substitute "person".

(6) The heading to the section becomes "Integration loans for refugees and others".

Appointment
30 June 2006: see SI 2006/1497, art 4.

46 Inspection of detention facilities

(1) For section 5A(5A) of the Prison Act 1952 (c 52) (removal centres: inspection) substitute—

"(5A) Subsections (2) to (5) shall apply—

(a) in relation to removal centres within the meaning of section 147 of the Immigration and Asylum Act 1999 (c 33),
(b) in relation to short-term holding facilities within the meaning of that section, and
(c) in relation to escort arrangements within the meaning of that section.

(5B) In their application by virtue of subsection (5A) subsections (2) to (5)—

(a) shall apply to centres, facilities and arrangements anywhere in the United Kingdom, and

(b) shall have effect—
(i) as if a reference to prisons were a reference to removal centres, short-term holding facilities and escort arrangements,
(ii) as if a reference to prisoners were a reference to detained persons and persons to whom escort arrangements apply, and
(iii) with any other necessary modifications."

(2) In section 55 of that Act (extent)—

(a) omit subsection (4A), and
(b) after subsection (5) insert—

"(6) But (despite subsections (4) and (5)) the following shall extend to England and Wales, Scotland and Northern Ireland—

(a) section 5A(5A) and (5B), and
(b) section 5A(2) to (5) in so far as they apply by virtue of section 5A(5A)."

Appointment
31 August 2006: see SI 2006/2226, art 3, Sch 1.

47 Removal: persons with statutorily extended leave

(1) Where a person's leave to enter or remain in the United Kingdom is extended by section 3C(2)(b) or 3D(2)(a) of the Immigration Act 1971 (c 77) (extension pending appeal), the Secretary of State may decide that the person is to be removed from the United Kingdom, in accordance with directions to be given by an immigration officer if and when the leave ends.

(2) Directions under this section may impose any requirements of a kind prescribed for the purpose of section 10 of the Immigration and Asylum Act 1999 (c 33) (removal of persons unlawfully in United Kingdom).

(3) In relation to directions under this section, paragraphs 10, 11, 16 to 18, 21 and 22 to 24 of Schedule 2 to the Immigration Act 1971 (administrative provisions as to control of entry) apply as they apply in relation to directions under paragraph 8 of that Schedule.

(4) The costs of complying with a direction given under this section (so far as reasonably incurred) must be met by the Secretary of State.

(5) A person shall not be liable to removal from the United Kingdom under this section at a time when section 7(1)(b) of the Immigration Act 1971 (Commonwealth and Irish citizens ordinarily resident in United Kingdom) would prevent a decision to deport him.

(6) In section 82(2) of the Nationality, Immigration and Asylum Act 2002 (c 41) (right of appeal: general) after paragraph (h) insert—

"(ha)a decision that a person is to be removed from the United Kingdom by way of directions under section 47 of the Immigration, Asylum and Nationality Act 2006 (removal: persons with statutorily extended leave),".

(7) In section 92(2) of that Act (appeal from within United Kingdom) after " (f)" insert ", (ha)".

(8) In section 94(1A) of that Act (appeal from within United Kingdom: unfounded claim) for "or (e)" substitute "(e) or (ha)".

Appointment
To be appointed: see s 62(1).

48 Removal: cancellation of leave

For section 10(8) of the Immigration and Asylum Act 1999 (c 33) (removal directions: cancellation of leave to enter or remain in UK) substitute—

"(8) When a person is notified that a decision has been made to remove him in accordance with this section, the notification invalidates any leave to enter or remain in the United Kingdom previously given to him."

Appointment
16 June 2006: see SI 2006/1497, art 3, Schedule.

49 Capacity to make nationality application

After section 44 of the British Nationality Act 1981 (c 61) (decisions involving discretion) insert—

"44A Waiver of requirement for full capacity

Where a provision of this Act requires an applicant to be of full capacity, the Secretary of State may waive the requirement in respect of a specified applicant if he thinks it in the applicant's best interests."

Appointment
31 August 2006: see SI 2006/2226, art 3, Sch 1.

50 Procedure

(1) Rules under section 3 of the Immigration Act 1971 (c 77)—

- (a) may require a specified procedure to be followed in making or pursuing an application or claim (whether or not under those rules or any other enactment),
- (b) may, in particular, require the use of a specified form and the submission of specified information or documents,
- (c) may make provision about the manner in which a fee is to be paid, and
- (d) may make provision for the consequences of failure to comply with a requirement under paragraph (a), (b) or (c).

(2) In respect of any application or claim in connection with immigration (whether or not under the rules referred to in subsection (1) or any other enactment) the Secretary of State—

- (a) may require the use of a specified form,
- (b) may require the submission of specified information or documents, and
- (c) may direct the manner in which a fee is to be paid;

and the rules referred to in subsection (1) may provide for the consequences of failure to comply with a requirement under paragraph (a), (b) or (c).

(3) The following shall cease to have effect—

- (a) section 31A of the Immigration Act 1971 (procedure for applications), and
- (b) section 25 of the Asylum and Immigration (Treatment of Claimants etc) Act 2004 (c 19) (marriage: application for permission).

(4) At the end of section 41(1) of the British Nationality Act 1981 (procedure) add—

"(j) as to the consequences of failure to comply with provision made under any of paragraphs (a) to (i)."

(5) In section 10(2)(c) of the Nationality, Immigration and Asylum Act 2002 (c 41) (right of abode: certificate of entitlement: procedure) for "made in a specified form;" substitute "accompanied by specified information;".

(6) Paragraph 2(3) of Schedule 23 to the Civil Partnership Act 2004 (c 33) (immigration: procedure) shall cease to have effect.

Appointment
To be appointed: see s 62(1).

51 Fees

(1) The Secretary of State may by order require an application or claim in connection with immigration or nationality (whether or not under an enactment) to be accompanied by a specified fee.

(2) The Secretary of State may by order provide for a fee to be charged by him, by an immigration officer or by another specified person in respect of—

(a) the provision on request of a service (whether or not under an enactment) in connection with immigration or nationality,
(b) a process (whether or not under an enactment) in connection with immigration or nationality,
(c) the provision on request of advice in connection with immigration or nationality, or
(d) the provision on request of information in connection with immigration or nationality.

(3) Where an order under this section provides for a fee to be charged, regulations made by the Secretary of State—

(a) shall specify the amount of the fee,
(b) may provide for exceptions,
(c) may confer a discretion to reduce, waive or refund all or part of a fee,
(d) may make provision about the consequences of failure to pay a fee,
(e) may make provision about enforcement, and
(f) may make provision about the time or period of time at or during which a fee may or must be paid.

(4) Fees paid by virtue of this section shall—

(a) be paid into the Consolidated Fund, or
(b) be applied in such other way as the relevant order may specify.

Appointment
To be appointed: see s 62(1).

52 Fees: supplemental

(1) A fee imposed under section 51 may relate to a thing whether or not it is done wholly or partly outside the United Kingdom; but that section is without prejudice to—

(a) section 1 of the Consular Fees Act 1980 (c 23), and
(b) any other power to charge a fee.

(2) Section 51 is without prejudice to the application of section 102 of the Finance (No 2) Act 1987 (c 51) (government fees and charges); and an order made under that section in respect of a power repealed by Schedule 2 to this Act shall have effect as if it related to the powers under section 51 above in so far as they relate to the same matters as the repealed power.

(3) An order or regulations under section 51—

(a) may make provision generally or only in respect of specified cases or circumstances,
(b) may make different provision for different cases or circumstances,
(c) may include incidental, consequential or transitional provision, and
(d) shall be made by statutory instrument.

(4) An order under section 51—

(a) may be made only with the consent of the Treasury, and
(b) may be made only if a draft has been laid before and approved by resolution of each House of Parliament.

(5) Regulations under section 51—

(a) may be made only with the consent of the Treasury, and
(b) shall be subject to annulment in pursuance of a resolution of either House of Parliament.

(6) A reference in section 51 to anything in connection with immigration or nationality includes a reference to anything in connection with an enactment (including an enactment of a jurisdiction outside the United Kingdom) that relates wholly or partly to immigration or nationality.

(7) Schedule 2 (consequential amendments) shall have effect.

Appointment
To be appointed: see s 62(1).

MISCELLANEOUS

53 Arrest pending deportation

At the end of paragraph 2(4) of Schedule 3 to the Immigration Act 1971 (c 77) (deportation: power to detain) insert "; and for that purpose the reference in paragraph 17(1) to a person liable to detention includes a reference to a person who would be liable to detention upon receipt of a notice which is ready to be given to him."

Appointment
31 August 2006: see SI 2006/2226, art 3, Sch 1.

54 Refugee Convention: construction

(1) In the construction and application of Article 1(F)(c) of the Refugee Convention the reference to acts contrary to the purposes and principles of the United Nations shall be taken as including, in particular—

(a) acts of committing, preparing or instigating terrorism (whether or not the acts amount to an actual or inchoate offence), and
(b) acts of encouraging or inducing others to commit, prepare or instigate terrorism (whether or not the acts amount to an actual or inchoate offence).

(2) In this section—

"the Refugee Convention" means the Convention relating to the Status of Refugees done at Geneva on 28th July 1951, and
"terrorism" has the meaning given by section 1 of the Terrorism Act 2000 (c 11).

Appointment
31 August 2006: see SI 2006/2226, art 3, Sch 1.

55 Refugee Convention: certification

(1) This section applies to an asylum appeal where the Secretary of State issues a certificate that the appellant is not entitled to the protection of Article 33(1) of the Refugee Convention because—

(a) Article 1(F) applies to him (whether or not he would otherwise be entitled to protection), or
(b) Article 33(2) applies to him on grounds of national security (whether or not he would otherwise be entitled to protection).

(2) In this section—

(a) "asylum appeal" means an appeal—
 (i) which is brought under section 82, 83 or 101 of the Nationality, Immigration and Asylum Act 2002 (c 41) or section 2 of the Special Immigration Appeals Commission Act 1997 (c 68), and
 (ii) in which the appellant claims that to remove him from or require him to leave the United Kingdom would be contrary to the United Kingdom's obligations under the Refugee Convention, and
(b) "the Refugee Convention" means the Convention relating to the Status of Refugees done at Geneva on 28th July 1951.

(3) The Asylum and Immigration Tribunal or the Special Immigration Appeals Commission must begin substantive deliberations on the asylum appeal by considering the statements in the Secretary of State's certificate.

(4) If the Tribunal or Commission agrees with those statements it must dismiss such part of the asylum appeal as amounts to an asylum claim (before considering any other aspect of the case).

(5) Section 72(10)(a) of the Nationality, Immigration and Asylum Act 2002 (serious criminal: Tribunal or Commission to begin by considering certificate) shall have effect subject to subsection (3) above.

(6) Section 33 of the Anti-terrorism, Crime and Security Act 2001 (c 24) (certificate of non-application of Refugee Convention) shall cease to have effect.

Appointment
31 August 2006: see SI 2006/2226, art 3, Sch 1; for transitional provisions see art 4(8) thereof.

56 Deprivation of citizenship

(1) For section 40(2) of the British Nationality Act 1981 (c 61) (deprivation of citizenship: prejudicing UK interests) substitute—

"(2) The Secretary of State may by order deprive a person of a citizenship status if the Secretary of State is satisfied that deprivation is conducive to the public good."

(2) At the end of section 40A(3) of that Act (deprivation: appeal) add—

", and
(e) section 108 (forged document: proceedings in private).";

(and omit the word "and" before section 40A(3)(d)).

Appointment
16 June 2006: see SI 2006/1497, art 3, Schedule.

57 Deprivation of right of abode

(1) After section 2 of the Immigration Act 1971 (c 77) (right of abode) insert—

"2A Deprivation of right of abode

(1) The Secretary of State may by order remove from a specified person a right of abode in the United Kingdom which he has under section 2(1)(b).

(2) The Secretary of State may make an order under subsection (1) in respect of a person only if the Secretary of State thinks that it would be conducive to the public good for the person to be excluded or removed from the United Kingdom.

(3) An order under subsection (1) may be revoked by order of the Secretary of State.

(4) While an order under subsection (1) has effect in relation to a person—

(a) section 2(2) shall not apply to him, and
(b) any certificate of entitlement granted to him shall have no effect."

(2) In section 82(2) of the Nationality, Immigration and Asylum Act 2002 (c 41) (right of appeal: definition of immigration decision) after paragraph (ia) insert—

"(ib) a decision to make an order under section 2A of that Act (deprivation of right of abode),".

Appointment
16 June 2006: see SI 2006/1497, art 3, Schedule.

58 Acquisition of British nationality, &c

(1) The Secretary of State shall not grant an application for registration of an adult or young person as a citizen of any description or as a British subject under a provision listed in subsection (2) unless satisfied that the adult or young person is of good character.

(2) Those provisions are—

(a) sections 1(3) and (4), 3(1) and (5), 4(2) and (5), 4A, 4C, 5, 10(1) and (2), 13(1) and (3) of the British Nationality Act 1981 (c 61) (registration as British citizen),
(b) sections 15(3) and (4), 17(1) and (5), 22(1) and (2), 24, 27(1) and 32 of that Act (registration as British overseas territories citizen, &c),
(c) section 1 of the Hong Kong (War Wives and Widows) Act 1996 (c 41) (registration as British citizen), and
(d) section 1 of the British Nationality (Hong Kong) Act 1997 (c 20) (registration as British citizen).

(3) In subsection (1) "adult or young person" means a person who has attained the age of 10 at the time when the application is made.

(4) Where the Secretary of State makes arrangements under section 43 of the British Nationality Act 1981 for a function to be exercised by some other person, subsection (1) above shall have effect in relation to that function as if the reference to the Secretary of State were a reference to that other person.

Appointment
To be appointed: see s 62(1).

59 Detained persons: national minimum wage

(1) After section 153 of the Immigration and Asylum Act 1999 (c 33) (removal centres: rules) insert—

"153A Detained persons: national minimum wage

A detained person does not qualify for the national minimum wage in respect of work which he does in pursuance of removal centre rules."

(2) After section 45A of the National Minimum Wage Act 1998 (c 39) (exemptions from national minimum wage: persons discharging fines) insert—

"45B Immigration: detained persons

Section 153A of the Immigration and Asylum Act 1999 (c 33) (persons detained in removal centres) disqualifies certain persons for the national minimum wage."

Appointment
31 August 2006: see SI 2006/2226, art 3, Sch 1.

GENERAL

60 Money

There shall be paid out of money provided by Parliament—

(a) any expenditure of the Secretary of State in connection with this Act, and
(b) any increase attributable to this Act in sums payable under another enactment out of money provided by Parliament.

Appointment
16 June 2006: see SI 2006/1497, art 3, Schedule.

61 Repeals

Schedule 3 (repeals) shall have effect.

Appointment
Appointment (for certain purposes): 16 June 2006: see SI 2006/1497, art 3, Schedule. Appointment (for certain purposes): 31 August 2006: see SI 2006/2226, art 3, Sch 1, Sch 2.

62 Commencement

(1) The preceding provisions of this Act shall come into force in accordance with provision made by order of the Secretary of State.

(2) An order under subsection (1)—

(a) may make provision generally or only for specified purposes,
(b) may make different provision for different purposes,
(c) may include transitional or incidental provision or savings, and
(d) shall be made by statutory instrument.

Appointment
Royal Assent: 30 March 2006: (no specific commencement provision).

63 Extent

(1) This Act extends to—

(a) England and Wales,
(b) Scotland, and
(c) Northern Ireland.

(2) But—

(a) an amendment by this Act of another Act has the same extent as that Act or as the relevant part of that Act (ignoring extent by virtue of an Order in Council), and
(b) a provision of this Act shall, so far as it relates to nationality, have the same extent as the British Nationality Act 1981 (c 61) (disregarding excepted provisions under section 53(7) of that Act).

(3) Her Majesty may by Order in Council direct that a provision of this Act is to extend, with or without modification or adaptation, to—

(a) any of the Channel Islands;
(b) the Isle of Man.

(4) Subsection (3) does not apply in relation to the extension to a place of a provision which extends there by virtue of subsection (2)(b).

Appointment
Royal Assent: 30 March 2006: (no specific commencement provision).

64 Citation

(1) This Act may be cited as the Immigration, Asylum and Nationality Act 2006.

(2) A reference (in any enactment, including one passed or made before this Act) to "the Immigration Acts" is to—

(a) the Immigration Act 1971 (c 77),
(b) the Immigration Act 1988 (c 14),
(c) the Asylum and Immigration Appeals Act 1993 (c 23),
(d) the Asylum and Immigration Act 1996 (c 49),
(e) the Immigration and Asylum Act 1999 (c 33),
(f) the Nationality, Immigration and Asylum Act 2002 (c 41),
(g) the Asylum and Immigration (Treatment of Claimants, etc) Act 2004 (c 19), and
(h) this Act.

(3) The following shall cease to have effect—

(a) section 32(5) of the Immigration Act 1971 ("the Immigration Acts"),
(b) in section 167(1) of the Immigration and Asylum Act 1999, the definition of "the Immigration Acts",
(c) section 158 of the Nationality, Immigration and Asylum Act 2002 ("the Immigration Acts"), and
(d) section 44 of the Asylum and Immigration (Treatment of Claimants, etc) Act 2004 ("the Immigration Acts").

(4) In Schedule 1 to the Interpretation Act 1978 (c 30) (defined expressions) at the appropriate place insert—

""The Immigration Acts" has the meaning given by section 64 of the Immigration, Asylum and Nationality Act 2006."

Appointment
Royal Assent: 30 March 2006: (no specific commencement provision).

SCHEDULE 1
IMMIGRATION AND ASYLUM APPEALS: CONSEQUENTIAL AMENDMENTS

Section 14

NATIONALITY, IMMIGRATION AND ASYLUM ACT 2002 (C 41)

1 The Nationality, Immigration and Asylum Act 2002 (appeals) shall be amended as follows.

2 In section 72(9) (serious criminal) after ", 83" insert ", 83A".

3 In section 85(4) (matters to be considered) for "or 83(2)" substitute ", 83(2) or 83A(2)".

4 In section 86(1) (determination of appeal) for "or 83." substitute ", 83 or 83A."

5 In section 87(1) (successful appeal: direction) for "or 83" substitute ", 83 or 83A".

6 In section 97(1) and (3) (national security, &c) for "or 83(2)" substitute ", 83(2) or 83A(2)".

7 In section 103A(1) (review of Tribunal's decision) for "or 83" substitute ", 83 or 83A".

8 In section 103E(1) (appeal from Tribunal sitting as panel) for "or 83" substitute ", 83 or 83A".

9 In section 106(1)(a) and (b) (rules) for "or 83" substitute ", 83 or 83A".

10 In section 108(1)(a) (forged document: proceedings in private) for "or 83" substitute ", 83 or 83A".

11 In section 112 (regulations and orders) in subsection (5) for "94(6)" substitute "94(6) or (6B)".

Race Relations Act 1976 (c 74)

12 In section 57A(5) of the Race Relations Act 1976 (discrimination claims in immigration cases) in the definition of "immigration appellate body" for "an adjudicator appointed for the purposes of Part 5 of the 2002 Act, the Immigration Appeal Tribunal," substitute "the Asylum and Immigration Tribunal,".

British Nationality Act 1981 (c 61)

13 In section 40A(3) of the British Nationality Act 1981 (deprivation of citizenship: appeal) for "or 83" substitute ", 83 or 83A".

Special Immigration Appeals Commission Act 1997 (c 68)

14 In section 2 of the Special Immigration Appeals Commission Act 1997 (jurisdiction: appeals)—

- (a) in subsection (1)(a) and (b) for "or 83(2)" substitute ", 83(2) or 83A(2)",
- (b) in subsection (2)(a)—
  - (i) after "3C" insert "or 3D", and
  - (ii) for "(continuation of leave pending variation decision)" substitute "continuation of leave", and
- (c) in subsection (3)—
  - (i) for "an appeal against the rejection of a claim for asylum" substitute "an appeal against a decision other than an immigration decision", and
  - (ii) after "83(2)" insert "or 83A(2)".

Appointment
Paras 1–10, 12–14: Appointment: 31 August 2006: see SI 2006/2226, art 3, Sch 1.

SCHEDULE 2
Fees: Consequential Amendments

Section 52

British Nationality Act 1981 (c 61)

1 In section 41 of the British Nationality Act 1981 (regulations and Orders in Council)—

(a) omit subsection (2), and
(b) in subsection (3)—
(i) omit "or (2)", and
(ii) omit paragraph (b).

2 Section 42A of the British Nationality Act 1981 (registration and naturalisation: fee) shall cease to have effect.

IMMIGRATION AND ASYLUM ACT 1999 (C 33)

3 Sections 5 and 27 of the Immigration and Asylum Act 1999 (charges) shall cease to have effect.

NATIONALITY, IMMIGRATION AND ASYLUM ACT 2002 (C 41)

4 In section 10(2) (right of abode: certificate of entitlement)—

(a) paragraph (e) shall cease to have effect, and
(b) in paragraph (f) for "(a) to (e)" substitute "(a) to (d)".

5 Section 122 (fee for work permit, &c) shall cease to have effect.

ASYLUM AND IMMIGRATION (TREATMENT OF CLAIMANTS, ETC) ACT 2004 (C 19)

6 (1) Section 42 of the Asylum and Immigration (Treatment of Claimants, etc) Act 2004 (amount of fees) shall be amended as follows.

(2) In subsection (1)—

(a) for "In prescribing a fee for an application or process under a provision specified in subsection (2)" substitute "In prescribing a fee under section 51 of the Immigration, Asylum and Nationality Act 2006 (fees) in connection with a matter specified in subsection (2)", and
(b) omit ", with the consent of the Treasury,".

(3) For subsection (2) substitute—

"(2) Those matters are—

(a) anything done under, by virtue of or in connection with a provision of the British Nationality Act 1981 (c 61) or of the former nationality Acts (within the meaning given by section 50(1) of that Act),
(b) an application for leave to remain in the United Kingdom,
(c) an application for the variation of leave to enter, or remain in, the United Kingdom,
(d) section 10 of the Nationality, Immigration and Asylum Act 2002 (c 41) (right of abode: certificate of entitlement),
(e) a work permit, and
(f) any other document which relates to employment and is issued for a purpose of immigration rules or in connection with leave to enter or remain in the United Kingdom."

Appointment
To be appointed: see s 62(1).

SCHEDULE 3
REPEALS

Section 61

Short title and chapter	Extent of repeal
Prison Act 1952 (c 52)	Section 55(4A).
Immigration Act 1971 (c 77)	In section 27, in paragraph (c) the words "as owner or agent of a ship or aircraft or".
	Section 31A.
	Section 32(5).
	In Schedule 2, paragraph 4(2A).
British Nationality Act 1981 (c 61)	In section 40A(3), the word "and" before paragraph (d).
	Section 41(2).
	In section 41(3)— (a) the words "or (2)", and (b) paragraph (b).
	Section 42A.
Asylum and Immigration Act 1996 (c 49)	Sections 8 and 8A.
Immigration and Asylum Act 1999 (c 33)	Section 5.
	Section 27.
	In section 167(1), the definition of "the Immigration Acts".
Anti-terrorism, Crime and Security Act 2001 (c 24)	Section 33.
Nationality, Immigration and Asylum Act 2002 (c 41)	Section 10(2)(e)
	Section 82(3)
	Section 110
	Section 122
	Section 158.
Asylum and Immigration (Treatment of Claimants, etc) Act 2004 (c 19)	Section 25.
	In section 42(1) the words ", with the consent of the Treasury,".
	Section 44.
Civil Partnership Act 2004 (c 33)	Paragraph 2(3) of Schedule 23.

Appointment

Appointment (in part): 16 June 2006: by virtue of SI 2006/1497, art 3, Schedule.

Appointment (in part): 31 August 2006: see SI 2006/2226, art 3, Sch 1, Sch 2; for transitional provisions see art 4(5), (6), (8) thereof.

OTHER RELEVANT LEGISLATION

CIVIL PARTNERSHIP ACT 2004

2004 CHAPTER 33

An Act to make provision for and in connection with civil partnership.

[18th November 2004]

Be it enacted by the Queen's most Excellent Majesty, by and with the advice and consent of the Lords Spiritual and Temporal, and Commons, in this present Parliament assembled, and by the authority of the same, as follows:—

PART 1
INTRODUCTION

1 Civil partnership

(1) A civil partnership is a relationship between two people of the same sex ("civil partners")—

(a) which is formed when they register as civil partners of each other—
   (i) in England or Wales (under Part 2),
   (ii) in Scotland (under Part 3),
   (iii) in Northern Ireland (under Part 4), or
   (iv) outside the United Kingdom under an Order in Council made under Chapter 1 of Part 5 (registration at British consulates etc or by armed forces personnel), or

(b) which they are treated under Chapter 2 of Part 5 as having formed (at the time determined under that Chapter) by virtue of having registered an overseas relationship.

(2) Subsection (1) is subject to the provisions of this Act under or by virtue of which a civil partnership is void.

(3) A civil partnership ends only on death, dissolution or annulment.

(4) The references in subsection (3) to dissolution and annulment are to dissolution and annulment having effect under or recognised in accordance with this Act.

(5) References in this Act to an overseas relationship are to be read in accordance with Chapter 2 of Part 5.

Appointment
5 December 2005: see SI 2005/3175, art 3, Sch 2.

PART 5
CIVIL PARTNERSHIP FORMED OR DISSOLVED ABROAD ETC

CHAPTER 1
REGISTRATION OUTSIDE UK UNDER ORDER IN COUNCIL

210 Registration at British consulates etc

(1) Her Majesty may by Order in Council make provision for two people to register as civil partners of each other—

(a) in prescribed countries or territories outside the United Kingdom, and
(b) in the presence of a prescribed officer of Her Majesty's Diplomatic Service,

in cases where the officer is satisfied that the conditions in subsection (2) are met.

(2) The conditions are that—

(a) at least one of the proposed civil partners is a United Kingdom national,
(b) the proposed civil partners would have been eligible to register as civil partners of each other in such part of the United Kingdom as is determined in accordance with the Order,
(c) the authorities of the country or territory in which it is proposed that they register as civil partners will not object to the registration, and
(d) insufficient facilities exist for them to enter into an overseas relationship under the law of that country or territory.

(3) An officer is not required to allow two people to register as civil partners of each other if in his opinion the formation of a civil partnership between them would be inconsistent with international law or the comity of nations.

(4) An Order in Council under this section may make provision for appeals against a refusal, in reliance on subsection (3), to allow two people to register as civil partners of each other.

(5) An Order in Council under this section may provide that two people who register as civil partners of each other under such an Order are to be treated for the purposes of sections 221(1)(c)(i) and (2)(c)(i), 222(c), 224(b), 225(1)(c)(i) and (3)(c)(i), 229(1)(c)(i) and (2)(c)(i), 230(c) and 232(b) and section 1(3)(c)(i) of the Presumption of Death (Scotland) Act 1977 (c 27) as if they had done so in the part of the United Kingdom determined as mentioned in subsection (2)(b).

Appointment
Sub-ss (1), (2), (4), (5): Appointment: 15 April 2005: see SI 2005/1112, art 2, Sch 2.
Sub-s (3): Appointment: 5 December 2005: see SI 2005/3175, art 3, Sch 2.

211 Registration by armed forces personnel

(1) Her Majesty may by Order in Council make provision for two people to register as civil partners of each other—

(a) in prescribed countries or territories outside the United Kingdom, and
(b) in the presence of an officer appointed by virtue of the Registration of Births, Deaths and Marriages (Special Provisions) Act 1957 (c 58),

in cases where the officer is satisfied that the conditions in subsection (2) are met.

(2) The conditions are that—

(a) at least one of the proposed civil partners—
  (i) is a member of a part of Her Majesty's forces serving in the country or territory,
  (ii) is employed in the country or territory in such other capacity as may be prescribed, or
  (iii) is a child of a person falling within sub-paragraph (i) or (ii) and has his home with that person in that country or territory,
(b) the proposed civil partners would have been eligible to register as civil partners of each other in such part of the United Kingdom as is determined in accordance with the Order, and
(c) such other requirements as may be prescribed are complied with.

(3) In determining for the purposes of subsection (2) whether one person is the child of another, a person who is or was treated by another as a child of the family in relation to—

(a) a marriage to which the other is or was a party, or

(b) a civil partnership in which the other is or was a civil partner,

is to be regarded as the other's child.

(4) An Order in Council under this section may provide that two people who register as civil partners of each other under such an Order are to be treated for the purposes of section 221(1)(c)(i) and (2)(c)(i), 222(c), 224(b), 225(1)(c)(i) and (3)(c)(i), 229(1)(c)(i) and (2)(c)(i), 230(c) and 232(b) and section 1(3)(c)(i) of the Presumption of Death (Scotland) Act 1977 (c 27) as if they had done so in the part of the United Kingdom determined in accordance with subsection (2)(b).

(5) Any references in this section—

(a) to a country or territory outside the United Kingdom,
(b) to forces serving in such a country or territory, and
(c) to persons employed in such a country or territory,

include references to ships which are for the time being in the waters of a country or territory outside the United Kingdom, to forces serving in any such ship and to persons employed in any such ship.

Appointment
15 April 2005: see SI 2005/1112, art 2, Sch 2.

CHAPTER 2
OVERSEAS RELATIONSHIPS TREATED AS CIVIL PARTNERSHIPS

212 Meaning of "overseas relationship"

(1) For the purposes of this Act an overseas relationship is a relationship which—

(a) is either a specified relationship or a relationship which meets the general conditions, and
(b) is registered (whether before or after the passing of this Act) with a responsible authority in a country or territory outside the United Kingdom, by two people—
  (i) who under the relevant law are of the same sex at the time when they do so, and
  (ii) neither of whom is already a civil partner or lawfully married.

(2) In this Chapter, "the relevant law" means the law of the country or territory where the relationship is registered (including its rules of private international law).

Appointment
5 December 2005: see SI 2005/3175, art 3, Sch 2.

213 Specified relationships

(1) A specified relationship is a relationship which is specified for the purposes of section 212 by Schedule 20.

(2) The Secretary of State may by order amend Schedule 20 by—

(a) adding a relationship,
(b) amending the description of a relationship, or
(c) omitting a relationship.

(3) No order may be made under this section without the consent of the Scottish Ministers and the Department of Finance and Personnel.

(4) The power to make an order under this section is exercisable by statutory instrument.

(5) An order which contains any provision (whether alone or with other provisions) amending Schedule 20 by—

- (a) amending the description of a relationship, or
- (b) omitting a relationship,

may not be made unless a draft of the statutory instrument containing the order is laid before, and approved by a resolution of, each House of Parliament.

(6) A statutory instrument containing any other order under this section is subject to annulment in pursuance of a resolution of either House of Parliament.

Appointment
Sub-s (1): 5 December 2005: see SI 2005/3175, art 3, Sch 2.

214 The general conditions

The general conditions are that, under the relevant law—

- (a) the relationship may not be entered into if either of the parties is already a party to a relationship of that kind or lawfully married,
- (b) the relationship is of indeterminate duration, and
- (c) the effect of entering into it is that the parties are—
  - (i) treated as a couple either generally or for specified purposes, or
  - (ii) treated as married.

Appointment
5 December 2005: see SI 2005/3175, art 3, Sch 2.

215 Overseas relationships treated as civil partnerships: the general rule

(1) Two people are to be treated as having formed a civil partnership as a result of having registered an overseas relationship if, under the relevant law, they—

- (a) had capacity to enter into the relationship, and
- (b) met all requirements necessary to ensure the formal validity of the relationship.

(2) Subject to subsection (3), the time when they are to be treated as having formed the civil partnership is the time when the overseas relationship is registered (under the relevant law) as having been entered into.

(3) If the overseas relationship is registered (under the relevant law) as having been entered into before this section comes into force, the time when they are to be treated as having formed a civil partnership is the time when this section comes into force.

(4) But if—

- (a) before this section comes into force, a dissolution or annulment of the overseas relationship was obtained outside the United Kingdom, and
- (b) the dissolution or annulment would be recognised under Chapter 3 if the overseas relationship had been treated as a civil partnership at the time of the dissolution or annulment,

subsection (3) does not apply and subsections (1) and (2) have effect subject to subsection (5).

(5) The overseas relationship is not to be treated as having been a civil partnership for the purposes of any provisions except—

- (a) Schedules 7, 11 and 17 (financial relief in United Kingdom after dissolution or annulment obtained outside the United Kingdom);

(b) such provisions as are specified (with or without modifications) in an order under section 259;
(c) Chapter 3 (so far as necessary for the purposes of paragraphs (a) and (b)).

(6) This section is subject to sections 216, 217 and 218.

Appointment
5 December 2005: see SI 2005/3175, art 3, Sch 2.

216 The same-sex requirement

(1) Two people are not to be treated as having formed a civil partnership as a result of having registered an overseas relationship if, at the critical time, they were not of the same sex under United Kingdom law.

(2) But if a full gender recognition certificate is issued under the 2004 Act to a person who has registered an overseas relationship which is within subsection (4), after the issue of the certificate the relationship is no longer prevented from being treated as a civil partnership on the ground that, at the critical time, the parties were not of the same sex.

(3) However, subsection (2) does not apply to an overseas relationship which is within subsection (4) if either of the parties has formed a subsequent civil partnership or lawful marriage.

(4) An overseas relationship is within this subsection if (and only if), at the time mentioned in section 215(2)—

(a) one of the parties ("A") was regarded under the relevant law as having changed gender (but was not regarded under United Kingdom law as having done so), and
(b) the other party was (under United Kingdom law) of the gender to which A had changed under the relevant law.

(5) In this section—

"the critical time" means the time determined in accordance with section 215(2) or (as the case may be) (3);
"the 2004 Act" means the Gender Recognition Act 2004 (c 7);
"United Kingdom law" means any enactment or rule of law applying in England and Wales, Scotland and Northern Ireland.

(6) Nothing in this section prevents the exercise of any enforceable Community right.

Appointment
5 December 2005: see SI 2005/3175, art 3, Sch 2.

217 Person domiciled in a part of the United Kingdom

(1) Subsection (2) applies if an overseas relationship has been registered by a person who was at the time mentioned in section 215(2) domiciled in England and Wales.

(2) The two people concerned are not to be treated as having formed a civil partnership if, at the time mentioned in section 215(2)—

(a) either of them was under 16, or
(b) they would have been within prohibited degrees of relationship under Part 1 of Schedule 1 if they had been registering as civil partners of each other in England and Wales.

(3) Subsection (4) applies if an overseas relationship has been registered by a person who at the time mentioned in section 215(2) was domiciled in Scotland.

(4) The two people concerned are not to be treated as having formed a civil partnership if, at the time mentioned in section 215(2), they were not eligible by virtue of paragraph (b), (c) or (e) of section 86(1) to register in Scotland as civil partners of each other.

(5) Subsection (6) applies if an overseas relationship has been registered by a person who at the time mentioned in section 215(2) was domiciled in Northern Ireland.

(6) The two people concerned are not to be treated as having formed a civil partnership if, at the time mentioned in section 215(2)—

- (a) either of them was under 16, or
- (b) they would have been within prohibited degrees of relationship under Schedule 12 if they had been registering as civil partners of each other in Northern Ireland.

Appointment
5 December 2005: see SI 2005/3175, art 3, Sch 2.

218 The public policy exception

Two people are not to be treated as having formed a civil partnership as a result of having entered into an overseas relationship if it would be manifestly contrary to public policy to recognise the capacity, under the relevant law, of one or both of them to enter into the relationship.

Appointment
5 December 2005: see SI 2005/3175, art 3, Sch 2.

PART 7
MISCELLANEOUS

249 Immigration control and formation of civil partnerships

Schedule 23 contains provisions relating to the formation of civil partnerships in the United Kingdom by persons subject to immigration control.

Appointment
Appointment (for certain purposes): 15 April 2005: by virtue of SI 2005/1112, art 2, Sch 1. Appointment (for remaining purposes): 5 December 2005: see SI 2005/3175, art 2(1), Sch 1.

SCHEDULE 20
MEANING OF OVERSEAS RELATIONSHIP: SPECIFIED RELATIONSHIPS

Section 213

A relationship is specified for the purposes of section 213 (meaning of "overseas relationship") if it is registered in a country or territory given in the first column of the table and fits the description given in relation to that country or territory in the second column—

Country or territory	**Description**
[Andorra	unió estable de parella
Australia: Tasmania	significant relationship]
Belgium	[the relationship referred to as cohabitation légale, wettelijke samenwoning or gesetzliches zusammenwohnen]

Belgium	marriage
[Canada	marriage]
Canada: Nova Scotia	domestic partnership
Canada: Quebec	[the relationship referred to as union civile or as civil union]
Denmark	registreret partnerskab
Finland	[the relationship referred to as rekisteröity parisuhde or as registrerad partnerskap]
France	[pacte civil de solidarité]
Germany	Lebenspartnerschaft
Iceland	staðfesta samvist
[Luxembourg	the relationship referred to as partenariat enregistré or eingetragene partnerschaft]
Netherlands	[geregistreerd partnerschap]
Netherlands	marriage
[New Zealand	civil union]
Norway	registrert partnerskap
[Spain	marriage]
Sweden	registrerat partnerskap
[United States of America: California	domestic partnership
United States of America: Connecticut	civil union
United States of America: Maine	domestic partnership
United States of America: Massachusetts	marriage
United States of America: New Jersey	domestic partnership]
United States of America: Vermont	civil union

Appointment
5 December 2005: see SI 2005/3175, art 3, Sch 2.

Amendment
SI 2005/3129, art 3; SI 2005/3135, art 2.

SCHEDULE 23
IMMIGRATION CONTROL AND FORMATION OF CIVIL PARTNERSHIPS

Section 249

PART 1
INTRODUCTION

APPLICATION OF SCHEDULE

1 (1) This Schedule applies if—

(a) two people wish to register as civil partners of each other, and

(b) one of them is subject to immigration control.

(2) For the purposes of this Schedule a person is subject to immigration control if—

(a) he is not an EEA national, and
(b) under the Immigration Act 1971 (c 77) he requires leave to enter or remain in the United Kingdom (whether or not leave has been given).

(3) "EEA national" means a national of a State which is a contracting party to the Agreement on the European Economic Area signed at Oporto on 2nd May 1992 (as it has effect from time to time).

The qualifying condition

2 (1) For the purposes of this Schedule the qualifying condition, in relation to a person subject to immigration control, is that the person—

(a) has an entry clearance granted expressly for the purpose of enabling him to form a civil partnership in the United Kingdom,
(b) has the written permission of the Secretary of State to form a civil partnership in the United Kingdom, or
(c) falls within a class specified for the purpose of this paragraph by regulations made by the Secretary of State.

(2) "Entry clearance" has the meaning given by section 33(1) of the Immigration Act 1971.

(3) *Section 25 of the Asylum and Immigration (Treatment of Claimants, etc) Act 2004 (c 19) (regulations about applications for permission to marry) applies in relation to the permission referred to in sub-paragraph (1)(b) as it applies in relation to permission to marry under sections 19(3)(b), 21(3)(b) and 23(3)(b) of that Act.*

Appointment
Paras 1, 2(2): 5 December 2005: see SI 2005/3175, art 2(1), Sch 1.
Para 2(1), (3): Appointment (for the purpose of making regulations and issuing guidance): 15 April 2005: see SI 2005/1112, art 2, Sch 1.
Para 2(1), (3): Appointment (for remaining purposes): 5 December 2005: see SI 2005/3175, art 2(1), Sch 1.

Amendment
Immigration, Asylum and Nationality Act 2006, ss 50(6), 61, Sch 3.

Part 2
England and Wales

Application of this Part

3 This Part of this Schedule applies if the civil partnership is to be formed in England and Wales by signing a civil partnership schedule.

Procedure for giving notice of proposed civil partnership

4 (1) Each notice of proposed civil partnership under Chapter 1 of Part 2 of this Act—

(a) must be given to a registration authority specified for the purposes of this paragraph by regulations made by the Secretary of State, ...
(b) must be delivered to the relevant individual in person by the two proposed civil partners,
[(c) may be given only if each of the proposed civil partners has been resident in the area of a registration authority for the period of 7 days immediately before

the giving of his or her notice (but the area need not be that of the registration authority to which the notice is given and the proposed civil partners need not have resided in the area of same registration authority), and

(d) must state, in relation to each of the proposed civil partners, the registration authority by reference to the area of which paragraph (c) is satisfied].

(2) "The relevant individual" means such employee or officer or other person provided by the specified registration authority as is determined in accordance with regulations made by the Secretary of State for the purposes of this sub-paragraph.

(3) Regulations under sub-paragraph (2) may, in particular, describe a person by reference to the location or office where he works.

(4) Before making any regulations under this paragraph the Secretary of State must consult the Registrar General.

Declaration

5 The necessary declaration under section 8 must include a statement that the person subject to immigration control fulfils the qualifying condition (and the reason why).

Recording of notice

6 (1) The fact that a notice of proposed civil partnership has been given must not be recorded in the register unless the registration authority is satisfied by the production of specified evidence that the person fulfils the qualifying condition.

(2) "Specified evidence" means such evidence as may be specified in guidance issued by the Registrar General.

Supplementary

7 (1) Part 2 of this Act has effect in any case where this Part of this Schedule applies subject to any necessary modification.

(2) In particular[—

(a) section 8(4)(b) has effect as if it required a declaration that the notice of proposed civil partnership is given in compliance with paragraph 4(1) above, and

(b)] section 52 has effect as if the matters proof of which is not necessary in support of the civil partnership included compliance with this Part of this Schedule.

(3) An expression used in this Part of this Schedule and in Chapter 1 of Part 2 of this Act has the same meaning as in that Chapter.

Appointment

Paras 3, 5, 7: Appointment: 5 December 2005: see SI 2005/3175, art 2(1), Sch 1.

Paras 4, 6: Appointment (for the purpose of making regulations and issuing guidance): 15 April 2005: see SI 2005/1112, art 2, Sch 1.

Paras 4, 6: Appointment (for remaining purposes): 5 December 2005: see SI 2005/3175, art 2(1), Sch 1.

Amendment

SI 2005/2000, art 3, Schedule.

PART 3
SCOTLAND

APPLICATION OF THIS PART

8 This Part of this Schedule applies if the civil partnership is to be formed in Scotland.

PROCEDURE FOR GIVING NOTICE OF PROPOSED CIVIL PARTNERSHIP

9 (1) Notice under section 88—

(a) may be submitted to the district registrar of a district specified for the purposes of this paragraph by regulations made by the Secretary of State, and
(b) may not be submitted to the district registrar of any other registration district.

(2) Before making any regulations under this paragraph the Secretary of State must consult the Registrar General.

PRE-CONDITION FOR MAKING ENTRY IN CIVIL PARTNERSHIP NOTICE BOOK ETC

10 (1) Where the district registrar to whom notice is submitted by virtue of paragraph 9(1) is the district registrar for the proposed place of registration, he shall neither—

(a) make an entry under section 89, nor
(b) complete a civil partnership schedule under section 94,

in respect of the proposed civil partnership unless satisfied, by the provision of specified evidence, that the intended civil partner subject to immigration control fulfils the qualifying condition.

(2) Where the district registrar to whom notice is so submitted (here the "notified registrar") is not the district registrar for the proposed place of registration (here the "second registrar")—

(a) the notified registrar shall, if satisfied as is mentioned in sub-paragraph (1), send the notices and any fee, *certificate or declaration which accompanied them* [paid, or any certificate or declaration submitted, in pursuance of section 88 in relation to the proposed civil partnership], to the second registrar, and
(b) the second registrar shall be treated as having received the notices from the intended partners on the dates on which the notified registrar received them.

(3) "Specified evidence" means such evidence as may be specified in guidance issued by the Secretary of State after consultation with the Registrar General.

SUPPLEMENTARY

11 (1) Part 3 of this Act has effect in any case where this Part of this Schedule applies subject to any necessary modification.

(2) An expression used in this Part of this Schedule and in Part 3 of this Act has the same meaning as in that Part.

Appointment
Paras 8, 10(2), 11: 5 December 2005: see SI 2005/3175, art 2(1), Sch 1.
Paras 9, 10(1), (3): Appointment (for the purpose of making regulations and issuing guidance): 15 April 2005: see SI 2005/1112, art 2, Sch 1.
Paras 9, 10(1), (3): Appointment (for remaining purposes): 5 December 2005: see SI 2005/3175, art 2(1), Sch 1.

Amendment
Local Electoral Administration and Registration Services (Scotland) Act 2006, s 59(5) – Date in force: to be appointed.

PART 4
NORTHERN IRELAND

APPLICATION OF THIS PART

12 This Part of this Schedule applies if the civil partnership is to be formed in Northern Ireland.

PROCEDURE FOR GIVING CIVIL PARTNERSHIP NOTICES

13 (1) The civil partnership notices must be given—

(a) only to a prescribed registrar, and
(b) in prescribed cases by both parties together in person at a prescribed register office.

(2) Before making any regulations under this paragraph the Secretary of State must consult the Registrar General.

ACCOMPANYING STATEMENT AS TO THE QUALIFYING CONDITION

14 A civil partnership notice given by a person subject to immigration control must be accompanied by a statement that the person fulfils the qualifying condition (and the reason why).

CIVIL PARTNERSHIP NOTICE BOOK AND CIVIL PARTNERSHIP SCHEDULE

15 (1) No action must be taken under section 140(1) or 143 (civil partnership notice book and civil partnership schedule) unless the prescribed registrar is satisfied by the production of specified evidence that the person fulfils the qualifying condition.

(2) If the prescribed registrar is satisfied as mentioned in sub-paragraph (1) but is not the registrar for the purposes of section 140(1), the prescribed registrar must send him the civil partnership notices and he is to be treated as having received them when the prescribed registrar received them.

(3) "Specified evidence" means such evidence as may be specified in guidance issued by the Secretary of State after consultation with the Registrar General.

SUPPLEMENTARY

16 (1) Part 4 of this Act has effect in any case where this Part of this Schedule applies subject to any necessary modification.

(2) In particular, section 176 has effect as if the matters proof of which is not necessary in support of the civil partnership included compliance with this Part of this Schedule.

(3) In this Part of this Schedule—

(a) "prescribed" means prescribed by regulations made by the Secretary of State;
(b) "registrar" means a person appointed under section 152(1)(a) or (b) or (3);
(c) other expressions have the same meaning as in Chapter 1 of Part 4 of this Act.

(4) Section 18(3) of the Interpretation Act (Northern Ireland) 1954 (c 33 (NI)) (provisions as to holders of offices) shall apply to this Part of this Schedule as if it were an enactment within the meaning of that Act.

Appointment
Paras 12, 14, 15(2), 16(1), (2), (3)(b), (c), (4): 5 December 2005: see SI 2005/3175, art 2(1), Sch 1.
Paras 13, 15(1), (3), 16(3)(a): Appointment (for the purpose of making regulations and issuing guidance): 15 April 2005: see SI 2005/1112, art 2, Sch 1.
Paras 13, 15(1), (3), 16(3)(a): Appointment (for remaining purposes): 5 December 2005: see SI 2005/3175, art 2(1), Sch 1.

PART 5
REGULATIONS

17 Any power to make regulations under this Schedule is exercisable by statutory instrument which is subject to annulment in pursuance of a resolution of either House of Parliament.

Appointment
15 April 2005: see SI 2005/1112, art 2, Sch 1.

EUROPEAN UNION (ACCESSIONS) ACT 2006

2006 CHAPTER 2

An Act to make provision consequential on the treaty concerning the accession of the Republic of Bulgaria and Romania to the European Union, signed at Luxembourg on 25th April 2005; and to make provision in relation to the entitlement of nationals of those states to enter or reside in the United Kingdom as workers.

[16th February 2006]

BE IT ENACTED by the Queen's most Excellent Majesty, by and with the advice and consent of the Lords Spiritual and Temporal, and Commons, in this present Parliament assembled, and by the authority of the same, as follows:—

1 Accession treaty

(1) In section 1(2) of the European Communities Act 1972 (c 68), in the definition of "The Treaties" and "the Community Treaties", after paragraph (q) insert—

"and
(r) the treaty concerning the accession of the Republic of Bulgaria and Romania to the European Union, signed at Luxembourg on 25th April 2005;".

(2) For the purposes of section 12 of the European Parliamentary Elections Act 2002 (c 24) (ratification of treaties), the treaty concerning the accession of the Republic of Bulgaria and Romania to the European Union, signed at Luxembourg on 25th April 2005, is approved.

Appointment
Royal Assent: 16 February 2006: (no specific commencement provision).

2 Freedom of movement for workers

(1) The Secretary of State may by regulations make provision concerning—

(a) the entitlement of a national of an acceding State to enter or reside in the United Kingdom as a worker;
(b) any matter ancillary to that entitlement.

(2) The provision that may be made by regulations under this section includes provision which applies (with or without modification) a specified enactment relating to—

(a) the entitlement of a national of an EEA State to enter or reside in the United Kingdom as a worker, or
(b) any matter ancillary to that entitlement,

to a national of an acceding State as it applies in relation to a national of an EEA State.

(3) Regulations under this section may (in particular) include provision the effect of which is—

(a) to make it a requirement that a national of an acceding State working in the United Kingdom be registered in accordance with the regulations;
(b) to make it a requirement that a fee is payable in respect of applications or registration under the regulations;
(c) to make it an offence for an employer to employ a national of an acceding State unless his employment of that person is authorised by the regulations.

(4) An offence by virtue of regulations under this section—

(a) may be a summary offence or an offence triable either way; and
(b) is not to be punishable by imprisonment or, on summary conviction, by a fine exceeding the statutory maximum.

(5) Regulations under this section—

(a) may include incidental, supplementary, consequential or transitional provision; and
(b) may make different provision for different cases.

(6) The power to make regulations under this section is exercisable by statutory instrument.

(7) No regulations may be made containing (with or without other provision) any provision the power to make which is conferred by this section unless—

(a) a draft of the regulations has been laid before Parliament and approved by a resolution of each House; or
(b) the regulations contain a declaration by the Secretary of State that the urgency of the matter makes it necessary for the regulations to be made without that approval.

(8) Regulations under this section that contain such a declaration—

(a) must be laid before Parliament after being made; and
(b) if not approved by a resolution of each House before the end of 40 days beginning with the day on which they were made, shall cease to have effect at the end of that period;

but, where regulations cease to have effect in accordance with this subsection, that does not affect anything previously done under them, or prevent the making of new regulations to the same or similar effect.

(9) In subsection (8) "40 days" means 40 days computed as provided for in section 7(1) of the Statutory Instruments Act 1946 (c 36).

(10) In this section—

"acceding State" means the Republic of Bulgaria or Romania;

"EEA State" means—

(a) a member State, other than the United Kingdom and the acceding States; or

(b) Norway, Iceland or Liechtenstein;

"enactment" includes a provision of any subordinate legislation (within the meaning of the Interpretation Act 1978 (c 30));

"modification" includes omissions, additions and alterations;

"specified" means specified in regulations made under this section;

"worker" has the same meaning as it does for the purposes of Article 39 of the Treaty establishing the European Community.

Appointment

Royal Assent: 16 February 2006: (no specific commencement provision).

3 Short title

This Act may be cited as the European Union (Accessions) Act 2006.

Appointment

Royal Assent: 16 February 2006: (no specific commencement provision).

IMMIGRATION RULES

The changes to the Rules have been summarised in the following table. The consolidated Rules (containing all the amendments noted below) can be viewed on the Home Office website at:

http://www.ind.homeoffice.gov.uk/lawandpolicy/immigrationrules/

SI No	Title	Brief Description of Changes
2006/ 6918	Statement of Changes to the Immigration Rules CM 6918 – September 2006	This Statement of Changes in the Immigration Rules together with the introduction of The Refugee or Person in Need of International Protection (Qualification) Regulations 2006 in part implement Council Directive 2004/83/EC of 29 April 2004 on minimum standards for the qualification and status of third country nationals or stateless persons as refugees or as persons who otherwise need international protection and the content of the protection granted (OJ L304, 30.9.2004, p 12) ('the Directive').
2006/ 1337	Statement of Changes to the Immigration Rules HC 1337 – July 2006	This Statement of Changes in Immigration Rules amends para 364 to make it clear that where a person is liable to deportation then the presumption shall be that the public interest requires deportation and that it will only be in exceptional circumstances that the public interest in deportation will be outweighed in a case where it would not be contrary to the European Convention on Human Rights and the Refugee Convention to deport.
2006/ 1053	Statement of Changes to the Immigration Rules HC 1053 – April 2006	This Statement of Changes in Immigration Rules revokes the existing provision of the right for European Economic Area (EEA) nationals and their family members to apply for permission to remain indefinitely under United Kingdom domestic law under certain conditions given in paras 255 to 257 of the Immigration Rules and makes amendments consequential to the making of the 2006 Regulations.

2006/ 1016	Statement of Changes to the Immigration Rules HC 1016 – March 2006	This Statement of Changes in Immigration Rules replaces the Statement of Changes in Immigration Rules HC 974, laid on 13 March but is to take effect on the same date as the instrument it replaces. It contains the following six policy changes: – For all employment related categories of entry to the UK the qualifying period for settlement ('indefinite leave to remain') is now five years. – A change to the provisions for Postgraduate Doctors and Dentists, so that only those doctors and dentists who have completed their medical or dental degree in the UK will be eligible for leave in this category, and then only to complete the two-year Foundation Programme. – A change to the Science and Engineering Graduates scheme to incorporate provisions announced in the Chancellor's Pre Budget Report on 5 December. This will enable all Master's and PhD students to apply to work in the UK for 12 months after they complete their studies, regardless of the subject they have studied. – A change to prevent non-visa nationals in the UK as visitors from being able to switch into the student category for courses above degree level. This change also moves the transitional provisions for the October 2004 (CM 6339) Rules change from guidance notes into the Immigration Rules. – A technical amendment to the civil partner provisions to include the term 'proposed civil partner' in one paragraph which was omitted when the civil partners changes were originally laid on 24 October 2005 (HC 582).

		– A technical amendment to allow work permit holders to switch into the Overseas Nurses Programme to undertake a period of supervised practice or midwife adaptation training. There are three key differences between the previous Statement of Changes laid on 13 March and this Statement of Changes. They are as follows: – Applicants coming to the UK under the ancestry provisions must have leave in this capacity for five years in order to qualify for settlement. The previous Statement of Changes provided for leave to be granted in the following pattern: two years' leave to enter, followed by three years' leave to remain, rather than allowing one single period all the way up to the settlement qualifying period. This Statement of Changes allows for one single period to be granted all the way up to the settlement qualifying period. So, leave to enter and leave to remain under the ancestry provisions may now be granted for up to five years at a time. – Prospective students need to have sought prior entry clearance if they subsequently wish to switch to student status in the UK. – The rules for postgraduate doctors and dentists have been amended to clarify that applicants need not have completed their medical or dental degree in the 12 months preceding their application, if they are applying for leave to enter and have previously been granted leave in this category.

2006/ 974	Statement of Changes to the Immigration Rules HC 974 – March 2006	This Statement of Changes in Immigration Rules contains the following six policy changes: – For all employment related categories of entry to the UK the qualifying period for settlement ('Indefinite leave to remain') is now five years. – A change to the provisions for Postgraduate Doctors and Dentists, so that only those doctors and dentists who have completed their medical or dental degree in the UK will be eligible for leave in this category, and then only to complete the two-year Foundation Programme. – A change to the Science and Engineering Graduates scheme to incorporate provisions announced in the Chancellor's Pre-Budget Report on 5 December. This will enable all Master's and PhD students to apply to work in the UK for 12 months after they complete their studies, regardless of the subject they have studied. – A change to prevent non-visa nationals in the UK as visitors from being able to switch into the student category for courses above degree level. This change also moves the transitional provisions for the October 2004 (CM 6339) Rules change from guidance notes into the Immigration Rules. – A technical amendment to the civil partner provisions to include the term 'proposed civil partner' in one paragraph which was omitted when the civil partners changes were originally laid on 24 October 2005 (HC 582). – A technical amendment to allow work permit holders to switch into the Overseas Nurses Programme to undertake a period of supervised practice or midwife adaptation training.

2006/ 949	Statement of Changes in Immigration Rules HC 949 – March 2006	This Statement of Changes in the Immigration Rules introduces the following changes: (1) With effect from 2 March, nationals of Malawi will require a visa to travel to the UK. (2) With effect from 2 March, nationals of Malawi will require a visa to travel to the UK.
2006/ 819	Statement of Changes in Immigration Rules HC 819 – January 2006	This Statement of Changes in Immigration Rules contains the following: (i) a provision requiring that a child under the age of 18 who is travelling alone should be able to demonstrate that suitable arrangements have been made for his travel to, and reception and care in the United Kingdom and that he has a parent or guardian in his home country or country of habitual residence who is responsible for his care. (ii) a provision requiring that children who are visa nationals and accompanied should have the name of that adult entered on their visa, and can only be given leave to enter on the same occasion as that accompanying adult.
2005/ 769	Statement of Changes in Immigration Rules HC 769 – December 2005	This Statement of Changes in Immigration Rules contains a new category for visiting religious workers and religious workers in non-pastoral roles.
2005/ 697	Statement of Changes in Immigration Rules HC 697 – November 2005	This Statement of Changes in Immigration Rules contains the following change: The addition of Appendix 3 containing the list of countries participating in the Working Holidaymaker scheme which was inadvertently deleted by the last Statement of Changes in Immigration Rules (HC 645).

2005/645	Statement of Changes in Immigration Rules HC 645 – November 2005	This Statement of Changes in Immigration Rules contains the following three changes: – A new provision to allow overseas trained nurses to enter the UK to undertake a period of supervised practice leading to registration with the Nursing and Midwifery Council. – An extension of the mandatory entry clearance requirement for non-visa nationals seeking leave to enter the UK for a period of more than six months and the deletion of Appendix 3 from the Rules. – Incorporation of age eligibility of candidates for the Sectors Based Scheme.
2005/582	Statement of Changes in Immigration Rules HC 582 – October 2005	This Statement of Changes in Immigration Rules amends all existing provision for spouses and fiancés to also cover civil partners and proposed civil partners.
2005/299	Statement of Changes in Immigration Rules HC 299 – July 2005	This Statement of Changes in Immigration Rules contains the following two changes: – An amendment to the postgraduate doctors and dentists training structure, which has been subsequently re-amended by HC 1016. – An amendment to extend the non-compliance provisions beyond asylum applications to cover human rights claims.
2005/104	Statement of Changes in Immigration Rules HC 104 – June 2005	This Statement of Changes in Immigration Rules contains the following three changes: – A new provision for a 'Fresh Talent: Working in Scotland' scheme. This is a scheme to enable non-EEA nationals who have been awarded an HND, an undergraduate, or Master's degree, or a PhD, by a relevant Scottish institution, to apply to stay in Scotland for up to two years after completing their studies to seek and take work.

		– A minor change to reinstate a reference to the Working Holidaymaker Rules about the maximum period of leave which can be granted to working holidaymakers in their entry clearances. – A small amendment to the Rules to clarify that an application for variation of leave to enter or remain in the UK can be refused if the applicant fails to produce information required by the Secretary of State.

STATUTORY INSTRUMENTS

REPORTING OF SUSPICIOUS MARRIAGES AND REGISTRATION OF MARRIAGES (MISCELLANEOUS AMENDMENTS) REGULATIONS 2000

SI 2000/3164

Made ...29th November 2000

Coming into force ...1st January 2001

The Registrar General, in exercise of the powers conferred on him by section 27(1), 27B(2)(b), 31(2), (5) and (5D), and 74 of the Marriage Act 1949 (as extended by section 26(3) of the Welsh Language Act 1993), section 20(a) of the Registration Service Act 1953 and section 24(3) of the Immigration and Asylum Act 1999 and of all other powers enabling him in that behalf, with the approval of the Chancellor of the Exchequer, hereby makes the following Regulations:—

1 Citation, commencement and interpretation

(1) These Regulations may be cited as the Reporting of Suspicious Marriages and Registration of Marriages (Miscellaneous Amendments) Regulations 2000 and shall come into force on 1st January 2001.

(2) In these Regulations, unless the context otherwise requires—

"registration officer" means one of the persons referred to in section 24(1)(a) or (b) of the 1999 Act or a registrar of marriages as referred to in section 24(2)(a) of that Act;
"the 1949 Act" means the Marriage Act 1949;
"the 1970 Act" means the Marriage (Registrar General's Licence) Act 1970;
"the 1999 Act" means the Immigration and Asylum Act 1999;
"the Authorised Persons Regulations" means the Marriage (Authorised Persons) Regulations 1952;
"the principal Regulations" means the Registration of Marriages Regulations 1986; and
"the Welsh Regulations" means the Registration of Marriages (Welsh Language) Regulations 1999.

Appointment
1 January 2001: see para (1) above.

2 Reporting suspicious marriages

For the purposes of section 24 of the 1999 Act (reporting suspicious marriages) a registration officer shall—

(a) report his suspicions to the Secretary of State by making a report in writing or other permanent form giving the information specified in Schedule 1 to these Regulations, and
(b) forward that report to the Home Office, Immigration and Nationality Directorate, Intelligence Section, Status 3, 4 Nobel Drive, Hayes, Middlesex UB3 5EY or, where the Secretary of State has notified the Registrar General of another address to be used in relation to any particular registration district, that address.

Appointment
1 January 2001: see para (1) above.

3 Amendment of the Authorised Persons Regulations

(1) In regulation 9 (production and disposal of certificates, etc)—

(a) in paragraph (2) omit the words "or certificate and licence" and "or certificate and licence," where they appear; and
(b) omit the words "for transmission to the Registrar General".

(2) In regulation 19 (residence) omit paragraph (2).

(3) In regulation 22 (attestation) omit the words "or "licence" as the case may be".

(4) In the Schedule for "19", wherever it appears as part of a date to be inserted, substitute "20".

Appointment
1 January 2001: see para (1) above.

4 Amendment of the Principal Regulations

(1) In regulation 3 (forms of notice of marriage)—

(a) for paragraph (a) substitute—
"(a) where—
(i) both parties are aged eighteen or over, form 1, and
(ii) either party is, or both parties are, aged under eighteen, form 1A;"
and
(b) omit paragraph (b).

(2) In regulation 6(1) (declaration for intended marriage of certain persons related by affinity) for "a certificate" substitute "certificates".

(3) After regulation 6 insert—

6A

"Application to reduce the 15 day waiting period

(1) For the purposes of section 31(5A) of the 1949 Act (application to the Registrar General to reduce the 15 day waiting period) where—

(a) a marriage is intended to be solemnized on the authority of certificates of a superintendent registrar,
(b) each person has given notice of marriage, and
(c) either of them has, or they each have, a reason for applying for a reduction of the 15 day period,

the following paragraphs of this regulation shall apply.

(2) The applicant shall—

(a) complete form 8A, and
(b) pass the completed application together with the fee to the superintendent registrar of the registration district in which that person has given notice of marriage.

(3) The superintendent registrar shall immediately forward the completed application and fee to the Registrar General.

(4) If, upon receipt of a completed application, the Registrar General requires further information, which may include documents, before making his decision he may—

(a) request that the superintendent registrar who forwarded the completed application obtain the information from the applicant and forward it to him, or

(b) request it from the applicant.

(5) After the Registrar General has considered the completed application and, where relevant, any further information obtained, and he is satisfied that there are, or are not, as the case may be, compelling reasons for reducing the 15 day period, he shall notify his decision both to the applicant and the superintendent registrar who forwarded the completed application to him.

(6) In this regulation "the applicant" means the person seeking a reduction in the 15 day period and "the completed application" means the completed form 8A together with any copy documents which support the reason given in that form for applying for a reduction of the 15 day period.".

(4) In regulation 7 (authorities for marriage issued by a superintendent registrar and by the Registrar General)—

(a) in paragraph (1) omit "(marriage without licence)"; and
(b) omit paragraph 2.

(5) In regulation 8 (form of instructions for solemnization of a marriage etc) for "section 31(5) or 32(4) of the Act, as the case may be," substitute "section 31(5) of the Act".

(6) In regulation 11 (manner of registration) omit paragraph (3).

(7) In regulation 12 (entry of attestation) in paragraphs (a), (b) and (bb) respectively omit the words "or, as the case may be, "licence"".

(8) In Schedule 1 (prescribed forms)—

(a) for the list headed "Contents" substitute the list headed "Contents" in Schedule 2 to these Regulations;
(b) for form 1 (notice of marriage without licence) substitute the forms which appear as forms 1 and 1A in Schedule 2 to these Regulations;
(c) in form 9 (certificate for marriage)—
  (i) for "of the district of ......, in the ......" substitute "of the district of ......";
  (ii) after the words "notice was" insert "given by ...... and"; and
  (iii) for the heading to column (8) substitute "Nationality and District of residence";
(d) in form 12 (instructions for the solemnization of a marriage in a registered building without the presence of a registrar) for paragraphs 1, 2 and 4 substitute the following paragraphs—

"**1** This marriage must take place in the registered building named in the superintendent registrar's certificates for marriage, **and nowhere else**.

2 The authorised person duly appointed for the registered building named in the certificates, or an authorised person for some other registered building in the same registration district, must be present at the marriage.

4 Each certificate issued by a superintendent registrar as the legal authority for the marriage must be delivered to the authorised person in whose presence the marriage is to be solemnized. Unless these certificates are in his possession the authorised person must on no account allow the marriage to take place.";

(e) after form 8 (declaration for marriages of certain persons related by affinity) insert the form which appears as form 8A in Schedule 2 to these Regulations;
(f) omit forms 2 (notice of marriage with licence) and 10 (certificate and licence for marriage); and
(g) where in any of the prescribed forms "19" appears as part of a date to be inserted, substitute "20".

Appointment
1 January 2001: see para (1) above.

5 Amendment of the Welsh Regulations

(1) For regulation 2 (forms of notice of marriage and of endorsement on notice) substitute—

"2 In relation to a notice of marriage attested in Wales regulation 3(a) and 4 of the principal Regulations (forms of notice of marriage and endorsement on notice of marriage) shall have effect as if they referred respectively not to forms 1 or 1A and 4 in Schedule 1 to those Regulations but to forms 1 or 1A and 3 respectively in Schedule 1 to these Regulations.".

(2) After regulation 4 (declaration of certain affinal relationships) insert—

4A

"Application to reduce the 15 day waiting period

In relation to a notice of marriage given in Wales, regulation 6A of the principal Regulations (application to reduce the 15 day waiting period) shall have effect as if it referred not to form 8A in Schedule 1 to those Regulations but to form 8A in Schedule 1 to these Regulations.".

(3) For regulation 5 (authorities for marriage issued by a superintendent registrar etc) substitute—

"5 In relation to a certificate for marriage issued in Wales regulations 7(1) and 8 of the principal Regulations (authorities for marriage issued by a superintendent registrar etc and form of instructions for solemnization of a marriage etc) shall have effect as if they referred respectively not to forms 9 and 12 in Schedule 1 to those Regulations but to forms 6 and 8 in Schedule 1 to these Regulations.".

(4) In regulation 7 (completion of forms)—

- (a) in paragraph (1) for "Forms 1 to 7" substitute "Forms 1 to 6 and 8A"; and
- (b) in paragraph 1(a)(i) for "forms 1 to 4, 6 and 7" substitute "forms 1 to 4, 6 and 8A".

(5) In Schedule 1 (prescribed forms)—

- (a) for the list headed "Prescribed forms" substitute the list headed "Prescribed forms" in Schedule 3 to these Regulations;
- (b) for form 1 (notice of marriage without licence), substitute the forms which appear as forms 1 and 1A in Schedule 3 to these Regulations;
- (c) in form 6 (certificate for marriage)—
  - (i) in the titles delete "without licence" and "heb drwydded";
  - (ii) for "of the district of .... in the county of ...." substitute "of the district of ....";
  - (iii) for "dosbarth .... yn sir ...." substitute "dosbarth ....";
  - (iv) after the words "notice was" insert "given by .... and";
  - (v) after the words "hysbysiad gael ei" insert "roddi gan .... a'i"; and
  - (vi) for the headings to column (8) substitute "Nationality and District of residence" and "Cenedligrwydd a Dosbarth y breswylfa";
- (d) in form 8 (form of instructions) for paragraphs 1, 2 and 4 substitute the following paragraphs—

"1 This marriage must take place in the registered building named in the superintendent registrar's certificates for marriage, **and nowhere else**.

2 The authorised person duly appointed for the registered building named in the certificates, or an authorised person for some other registered building in the same registration district, must be present at the marriage.

4 Each certificate issued by a superintendent registrar as the legal authority for the marriage must be delivered to the authorised person in whose presence the marriage is to be solemnized. Unless these certificates are in his possession the authorised person must on no account allow the marriage to take place."

and

"**1** Mae'n rhaid cynnal y briodas hon yn yr adeilad cofrestredig a enwir ar dystysgrifau priodas y cofrestrydd arolygol, **ac yn unman arall**.

2 Mae'n rhaid i'r person awdurdodedig a benodwyd ar gyfer yr adeilad cofrestredig a enwir ar y tystysgrifau neu berson awdurdodedig ar gyfer adeilad cofrestredig arall yn yr un dosbarth cofrestru fod yn bresennol yn y briodas.

4 Mae'n rhaid danfon pob tystysgrif a gyflwynir gan gofrestrydd arolygol fel awdurdod cyfreithiol y briodas i'r person awdurdodedig y bydd y briodas yn cael ei gweinyddu yn ei (g)wydd. Oni fydd y tystysgrifau hyn yn ei m/feddiant ni ddylai'r person awdurdodedig ar unrhyw gyfrif ganiatáu i'r briodas gael ei chynnal.";

(e) after form 8 insert the form which appears as form 8A in Schedule 3 to these Regulations; and

(f) forms 2 (notice of marriage with licence) and 7 (certificate and licence for marriage) shall be omitted.

(6) In Schedule 2 in column 1 omit "licence" and in column 2 omit "trwydded".

Appointment
1 January 2001: see para (1) above.

6 Transitional provision

Regulations 3, 4 and 5 shall not apply in respect of any marriage, notice of which has been entered in the marriage notice book for—

(a) the registration district referred to in section 27(1)(a) or (2) of the 1949 Act, or

(b) each registration district referred to in section 27(1)(b) of the 1949 Act,

before 1st January 2001.

Appointment
1 January 2001: see para (1) above.

SCHEDULE 1
INFORMATION TO BE PROVIDED WHEN REPORTING A SUSPICIOUS MARRIAGE

Regulation 2

Name and surname of each party to the marriage

Date of birth and/or age of each party to the marriage

[Condition] of each party to the marriage

Address (and district of residence) of each party to the marriage

Nationality of each party to the marriage

Date of marriage

Place of marriage

Time of marriage

Nature of evidence produced in respect of—

(i) name and age
(ii) [condition]
(iii) nationality

of the parties to the marriage

Reason for making the report

Full name of registration officer making the report

Date report made

Appointment
1 January 2001: see para (1) above.

Amendment
SI 2005/3177, reg 8.

SCHEDULE 2

Regulation 4(8)

"CONTENTS

Form	*Relevant regulation*	*Description*	*Statutory purpose*
1	3(a)(i)	Notice of marriage where both parties aged 18 or over	Marriage Act 1949, section 27(1)
1A	3(a)(ii)	Notice of marriage where either or both parties under 18	Marriage Act 1949, section 27(1)
3	3(c)	Notice of marriage by Registrar General's licence	Marriage (Registrar General's Licence) Act 1970, section 2(1)
4	4	Endorsement on notice of marriage	Marriage Act 1949, section 35(1)
5	5(a)	Statement by registered medical practitioner	Marriage Act 1949, section 27A(2) and (7)
6	5(b)	Statement by responsible authority	Marriage Act 1949, section 27A(3)
7	5(c)	Particulars of person by or before whom marriage intended to be solemnized	Marriage Act 1949, section 27A(4)
8	6	Declaration for marriages of certain persons related by affinity	Marriage Act 1949, section 27B(2)(b)
8A	6A	Application to reduce the 15 day waiting period	Marriage Act 1949, section 31(5D)
9	7(1)	Certificate for marriage	Marriage Act 1949, section 31(2)
11	7(3)	Registrar General's licence for marriage	Marriage (Registrar General's Licence) Act 1970, section 7

12	8	Form of instructions	Marriage Act 1949, sections 31(5) and 32(4)
13	10(1)	Form of marriage entry	Marriage Act 1949, section 55(1)
14	18(a)	Quarterly return of marriages	Marriage Act 1949, section 57(2)
15	18(b)	Certificate of no registration	Marriage Act 1949, section 57(2)"

FORM 1
NOTICE OF MARRIAGE

Regulation 3(a)(i)
Marriage Act 1949, s 27(1)

PARTICULARS RELATING TO THE PERSONS TO BE MARRIED

(The full text of this form is currently unavailable. Please see the original.)

FORM 1A
NOTICE OF MARRIAGE

Regulation 3(a)(i)
Marriage Act 1949, s 27(1)

PARTICULARS RELATING TO THE PERSONS TO BE MARRIED

(The full text of this form is currently unavailable. Please see the original.)

FORM 8A
APPLICATION TO REDUCE THE 15 DAY WAITING PERIOD

Regulation 6A(2)
Marriage Act 1949, s 31(5A)

(The full text of this form is currently unavailable. Please see the original.)

Appointment
1 January 2001: see para (1) above.

SCHEDULE 3

Regulation 5(5)

"PRESCRIBED FORMS

CONTENTS

Form	*Relevant regulation*	*Description*	*Statutory purpose*
1	2	Notice of marriage where both parties aged 18 or over	Marriage Act 1949, section 27(1)
1A	2	Notice of marriage where either or both parties under 18	Marriage Act 1949, section 27(1)
3	2	Endorsement on notice of marriage	Marriage Act 1949, section 35(1)

4	3	Particulars of person by or before whom marriage intended to be solemnized	Marriage Act 1949, section 27A(4)
5	4	Declaration for marriages of certain persons related by affinity	Marriage Act 1949, section 27B(2)(b)
6	5	Certificate for marriage	Marriage Act 1949, section 31(2)
8	5	Form of instructions	Marriage Act 1949, sections 31(5D) and 32(4)
8A	4A	Application to reduce the 15 day waiting period	Marriage Act 1949, section 31(5)
9	6	Form of marriage entry	Marriage Act 1949, section 55(1)"

FORM 1
NOTICE OF MARRIAGEHYSBYSIAD PRIODAS

Regulation 2
Marriage Act 1949, s 27(1)

PARTICULARS RELATING TO THE PERSONS TO BE MARRIED
MANYLION YNGLYN Â'R PERSONAU A BRIODIR

(*The full text of this form is currently unavailable. Please see the original.*)

FORM 1A
NOTICE OF MARRIAGEHYSBYSIAD PRIODAS

Regulation 2
Marriage Act 1949, s 27(1)

PARTICULARS RELATING TO THE PERSONS TO BE MARRIED
MANYLION YNGLYN Â'R PERSONAU A BRIODIR

(*The full text of this form is currently unavailable. Please see the original.*)

FORM 8A
APPLICATION TO REDUCE THE 15 DAY WAITING PERIOD
CAIS I LEIHAU'R CYFNOD AROS O 15 DIWRNOD

Regulation 6A(2)
Marriage Act 1949, s 31(5A)

(*The full text of this form is currently unavailable. Please see the original.*)

Appointment
1 January 2001: see para (1) above.

IMMIGRATION (NOTICES) REGULATIONS 2003

SI 2003/658

Made ...11th March 2003

Laid before Parliament ...11th March 2003

Coming into force ...1st April 2003

The Secretary of State, in exercise of the powers conferred on him by section 105 and 112(1) to (3) of the Nationality, Immigration and Asylum Act 2002, hereby makes the following Regulations:

1 Citation and commencement

These Regulations may be cited as the Immigration (Notices) Regulations 2003 and shall come into force on the 1st April 2003.

Initial Commencement
Specified date: 1 April 2003: see above.

2 Interpretation

In these Regulations—

"the 1971 Act" means the Immigration Act 1971;
"the 1997 Act" means the Special Immigration Appeals Commission Act 1997;
"the 1999 Act" means the Immigration and Asylum Act 1999;
"the 2002 Act" means the Nationality, Immigration and Asylum Act 2002;
"decision-maker" means—
(a) the Secretary of State;
(b) an immigration officer;
(c) an entry clearance officer;
"EEA decision" means an immigration decision within the meaning of section 109(3) of the 2002 Act or a decision under Regulation 1251/70 which concerns a person's—
(a) removal from the United Kingdom;
(b) entitlement to be admitted to the United Kingdom; ...
(c) entitlement to be issued with or to have removed, or not to have removed, a residence permit or residence document; [or]
[(d) on or after 30th April 2006, entitlement to be issued with or have renewed, or not to have revoked, a registration certificate, residence card, document certifying permanent residence or permanent residence card;]
"entry clearance officer" means a person responsible for the grant or refusal of entry clearance;
"immigration decision" has the same meaning as in section 82(2) of the 2002 Act;
"minor" means a person who is under 18 years of age;
"notice of appeal" means a notice in the appropriate prescribed form in accordance with the rules for the time being in force under section 106(1) of the 2002 Act;
"Procedure Rules" means rules made under section 106(1) of the 2002 Act;
"representative" means a person who appears to the decision-maker—
(a) to be the representative of a person referred to in regulation 4(1) below; and
(b) not to be prohibited from acting as a representative by section 84 of the 1999 Act.

Initial Commencement
Specified date: 1 April 2003: see reg 1.

Amendment
SI 2006/1003, reg 31, Sch 5.

3 Transitional provision

These Regulations apply to a decision to make a deportation order which, by virtue of paragraph 12 of Schedule 15 to the 1999 Act,—

(a) is appealable under section 15 of the 1971 Act (appeals in respect of deportation orders); or
(b) would be appealable under section 15 of the 1971 Act, but for section 15(3) (deportation conducive to public good), and is appealable under section 2(1)(c) of the 1997 Act (appeal to Special Immigration Appeals Commission against a decision to make a deportation order).

Initial Commencement
Specified date: 1 April 2003: see reg 1.

4 Notice of decisions

(1) Subject to regulation 6, the decision-maker must give written notice to a person of any immigration decision or EEA decision taken in respect of him which is appealable.

(2) The decision-maker must give written notice to a person of the relevant grant of leave to enter or remain if, as a result of that grant, a right of appeal arises under section 83(2) of the 2002 Act.

[(2A) The decision-maker must give written notice to a person of a decision that they are no longer a refugee if as a result of that decision a right of appeal arises under section 83A(2) of the 2002 Act.]

(3) If the notice is given to the representative of the person, it is to be taken to have been given to the person.

Initial Commencement
Specified date: 1 April 2003: see reg 1.

Amendment
SI 2006/2168, regs 2, 3.

5 Contents of notice

[(1) A notice given under regulation 4(1)—

(a) is to include or be accompanied by a statement of the reasons for the decision to which it relates; and
(b) if it relates to an immigration decision specified in section 82(2)(a), (g), (h), (i), (ia) or (j) of the 2002 Act—
    (i) shall state the country or territory to which it is proposed to remove the person; or
    (i) may, if it appears to the decision-maker that the person to whom the notice is to be given may be removable to more than one country or territory, state any such countries or territories.]

(2) A notice given under regulation 4(2) is to include or be accompanied by a statement of the reasons for the rejection of the claim for asylum.

(3) Subject to paragraph (6), the notice given under regulation 4 shall also include, or be accompanied by, a statement which advises the person of—

- (a) his right of appeal and the statutory provision on which his right of appeal is based;
- (b) whether or not such an appeal may be brought while in the United Kingdom;
- (c) the grounds on which such an appeal may be brought; and
- (d) the facilities available for advice and assistance in connection with such an appeal.

(4) Subject to paragraph (6), the notice given under regulation 4 shall be accompanied by a notice of appeal which indicates the time limit for bringing the appeal, the address to which it should be sent or may be taken by hand and a fax number for service by fax.

(5) Subject to paragraph (6), where the exercise of the right is restricted by an exception or limitation by virtue of a provision of Part 5 of the 2002 Act, the notice given under regulation 4 shall include or be accompanied by a statement which refers to the provision limiting or restricting the right of appeal.

(6) The notice given under regulation 4 need not comply with paragraphs (3), (4) and (5) where a right of appeal may only be exercised on the grounds referred to in section 84(1)(b), (c) or (g) of the 2002 Act by virtue of the operation of section 88(4), 89(3), 90(4), 91(2), 98(4) or (5) of that Act.

(7) Where notice is given under regulation 4 and paragraph (6) applies, if the person claims in relation to the immigration decision or the EEA decision that—

- (a) the decision is unlawful by virtue of section 19B of the Race Relations Act 1976 (discrimination by public authorities);
- (b) the decision is unlawful under section 6 of the Human Rights Act 1998 (public authority not to act contrary to the Human Rights Convention) as being incompatible with the person's Convention rights; or
- (c) removal of the person from the United Kingdom in consequence of the immigration decision would breach the United Kingdom's obligations under the Refugee Convention or would be unlawful under section 6 of the Human Rights Act 1998 as being incompatible with the person's Convention rights,

the decision-maker must as soon as practicable re-serve the notice of decision under regulation 4 and paragraph (6) of this regulation shall not apply.

(8) Where a notice is re-served under paragraph (7), the time limit for appeal under the Procedure Rules shall be calculated as if the notice of decision had been served on the date on which it was re-served.

Initial Commencement
Specified date: 1 April 2003: see reg 1.

Amendment
SI 2006/2168, regs, 2, 4.

6 Certain notices under the 1971 Act deemed to comply with the Regulations

(1) This regulation applies where the power to—

- (a) refuse leave to enter; or
- (b) vary leave to enter or remain in the United Kingdom;

is exercised by notice in writing under section 4 of (administration of control), or paragraph 6(2) (notice of decisions of leave to enter or remain) of Schedule 2 to, the 1971 Act.

(2) If—

- (a) the statement required by regulation 5(3) is included in or accompanies that notice; and
- (b) the notice is given in accordance with the provision of regulation 7;

the notice is to be taken to have been given under regulation 4(1) for the purposes of these Regulations.

Initial Commencement
Specified date: 1 April 2003: see reg 1.

7 Service of notice

(1) A notice required to be given under regulation 4 may be—

- (a) given by hand;
- (b) sent by fax;
- (c) sent by postal service in which delivery or receipt is recorded to:-
  - (i) an address provided for correspondence by the person or his representative; or
  - (ii) where no address for correspondence has been provided by the person, the last-known or usual place of abode or place of business of the person or his representative.

(2) Where—

- (a) a person's whereabouts are not known; and
- (b)
  - (i) no address has been provided for correspondence and the decision-maker does not know the last-known or usual place of abode or place of business of the person; or
  - (ii) the address provided to the decision-maker is defective, false or no longer in use by the person; and
- (c) no representative appears to be acting for the person,

the notice shall be deemed to have been given when the decision-maker enters a record of the above circumstances and places the signed notice on the relevant file.

(3) Where a notice has been given in accordance with paragraph (2) and then subsequently the person is located, he shall be given a copy of the notice and details of when and how it was given as soon as is practicable.

(4) Where a notice is sent by post in accordance with paragraph (1)(c) it shall be deemed to have been served, unless the contrary is proved,—

- (a) on the second day after it was posted if it is sent to a place within the United Kingdom;
- (b) on the twenty-eighth day after it was posted if it is sent to a place outside the United Kingdom.

(5) For the purposes of paragraph (4) the period is to be calculated—

- (a) excluding the day on which the notice is posted; and
- (b) in the case of paragraph (4)(a), excluding any day which is not a business day.

(6) In this regulation, "business day" means any day other than Saturday or Sunday, a day which is a bank holiday under the Banking and Financial Dealings Act 1971 in the part of the United Kingdom to which the notice is sent, Christmas Day or Good Friday.

(7) A notice given under regulation 4 may, in the case of a minor who does not have a representative, be given to the parent, guardian or another adult who for the time being takes responsibility for the child.

Initial Commencement
Specified date: 1 April 2003: see reg 1.

ADOPTIONS WITH A FOREIGN ELEMENT REGULATIONS 2005

SI 2005/392

Made ...24th February 2005

Laid before Parliament ...2nd March 2005

Coming into force ...30th December 2005

The Secretary of State for Education and Skills, in exercise of the powers conferred on her by section 1(1), (3) and (5) of the Adoption (Intercountry Aspects) Act 1999 and sections 83(4), (5), (6) and (7), 84(3) and (6), 140(7) and (8), 142(4) and (5) of the Adoption and Children Act 2002, and of all other powers enabling her in that behalf, after consultation with the National Assembly for Wales, hereby makes the following Regulations:—

PART 1
GENERAL

1 Citation, commencement and application

(1) These Regulations may be cited as the Adoptions with a Foreign Element Regulations 2005 and shall come into force on 30th December 2005.

(2) These Regulations apply to England and Wales.

Initial Commencement
Specified date: 30 December 2005: see para (1) above.

2 Interpretation

In these Regulations—

"the Act" means the Adoption and Children Act 2002;
"adoption support services" has the meaning given in section 2(6)(a) of the Act and any regulations made under section 2(6)(b) of the Act;
"adoptive family" has the same meaning as in regulation 31(2)(a) of the Agencies Regulations or corresponding Welsh provision;
"adoption panel" means a panel established in accordance with regulation 3 of the Agencies Regulations or corresponding Welsh provision;
"the Agencies Regulations" means the Adoption Agencies Regulations 2005;
"child's case record" has the same meaning as in regulation 12 of the Agencies Regulations or corresponding Welsh provision;
"CA of the receiving State" means, in relation to a Convention country other than the United Kingdom, the Central Authority of the receiving State;

"CA of the State of origin" means, in relation to a Convention country other than the United Kingdom, the Central Authority of the State of origin;
"Convention adoption" is given a meaning by virtue of section 66(1)(c) of the Act;
"Convention country" has the same meaning as in section 144(1) of the Act;
"Convention list" means—
- (a) in relation to a relevant Central Authority, a list of children notified to that Authority in accordance with regulation 40; or
- (b) in relation to any other Central Authority within the British Islands, a list of children notified to that Authority in accordance with provisions, which correspond to regulation 40.

"corresponding Welsh provision" in relation to a Part or a regulation of the Agencies Regulations means the provision of regulations made by the Assembly under section 9 of the Act which corresponds to that Part or regulation;
"prospective adopter's case record" has the same meaning as in regulation 22(1) of the Agencies Regulations or corresponding Welsh provision;
"prospective adopter's report" has the same meaning as in regulation 25(5) of the Agencies Regulations or corresponding Welsh provisions;
"receiving State" has the same meaning as in Article 2 of the Convention;
"relevant Central Authority" means—
- (a) in Chapter 1 of Part 3, in relation to a prospective adopter who is habitually resident in—
  - (i) England, the Secretary of State; and
  - (ii) Wales, the National Assembly for Wales; and
- (b) in Chapter 2 of Part 3 in relation to a local authority in—
  - (i) England, the Secretary of State; and
  - (ii) Wales, the National Assembly for Wales;

"relevant local authority" means in relation to a prospective adopter—
- (a) the local authority within whose area he has his home; or
- (b) in the case where he no longer has a home in England or Wales, the local authority for the area in which he last had his home;

"relevant foreign authority" means a person, outside the British Islands performing functions in the country in which the child is, or in which the prospective adopter is, habitually resident which correspond to the functions of an adoption agency or to the functions of the Secretary of State in respect of adoptions with a foreign element;
"State of origin" has the same meaning as in Article 2 of the Convention.

Initial Commencement
Specified date: 30 December 2005: see reg 1(1).

PART 2
BRINGING CHILDREN INTO AND OUT OF THE UNITED KINGDOM

CHAPTER 1
BRINGING CHILDREN INTO THE UNITED KINGDOM

3 Requirements applicable in respect of bringing or causing a child to be brought into the United Kingdom

A person intending to bring, or to cause another to bring, a child into the United Kingdom in circumstances where section 83(1) of the Act applies must—

- (a) apply in writing to an adoption agency for an assessment of his suitability to adopt a child; and
- (b) give the adoption agency any information it may require for the purpose of the assessment.

Initial Commencement
Specified date: 30 December 2005: see reg 1(1).

4 Conditions applicable in respect of a child brought into the United Kingdom

(1) This regulation prescribes the conditions for the purposes of section 83(5) of the Act in respect of a child brought into the United Kingdom in circumstances where section 83 applies.

(2) Prior to the child's entry into the United Kingdom, the prospective adopter must—

- (a) receive in writing, notification from the Secretary of State that she has issued a certificate confirming to the relevant foreign authority—
  - (i) that the person has been assessed and approved as eligible and suitable to be an adoptive parent in accordance with Part 4 of the Agencies Regulations or corresponding Welsh provision; and
  - (ii) that if entry clearance and leave to enter and remain, as may be necessary, is granted and not revoked or curtailed, and an adoption order is made or an overseas adoption is effected, the child will be authorised to enter and reside permanently in the United Kingdom;
- (b) before visiting the child in the State of origin—
  - (i) notify the adoption agency of the details of the child to be adopted;
  - (ii) provide the adoption agency with any information and reports received from the relevant foreign authority; and
  - (iii) meet with the adoption agency to discuss the proposed adoption and information received from the relevant foreign authority;
- (c) visit the child in the State of origin (and where the prospective adopters are a couple each of them); and
- (d) after that visit—
  - (i) confirm in writing to the adoption agency that he has done so and wishes to proceed with the adoption;
  - (ii) provide the adoption agency with any additional reports and information received on or after that visit; and
  - (iii) notify the adoption agency of his expected date of entry into the United Kingdom with the child.

(3) The prospective adopter must accompany the child on entering the United Kingdom unless, in the case of a couple, the adoption agency and the relevant foreign authority have agreed that it is necessary for only one of them to do so.

(4) Except where an overseas adoption is or is to be effected, the prospective adopter must within the period of 14 days beginning with the date on which the child is brought into the United Kingdom give notice to the relevant local authority—

- (a) of the child's arrival in the United Kingdom; and
- (b) of his intention—
  - (i) to apply for an adoption order in accordance with section 44(2) of the Act; or
  - (ii) not to give the child a home.

(5) In a case where a prospective adopter has given notice in accordance with paragraph (4) and subsequently moves his home into the area of another local authority, he must within 14 days of that move confirm in writing to that authority, the child's entry into the United Kingdom and that notice of his intention—

- (a) to apply for an adoption order in accordance with section 44(2) of the Act has been given to another local authority; or
- (b) not to give the child a home,

has been given.

Initial Commencement
Specified date: 30 December 2005: see reg 1(1).

5 Functions imposed on the local authority

(1) Where notice of intention to adopt has been given to the local authority, that authority must—

(a) if it has not already done so, set up a case record in respect of the child and place on it any information received from the—
 (i) relevant foreign authority;
 (ii) adoption agency, if it is not the local authority;
 (iii) prospective adopter;
 (iv) entry clearance officer; and
 (v) Secretary of State, or as the case may be, the Assembly;

(b) send the prospective adopter's general practitioner written notification of the arrival in England or Wales of the child and send with that notification a written report of the child's health history and current state of health, so far as is known;

(c) send to the Primary Care Trust or Local Health Board (Wales), in whose area the prospective adopter has his home, written notification of the arrival in England or Wales of the child;

(d) where the child is of compulsory school age, send to the local education authority, in whose area the prospective adopter has his home, written notification of the arrival of the child in England or Wales and information, if known, about the child's educational history and whether he is likely to be assessed for special educational needs under the Education Act 1996;

(e) ensure that the child and the prospective adopter are visited within one week of receipt of the notice of intention to adopt and thereafter not less than once a week until the review referred to in sub-paragraph (f) and thereafter at such frequency as the authority may decide;

(f) carry out a review of the child's case not more than 4 weeks after receipt of the notice of intention to adopt and—
 (i) visit and, if necessary, review not more than 3 months after that initial review; and
 (ii) thereafter not more than 6 months after the date of the previous visit,

unless the child no longer has his home with the prospective adopter or an adoption order is made;

(g) when carrying out a review consider—
 (i) the child's needs, welfare and development, and whether any changes need to be made to meet his needs or assist his development;
 (ii) the arrangements for the provision of adoption support services and whether there should be any re-assessment of the need for those services; and
 (iii) the need for further visits and reviews; and

(h) ensure that—
 (i) advice is given as to the child's needs, welfare and development;
 (ii) written reports are made of all visits and reviews of the case and placed on the child's case record; and
 (iii) on such visits, where appropriate, advice is given as to the availability of adoption support services.

(2) Part 7 of the Agencies Regulations or corresponding Welsh provision (case records) shall apply to the case record set up in respect of the child as a consequence of this regulation as if that record had been set up under the Agencies Regulations or corresponding Welsh provision.

(3) In a case where the prospective adopter fails to make an application under section 50 or 51 of the Act within two years of the receipt by a local authority of the notice of intention to adopt the local authority must review the case.

(4) For the purposes of the review referred to in paragraph (3), the local authority must consider—

- (a) the child's needs, welfare and development, and whether any changes need to be made to meet his needs or assist his development;
- (b) the arrangements, if any, in relation to the exercise of parental responsibility for the child;
- (c) the terms upon which leave to enter the United Kingdom is granted and the immigration status of the child;
- (d) the arrangements for the provision of adoption support services for the adoptive family and whether there should be any re-assessment of the need for those services; and
- (e) in conjunction with the appropriate agencies, the arrangements for meeting the child's health care and educational needs.

(5) In a case where the local authority to which notice of intention to adopt is given ("the original authority") is notified by the prospective adopter that he intends to move or has moved his home into the area of another local authority, the original authority must notify the local authority into whose area the prospective adopter intends to move or has moved, within 14 days of receiving information in respect of that move, of—

- (a) the name, sex, date and place of birth of child;
- (b) the prospective adopter's name, sex and date of birth;
- (c) the date on which the child entered the United Kingdom;
- (d) where the original authority received notification of intention to adopt, the date of receipt of such notification whether an application for an adoption order has been made and the stage of those proceedings; and
- (e) any other relevant information.

Initial Commencement
Specified date: 30 December 2005: see reg 1(1).

6 Application of Chapter 3 of the Act

In the case of a child brought into the United Kingdom for adoption in circumstances where section 83 of the Act applies—

- (a) the modifications in regulations 7 to 9 apply;
- (b) section 36(2) and (5) (restrictions on removal) and section 39(3)(a) (partners of parents) of the Act shall not apply.

Initial Commencement
Specified date: 30 December 2005: see reg 1(1).

7 Change of name and removal from the United Kingdom

Section 28(2) of the Act (further consequences of placement) shall apply as if from the words "is placed" to "then", there is substituted "enters the United Kingdom in the circumstances where section 83(1)(a) of this Act applies".

Initial Commencement
Specified date: 30 December 2005: see reg 1(1).

8 Return of the child

(1) Section 35 of the Act (return of child) shall apply with the following modifications.

(2) Subsections (1), (2) and (3) shall apply as if in each place where—

- (a) the words "is placed for adoption by an adoption agency" occur there were substituted "enters the United Kingdom in circumstances where section 83(1) applies";
- (b) the words "the agency" occur there were substituted the words "the local authority"; and
- (c) the words "any parent or guardian of the child" occur there were substituted "the Secretary of State or, as the case may be, the Assembly".

(3) Subsection (5) shall apply as if for the words "an adoption agency" or "the agency" there were substituted the words "the local authority".

Initial Commencement
Specified date: 30 December 2005: see reg 1(1).

9 Child to live with adopters before application

(1) In a case where the requirements imposed by section 83(4) of the Act have been complied with and the conditions required by section 83(5) of the Act have been met, section 42 shall apply as if—

- (a) subsection (3) is omitted; and
- (b) in subsection (5) the words from "three years" to "preceding" there were substituted "six months".

(2) In a case where the requirements imposed by section 83(4) of the Act have not been complied with or the conditions required by section 83(5) have not been met, section 42 shall apply as if—

- (a) subsection (3) is omitted; and
- (b) in subsection (5) the words from "three years" to "preceding" there were substituted "twelve months".

Initial Commencement
Specified date: 30 December 2005: see reg 1(1).

CHAPTER 2
TAKING CHILDREN OUT OF THE UNITED KINGDOM

10 Requirements applicable in respect of giving parental responsibility prior to adoption abroad

The prescribed requirements for the purposes of section 84(3) of the Act (requirements to be satisfied prior to the making of an order) are that—

- (a) in the case of a child placed by an adoption agency, that agency has—
  - (i) confirmed to the court that it has complied with the requirements imposed in accordance with Part 3 of the Agencies Regulations or corresponding Welsh provision;
  - (ii) submitted to the court—
    - (aa) the reports and information referred to in regulation 17(2) and (3) of the Agencies Regulations or corresponding Welsh provision;

(bb) the recommendations made by the adoption panel in accordance with regulations 18 (placing child for adoption) and 33 (proposed placement) of the Agencies Regulations or corresponding Welsh provision;
(cc) the adoption placement report prepared in accordance with regulation 31(2)(d) of the Agencies Regulations or corresponding Welsh provision;
(dd) the reports of and information obtained in respect of the visits and reviews referred to in regulation 36 of the Agencies Regulations or corresponding Welsh provision; and
(ee) the report referred to in section 43 of the Act as modified by regulation 11;

(b) in the case of a child placed by an adoption agency the relevant foreign authority has—
(i) confirmed in writing to that agency that the prospective adopter has been counselled and the legal implications of adoption have been explained to him;
(ii) prepared a report on the suitability of the prospective adopter to be an adoptive parent;
(iii) determined and confirmed in writing to that agency that he is eligible and suitable to adopt in the country or territory in which the adoption is to be effected; and
(iv) confirmed in writing to that agency that the child is or will be authorised to enter and reside permanently in that foreign country or territory; and

(c) in the case of a child placed by an adoption agency the prospective adopter has confirmed in writing to the adoption agency that he will accompany the child on taking him out of the United Kingdom and entering the country or territory where the adoption is to be effected, or in the case of a couple, the agency and relevant foreign authority have confirmed that it is necessary for only one of them to do so.

Initial Commencement
Specified date: 30 December 2005: see reg 1(1).

11 Application of the Act in respect of orders under section 84

(1) The following provisions of the Act which refer to adoption orders shall apply to orders under section 84 as if in each place where the words "adoption order" appear there were substituted "order under section 84"—

(a) section 1(7)(a) (coming to a decision relating to adoption of a child);
(b) section 18(4) (placement for adoption by agencies);
(c) section 21(4)(b) (placement orders);
(d) section 22(5)(a) and (b) (application for placement orders);
(e) section 24(4) (revoking placement orders);
(f) section 28(1) (further consequences of placement);
(g) section 29(4)(a) and (5)(a) (further consequences of placement orders);
(h) section 32(5) (recovery by parent etc where child placed and consent withdrawn);
(i) section 42(7) (sufficient opportunity for adoption agency to see the child);
(j) section 43 (reports where child placed by agency);
(k) section 44(2) (notice of intention to adopt);
(l) section 47(1) to (5), (8) and (9) (conditions for making orders);
(m) section 48(1) (restrictions on making applications);
(n) section 50(1) and (2) (adoption by a couple);
(o) section 51(1) to (4) (adoption by one person);
(p) section 52(1) to (4) (parental etc consent);

(q) section 53(5) (contribution towards maintenance); and
(r) section 141(3) and (4)(c) (rules of procedure).

(2) Section 35(5) of the Act (return of child in other cases) shall apply to orders under section 84 of that Act as if in paragraph (b) of that subsection—

(a) for the first reference to "adoption order" there were substituted "order under section 84(1)"; and
(b) the words in brackets were omitted.

Initial Commencement
Specified date: 30 December 2005: see reg 1(1).

PART 3
ADOPTIONS UNDER THE CONVENTION

CHAPTER 1
REQUIREMENTS, PROCEDURE, RECOGNITION AND EFFECT OF ADOPTIONS WHERE THE UNITED KINGDOM IS THE RECEIVING STATE

12 Application of Chapter 1

The provisions in this Chapter shall apply where a couple or a person, habitually resident in the British Islands, wishes to adopt a child who is habitually resident in a Convention country outside the British Islands in accordance with the Convention.

Initial Commencement
Specified date: 30 December 2005: see reg 1(1).

13 Requirements applicable in respect of eligibility and suitability

(1) A couple or a person who wishes to adopt a child habitually resident in a Convention country outside the British Islands shall—

(a) apply in writing to an adoption agency for a determination of eligibility, and an assessment of his suitability, to adopt; and
(b) give the agency any information it may require for the purposes of the assessment.

(2) An adoption agency may not consider an application under paragraph (1) unless at the date of that application—

(a) in the case of an application by a couple, they have both—
 (i) attained the age of 21 years; and
 (ii) been habitually resident in a part of the British Islands for a period of not less than one year ending with the date of application; and
(b) in the case of an application by one person, he has—
 (i) attained the age of 21 years; and
 (ii) been habitually resident in a part of the British Islands for a period of not less than one year ending with the date of application.

Initial Commencement
Specified date: 30 December 2005: see reg 1(1).

14 Counselling and information

(1) An adoption agency must provide a counselling service in accordance with regulation 21(1)(a) of the Agencies Regulations or corresponding Welsh provision and must—

(a) explain to the prospective adopter the procedure in relation to, and the legal implications of, adopting a child from the State of origin from which the prospective adopter wishes to adopt in accordance with the Convention; and
(b) provide him with written information about the matters referred to in sub-paragraph (a).

(2) Paragraph (1) does not apply if the adoption agency is satisfied that the requirements set out in that paragraph have been carried out in respect of the prospective adopter by another agency.

Initial Commencement
Specified date: 30 December 2005: see reg 1(1).

15 Procedure in respect of carrying out an assessment

(1) Regulation 22 of the Agencies Regulations (requirement to consider application for an assessment of suitability) or corresponding Welsh provision shall apply as if the reference to an application in those Regulations or corresponding Welsh provision was to an application made in accordance with regulation 13.

(2) Where the adoption agency is satisfied that the requirements in—

(a) regulation 14; and
(b) regulations 23 (police checks) and 24 (preparation for adoption) of the Agencies Regulations or corresponding Welsh provision,

have been meet, regulations 25 (prospective adopter's report) and 26 (adoption panel) of the Agencies Regulations or corresponding Welsh provisions shall apply.

(3) The adoption agency must place on the prospective adopter's case record any information obtained as a consequence of this Chapter.

(4) The adoption agency must include in the prospective adopter's report—

(a) the State of origin from which the prospective adopter wishes to adopt a child;
(b) confirmation that the prospective adopter is eligible to adopt a child under the law of that State;
(c) any additional information obtained as a consequence of the requirements of that State; and
(d) the agency's assessment of the prospective adopter's suitability to adopt a child who is habitually resident in that State.

(5) The references to information in regulations 25(5) and 26(2) of the Agencies Regulations or corresponding Welsh provisions shall include information obtained by the adoption agency or adoption panel as a consequence of this regulation.

Initial Commencement
Specified date: 30 December 2005: see reg 1(1).

16 Adoption agency decision and notification

The adoption agency must make a decision about whether the prospective adopter is suitable to adopt a child in accordance with regulation 27 of the Agencies Regulations and regulations made under section 45 of the Act, or corresponding Welsh provisions.

Initial Commencement
Specified date: 30 December 2005: see reg 1(1).

17 Review and termination of approval

The adoption agency must review the approval of each prospective adopter in accordance with regulation 29 of the Agencies Regulations or corresponding Welsh provision unless the agency has received written notification from the relevant Central Authority that the agreement under Article 17(c) of the Convention has been made.

Initial Commencement
Specified date: 30 December 2005: see reg 1(1).

18 Procedure following decision as to suitability to adopt

(1) Where an adoption agency has made a decision that the prospective adopter is suitable to adopt a child in accordance with regulation 16, it must send to the relevant Central Authority—

(a) written confirmation of the decision and any recommendation the agency may make in relation to the number of children the prospective adopter may be suitable to adopt, their age range, sex, likely needs and background;
(b) the enhanced criminal record certificate obtained under regulation 23 of the Agencies Regulations or corresponding Welsh provision;
(c) all the documents and information which were passed to the adoption panel in accordance with regulation 25(9) of the Agencies Regulations or corresponding Welsh provision;
(d) the record of the proceedings of the adoption panel, its recommendation and the reasons for its recommendation; and
(e) any other information relating to the case as the relevant Central Authority or the CA of the State of origin may require.

(2) If the relevant Central Authority is satisfied that the adoption agency has complied with the duties and procedures imposed by the Agencies Regulations or corresponding Welsh provision, and that all the relevant information has been supplied by that agency, the Authority must send to the CA of the State of origin—

(a) the prospective adopter's report prepared in accordance with regulation 25 of the Agencies Regulations or corresponding Welsh provision;
(b) ...
(c) a copy of the adoption agency's decision and the adoption panel's recommendation;
(d) any other information that the CA of the State of origin may require; ...
[(da) if the prospective adopter applied to the appropriate Minister for a review under section 12 of the Adoption and Children Act 2002, the record of the proceedings of the panel, its recommendation and the reasons for its recommendation; and]
(e) a certificate in the form set out in Schedule 1 confirming that the—
  (i) prospective adopter is eligible to adopt;
  (ii) prospective adopter has been assessed in accordance with this Chapter;
  (iii) prospective adopter has been approved as suitable to adopt a child; and
  (iv) child will be authorised to enter and reside permanently in the United Kingdom if entry clearance, and leave to enter or remain as may be necessary, is granted and not revoked or curtailed and a Convention adoption order or Convention adoption is made.

(3) The relevant Central Authority must notify the adoption agency and the prospective adopter in writing that the certificate and the documents referred to in paragraph (2) have been sent to the CA of the State of origin.

Initial Commencement
Specified date: 30 December 2005: see reg 1(1).

Amendment
SI 2005/3482, reg 6.

19 Procedure following receipt of the Article 16 Information from the CA of the State of origin

(1) Where the relevant Central Authority receives from the CA of the State of origin, the Article 16 Information relating to the child whom the CA of the State of origin considers should be placed for adoption with the prospective adopter, the relevant Central Authority must send that Information to the adoption agency.

(2) The adoption agency must consider the Article 16 Information and—

(a) send that Information to the prospective adopter;
(b) meet with him to discuss—
  (i) that Information;
  (ii) the proposed placement;
  (iii) the availability of adoption support services; and
(c) if appropriate, offer a counselling service and further information as required.

(3) Where—

(a) the procedure in paragraph (2) has been followed;
(b) the prospective adopter (and where the prospective adopters are a couple each of them) has visited the child in the State of origin; and
(c) after that visit to the child, the prospective adopter has confirmed in writing to the adoption agency that—
  (i) he has visited the child;
  (ii) he has provided the adoption agency with additional reports and information received on or after that visit; and
  (iii) he wishes to proceed to adopt that child,

the agency must notify the relevant Central Authority in writing that the requirements specified in sub-paragraphs (a) to (c) have been satisfied and at the same time it must confirm that it is content for the adoption to proceed.

(4) Where the relevant Central Authority has received notification from the adoption agency under paragraph (3), the relevant Central Authority shall—

(a) notify the CA of the State of origin that—
  (i) the prospective adopter wishes to proceed to adopt the child;
  (ii) it is prepared to agree with the CA of the State of origin that the adoption may proceed; and
(b) confirm to the CA of the State of origin that—
  (i) in the case where the requirements specified in section 1(5A) of the British Nationality Act 1981 are met that the child will be authorised to enter and reside permanently in the United Kingdom; or
  (ii) in any other case, if entry clearance and leave to enter and remain, as may be necessary, is granted and not revoked or curtailed and a Convention adoption order or a Convention adoption is made, the child will be authorised to enter and reside permanently in the United Kingdom.

(5) The relevant Central Authority must inform the adoption agency and the prospective adopter when the agreement under Article 17(c) of the Convention has been made.

(6) For the purposes of this regulation and regulation 20 "the Article 16 Information" means—

(a) the report referred to in Article 16(1) of the Convention including information about the child's identity, adoptability, background, social environment, family history, medical history including that of the child's family and any special needs of the child;

(b) proof of confirmation that the consents of the persons, institutions and authorities whose consents are necessary for adoption have been obtained in accordance with Article 4 of the Convention; and
(c) the reasons for the CA of the State of origin's determination on the placement.

Initial Commencement
Specified date: 30 December 2005: see reg 1(1).

20 Procedure where proposed adoption is not to proceed

(1) If, at any stage before the agreement under Article 17(c) of the Convention is made, the CA of the State of origin notifies the relevant Central Authority that it has decided the proposed placement should not proceed—

(a) the relevant Central Authority must inform the adoption agency of the CA of the State of origin's decision;
(b) the agency must then inform the prospective adopter and return the Article 16 Information to the relevant Central Authority; and
(c) the relevant Central Authority must then return those documents to the CA of the State of origin.

(2) Where at any stage before the adoption agency receives notification of the agreement under Article 17(c) of the Convention the approval of the prospective adopter is reviewed under regulation 29 of the Agencies Regulations or corresponding Welsh provision, and as a consequence, the agency determines that the prospective adopter is no longer suitable to adopt a child—

(a) the agency must inform the relevant Central Authority and return the documents referred to in regulation 19(1);
(b) the relevant Central Authority must notify the CA of the State of origin and return those documents.

(3) If, at any stage before the child is placed with him, the prospective adopter notifies the adoption agency that he does not wish to proceed with the adoption of the child—

(a) that agency must inform the relevant Central Authority and return the documents to that Authority; and
(b) the relevant Central Authority must notify the CA of the State of origin of the prospective adopter's decision and return the documents to the CA of the State of origin.

Initial Commencement
Specified date: 30 December 2005: see reg 1(1).

21 Applicable requirements in respect of prospective adopter entering the United Kingdom with a child

Following any agreement under Article 17(c) of the Convention, the prospective adopter must—

(a) notify the adoption agency of his expected date of entry into the United Kingdom with the child;
(b) confirm to the adoption agency when the child is placed with him by the competent authority in the State of origin; and
(c) accompany the child on entering the United Kingdom unless, in the case of a couple, the adoption agency and the CA of the State of origin have agreed that it is necessary for only one of them to do so.

Initial Commencement
Specified date: 30 December 2005: see reg 1(1).

22 Applicable requirements in respect of an adoption agency before the child enters the United Kingdom

Where the adoption agency is informed by the relevant Central Authority that the agreement under Article 17(c) of the Convention has been made and the adoption may proceed, before the child enters the United Kingdom that agency must—

(a) send the prospective adopter's general practitioner written notification of the proposed placement and send with that notification a written report of the child's health history and current state of health, so far as it is known;
(b) send the local authority (if that authority is not the adoption agency) and the Primary Care Trust or Local Health Board (Wales), in whose area the prospective adopter has his home, written notification of the proposed arrival of the child into England or Wales; and
(c) where the child is of compulsory school age, send the local education authority, in whose area the prospective adopter has his home, written notification of the proposed arrival of the child into England or Wales and information about the child's educational history if known and whether he is likely to be assessed for special educational needs under the Education Act 1996.

Initial Commencement
Specified date: 30 December 2005: see reg 1(1).

23 Applicable provisions following the child's entry into the United Kingdom where no Convention adoption is made

Regulations 24 to 27 apply where—

(a) following the agreement between the relevant Central Authority and the CA of the State of origin under Article 17(c) of the Convention that the adoption may proceed, no Convention adoption is made, or applied for, in the State of origin; and
(b) the child is placed with the prospective adopter in the State of origin who then returns to England or Wales with that child.

Initial Commencement
Specified date: 30 December 2005: see reg 1(1).

24 Applicable requirements in respect of prospective adopter following child's entry into the United Kingdom

(1) A prospective adopter must within the period of 14 days beginning with the date on which the child enters the United Kingdom give notice to the relevant local authority—

(a) of the child's arrival in the United Kingdom; and
(b) of his intention—
  (i) to apply for an adoption order in accordance with section 44(2) of the Act; or
  (ii) not to give the child a home.

(2) In a case where a prospective adopter has given notice in accordance with paragraph (1) and he subsequently moves his home into the area of another local authority, he must within 14 days of that move confirm to that authority in writing the child's entry into the United Kingdom and that notice of his intention—

(a) to apply for an adoption order in accordance with section 44(2) of the Act has been given to another local authority; or
(b) not to give the child a home,

has been given.

Initial Commencement
Specified date: 30 December 2005: see reg 1(1).

25 Functions imposed on the local authority following the child's entry into the United Kingdom

(1) Where notice is given to a local authority in accordance with regulation 24, the functions imposed on the local authority by virtue of regulation 5 shall apply subject to the modifications in paragraph (2).

(2) Paragraph (1) of regulation 5 shall apply as if—

(a) in sub-paragraph (a)—
 (i) in head (i) for the words "relevant foreign authority" there is substituted "CA of the State of origin and competent foreign authority";
 (ii) in head (v) there is substituted "the relevant Central Authority"; and
(b) sub-paragraphs (b) to (d) were omitted.

Initial Commencement
Specified date: 30 December 2005: see reg 1(1).

[26 Prospective adopter unable to proceed with adoption]

[(1) Where the prospective adopter gives notice to the relevant local authority that he does not wish to proceed with the adoption and no longer wishes to give the child a home, he must return the child to that authority not later than the end of the period of seven days beginning with the date on which notice was given.

(2) Where a relevant local authority have received a notice in accordance with paragraph (1), that authority must give notice to the relevant Central Authority of the decision of the prospective adopter not to proceed with the adoption.]

Amendment
Substituted by SI 2005/3482, reg 6 as from 30 December 2005.

27 Withdrawal of child from prospective adopter

(1) Where the relevant local authority are of the opinion that the continued placement of the child is not in the child's best interests—

(a) that authority must give notice to the prospective adopter of their opinion and request the return of the child to them; and
(b) subject to paragraph (3), the prospective adopter must, not later than the end of the period of seven days beginning with the date on which notice was given, return the child to that authority.

(2) Where the relevant local authority has given notice under paragraph (1), that authority must at the same time notify the relevant Central Authority that they have requested the return of the child.

(3) Where notice is given under paragraph (1) but—

(a) an application for a Convention adoption order was made prior to the giving of that notice; and
(b) the application has not been disposed of,

the prospective adopter is not required by virtue of paragraph (1) to return the child unless the court so orders.

(4) This regulation does not affect the exercise by any local authority or other person of any power conferred by any enactment or the exercise of any power of arrest.

Initial Commencement
Specified date: 30 December 2005: see reg 1(1).

28 Breakdown of placement

(1) This regulation applies where—

(a) notification is given by the prospective adopter under regulation 26 (unable to proceed with adoption);
(b) the child is withdrawn from the prospective adopter under regulation 27 (withdrawal of child from prospective adopter);
(c) an application for a Convention adoption order is refused;
(d) a Convention adoption which is subject to a probationary period cannot be made; or
(e) a Convention adoption order or a Convention adoption is annulled pursuant to section 89(1) of the Act.

(2) Where the relevant local authority are satisfied that it would be in the child's best interests to be placed for adoption with another prospective adopter habitually resident in the United Kingdom they must take the necessary measures to identify a suitable adoptive parent for that child.

(3) Where the relevant local authority have identified and approved another prospective adopter who is eligible, and has been assessed as suitable, to adopt in accordance with these Regulations—

(a) that authority must notify the relevant Central Authority in writing that—
 (i) another prospective adopter has been identified; and
 (ii) the provisions in regulations 14, 15 and 16 have been complied with; and
(b) the requirements specified in regulations 18 and 19 have been complied with.

(4) Where the relevant Central Authority has been notified in accordance with paragraph (3)(a)—

(a) it shall inform the CA of the State of origin of the proposed placement; and
(b) it shall agree the placement with the CA of the State of origin in accordance with the provisions in this Chapter.

(5) Subject to paragraph (2), where the relevant local authority is not satisfied it would be in the child's best interests to be placed for adoption with another prospective adopter in England or Wales, it must liaise with the relevant Central Authority to arrange for the return of the child to his State of origin.

(6) Before coming to any decision under this regulation, the relevant local authority must have regard to the wishes and feelings of the child, having regard to his age and understanding, and where appropriate, obtain his consent in relation to measures to be taken under this regulation.

Initial Commencement
Specified date: 30 December 2005: see reg 1(1).

29 Convention adoptions subject to a probationary period

(1) This regulation applies where—

(a) the child has been placed with the prospective adopters by the competent authority in the State of origin and a Convention adoption has been applied for by the prospective adopters in the State of origin but the child's placement with the prospective adopter is subject to a probationary period before the Convention adoption is made; and

(b) the prospective adopter returns to England or Wales with the child before that probationary period is completed and the Convention adoption is made in the State of origin.

(2) The relevant local authority must, if requested by the competent authority of the State of origin, submit a report about the placement to that authority and such a report must be prepared within such timescales and contain such information as the competent authority may reasonably require.

Initial Commencement
Specified date: 30 December 2005: see reg 1(1).

30 Report of local authority investigation

The report of the investigation which a local authority must submit to the court in accordance with section 44(5) of the Act must include—

(a) confirmation that the Certificate of eligibility and approval has been sent to the CA of the State of origin in accordance with regulation 18;

(b) the date on which the agreement under Article 17(c) of the Convention was made; and

(c) details of the reports of the visits and reviews made in accordance with regulation 5 as modified by regulation 25.

Initial Commencement
Specified date: 30 December 2005: see reg 1(1).

31 Convention adoption order

An adoption order shall not be made as a Convention adoption order unless—

(a) in the case of—
 (i) an application by a couple, both members of the couple have been habitually resident in any part of the British Islands for a period of not less than one year ending with the date of the application; or
 (ii) an application by one person, the applicant has been habitually resident in any part of the British Islands for a period of not less than one year ending with the date of the application;

(b) the child to be adopted was, on the date on which the agreement under Article 17(c) of the Convention was made, habitually resident in a Convention country outside the British Islands; and

(c) in a case where one member of a couple (in the case of an application by a couple) or the applicant (in the case of an application by one person) is not a British citizen, the Home Office has confirmed that the child is authorised to enter and reside permanently in the United Kingdom.

Initial Commencement
Specified date: 30 December 2005: see reg 1(1).

32 Requirements following a Convention adoption order or Convention adoption

(1) Where the relevant Central Authority receives a copy of a Convention adoption order made by a court in England or Wales that Authority must issue a certificate in the form set out in Schedule 2 certifying that the adoption has been made in accordance with the Convention.

(2) A copy of the certificate issued under paragraph (1) must be sent to the—

(a) CA of the State of origin;
(b) adoptive parent; and
(c) adoption agency and, if different, the relevant local authority.

(3) Where a Convention adoption is made and the relevant Central Authority receives a certificate under Article 23 of the Convention in respect of that Convention adoption, the relevant Central Authority must send a copy of that certificate to the—

(a) adoptive parent; and
(b) adoption agency and, if different, the relevant local authority.

Initial Commencement
Specified date: 30 December 2005: see reg 1(1).

33 Refusal of a court in England or Wales to make a Convention adoption order

Where an application for a Convention adoption order is refused by the court or is withdrawn, the prospective adopter must return the child to the relevant local authority within the period determined by the court.

Initial Commencement
Specified date: 30 December 2005: see reg 1(1).

34 Annulment of a Convention adoption order or a Convention adoption

Where a Convention adoption order or a Convention adoption is annulled under section 89(1) of the Act and the relevant Central Authority receives a copy of the order from the court, it must forward a copy of that order to the CA of the State of origin.

Initial Commencement
Specified date: 30 December 2005: see reg 1(1).

CHAPTER 2
REQUIREMENTS, PROCEDURE, RECOGNITION AND EFFECT OF ADOPTIONS IN ENGLAND AND WALES WHERE THE UNITED KINGDOM IS THE STATE OF ORIGIN

35 Application of Chapter 2

The provisions in this Chapter shall apply where a couple or a person habitually resident in a Convention country outside the British Islands, wishes to adopt a child who is habitually resident in the British Islands in accordance with the Convention.

Initial Commencement
Specified date: 30 December 2005: see reg 1(1).

36 Counselling and information for the child

(1) Where an adoption agency is considering whether a child is suitable for an adoption in accordance with the Convention, it must provide a counselling service for and information to that child in accordance with regulation 13 of the Agencies Regulations or corresponding Welsh provision and it must—

(a) explain to the child in an appropriate manner the procedure in relation to, and the legal implications of, adoption under the Convention for that child by a prospective adopter habitually resident in the receiving State; and
(b) provide him with written information about the matters referred to in sub-paragraph (a).

(2) Paragraph (1) does not apply if the adoption agency is satisfied that the requirements set out in that paragraph have been carried out in respect of the prospective adopter by another agency.

Initial Commencement
Specified date: 30 December 2005: see reg 1(1).

37 Counselling and information for the parent or guardian of the child etc

(1) An adoption agency must provide a counselling service and information in accordance with regulation 14 of the Agencies Regulations or corresponding Welsh provision for the parent or guardian of the child and, where regulation 14(4) of the Agencies Regulations or corresponding Welsh provision applies, for the father.

(2) The adoption agency must also—

- (a) explain to the parent or guardian, and, where regulation 14(4) of the Agencies Regulations or corresponding Welsh provision applies, the father the procedure in relation to, and the legal implications of, adoption under the Convention by a prospective adopter in a receiving State; and
- (b) provide him with written information about the matters referred to in sub-paragraph (a).

(3) Paragraphs (1) and (2) do not apply if the adoption agency is satisfied that the requirements set out in that paragraph have been carried out in respect of the prospective adopter by another agency.

Initial Commencement
Specified date: 30 December 2005: see reg 1(1).

38 Requirements in respect of the child's permanence report and information for the adoption panel

(1) The child's permanence report which the adoption agency is required to prepare in accordance with regulation 17 of the Agencies Regulations or corresponding Welsh provision must include—

- (a) a summary of the possibilities for placement of the child within the United Kingdom; and
- (b) an assessment of whether an adoption by a person in a particular receiving State is in the child's best interests.

(2) The adoption agency must send—

- (a) if received, the Article 15 Report; and
- (b) their observations on that Report,

together with the reports and information referred to in regulation 17(2) of the Agencies Regulations or corresponding Welsh provision to the adoption panel.

Initial Commencement
Specified date: 30 December 2005: see reg 1(1).

39 Recommendation of adoption panel

Where an adoption panel make a recommendation in accordance with regulation 18(1) of the Agencies Regulations or corresponding Welsh provision it must consider and take into account the Article 15 Report, if available, and the observations thereon together with the information passed to it as a consequence of regulation 38.

Initial Commencement
Specified date: 30 December 2005: see reg 1(1).

40 Adoption agency decision and notification

Where the adoption agency decides in accordance with regulation 19 of the Agencies Regulations or corresponding Welsh provision that the child should be placed for an adoption in accordance with the Convention it must notify the relevant Central Authority of—

(a) the name, sex and age of the child;
(b) the reasons why they consider that the child may be suitable for such an adoption;
(c) whether a prospective adopter has been identified and, if so, provide any relevant information; and
(d) any other information that Authority may require.

Initial Commencement
Specified date: 30 December 2005: see reg 1(1).

41 Convention list

(1) The relevant Central Authority is to maintain a Convention list of children who are notified to that Authority under regulation 40 and shall make the contents of that list available for consultation by other Authorities within the British Islands.

(2) Where an adoption agency—

(a) places for adoption a child whose details have been notified to the relevant Central Authority under regulation 40; or
(b) determines that an adoption in accordance with the Convention is no longer in the best interests of the child,

it must notify the relevant Central Authority accordingly and that Authority must remove the details relating to that child from the Convention list.

Initial Commencement
Specified date: 30 December 2005: see reg 1(1).

42 Receipt of the Article 15 Report from the CA of the receiving State

(1) This regulation applies where—

(a) the relevant Central Authority receives a report from the CA of the receiving State which has been prepared for the purposes of Article 15 of the Convention ("the Article 15 Report");
(b) the Article 15 Report relates to a prospective adopter who is habitually resident in that receiving State; and
(c) the prospective adopter named in the Article 15 Report wishes to adopt a child who is habitually resident in the British Islands.

(2) Subject to paragraph (3), if the relevant Central Authority is satisfied the prospective adopter meets the following requirements—

(a) the age requirements as specified in section 50 of the Act in the case of adoption by a couple, or section 51 of the Act in the case of adoption by one person; and
(b) in the case of a couple, both are, or in the case of adoption by one person, that person is habitually resident in a Convention country outside the British Islands,

that Authority must consult the Convention list and may, if the Authority considers it appropriate, consult any Convention list maintained by another Central Authority within the British Islands.

(3) Where a prospective adopter has already been identified in relation to a proposed adoption of a particular child and the relevant Central Authority is satisfied that prospective adopter meets the requirements referred to in paragraph (2)(a) and (b), that Authority—

(a) need not consult the Convention list; and
(b) must send the Article 15 Report to the local authority which referred the child's details to the Authority.

(4) The relevant Central Authority may pass a copy of the Article 15 Report to any other Central Authority within the British Islands for the purposes of enabling that Authority to consult its Convention list.

(5) Where the relevant Central Authority identifies a child on the Convention list who may be suitable for adoption by the prospective adopter, that Authority must send the Article 15 Report to the local authority which referred the child's details to that Authority.

Initial Commencement
Specified date: 30 December 2005: see reg 1(1).

43 Proposed placement and referral to adoption panel

(1) Where the adoption agency is considering whether a proposed placement should proceed in accordance with the procedure provided for in regulation 31 of the Agencies Regulations or corresponding Welsh provision it must take into account the Article 15 Report.

(2) Where the adoption agency refers the proposal to place the child with the particular prospective adopter to the adoption panel in accordance with regulation 31 of the Agencies Regulations or corresponding Welsh provision, it must also send the Article 15 Report to the panel.

Initial Commencement
Specified date: 30 December 2005: see reg 1(1).

44 Consideration by adoption panel

The adoption panel must take into account when considering what recommendation to make in accordance with regulation 32(1) of the Agencies Regulations or corresponding Welsh provision the Article 15 Report and any other information passed to it as a consequence of the provisions in this Chapter.

Initial Commencement
Specified date: 30 December 2005: see reg 1(1).

45 Adoption agency's decision in relation to the proposed placement

(1) Regulation 33 of the Agencies Regulations or corresponding Welsh provision shall apply as if paragraph (3) of that regulation or corresponding Welsh provision was omitted.

(2) As soon as possible after the agency makes its decision, it must notify the relevant Central Authority of its decision.

(3) If the proposed placement is not to proceed—

(a) the adoption agency must return the Article 15 Report and any other documents or information sent to it by the relevant Central Authority to that Authority; and
(b) the relevant Central Authority must then send that Report, any such documents or such information to the CA of the receiving State.

Initial Commencement
Specified date: 30 December 2005: see reg 1(1).

46 Preparation of the Article 16 Information

(1) If the adoption agency decides that the proposed placement should proceed, it must prepare a report for the purposes of Article 16(1) of the Convention which must include—

(a) the information about the child which is specified in Schedule 1 to the Agencies Regulations or corresponding Welsh provision; and
(b) the reasons for their decision.

(2) The adoption agency must send the following to the relevant Central Authority—

(a) the report referred to in paragraph (1);
(b) details of any placement order or other orders, if any, made by the courts; and
(c) confirmation that the parent or guardian consents to the proposed adoption.

(3) The relevant Central Authority must then send the documents referred to in paragraph (2) to the CA of the receiving State.

Initial Commencement
Specified date: 30 December 2005: see reg 1(1).

47 Requirements to be met before the child is placed for adoption with prospective adopter

(1) The relevant Central Authority may notify the CA of the receiving State that it is prepared to agree that the adoption may proceed provided that CA has confirmed that—

(a) the prospective adopter has agreed to adopt the child and has received such counselling as may be necessary;
(b) the prospective adopter has confirmed that he will accompany the child to the receiving State, unless in the case of a couple, the adoption agency and the CA of the receiving State have agreed that it is only necessary for one of them to do so;
(c) it is content for the adoption to proceed;
(d) in the case where a Convention adoption is to be effected, it has explained to the prospective adopter the need to make an application under section 84(1) of the Act; and
(e) the child is or will be authorised to enter and reside permanently in the Convention country if a Convention adoption is effected or a Convention adoption order is made.

(2) The relevant Central Authority may not make an agreement under Article 17(c) of the Convention with the CA of the receiving State unless—

(a) confirmation has been received in respect of the matters referred to in paragraph (1); and
(b) the adoption agency has confirmed to the relevant Central Authority that—

(i) it has met the prospective adopter and explained the requirement to make an application for an order under section 84 of the Act before the child can be removed from the United Kingdom;
(ii) the prospective adopter has visited the child; and
(iii) the prospective adopter is content for the adoption to proceed.

(3) An adoption agency may not place a child for adoption unless the agreement under Article 17(c) of the Convention has been made and the relevant Central Authority must advise that agency when that agreement has been made.

(4) In this regulation, the reference to "prospective adopter" means in the case of a couple, both of them.

Initial Commencement
Specified date: 30 December 2005: see reg 1(1).

48 Requirements in respect of giving parental responsibility prior to a proposed Convention adoption

In the case of a proposed Convention adoption, the prescribed requirements for the purposes of section 84(3) of the Act (requirements to be satisfied prior to making an order) are—

(a) the competent authorities of the receiving State have—
  (i) prepared a report for the purposes of Article 15 of the Convention;
  (ii) determined and confirmed in writing that the prospective adoptive parent is eligible and suitable to adopt;
  (iii) ensured and confirmed in writing that the prospective adoptive parent has been counselled as may be necessary; and
  (iv) determined and confirmed in writing that the child is or will be authorised to enter and reside permanently in that State;
(b) the report required for the purposes of Article 16(1) of the Convention has been prepared by the adoption agency;
(c) the adoption agency confirms in writing that it has complied with the requirements imposed upon it under Part 3 of the Agencies Regulations or corresponding Welsh provision and this Chapter;
(d) the adoption agency has obtained and made available to the court—
  (i) the reports and information referred to in regulation 17(1) and (2) of the Agencies Regulations or corresponding Welsh provision;
  (ii) the recommendation made by the adoption panel in accordance with regulations 18 and 33 of the Agencies Regulations or corresponding Welsh provisions; and
  (iii) the adoption placement report prepared in accordance with regulation 31(2) of the Agencies Regulations or corresponding Welsh provision;
(e) the adoption agency includes in their report submitted to the court in accordance with section 43(a) or 44(5) of the Act as modified respectively by regulation 11, details of any reviews and visits carried out as consequence of Part 6 of the Agencies Regulations or corresponding Welsh provision; and
(f) the prospective adopter has confirmed in writing that he will accompany the child on taking the child out of the United Kingdom to travel to the receiving State or in the case of a couple the agency and competent foreign authority have confirmed that it is necessary for only one of them to do so.

Initial Commencement
Specified date: 30 December 2005: see reg 1(1).

49 Local authority report

In the case of a proposed application for a Convention adoption order, the report which a local authority must submit to the court in accordance with section 43(a) or 44(5) of the Act must include a copy of the—

(a) Article 15 Report;
(b) report prepared for the purposes of Article 16(1); and
(c) written confirmation of the agreement under Article 17(c) of the Convention.

Initial Commencement
Specified date: 30 December 2005: see reg 1(1).

50 Convention adoption order

An adoption order shall not be made as a Convention adoption order unless—

(a) in the case of—
  (i) an application by a couple, both members of the couple have been habitually resident in a Convention country outside the British Islands for a period of not less than one year ending with the date of the application; or
  (aa) an application by one person, the applicant has been habitually resident in a Convention country outside the British Islands for a period of not less than one year ending with the date of the application;
(b) the child to be adopted was, on the date on which the agreement under Article 17(c) of the Convention was made, habitually resident in any part of the British Islands; and
(c) the competent authority has confirmed that the child is authorised to enter and remain permanently in the Convention country in which the applicant is habitually resident.

Initial Commencement
Specified date: 30 December 2005: see reg 1(1).

51 Requirements following a Convention adoption order or Convention adoption

(1) Where the relevant Central Authority receives a copy of a Convention adoption order made by a court in England or Wales, that Authority must issue a certificate in the form set out in Schedule 2 certifying that the adoption has been made in accordance with the Convention.

(2) A copy of the certificate must be sent to the—

(a) CA of the receiving State; and
(b) the relevant local authority.

(3) Where a Convention adoption is made and the Central Authority receives a certificate under Article 23 in respect of that Convention adoption, the relevant Central Authority must send a copy of that certificate to the relevant local authority.

Initial Commencement
Specified date: 30 December 2005: see reg 1(1).

CHAPTER 3
MISCELLANEOUS PROVISIONS

52 Application, with or without modifications, of the Act

(1) Subject to the modifications provided for in this Chapter, the provisions of the Act shall apply to adoptions within the scope of the Convention so far as the nature of the provision permits and unless the contrary intention is shown.

Initial Commencement
Specified date: 30 December 2005: see reg 1(1).

53 Change of name and removal from the United Kingdom

In a case falling within Chapter 1 of this Part, section 28(2) of the Act shall apply as if—

(a) at the end of paragraph (a), "or" was omitted;
(b) at the end of paragraph (b) there were inserted "or (c) a child is placed by a competent foreign authority for the purposes of an adoption under the Convention,"; and
(c) at the end of subsection (2) there were inserted "or the competent foreign authority consents to a change of surname.".

Initial Commencement
Specified date: 30 December 2005: see reg 1(1).

54 Removal of children

(1) In a case falling within Chapter 1 of this Part, sections 36 to 40 of the Act shall not apply.

(2) In a case falling within Chapter 2 of this Part—

(a) section 36 of the Act shall apply, as if—
 (i) for the words "an adoption order" in paragraphs (a) and (c) in subsection (1) there were substituted "a Convention adoption order"; and
 (ii) subsection (2) was omitted; and
(b) section 39 of the Act shall apply as if subsection (3)(a) was omitted.

Initial Commencement
Specified date: 30 December 2005: see reg 1(1).

55 Modifications of the Act in respect of orders under section 84 where child is to be adopted under the Convention

The modifications set out in regulation 11 shall apply in the case where a couple or person habitually resident in a Convention country outside the British Islands intend to adopt a child who is habitually resident in England or Wales in accordance with the Convention.

Initial Commencement
Specified date: 30 December 2005: see reg 1(1).

56 Child to live with adopters before application for a Convention adoption order

Section 42 of the Act shall apply as if—

(a) subsections (1)(b) and (3) to (6) were omitted; and

(b) in subsection (2) from the word "If" to the end of paragraph (b) there were substituted "In the case of an adoption under the Convention,".

Initial Commencement
Specified date: 30 December 2005: see reg 1(1).

57 Notice of intention to adopt

Section 44 of the Act shall apply as if subsection (3) was omitted.

Initial Commencement
Specified date: 30 December 2005: see reg 1(1).

58 Application for Convention adoption order

Section 49 of the Act shall apply as if—

(a) in subsection (1), the words from "but only" to the end were omitted;
(b) subsections (2) and (3) were omitted.

Initial Commencement
Specified date: 30 December 2005: see reg 1(1).

59 Offences

Any person who contravenes or fails to comply with—

[(a) regulation 24 (requirements in respect of prospective adopter following child's entry into the United Kingdom);
(b) regulation 26(1) (return of child to relevant local authority where prospective adopter does not wish to proceed);
(c) regulation 27(1)(b) (return of child to relevant local authority on request of local authority or by order of court); or
(d) regulation 33 (refusal of a court in England or Wales to make a Convention adoption order)]

is guilty of an offence and liable on summary conviction to imprisonment for a term not exceeding three months, or a fine not exceeding level 5 on the standard scale, or both.

Initial Commencement
Specified date: 30 December 2005: see reg 1(1).

Amendment
SI 2005/3482, reg 6.

SCHEDULE 1
Certificate of Eligibility and Approval

Regulation 18

To the Central Authority of the State of origin

Re ... [name of applicant]

In accordance with Article 5 of the Convention, I hereby certify on behalf of the Central Authority for [England] [Wales] that ... [name of applicant] has been counselled, is eligible to adopt and has been assessed and approved as suitable to adopt a child from ... [State of origin] by ... [public authority or accredited body for the purposes of the Convention].

The attached report has been prepared in accordance with Article 15 of the Convention for presentation to the competent authority in ... [State of origin].

This certificate of eligibility and approval and the report under Article 15 of the Convention are provided on the condition that a Convention adoption or Convention adoption order will not be made until the agreement under Article 17(c) of the Convention has been made.
I confirm on behalf of the Central Authority that if following the agreement under Article 17(c) of the Convention that—

[in the case, where the requirements specified in section 1(5A) of the British Nationality Act 1981 are met that the child ... [name] will be authorised to enter and reside permanently in the United Kingdom]; or

[in any other case, if entry clearance and leave to enter and remain, as may be necessary, is granted and not revoked, or curtailed and a Convention adoption order or Convention adoption is made, the child ... [name] will be authorised to enter and reside permanently in the United Kingdom.]

Name
[On behalf of the Secretary of State, the Central Authority for England]

Date

[the National Assembly for Wales, the Central Authority for Wales] NOTES

Initial Commencement
Specified date: 30 December 2005: see reg 1(1).

SCHEDULE 2
CERTIFICATE THAT THE CONVENTION ADOPTION ORDER HAS BEEN MADE IN ACCORDANCE WITH THE CONVENTION

Regulations 32 and 51

1 The Central Authority as the competent authority for [England] [Wales] being the country in which the Convention adoption order was made hereby certifies, in accordance with Article 23(1) of the Convention, that the child:

(a) name ... [name on birth certificate, also known as/now known as ...]
sex: ...
date and place of birth: ...
habitual residence at the time of the adoption: ...
State of origin: ...
(b) was adopted on: ...
by order made by: ... court in [England] [Wales]
(c) by the following person(s):
(i) family name and first name(s): ...
sex: ...
date and place of birth: ...
Habitual residence at the time adoption order was made: ...
(ii)family name and first name(s): ...
sex: ...
date and place of birth: ...
habitual residence at the time adoption order made: ...

2 The competent authority for [England] [Wales] in pursuance of Article 23(1) of the Convention hereby certifies that the adoption was made in accordance with the Convention and that the agreement under Article 17(c) was given by:

(a) name and address of the Central Authority in State of origin: ...

date of the agreement: ...
(b) name and address of the Central Authority of receiving State: ...
date of the agreement: ...

Signed

Date

Initial Commencement
Specified date: 30 December 2005: see reg 1(1).

COMMUNITY LEGAL SERVICE (ASYLUM AND IMMIGRATION APPEALS) REGULATIONS 2005

SI 2005/966

Made ...27th March 2005

Coming into force ...4th April 2005

The Secretary of State, in exercise of the powers conferred upon him by section 103D of the Nationality, Immigration and Asylum Act 2002, after consulting in accordance with section 103D(7), makes the following Regulations, a draft of which has in accordance with section 112(6) of the Nationality, Immigration and Asylum Act 2002 been laid before and approved by resolution of each House of Parliament:

1 Citation and commencement

These Regulations may be cited as the Community Legal Service (Asylum and Immigration Appeals) Regulations 2005 and shall come into force on 4th April 2005.

Initial Commencement
Specified date: 4 April 2005: see reg 1.

2 Scope of these Regulations

These Regulations have effect only in relation to appeals decided in England and Wales.

Initial Commencement
Specified date: 4 April 2005: see reg 1.

3 Interpretation

(1) In these Regulations—

"the 1999 Act" means the Access to Justice Act 1999;
"the 2002 Act" means the Nationality, Immigration and Asylum Act 2002;
"the 2004 Act" means the Asylum and Immigration (Treatment of Claimants, etc) Act 2004;
"business day" means any day other than a Saturday or Sunday, a bank holiday, Christmas Day, 27th to 31st December or Good Friday;
"Commission" means the Legal Services Commission established under section 1 of the 1999 Act;

"contract" means a contract between the Commission and a supplier under section 6(3)(a) of the 1999 Act;

"counsel" means a barrister in independent practice;

"fast track proceedings" means any immigration review proceedings in relation to which, pursuant to an order under section 26(8) of the 2004 Act, the time period for making an application under section 103A(1) of the 2002 Act is a period of less than 5 days;

"Funding Code" means the code approved under section 9 of the 1999 Act;

"immigration review proceedings" means—

(i) applications to the High Court under section 103A of the 2002 Act (including applications which are considered by a member of the Tribunal pursuant to paragraph 30 of Schedule 2 to the 2004 Act); and

(ii) proceedings for the reconsideration of an appeal by the Tribunal pursuant to an order under section 103A of the 2002 Act;

"Legal Representation" has the meaning given in the Funding Code;

"section 103D order" means an order under section 103D(1) or 103D(3) of the 2002 Act;

"supplier" means a solicitor or other person who is an authorised litigator within the meaning of section 119(1) of the Courts and Legal Services Act 1990, having a contract for the provision of services including Legal Representation in immigration review proceedings;

"Tribunal" means the Asylum and Immigration Tribunal.

(2) References to a section by number alone refer to the section so numbered in the 2002 Act.

Initial Commencement

Specified date: 4 April 2005: see reg 1.

4 General restrictions on power to make section 103D orders

(1) The High Court or the Tribunal shall only make a section 103D order in immigration review proceedings where an appellant is represented by a supplier acting pursuant to a grant of Legal Representation.

(2) The High Court or the Tribunal shall not make a section 103D order in fast track proceedings.

(3) Regulations 5 to 8 apply in relation to immigration review proceedings in which the High Court or the Tribunal has power, under section 103D(1)–(3) and this regulation, to make a section 103D order.

Initial Commencement

Specified date: 4 April 2005: see reg 1.

5 Criteria for making orders under section 103D(1)

(1) The appropriate court must exercise the power to make an order under section 103D(1) in accordance with this regulation.

(2) If, upon a section 103A application, the appropriate court makes an order for reconsideration, subject to paragraph (5) it must not make an order under section 103D(1).

(3) If the High Court makes a reference under section 103C of the 2002 Act, it must make an order under section 103D(1).

(4) If the appropriate court dismisses or makes no order on the section 103A application, it may make an order under section 103D(1) only if—

(a) there has been a change in any relevant circumstances or a change in the law since the application was made; and
(b) at the time when the application was made, there was a significant prospect that the appeal would be allowed upon reconsideration.

(5) The appropriate court may, on an application in writing by a supplier or counsel instructed by the supplier, make an order under section 103D(1) where it has made an order for reconsideration, but no reconsideration of the appeal takes place.

(6) In this regulation, "the appropriate court" means—

(a) the High Court; or
(b) a member of the Tribunal who considers a section 103A application by virtue of paragraph 30 of Schedule 2 to the 2004 Act.

Initial Commencement
Specified date: 4 April 2005: see reg 1.

6 Criteria for making orders under section 103D(3)

(1) The Tribunal must exercise the power to make an order under section 103D(3) in accordance with this regulation.

(2) If the Tribunal allows an appeal on reconsideration, it must make an order under section 103D(3).

(3) If the Tribunal does not allow an appeal, it must not make an order under section 103D(3) unless it is satisfied that, at the time when the appellant made the section 103A application, there was a significant prospect that the appeal would be allowed upon reconsideration.

(4) If, where paragraph (3) applies, the Tribunal decides not to make an order under section 103D(3), it must give reasons for its decision.

Initial Commencement
Specified date: 4 April 2005: see reg 1.

7 Review by Tribunal of decision not to make order under section 103D(3)

(1) A supplier, or counsel instructed by a supplier, may apply to the Tribunal in writing for a review of a decision by the Tribunal not to make an order under section 103D(3).

(2) An application under this regulation must be filed within 10 business days after the supplier is served with the Tribunal's decision not to make an order, or such longer period as the Tribunal may allow.

(3) A review shall be carried out by a senior immigration judge who was not the member of the Tribunal, or a member of the constitution of the Tribunal, which made the original decision.

(4) The senior immigration judge may—

(a) carry out the review without a hearing; or
(b) hold an oral hearing, if one is requested by the supplier or counsel.

(5) The senior immigration judge may—

(a) make an order under section 103D(3); or
(b) confirm the Tribunal's decision not to make an order.

(6) The senior immigration judge must give reasons for his decision on a review.

Initial Commencement
Specified date: 4 April 2005: see reg 1.

8 Terms and effect of section 103D orders

(1) Subject to paragraph (2), a section 103D order shall have effect as an order for payment of all the costs incurred by a supplier representing the appellant in the proceedings to which the order relates, including the fees of counsel instructed by the supplier, for which payment is allowable under the terms of the contract between the Commission and the supplier.

(2) In relation to proceedings in which a supplier has instructed counsel, the High Court or the Tribunal may in special circumstances make a section 103D order—

- (a) in respect of counsel's fees only; or
- (b) in respect of the costs incurred by the supplier excluding counsel's fees.

(3) A section 103D order must not specify—

- (a) the amount to be paid by the Commission; or
- (b) the person or persons to whom payment is to be made,

and the Commission shall determine those matters in accordance with the terms of its contract with the supplier.

Initial Commencement
Specified date: 4 April 2005: see reg 1.

9 Modification to the Funding Code, etc

(1) Where an appellant applies for Legal Representation to bring immigration review proceedings, the Funding Code shall apply subject to the modifications that—

- (a) in Section 5 of the Funding Code Criteria, the criteria in section 5.4 (standard criteria for Legal Representation and Support Funding) shall not apply; and
- (b) in Section 13 of the Funding Code Criteria, sections 13.4 (prospects of success) and 13.5 (cost benefit) shall not apply.

(2) Where Legal Representation is granted for immigration review proceedings to be brought by an appellant, the effect of the grant shall be that—

- (a) the Commission shall, subject to the provisions of its contract with the supplier, pay for—
  - (i) services consisting of advising on the merits of making an application under section 103A; and
  - (ii) any disbursements incurred by the supplier, other than counsel's fees,

  whether or not a section 103D order is made; but
- (b) otherwise, payment by the Commission for services provided by the supplier, or by counsel instructed by the supplier, shall be conditional upon the High Court or the Tribunal making a section 103D order.

(3) Where Legal Representation has been granted for immigration review proceedings to be brought by an appellant, section 10(1) of the 1999 Act shall apply, notwithstanding that payment by the Commission for services is conditional upon a section 103D order being made.

(4) This regulation does not apply in relation to fast track proceedings.

Initial Commencement
Specified date: 4 April 2005: see reg 1.

IMMIGRATION (LEAVE TO ENTER AND REMAIN) (AMENDMENT) ORDER 2005

SI 2005/1159

Made ...31st March 2005

Coming into force ...1st April 2005

Whereas a draft of this Order has been laid before Parliament and approved by a resolution of each House in accordance with sections 3A(13) and 3B(6) of the Immigration Act 1971;

Now, therefore, the Secretary of State, in exercise of the powers conferred upon him by sections 3A(1), (3) and (10) and 3B(1) of that Act, hereby makes the following Order:

1 Citation and commencement

This Order may be cited as the Immigration (Leave to Enter and Remain) (Amendment) Order 2005 and shall come into force on the day after the day on which it is made.

Initial Commencement
Specified date: 1 April 2005: see above.

2 Amendment of the Immigration (Leave to Enter and Remain) Order 2000

The Immigration (Leave to Enter and Remain) Order 2000 shall be amended as follows.

Initial Commencement
Specified date: 1 April 2005: see art 1.

3

In article 1(3), after the definition of "the Act", there shall be inserted the following definition:

> ""ADS Agreement with China" means the Memorandum of Understanding on visa and related issues concerning tourist groups from the People's Republic of China to the United Kingdom as an approved destination, signed on 21st January 2005;".

Initial Commencement
Specified date: 1 April 2005: see art 1.

4

(1) Article 4 shall be amended as follows.

(2) In paragraph (1), after the words "visit visa", there shall be inserted the words "(other than a visit visa granted pursuant to the ADS Agreement with China) unless endorsed with a statement that it is to have effect as a single-entry visa".

(3) After paragraph (2) there shall be inserted the following paragraphs:

"(2A) A visit visa granted pursuant to the ADS Agreement with China endorsed with a statement that it is to have effect as a dual-entry visa, shall have effect as leave to enter the United Kingdom on two occasions during its period of validity, in accordance with paragraph (2B).

(2B) On arrival in the United Kingdom on each occasion, the holder shall be treated for the purposes of the Immigration Acts as having been granted, before arrival, leave to enter the United Kingdom for a limited period, being the period beginning on the date on which the holder arrives in the United Kingdom and ending on the date of expiry of the entry clearance.".

(4) In paragraph (3), for the words "any other form of entry clearance" there shall be substituted the words "any form of entry clearance to which this paragraph applies".

(5) After paragraph (3) there shall be inserted the following paragraph:

"(3A) Paragraph (3) applies to—

(a) a visit visa (other than a visit visa granted pursuant to the ADS Agreement with China) endorsed with a statement that it is to have effect as a single entry visa;
(b) a visit visa granted pursuant to the ADS Agreement with China unless endorsed with a statement to the effect that it is to have effect as a dual entry visa; and
(c) any other form of entry clearance.".

Initial Commencement
Specified date: 1 April 2005: see art 1.

DISPLACED PERSONS (TEMPORARY PROTECTION) REGULATIONS 2005

SI 2005/1379

Made ...18th May 2005

Laid before Parliament ...24th May 2005

Coming into force ...15th June 2005

The Secretary of State, being a Minister designated for the purposes of section 2(2) of the European Communities Act 1972 in relation to measures relating to immigration, asylum, refugees and displaced persons, in exercise of the powers conferred upon him by that section, hereby makes the following Regulations:

1 Citation and commencement

These Regulations may be cited as the Displaced Persons (Temporary Protection) Regulations 2005 and shall come into force on 15th June 2005.

Initial Commencement
Specified date: 15 June 2005: see above.

2 Interpretation

(1) In these Regulations—

(a) "the 2002 Act" means the Nationality, Immigration and Asylum Act 2002;
(b) "claim for asylum" has the same meaning as in section 18 of the 2002 Act;
(c) "consular officer" has the same meaning as in article 2 of the Consular Fees (No2) Order 1999;

(d) "entry clearance" has the same meaning as in article 2 of the Consular Fees (No2) Order 1999;
(e) "local authority" means—
   (i) in England and Wales, a district council, a county council, a county borough council, a London borough council, the Common Council of the City of London or the Council of the Isles of Scilly; and
   (ii) in Scotland, a council constituted under section 2 of the Local Government etc (Scotland) Act 1994;
(f) "registered social landlord"—
   (i) in England and Wales, has the same meaning as in Part I of the Housing Act 1996; and
   (ii) in Scotland, means a body in the register maintained under section 57 of the Housing (Scotland) Act 2001;
(g) "registered housing association" has the same meaning, in relation to Northern Ireland, as in Part II of the Housing (Northern Ireland) Order 1992;
(h) "temporary protection" means limited leave to enter or remain granted pursuant to Part 11A of the Immigration Rules; and
(i) "Temporary Protection Directive" means Council Directive 2001/55/EC of 20 July 2001 on minimum standards for giving temporary protection in the event of a mass influx of displaced persons and on measures promoting a balance of efforts between member States in receiving such persons and bearing the consequences thereof.

Initial Commencement
Specified date: 15 June 2005: see reg 1.

3 Means of subsistence

(1) Any person granted temporary protection as a result of a decision of the Council of the European Union made pursuant to Article 5 of the Temporary Protection Directive shall be deemed for the purposes of the provision of means of subsistence to have been granted leave to enter or remain in the United Kingdom exceptionally, outside the Immigration Rules.

(2) Subject to paragraph (3), paragraph (1) shall cease to apply on the date when the period of mass influx of displaced persons to which the grant of temporary protection relates ends in accordance with Chapter II of the Temporary Protection Directive.

(3) Paragraph (1) shall continue to apply for a period not exceeding 28 days from the date referred to in paragraph (2) for as long as the conditions in paragraph (4) are satisfied and the person is in the United Kingdom.

(4) Those conditions are—

(a) the person's grant of temporary protection has expired; and
(b) the person is taking all reasonable steps to leave the United Kingdom or place himself in a position in which he is able to leave the United Kingdom, which may include co-operating with a voluntary return programme.

Initial Commencement
Specified date: 15 June 2005: see reg 1.

4

"Means of subsistence" in regulation 3 means any means of subsistence governed by—

(a) Part VII of the Social Security Contributions and Benefits Act 1992;
(b) Part VII of the Social Security Contributions and Benefits (Northern Ireland) Act 1992;

(c) sections 1 and 3 of Part I of the Jobseekers Act 1995;
(d) articles 3 and 5 of Part II of the Jobseekers (Northern Ireland) Order 1995;
(e) the State Pension Credit Act 2002; or
(f) the State Pension Credit Act (Northern Ireland) 2002.

Initial Commencement
Specified date: 15 June 2005: see reg 1.

5 Housing: provision of accommodation

(1) The Secretary of State may provide, or arrange for the provision of, accommodation for any person granted temporary protection.

(2) Subject to paragraph (3), paragraph (1) shall cease to apply on the date when the period of mass influx of displaced persons to which the grant of temporary protection relates ends in accordance with Chapter II of the Temporary Protection Directive.

(3) Paragraph (1) shall continue to apply for a period not exceeding 28 days from the date referred to in paragraph (2) for as long as the conditions in paragraph (4) are satisfied and the person is in the United Kingdom.

(4) Those conditions are—

(a) the person's grant of temporary protection has expired; and
(b) the person is taking all reasonable steps to leave the United Kingdom or place himself in a position in which he is able to leave the United Kingdom, which may include co-operating with a voluntary return programme.

Initial Commencement
Specified date: 15 June 2005: see reg 1.

6

A local authority or the Northern Ireland Housing Executive may provide accommodation for those granted temporary protection in accordance with arrangements made by the Secretary of State under regulation 5.

Initial Commencement
Specified date: 15 June 2005: see reg 1.

7

When exercising his power under regulation 5 to provide, or arrange for the provision of, accommodation, the Secretary of State—

(a) shall have regard to the desirability, in general, of providing, or arranging for the provision of, accommodation in areas in which there is a ready supply of accommodation; and
(b) shall not have regard to any preference that those who have been granted temporary protection or their dependants may have as to the locality in which the accommodation is to be provided.

Initial Commencement
Specified date: 15 June 2005: see reg 1.

8 Housing: requests for assistance

(1) This regulation applies if the Secretary of State asks—

(a) a local authority;
(b) the Northern Ireland Housing Executive;

(c) a registered social landlord; or
(d) a registered housing association in Northern Ireland

to assist him in the exercise of his power under regulation 5 to provide, or arrange for the provision of, accommodation.

(2) The body to whom the request is made shall co-operate in giving the Secretary of State such assistance in the exercise of that power as is reasonable in the circumstances.

(3) This regulation does not require a registered social landlord to act beyond his powers.

(4) The Secretary of State shall pay to a body listed in regulation 8(1) any costs reasonably incurred by that body in assisting the Secretary of State to provide, or arrange for the provision of, accommodation.

Initial Commencement
Specified date: 15 June 2005: see reg 1.

9

A local authority or the Northern Ireland Housing Executive shall supply to the Secretary of State such information about its housing accommodation (whether or not occupied) as the Secretary of State may request.

Initial Commencement
Specified date: 15 June 2005: see reg 1.

10 Housing: direction by the Secretary of State

(1) If the Secretary of State considers that a local authority or the Northern Ireland Housing Executive has suitable housing accommodation, the Secretary of State may direct the authority or the Executive to make available such accommodation as may be specified in the direction for a period so specified to the Secretary of State for the purpose of providing accommodation under regulation 5.

(2) The Secretary of State shall pay to a body to which a direction is given costs reasonably incurred by the body in complying with the direction.

(3) Any such direction is enforceable, on an application made on behalf of the Secretary of State, by injunction or, in Scotland, by an order under section 45(b) of the Court of Session Act 1988.

Initial Commencement
Specified date: 15 June 2005: see reg 1.

11

Housing accommodation shall be suitable for the purposes of regulation 10 if it is—

(a) unoccupied;
(b) likely to remain unoccupied for the foreseeable future if not made available; and
(c) appropriate for the accommodation of persons with temporary protection or is capable of being made so with minor work.

Initial Commencement
Specified date: 15 June 2005: see reg 1.

12

(1) If the housing accommodation specified in a direction under regulation 10 is not appropriate for the accommodation of persons with temporary protection but is capable of being made so with minor work, the Secretary of State may require the directed body to secure that the work is carried out without delay.

(2) The Secretary of State shall meet the reasonable cost of carrying out the minor work.

Initial Commencement
Specified date: 15 June 2005: see reg 1.

13

Before giving a direction under regulation 10, the Secretary of State shall consult—

- (a) such local authorities, local authority associations and other persons as he thinks appropriate in respect of a direction given to a local authority;
- (b) the Northern Ireland Housing Executive in respect of a direction given to the Executive;
- (c) the National Assembly of Wales in respect of a direction given to a local authority in Wales; and
- (d) the Scottish Ministers in respect of a direction given to a local authority in Scotland.

Initial Commencement
Specified date: 15 June 2005: see reg 1.

14 Housing: rent liability

A person with temporary protection who is provided with accommodation under regulation 5 shall be liable to make periodical payments of, or by way of, rent in respect of the accommodation provided and, in relation to any claim for housing benefit by virtue of regulation 3, such payments shall be regarded as rent for the purposes of [14(1)(a) of the Housing Benefit Regulations 2006, regulation 12(1)(a) of the Housing Benefit (Persons who have attained the qualifying age for state pension credit) Regulations 2006] and regulation 10(1)(a) of the Housing Benefit (General) Regulations (Northern Ireland) 1987.

Initial Commencement
Specified date: 15 June 2005: see reg 1.

Amendment
SI 2006/217, reg 5, Sch 2.

15 Housing: notice to vacate

(1) A tenancy, licence or right of occupancy granted in order to provide accommodation under regulation 5 shall end on the date specified in a notice to vacate complying with paragraph (2) regardless of when the tenancy, licence or right of occupancy could otherwise be brought to an end.

(2) A notice to vacate complies with this paragraph if it is in writing and it specifies as the notice period a period of at least 7 days from the date of service by post of the notice to vacate. NOTES

Initial Commencement
Specified date: 15 June 2005: see reg 1.

16 Claims for asylum

(1) This regulation shall apply when a person granted temporary protection makes a claim for asylum which is recorded by the Secretary of State.

(2) When considering under section 55(1)(b) of the 2002 Act whether he is satisfied that the person has made his claim for asylum as soon as reasonably practicable after his arrival in the United Kingdom, the Secretary of State may disregard any time during which the person benefited from a grant of temporary protection.

Initial Commencement
Specified date: 15 June 2005: see reg 1.

17 Consular fees

Where a consular officer is satisfied that a person outside the United Kingdom will benefit from a grant of temporary protection on arrival at a port of entry in the United Kingdom, that person shall not be required to pay any fee prescribed by the Consular Fees (No2) Order 1999 in connection with an application for entry clearance.

Initial Commencement
Specified date: 15 June 2005: see reg 1.

SCHEDULE
CONSEQUENTIAL AMENDMENTS

1 The Protection from Eviction Act 1977

In section 3A of the Protection from Eviction Act 1977 (excluded tenancies and licences), after subsection (7B) insert—

"(7C) A tenancy or licence is excluded if it is granted in order to provide accommodation under the Displaced Persons (Temporary Protection) Regulations 2005.".

2 The Housing (Northern Ireland) Order 1983

In Schedule 2 to the Housing (Northern Ireland) Order 1983 (tenancies which are not secure tenancies), after paragraph 3A insert—

"ACCOMMODATION FOR PERSONS WITH TEMPORARY PROTECTION

3B A tenancy is not a secure tenancy if it is granted in order to provide accommodation under the Displaced Persons (Temporary Protection) Regulations 2005."

3 The Rent (Scotland) Act 1984

In section 23A of the Rent (Scotland) Act 1984 (excluded tenancies and occupancy rights), after subsection (5A) insert—

"(5B) Nothing in section 23 of this Act applies to a tenancy or right of occupancy if it is granted in order to provide accommodation under the Displaced Persons (Temporary Protection) Regulations 2005."

4 The Housing Act 1985

In Schedule 1 to the Housing Act 1985 (tenancies which cannot be secure tenancies), after paragraph 4A insert—

"ACCOMMODATION FOR PERSONS WITH TEMPORARY PROTECTION

4B A tenancy is not a secure tenancy if it is granted in order to provide accommodation under the Displaced Persons (Temporary Protection) Regulations 2005."

5 The Housing (Scotland) Act 1988

In Schedule 4 to the Housing (Scotland) Act 1988 (tenancies which cannot be assured tenancies), after paragraph 11B insert—

"ACCOMMODATION FOR PERSONS WITH TEMPORARY PROTECTION

11C A tenancy granted under arrangements for the provision of accommodation for persons with temporary protection made under the Displaced Persons (Temporary Protection) Regulations 2005."

6 The Housing Act 1988

In Schedule 1 to the Housing Act 1988 (tenancies which are not assured tenancies), after paragraph 12A insert—

"ACCOMMODATION FOR PERSONS WITH TEMPORARY PROTECTION

12B (1) A tenancy granted by a private landlord under arrangements for the provision of accommodation for persons with temporary protection made under the Displaced Persons (Temporary Protection) Regulations 2005.

(2) "Private landlord" means a landlord who is not within section 80(1) of the Housing Act 1985."

7 The Homelessness (England) Regulations 2000

The Homelessness (England) Regulations 2000 shall be amended as follows.

8

In regulation 3 (classes of persons subject to immigration control who are eligible for housing assistance), for paragraph (1)(i) substitute—

"Class I—a person who is on an income-based jobseeker's allowance or in receipt of income support and is eligible for that benefit other than because—

(i) he has limited leave to enter or remain in the United Kingdom which was given in accordance with the relevant immigration rules and he is temporarily without funds because remittances to him from abroad have been disrupted; or

(ii) he has been deemed by regulation 3 of the Displaced Persons (Temporary Protection) Regulations 2005 to have been granted leave to enter or remain in the United Kingdom exceptionally for the purposes of the provision of means of subsistence.".

9

In regulation 3, after paragraph (3) insert—

"(4) In paragraph (1)(i) (Class I), "means of subsistence" has the same meaning as in regulation 4 of the Displaced Persons (Temporary Protection) Regulations 2005.".

10 The Persons subject to Immigration Control (Housing Authority Accommodation and Homelessness) Order 2000

The Persons subject to Immigration Control (Housing Authority Accommodation and Homelessness) Order 2000 shall be amended as follows.

11

In Article 8 (homelessness—Northern Ireland), for paragraph (1)(a) substitute—

"Class S—a person who is on an income-based jobseeker's allowance or in receipt of income support and is eligible for that benefit other than because—

(i) he has limited leave to enter or remain in the United Kingdom which was given in accordance with the relevant immigration rules and he is temporarily without funds because remittances to him from abroad have been disrupted; or

(ii) he has been deemed by regulation 3 of the Displaced Persons (Temporary Protection) Regulations 2005 to have been granted leave to enter or remain in the United Kingdom exceptionally for the purposes of the provision of means of subsistence.".

12

In article 8, after paragraph (2) insert—

"(3) In paragraph (1)(a) (Class S), "means of subsistence" has the same meaning as in regulation 4 of the Displaced Persons (Temporary Protection) Regulations 2005.".

13

In article 9 (homelessness—Scotland), for paragraph (1)(a) substitute—

"Class U—a person who is on an income-based jobseeker's allowance or in receipt of income support and is eligible for that benefit other than because—

(i) he has limited leave to enter or remain in the United Kingdom which was given in accordance with the relevant immigration rules and he is temporarily without funds because remittances to him from abroad have been disrupted; or

(ii) he has been deemed by regulation 3 of the Displaced Persons (Temporary Protection) Regulations 2005 to have been granted leave to enter or remain in the United Kingdom exceptionally for the purposes of the provision of means of subsistence.".

14

In article 9, after paragraph (2)(d) insert—

"(e) In paragraph (1)(a) (Class U), "means of subsistence" has the same meaning as in regulation 4 of the Displaced Persons (Temporary Protection) Regulations 2005.".

15 The Housing (Scotland) Act 2001

In Schedule 1 to the Housing (Scotland) Act 2001 (tenancies which are not Scottish secure tenancies), after paragraph 10 insert—

"ACCOMMODATION FOR PERSONS WITH TEMPORARY PROTECTION

11 A tenancy is not a Scottish secure tenancy if it is granted in order to provide accommodation under the Displaced Persons (Temporary Protection) Regulations 2005.".

Initial Commencement
Specified date: 15 June 2005: see reg 1.

ACCESSION (IMMIGRATION AND WORKER REGISTRATION) (AMENDMENT) REGULATIONS 2005

SI 2005/2400

Made ...24th August 2005

Laid before Parliament ...1st September 2005

Coming into force ...1st October 2005

The Secretary of State, being a Minister designated for the purposes of section 2(2) of the European Communities Act 1972 in relation to measures relating to access to the labour market of the United Kingdom, in exercise of the powers conferred upon him by the said section 2(2), hereby makes the following Regulations:

1 Citation and commencement

(1) These Regulations may be cited as the Accession (Immigration and Worker Registration) (Amendment) Regulations 2005 and shall come into force on 1st October 2005.

(2) Regulation 2 shall not have effect in relation to an application for a registration certificate under regulation 8 of the Accession (Immigration and Worker Registration) Regulations 2004 made before 1st October 2005.

Initial Commencement
Specified date: 1 October 2005: see para (1) above.

2 Amendment of the Accession (Immigration and Worker Registration) Regulations 2004

In regulation 8(4)(a) of the Accession (Immigration and Worker Registration) Regulations 2004, for "£50" substitute "£70".

Initial Commencement
Specified date: 1 October 2005: see reg 1 (1.

BRITISH NATIONALITY (GENERAL) (AMENDMENT) REGULATIONS 2005

SI 2005/2785

Made ...10th October 2005

Laid before Parliament ...11th October 2005

The Secretary of State makes the following Regulations in exercise of the powers conferred by section 41(1)(ba) and (bb), (1A) and (3) of the British Nationality Act 1981:

1

(1) These Regulations may be cited as the British Nationality (General) (Amendment) Regulations 2005.

(2) Subject to paragraph (3), these Regulations shall come into force on 1st November 2005.

(3) These Regulations shall come into force in the Islands on 1st May 2006.

Initial Commencement
Specified date: 1 November 2005: see para (2) above.

2

The British Nationality (General) Regulations 2003 shall be amended as follows.

Initial Commencement
Specified date: 1 November 2005: see reg 1(2).

3

For regulation 5A, substitute:

"5A Knowledge of language and life in the United Kingdom

(1) A person has sufficient knowledge of the English language and sufficient knowledge about life in the United Kingdom for the purpose of an application for naturalisation as a British citizen under section 6 of the Act if—

(a) he has attended a course which used teaching materials derived from the document entitled "Citizenship Materials for ESOL Learners" (ISBN 1–84478–5424) and he has thereby attained a relevant accredited qualification; or

(b) he has passed the test known as the "Life in the UK Test" administered by an educational institution or other person approved for this purpose by the Secretary of State; or

(c) in the case of a person who is ordinarily resident outside the United Kingdom, a person designated by the Secretary of State certifies in writing that he has sufficient knowledge of the English language and sufficient knowledge about life in the United Kingdom for this purpose.

(2) In this regulation, a "relevant accredited qualification" is—

(a) an ESOL "Skills for Life" qualification in speaking and listening at Entry Level approved by the Qualifications and Curriculum Authority; or

(b) two ESOL Units at Access Level under the Scottish Credit and Qualifications Framework approved by the Scottish Qualifications Authority.".

Initial Commencement
Specified date: 1 November 2005: see reg 1(2).

4

In Schedule 2—

(a) in paragraph 13(1)(a), after "knowledge of language" insert ", knowledge about life in the United Kingdom"; and
(b) in paragraph 14(1)(b), for the words from "immigration laws" to the end, substitute "immigration laws, good character, knowledge of language and knowledge about life in the United Kingdom".

Initial Commencement
Specified date: 1 November 2005: see reg 1(2).

5

The British Nationality (General) (Amendment) Regulations 2004 and the British Nationality (General) (Amendment No 2) Regulations 2004 are revoked.

Initial Commencement
Specified date: 1 November 2005: see reg 1(2).

IMMIGRATION (PROCEDURE FOR FORMATION OF CIVIL PARTNERSHIPS) REGULATIONS 2005

SI 2005/2917

Made ...19th October 2005

Laid before Parliament ...24th October 2005

The Secretary of State makes the following Regulations in exercise of the powers conferred by paragraphs 2(1), 4, 9, 13 and 16(3)(a) of Schedule 23 to the Civil Partnership Act 2004 and section 25 of the Asylum and Immigration (Treatment of Claimants, etc) Act 2004.

In accordance with paragraphs 4(4), 9(2) and 13(2) of Schedule 23 to the Civil Partnership Act 2004 he has consulted with the Registrar General.

1 Citation, commencement and interpretation

(1) These Regulations may be cited as the Immigration (Procedure for Formation of Civil Partnerships) Regulations 2005.

(2) Subject to paragraph (3), these Regulations shall come into force on 5th December 2005.

(3) This regulation, regulations 2 and 3 and Schedule 1 shall come into force on 14th November 2005.

Initial Commencement
Specified date: 14 November 2005: see para (3) above.

2

In these Regulations—

(a) "the 2004 Act" means the Civil Partnership Act 2004; and
(b) "civil partnership" means a civil partnership which exists under or by virtue of the 2004 Act.

Initial Commencement
Specified date: 14 November 2005: see para (3) above.

3 Application for permission

(1) A person seeking the permission of the Secretary of State to form a civil partnership in the United Kingdom under paragraph 2(1)(b) of Schedule 23 to the 2004 Act shall—

(a) make an application in writing; and
(b) pay a fee of £135 on the submission of the application.

(2) The information set out in Schedule 1 to these Regulations is to be contained in or provided with the application.

(3) The fee is to be paid to the Immigration and Nationality Directorate of the Home Office—

(a) by a cheque or postal order crossed and made payable to "Home Office Certificates of Approval"; or
(b) by means of any debit card or credit card which that Directorate accepts.

Initial Commencement
Specified date: 14 November 2005: see para (3) above.

4 Specified classes of person

(1) The following persons are specified for the purpose of paragraph 2(1)(c) of Schedule 23 to the 2004 Act—

(a) persons who are settled in the United Kingdom; and
(b) persons to whom Schedule 3 to the 2004 Act applies.

(2) In this regulation, "settled in the United Kingdom" has the meaning given in paragraph 6 of the immigration rules (which are the rules laid before Parliament under section 3(2) of the Immigration Act 1971).

Initial Commencement
Specified date: 5 December 2005: see reg 1(2).

5 Specified registration authorities in England and Wales

(1) The registration authorities in England and Wales listed in the left-hand column of Schedule 2 to these Regulations are specified for the purposes of paragraph 4(1)(a) of Schedule 23 to the 2004 Act.

(2) An employee or officer or other person provided by a specified registration authority is a "relevant individual" for the purposes of paragraph 4(1)(b) and (2) of Schedule 23 to the 2004 Act if he—

(a) is authorised by that authority to attest notices of proposed civil partnership; and

(b) is located at the office specified in relation to that authority in the right-hand column of Schedule 2 to these Regulations.

Initial Commencement
Specified date: 5 December 2005: see reg 1(2).

6 Specified registration districts in Scotland

Every registration district in Scotland is specified for the purposes of paragraph 9(1)(a) of Schedule 23 to the 2004 Act.

Initial Commencement
Specified date: 5 December 2005: see reg 1(2).

7 Prescribed registrars in Northern Ireland

The registrar of every register office in Northern Ireland is prescribed for the purposes of paragraph 13(1)(a) of Schedule 23 to the 2004 Act.

Initial Commencement
Specified date: 5 December 2005: see reg 1(2).

8 Amendment to the Immigration (Procedure for Marriage) Regulations 2005

(1) The Immigration (Procedure for Marriage) Regulations 2005 are amended as follows.

(2) In Schedule 2 to those Regulations, after the words "Whether he has previously been married", insert on both occasions "or formed a civil partnership".

Initial Commencement
Specified date: 5 December 2005: see reg 1(2).

SCHEDULE 1
Information to be Contained in or Provided with an Application for Permission to Form a Civil Partnership in the United Kingdom

Regulation 3

(a) Information to be provided in respect of the applicant

Name

Date of birth

Name at birth (if different)

Nationality

Full postal address

Daytime telephone number

Passport or travel document number

Home Office reference number

Current immigration status

Date on which current leave to enter or remain in the United Kingdom was granted

Date on which that leave expires

Whether he has previously been married or formed a civil partnership, and if so, information showing that he is now free to form a civil partnership

Two passport-sized photographs

Passport or travel document

(b) Information to be provided in respect of the other party to the proposed civil partnership

Name

Date of birth

Name at birth (if different)

Nationality

Full postal address

Daytime telephone number

Passport or travel document number

Whether he is subject to immigration control and, if so:

Home Office reference number

Current immigration status

Date on which current leave to enter or remain in the United Kingdom was granted

Date on which that leave expires

Whether he has previously been married or formed a civil partnership, and if so, information showing that he is now free to form a civil partnership

Two passport-sized photographs

Passport or travel document

Initial Commencement
Specified date: 14 November 2005: see para (3) above.

SCHEDULE 2
SPECIFIED REGISTRATION AUTHORITIES IN ENGLAND & WALES

Regulation 5

[Text omitted]

REPORTING OF SUSPICIOUS CIVIL PARTNERSHIPS REGULATIONS 2005

SI 2005/3174

Made ...15th November 2005

Coming into force ...5th December 2005

The Registrar General, in exercise of the powers conferred on him by section 24A(3) and (4)(a) of the Immigration and Asylum Act 1999, with the approval of the Chancellor of the Exchequer, makes the following Regulations:

1 Citation, commencement and interpretation

(1) These Regulations may be cited as the Reporting of Suspicious Civil Partnerships Regulations 2005 and shall come into force on 5th December 2005.

(2) In these Regulations, unless the context otherwise requires "the 1999 Act" means the Immigration and Asylum Act 1999.

Initial Commencement
Specified date: 5 December 2005: see para (1) above.

2 Reporting of suspicious civil partnerships

For the purpose of section 24A of the 1999 Act (duty to report suspicious civil partnerships) the person concerned shall—

- (a) report his suspicions to the Secretary of State by making a report in writing or other permanent form giving the information specified in the Schedule to these Regulations, and
- (b) forward that report to the Home Office, National Intelligence Unit, PO Box 1000, Hayes, Middlesex UB3 5WB or, where the Secretary of State has notified the Registrar General of another address to be used in relation to any particular registration authority, that address.

Initial Commencement
Specified date: 5 December 2005: see reg 1(1).

SCHEDULE

Regulation 2

Information to be provided when reporting a suspicious civil partnership

Name and surname of each of the civil partners

Date of birth and/or age of each of the civil partners

Sex of each of the civil partners

Condition of each of the civil partners

Address (and registration authority of residence) of each of the civil partners

Nationality of each of the civil partners

Date of formation of civil partnership

Place of formation of civil partnership

Time of formation of civil partnership

Nature of evidence produced in respect of—

(i) name and age
(ii) condition
(iii) nationality

of the civil partners

Reasons for making the report

Full name of person making the report

Name of registration authority on whose behalf the report is being made

Date report made

Initial Commencement
Specified date: 5 December 2005: see reg 1(1).

ASYLUM (DESIGNATED STATES) (NO 2) ORDER 2005

SI 2005/3306

Made ...1st December 2005

Coming into force ...2nd December 2005

The Secretary of State is satisfied that there is in general in the States to be added to section 94(4) of the Nationality, Immigration and Asylum Act 2002 by article 2 of this Order no serious risk of persecution of persons or men, as relevant, entitled to reside in those States and that removal to those States of persons or men, as relevant, entitled to reside there will not in general contravene the United Kingdom's obligations under the Human Rights Convention;

Therefore, the Secretary of State makes the following Order in exercise of the powers conferred on him by section 94(5) and (5A) of that Act;

In accordance with section 112(4)(b) of that Act, a draft of this instrument was laid before Parliament and approved by a resolution of each House of Parliament.

1 Citation and commencement

This Order may be cited as the Asylum (Designated States) (No 2) Order 2005 and shall come into force on the day after it is made, but shall not apply in relation to an asylum or human rights claim made prior to the commencement of this Order.

Initial Commencement
Specified date: 2 December 2005: see above.

2 Designated States

The States listed below shall be added to the list of States in section 94(4) of the Nationality, Immigration and Asylum Act 2002:

"(z) Mongolia,
(aa) Ghana (in respect of men),

(bb) Nigeria (in respect of men)."

Initial Commencement
Specified date: 2 December 2005: see art 1.

IMMIGRATION (DESIGNATION OF TRAVEL BANS) (AMENDMENT) ORDER 2005

SI 2005/3310

Made ...1st December 2005

Laid before Parliament ...5th December 2005

Coming into force ...6th December 2005

The Secretary of State, in exercise of the powers conferred upon him by section 8B(5) of the Immigration Act 1971, makes the following Order:

1

This Order may be cited as the Immigration (Designation of Travel Bans) (Amendment) Order 2005 and shall come into force on 6th December 2005.

Initial Commencement
Specified date: 6 December 2005: see above.

2

For the Schedule to the Immigration (Designation of Travel Bans) Order 2000 there shall be substituted the Schedule set out in the Schedule to this Order.

Initial Commencement
Specified date: 6 December 2005: see art 1.

3

The Immigration (Designation of Travel Bans) (Amendment No 2) Order 2003 and the Immigration (Designation of Travel Bans) (Amendment) Order 2004 are revoked.

Initial Commencement
Specified date: 6 December 2005: see art 1.

THE SCHEDULE
SCHEDULE SUBSTITUTED FOR THE SCHEDULE TO THE IMMIGRATION (DESIGNATION OF TRAVEL BANS) ORDER 2000

"SCHEDULE
DESIGNATED INSTRUMENTS

Article 2

PART 1
RESOLUTIONS OF THE SECURITY COUNCIL OF THE UNITED NATIONS

Resolution 1390 (2002) of 16th January 2002 (Al Qa'ida and the Taliban).

Resolution 1617 (2005) of 29th July 2005 (Al Qa'ida and the Taliban).

Resolution 1572 (2004) of 15th November 2004 (Côte d'Ivoire).

Resolution 1596 (2005) of 18th April 2005 (Democratic Republic of the Congo).

Resolution 1521 (2003) of 22nd December 2003 (Liberia) renewed by Resolution 1579 (2004) of 21st December 2004 (Liberia).

Resolution 1171 (1998) of 5th June 1998 (Sierra Leone).

Resolution 1591 (2005) of 29th March 2005 (Sudan).

Resolution 1636 (2005) of 31st October 2005 (Syria and the Lebanon).

PART 2
INSTRUMENTS MADE BY THE COUNCIL OF THE EUROPEAN UNION

Common Position 2002/402/CFSP of 27th May 2002 (Al Qa'ida and the Taliban).

Common Position 2004/661/CFSP of 24th September 2004 (Belarus) as amended by Common Position 2004/848/CFSP of 13th December 2004 (Belarus) and extended by Common Position 2005/666/CFSP of 20th September 2005 (Belarus).

Common Position 97/193/CFSP of 17th March 1997 (Bosnia-Herzegovina).

Common Position 2004/423/CFSP of 26th April 2004 (Burma) as amended by Common Position 2004/730/CFSP of 25th October 2004 (Burma) and Common Position 2005/340/CFSP of 25th April 2005 (Burma).

Common Position 2004/852/CFSP of 13th December 2004 (Côte d'Ivoire).

Common Position 2005/440/CFSP of 13th June 2005 (Democratic Republic of Congo).

Common Position 98/240/CFSP of 19th March 1998 (Federal Republic of Yugoslavia).

Common Position 1999/318/CFSP of 10th May 1999 (Federal Republic of Yugoslavia) as amended by Common Position 2000/56/CFSP of 24th January 2000 (Federal Republic of Yugoslavia).

Common Position 2000/696/CFSP of 10th November 2000 (Federal Republic of Yugoslavia) as amended by Common Position 2001/155/CFSP of 26th February 2001 (Federal Republic of Yugoslavia).

Common Position 2004/133/CFSP of 10th February 2004 (Former Yugoslav Republic of Macedonia) as amended by Common Position 2005/80/CFSP of 31st January 2005 (Former Yugoslav Republic of Macedonia).

Common Position 2004/293/CFSP of 30th March 2004 (International Criminal Tribunal for the former Yugoslavia) as implemented by Decision 2005/83/CFSP of 31st January 2005 (International Criminal Tribunal for the former Yugoslavia) and renewed by Common Position 2005/227/CFSP of 16th March 2005 (International Criminal Tribunal for the former Yugoslavia).

Common Position 2004/137/CFSP of 10th February 2004 (Liberia) as amended by Common Position 2004/902/CFSP of 22nd December 2004 (Liberia).

Common Position 2004/179/CFSP of 23rd February 2004 (Moldovan Republic) as amended by Common Position 2004/622/CFSP of 26th August 2004 (Moldovan Republic) and Common Position 2005/147/CFSP of 21st February 2005 (Moldovan Republic).

Common Position 98/409/CFSP of 29th June 1998 (Sierra Leone).

Common Position 2005/411/CFSP of 30th May 2005 (Sudan).

Common Position 2005/792/CFSP of 14th November 2005 (Uzbekistan).

Common Position 2004/161/CFSP of 19th February 2004 (Zimbabwe) as extended by Common Position 2005/146/CFSP of 21st February 2005 (Zimbabwe) and implemented by Decision 2005/592/CFSP of 29th July 2005 (Zimbabwe).".

Initial Commencement
Specified date: 6 December 2005: see art 1.

IMMIGRATION (PASSENGER TRANSIT VISA) (AMENDMENT) ORDER 2006

SI 2006/493

Made ...27th February 2006

Laid before Parliament ...1st March 2006

Coming into force ...2nd March 2006

The Secretary of State, in exercise of the powers conferred upon him by section 41 of the Immigration and Asylum Act 1999, makes the following Order:

1

This Order may be cited as the Immigration (Passenger Transit Visa) (Amendment) Order 2006 and shall come into force on 2nd March 2006.

Initial Commencement
Specified date: 2 March 2006: see above.

2

In the Immigration (Passenger Transit Visa) Order 2003, in Schedule 1, after "Liberia" there shall be inserted "Malawi".

Initial Commencement
Specified date: 2 March 2006: see art 1.

ASYLUM SUPPORT (AMENDMENT) REGULATIONS 2006

SI 2006/733

Made ...13th March 2006

Laid before Parliament ...17th March 2006

Coming into force ...10th April 2006

The Secretary of State, in exercise of the powers conferred on him by section 166(3) of, and paragraphs 1 and 3(a) of Schedule 8 to, the Immigration and Asylum Act 1999, makes the following Regulations:

1 Citation and commencement

These Regulations may be cited as the Asylum Support (Amendment) Regulations 2006 and shall come into force on 10th April 2006.

Initial Commencement
Specified date: 10 April 2006: see above.

2 Kind and levels of support for essential living needs

For the table at regulation 10(2) of the Asylum Support Regulations 2000 substitute:

"TABLE	
Qualifying couple	£63.07
Lone parent aged 18 or over	£40.22
Single person aged 25 or over	£40.22
Single person aged at least 18 but under 25	£31.85
Person aged at least 16 but under 18 (except a member of a qualifying couple)	£34.60
Person aged under 16	£45.58".

Initial Commencement
Specified date: 10 April 2006: see reg 1.

3 Revocation of the Asylum Support (Amendment) (No 2) Regulations 2005

The Asylum Support (Amendment) (No 2) Regulations 2005 are revoked.

Initial Commencement
Specified date: 10 April 2006: see reg 1.

IMMIGRATION (EUROPEAN ECONOMIC AREA) REGULATIONS 2006

SI 2006/1003

Made ...30th March 2006

Laid before Parliament ...4th April 2006

Coming into force ...30th April 2006

The Secretary of State, being a Minister designated for the purposes of section 2(2) of the European Communities Act 1972 in relation to measures relating to rights of entry into, and residence in, the United Kingdom, in exercise of the powers conferred upon him by that section, and of the powers conferred on him by section 109 of the Nationality, Immigration and Asylum Act 2002, makes the following Regulations:

PART 1
INTERPRETATION ETC

1 Citation and commencement

These Regulations may be cited as the Immigration (European Economic Area) Regulations 2006 and shall come into force on 30th April 2006.

Initial Commencement
Specified date: 30 April 2006: see above.

2 General interpretation

(1) In these Regulations—

"the 1971 Act" means the Immigration Act 1971;
"the 1999 Act" means the Immigration and Asylum Act 1999;
"the 2002 Act" means the Nationality, Immigration and Asylum Act 2002;
"civil partner" does not include a party to a civil partnership of convenience;
"decision maker" means the Secretary of State, an immigration officer or an entry clearance officer (as the case may be);
"document certifying permanent residence" means a document issued to an EEA national, in accordance with regulation 18, as proof of the holder's permanent right of residence under regulation 15 as at the date of issue;
"EEA decision" means a decision under these Regulations that concerns a person's—

(a) entitlement to be admitted to the United Kingdom;
(b) entitlement to be issued with or have renewed, or not to have revoked, a registration certificate, residence card, document certifying permanent residence or permanent residence card; or
(c) removal from the United Kingdom;

"EEA family permit" means a document issued to a person, in accordance with regulation 12, in connection with his admission to the United Kingdom;
"EEA national" means a national of an EEA State;
"EEA State" means—

(a) a member State, other than the United Kingdom;
(b) Norway, Iceland or Liechtenstein; or
(c) Switzerland;

"entry clearance" has the meaning given in section 33(1) of the 1971 Act;
"entry clearance officer" means a person responsible for the grant or refusal of entry clearance;

"immigration rules" has the meaning given in section 33(1) of the 1971 Act;
"military service" means service in the armed forces of an EEA State;
"permanent residence card" means a card issued to a person who is not an EEA national, in accordance with regulation 18, as proof of the holder's permanent right of residence under regulation 15 as at the date of issue;
"registration certificate" means a certificate issued to an EEA national, in accordance with regulation 16, as proof of the holder's right of residence in the United Kingdom as at the date of issue;
"relevant EEA national" in relation to an extended family member has the meaning given in regulation 8(6);
"residence card" means a card issued to a person who is not an EEA national, in accordance with regulation 17, as proof of the holder's right of residence in the United Kingdom as at the date of issue;
"spouse" does not include a party to a marriage of convenience;
"United Kingdom national" means a person who falls to be treated as a national of the United Kingdom for the purposes of the Community Treaties.

(2) Paragraph (1) is subject to paragraph 1(a) of Schedule 4 (transitional provisions).

Initial Commencement
Specified date: 30 April 2006: see reg 1.

3 Continuity of residence

(1) This regulation applies for the purpose of calculating periods of continuous residence in the United Kingdom under regulation 5(1) and regulation 15.

(2) Continuity of residence is not affected by—

(a) periods of absence from the United Kingdom which do not exceed six months in total in any year;
(b) periods of absence from the United Kingdom on military service; or
(c) any one absence from the United Kingdom not exceeding twelve months for an important reason such as pregnancy and childbirth, serious illness, study or vocational training or an overseas posting.

(3) But continuity of residence is broken if a person is removed from the United Kingdom under regulation 19(3).

Initial Commencement
Specified date: 30 April 2006: see reg 1.

4 "Worker", "self-employed person", "self-sufficient person" and "student"

(1) In these Regulations—

(a) "worker" means a worker within the meaning of Article 39 of the Treaty establishing the European Community;
(b) "self-employed person" means a person who establishes himself in order to pursue activity as a self-employed person in accordance with Article 43 of the Treaty establishing the European Community;
(c) "self-sufficient person" means a person who has—
  (i) sufficient resources not to become a burden on the social assistance system of the United Kingdom during his period of residence; and
  (ii) comprehensive sickness insurance cover in the United Kingdom;
(d) "student" means a person who—
  (i) is enrolled at a private or public establishment, included on the Department for Education and Skills' Register of Education and Training

Providers or financed from public funds, for the principal purpose of following a course of study, including vocational training;

(ii) has comprehensive sickness insurance cover in the United Kingdom; and

(iii) assures the Secretary of State, by means of a declaration, or by such equivalent means as the person may choose, that he has sufficient resources not to become a burden on the social assistance system of the United Kingdom during his period of residence.

(2) For the purposes of paragraph (1)(c), where family members of the person concerned reside in the United Kingdom and their right to reside is dependent upon their being family members of that person—

(a) the requirement for that person to have sufficient resources not to become a burden on the social assistance system of the United Kingdom during his period of residence shall only be satisfied if his resources and those of the family members are sufficient to avoid him and the family members becoming such a burden;

(b) the requirement for that person to have comprehensive sickness insurance cover in the United Kingdom shall only be satisfied if he and his family members have such cover.

(3) For the purposes of paragraph (1)(d), where family members of the person concerned reside in the United Kingdom and their right to reside is dependent upon their being family members of that person, the requirement for that person to assure the Secretary of State that he has sufficient resources not to become a burden on the social assistance system of the United Kingdom during his period of residence shall only be satisfied if he assures the Secretary of State that his resources and those of the family members are sufficient to avoid him and the family members becoming such a burden.

(4) For the purposes of paragraphs (1)(c) and (d) and paragraphs (2) and (3), the resources of the person concerned and, where applicable, any family members, are to be regarded as sufficient if they exceed the maximum level of resources which a United Kingdom national and his family members may possess if he is to become eligible for social assistance under the United Kingdom benefit system.

Initial Commencement

Specified date: 30 April 2006: see reg 1.

5 "Worker or self-employed person who has ceased activity"

(1) In these Regulations, "worker or self-employed person who has ceased activity" means an EEA national who satisfies the conditions in paragraph (2), (3), (4) or (5).

(2) A person satisfies the conditions in this paragraph if he—

(a) terminates his activity as a worker or self-employed person and—

(i) has reached the age at which he is entitled to a state pension on the date on which he terminates his activity; or

(ii) in the case of a worker, ceases working to take early retirement;

(b) pursued his activity as a worker or self-employed person in the United Kingdom for at least twelve months prior to the termination; and

(c) resided in the United Kingdom continuously for more than three years prior to the termination.

(3) A person satisfies the conditions in this paragraph if—

(a) he terminates his activity in the United Kingdom as a worker or self-employed person as a result of a permanent incapacity to work; and

(b) either—

(i) he resided in the United Kingdom continuously for more than two years prior to the termination; or

(ii) the incapacity is the result of an accident at work or an occupational disease that entitles him to a pension payable in full or in part by an institution in the United Kingdom.

(4) A person satisfies the conditions in this paragraph if—

(a) he is active as a worker or self-employed person in an EEA State but retains his place of residence in the United Kingdom, to which he returns as a rule at least once a week; and

(b) prior to becoming so active in that EEA State, he had been continuously resident and continuously active as a worker or self-employed person in the United Kingdom for at least three years.

(5) A person who satisfies the condition in paragraph (4)(a) but not the condition in paragraph (4)(b) shall, for the purposes of paragraphs (2) and (3), be treated as being active and resident in the United Kingdom during any period in which he is working or self-employed in the EEA State.

(6) The conditions in paragraphs (2) and (3) as to length of residence and activity as a worker or self-employed person shall not apply in relation to a person whose spouse or civil partner is a United Kingdom national.

(7) For the purposes of this regulation—

(a) periods of inactivity for reasons not of the person's own making;

(b) periods of inactivity due to illness or accident; and

(c) in the case of a worker, periods of involuntary unemployment duly recorded by the relevant employment office,

shall be treated as periods of activity as a worker or self-employed person, as the case may be.

Initial Commencement
Specified date: 30 April 2006: see reg 1.

6 "Qualified person"

(1) In these Regulations, "qualified person" means a person who is an EEA national and in the United Kingdom as—

(a) a jobseeker;

(b) a worker;

(c) a self-employed person;

(d) a self-sufficient person; or

(e) a student.

(2) A person who is no longer working shall not cease to be treated as a worker for the purpose of paragraph (1)(b) if—

(a) he is temporarily unable to work as the result of an illness or accident;

(b) he is in duly recorded involuntary unemployment after having been employed in the United Kingdom, provided that he has registered as a jobseeker with the relevant employment office and—

(i) he was employed for one year or more before becoming unemployed;

(ii) he has been unemployed for no more than six months; or

(iii) he can provide evidence that he is seeking employment in the United Kingdom and has a genuine chance of being engaged;

(c) he is involuntarily unemployed and has embarked on vocational training; or

(d) he has voluntarily ceased working and embarked on vocational training that is related to his previous employment.

(3) A person who is no longer in self-employment shall not cease to be treated as a self-employed person for the purpose of paragraph (1)(c) if he is temporarily unable to pursue his activity as a self-employed person as the result of an illness or accident.

(4) For the purpose of paragraph (1)(a), "jobseeker" means a person who enters the United Kingdom in order to seek employment and can provide evidence that he is seeking employment and has a genuine chance of being engaged.

Initial Commencement
Specified date: 30 April 2006: see reg 1.

7 Family member

(1) Subject to paragraph (2), for the purposes of these Regulations the following persons shall be treated as the family members of another person—

(a) his spouse or his civil partner;
(b) direct descendants of his, his spouse or his civil partner who are—
 (i) under 21; or
 (ii) dependants of his, his spouse or his civil partner;
(c) dependent direct relatives in his ascending line or that of his spouse or his civil partner;
(d) a person who is to be treated as the family member of that other person under paragraph (3).

(2) A person shall not be treated under paragraph (1)(b) or (c) as the family member of a student residing in the United Kingdom after the period of three months beginning on the date on which the student is admitted to the United Kingdom unless—

(a) in the case of paragraph (b), the person is the dependent child of the student or of his spouse or civil partner; or
(b) the student also falls within one of the other categories of qualified persons mentioned in regulation 6(1).

(3) Subject to paragraph (4), a person who is an extended family member and has been issued with an EEA family permit, a registration certificate or a residence card shall be treated as the family member of the relevant EEA national for as long as he continues to satisfy the conditions in regulation 8(2), (3), (4) or (5) in relation to that EEA national and the permit, certificate or card has not ceased to be valid or been revoked.

(4) Where the relevant EEA national is a student, the extended family member shall only be treated as the family member of that national under paragraph (3) if either the EEA family permit was issued under regulation 12(2), the registration certificate was issued under regulation 16(5) or the residence card was issued under regulation 17(4).

Initial Commencement
Specified date: 30 April 2006: see reg 1.

8 "Extended family member"

(1) In these Regulations "extended family member" means a person who is not a family member of an EEA national under regulation 7(1)(a), (b) or (c) and who satisfies the conditions in paragraph (2), (3), (4) or (5).

(2) A person satisfies the condition in this paragraph if the person is a relative of an EEA national, his spouse or his civil partner and—

(a) the person is residing in an EEA State in which the EEA national also resides and is dependent upon the EEA national or is a member of his household;
(b) the person satisfied the condition in paragraph (a) and is accompanying the EEA national to the United Kingdom or wishes to join him there; or
(c) the person satisfied the condition in paragraph (a), has joined the EEA national in the United Kingdom and continues to be dependent upon him or to be a member of his household.

(3) A person satisfies the condition in this paragraph if the person is a relative of an EEA national or his spouse or his civil partner and, on serious health grounds, strictly requires the personal care of the EEA national his spouse or his civil partner.

(4) A person satisfies the condition in this paragraph if the person is a relative of an EEA national and would meet the requirements in the immigration rules (other than those relating to entry clearance) for indefinite leave to enter or remain in the United Kingdom as a dependent relative of the EEA national were the EEA national a person present and settled in the United Kingdom.

(5) A person satisfies the condition in this paragraph if the person is the partner of an EEA national (other than a civil partner) and can prove to the decision maker that he is in a durable relationship with the EEA national.

(6) In these Regulations "relevant EEA national" means, in relation to an extended family member, the EEA national who is or whose spouse or civil partner is the relative of the extended family member for the purpose of paragraph (2), (3) or (4) or the EEA national who is the partner of the extended family member for the purpose of paragraph (5).

Initial Commencement
Specified date: 30 April 2006: see reg 1.

9 Family members of United Kingdom nationals

(1) If the conditions in paragraph (2) are satisfied, these Regulations apply to a person who is the family member of a United Kingdom national as if the United Kingdom national were an EEA national.

(2) The conditions are that—

(a) the United Kingdom national is residing in an EEA State as a worker or self-employed person or was so residing before returning to the United Kingdom; and
(b) if the family member of the United Kingdom national is his spouse or civil partner, the parties are living together in the EEA State or had entered into the marriage or civil partnership and were living together in that State before the United Kingdom national returned to the United Kingdom.

(3) Where these Regulations apply to the family member of a United Kingdom national the United Kingdom national shall be treated as holding a valid passport issued by an EEA State for the purpose of the application of regulation 13 to that family member.

Initial Commencement
Specified date: 30 April 2006: see reg 1.

10 "Family member who has retained the right of residence"

(1) In these Regulations, "family member who has retained the right of residence" means, subject to paragraph (8), a person who satisfies the conditions in paragraph (2), (3), (4) or (5).

(2) A person satisfies the conditions in this paragraph if—

(a) he was a family member of a qualified person when the qualified person died;
(b) he resided in the United Kingdom in accordance with these Regulations for at least the year immediately before the death of the qualified person; and
(c) he satisfies the condition in paragraph (6).

(3) A person satisfies the conditions in this paragraph if—

(a) he is the direct descendant of—
 (i) a qualified person who has died;
 (ii) a person who ceased to be a qualified person on ceasing to reside in the United Kingdom; or
 (iii) the person who was the spouse or civil partner of the qualified person mentioned in sub-paragraph (i) when he died or is the spouse or civil partner of the person mentioned in sub-paragraph (ii); and
(b) he was attending an educational course in the United Kingdom immediately before the qualified person died or ceased to be a qualified person and continues to attend such a course.

(4) A person satisfies the conditions in this paragraph if the person is the parent with actual custody of a child who satisfies the condition in paragraph (3).

(5) A person satisfies the conditions in this paragraph if—

(a) he ceased to be a family member of a qualified person on the termination of the marriage or civil partnership of the qualified person;
(b) he was residing in the United Kingdom in accordance with these Regulations at the date of the termination;
(c) he satisfies the condition in paragraph (6); and
(d) either—
 (i) prior to the initiation of the proceedings for the termination of the marriage or the civil partnership the marriage or civil partnership had lasted for at least three years and the parties to the marriage or civil partnership had resided in the United Kingdom for at least one year during its duration;
 (ii) the former spouse or civil partner of the qualified person has custody of a child of the qualified person;
 (iii) the former spouse or civil partner of the qualified person has the right of access to a child of the qualified person under the age of 18 and a court has ordered that such access must take place in the United Kingdom; or
 (iv) the continued right of residence in the United Kingdom of the person is warranted by particularly difficult circumstances, such as he or another family member having been a victim of domestic violence while the marriage or civil partnership was subsisting.

(6) The condition in this paragraph is that the person—

(a) is not an EEA national but would, if he were an EEA national, be a worker, a self-employed person or a self-sufficient person under regulation 6; or
(b) is the family member of a person who falls within paragraph (a).

(7) In this regulation, "educational course" means a course within the scope of Article 12 of Council Regulation (EEC) No 1612/68 on freedom of movement for workers.

(8) A person with a permanent right of residence under regulation 15 shall not become a family member who has retained the right of residence on the death or departure from the United Kingdom of the qualified person or the termination of the

marriage or civil partnership, as the case may be, and a family member who has retained the right of residence shall cease to have that status on acquiring a permanent right of residence under regulation 15.

Initial Commencement
Specified date: 30 April 2006: see reg 1.

PART 2
EEA RIGHTS

11 Right of admission to the United Kingdom

(1) An EEA national must be admitted to the United Kingdom if he produces on arrival a valid national identity card or passport issued by an EEA State.

(2) A person who is not an EEA national must be admitted to the United Kingdom if he is a family member of an EEA national, a family member who has retained the right of residence or a person with a permanent right of residence under regulation 15 and produces on arrival—

- (a) a valid passport; and
- (b) an EEA family permit, a residence card or a permanent residence card.

(3) An immigration officer may not place a stamp in the passport of a person admitted to the United Kingdom under this regulation who is not an EEA national if the person produces a residence card or permanent residence card.

(4) Before an immigration officer refuses admission to the United Kingdom to a person under this regulation because the person does not produce on arrival a document mentioned in paragraph (1) or (2), the immigration officer must give the person every reasonable opportunity to obtain the document or have it brought to him within a reasonable period of time or to prove by other means that he is—

- (a) an EEA national;
- (b) a family member of an EEA national with a right to accompany that national or join him in the United Kingdom; or
- (c) a family member who has retained the right of residence or a person with a permanent right of residence under regulation 15.

(5) But this regulation is subject to regulations 19(1) and (2).

Initial Commencement
Specified date: 30 April 2006: see reg 1.

12 Issue of EEA family permit

(1) An entry clearance officer must issue an EEA family permit to a person who applies for one if the person is a family member of an EEA national and—

- (a) the EEA national—
  - (i) is residing in the UK in accordance with these Regulations; or
  - (ii) will be travelling to the United Kingdom within six months of the date of the application and will be an EEA national residing in the United Kingdom in accordance with these Regulations on arrival in the United Kingdom; and
- (b) the family member will be accompanying the EEA national to the United Kingdom or joining him there and—
  - (i) is lawfully resident in an EEA State; or
  - (ii) would meet the requirements in the immigration rules (other than those relating to entry clearance) for leave to enter the United Kingdom as the

family member of the EEA national or, in the case of direct descendants or dependent direct relatives in the ascending line of his spouse or his civil partner, as the family member of his spouse or his civil partner, were the EEA national or the spouse or civil partner a person present and settled in the United Kingdom.

(2) An entry clearance officer may issue an EEA family permit to an extended family member of an EEA national who applies for one if—

(a) the relevant EEA national satisfies the condition in paragraph (1)(a);
(b) the extended family member wishes to accompany the relevant EEA national to the United Kingdom or to join him there; and
(c) in all the circumstances, it appears to the entry clearance officer appropriate to issue the EEA family permit.

(3) Where an entry clearance officer receives an application under paragraph (2) he shall undertake an extensive examination of the personal circumstances of the applicant and if he refuses the application shall give reasons justifying the refusal unless this is contrary to the interests of national security.

(4) An EEA family permit issued under this regulation shall be issued free of charge and as soon as possible.

(5) But an EEA family permit shall not be issued under this regulation if the applicant or the EEA national concerned falls to be excluded from the United Kingdom on grounds of public policy, public security or public health in accordance with regulation 21.

Initial Commencement
Specified date: 30 April 2006: see reg 1.

13 Initial right of residence

(1) An EEA national is entitled to reside in the United Kingdom for a period not exceeding three months beginning on the date on which he is admitted to the United Kingdom provided that he holds a valid national identity card or passport issued by an EEA State.

(2) A family member of an EEA national residing in the United Kingdom under paragraph (1) who is not himself an EEA national is entitled to reside in the United Kingdom provided that he holds a valid passport.

(3) But—

(a) this regulation is subject to regulation 19(3)(b); and
(b) an EEA national or his family member who becomes an unreasonable burden on the social assistance system of the United Kingdom shall cease to have the right to reside under this regulation.

Initial Commencement
Specified date: 30 April 2006: see reg 1.

14 Extended right of residence

(1) A qualified person is entitled to reside in the United Kingdom for so long as he remains a qualified person.

(2) A family member of a qualified person residing in the United Kingdom under paragraph (1) or of an EEA national with a permanent right of residence under regulation 15 is entitled to reside in the United Kingdom for so long as he remains the family member of the qualified person or EEA national.

(3) A family member who has retained the right of residence is entitled to reside in the United Kingdom for so long as he remains a family member who has retained the right of residence.

(4) A right to reside under this regulation is in addition to any right a person may have to reside in the United Kingdom under regulation 13 or 15.

(5) But this regulation is subject to regulation 19(3)(b).

Initial Commencement
Specified date: 30 April 2006: see reg 1.

15 Permanent right of residence

(1) The following persons shall acquire the right to reside in the United Kingdom permanently—

- (a) an EEA national who has resided in the United Kingdom in accordance with these Regulations for a continuous period of five years;
- (b) a family member of an EEA national who is not himself an EEA national but who has resided in the United Kingdom with the EEA national in accordance with these Regulations for a continuous period of five years;
- (c) a worker or self-employed person who has ceased activity;
- (d) the family member of a worker or self-employed person who has ceased activity;
- (e) a person who was the family member of a worker or self-employed person where—
  - (i) the worker or self-employed person has died;
  - (ii) the family member resided with him immediately before his death; and
  - (iii) the worker or self-employed person had resided continuously in the United Kingdom for at least the two years immediately before his death or the death was the result of an accident at work or an occupational disease;
- (f) a person who—
  - (i) has resided in the United Kingdom in accordance with these Regulations for a continuous period of five years; and
  - (ii) was, at the end of that period, a family member who has retained the right of residence.

(2) Once acquired, the right of permanent residence under this regulation shall be lost only through absence from the United Kingdom for a period exceeding two consecutive years.

(3) But this regulation is subject to regulation 19(3)(b).

Initial Commencement
Specified date: 30 April 2006: see reg 1.

PART 3
RESIDENCE DOCUMENTATION

16 Issue of registration certificate

(1) The Secretary of State must issue a registration certificate to a qualified person immediately on application and production of—

- (a) a valid identity card or passport issued by an EEA State;
- (b) proof that he is a qualified person.

(2) In the case of a worker, confirmation of the worker's engagement from his employer or a certificate of employment is sufficient proof for the purposes of paragraph (1)(b).

(3) The Secretary of State must issue a registration certificate to an EEA national who is the family member of a qualified person or of an EEA national with a permanent right of residence under regulation 15 immediately on application and production of—

- (a) a valid identity card or passport issued by an EEA State; and
- (b) proof that the applicant is such a family member.

(4) The Secretary of State must issue a registration certificate to an EEA national who is a family member who has retained the right of residence on application and production of—

- (a) a valid identity card or passport; and
- (b) proof that the applicant is a family member who has retained the right of residence.

(5) The Secretary of State may issue a registration certificate to an extended family member not falling within regulation 7(3) who is an EEA national on application if—

- (a) the relevant EEA national in relation to the extended family member is a qualified person or an EEA national with a permanent right of residence under regulation 15; and
- (b) in all the circumstances it appears to the Secretary of State appropriate to issue the registration certificate.

(6) Where the Secretary of State receives an application under paragraph (5) he shall undertake an extensive examination of the personal circumstances of the applicant and if he refuses the application shall give reasons justifying the refusal unless this is contrary to the interests of national security.

(7) A registration certificate issued under this regulation shall state the name and address of the person registering and the date of registration and shall be issued free of charge.

(8) But this regulation is subject to regulation 20(1).

Initial Commencement
Specified date: 30 April 2006: see reg 1.

17 Issue of residence card

(1) The Secretary of State must issue a residence card to a person who is not an EEA national and is the family member of a qualified person or of an EEA national with a permanent right of residence under regulation 15 on application and production of—

- (a) a valid passport; and
- (b) proof that the applicant is such a family member.

(2) The Secretary of State must issue a residence card to a person who is not an EEA national but who is a family member who has retained the right of residence on application and production of—

- (a) a valid passport; and
- (b) proof that the applicant is a family member who has retained the right of residence.

(3) On receipt of an application under paragraph (1) or (2) and the documents that are required to accompany the application the Secretary of State shall immediately

issue the applicant with a certificate of application for the residence card and the residence card shall be issued no later than six months after the date on which the application and documents are received.

(4) The Secretary of State may issue a residence card to an extended family member not falling within regulation 7(3) who is not an EEA national on application if—

- (a) the relevant EEA national in relation to the extended family member is a qualified person or an EEA national with a permanent right of residence under regulation 15; and
- (b) in all the circumstances it appears to the Secretary of State appropriate to issue the residence card.

(5) Where the Secretary of State receives an application under paragraph (4) he shall undertake an extensive examination of the personal circumstances of the applicant and if he refuses the application shall give reasons justifying the refusal unless this is contrary to the interests of national security.

(6) A residence card issued under this regulation may take the form of a stamp in the applicant's passport and shall be entitled "Residence card of a family member of an EEA national" and be valid for—

- (a) five years from the date of issue; or
- (b) in the case of a residence card issued to the family member or extended family member of a qualified person, the envisaged period of residence in the United Kingdom of the qualified person,

whichever is the shorter.

(7) A residence card issued under this regulation shall be issued free of charge.

(8) But this regulation is subject to regulation 20(1).

Initial Commencement
Specified date: 30 April 2006: see reg 1.

18 Issue of a document certifying permanent residence and a permanent residence card

(1) The Secretary of State must issue an EEA national with a permanent right of residence under regulation 15 with a document certifying permanent residence as soon as possible after an application for such a document and proof that the EEA national has such a right is submitted to the Secretary of State.

(2) The Secretary of State must issue a person who is not an EEA national who has a permanent right of residence under regulation 15 with a permanent residence card no later than six months after the date on which an application for a permanent residence card and proof that the person has such a right is submitted to the Secretary of State.

(3) Subject to paragraph (5) and regulation 20(3), a permanent residence card shall be valid for ten years from the date of issue and must be renewed on application.

(4) A document certifying permanent residence and a permanent residence card shall be issued free of charge.

(5) A document certifying permanent residence and a permanent residence card shall cease to be valid if the holder ceases to have a right of permanent residence under regulation 15.

Initial Commencement
Specified date: 30 April 2006: see reg 1.

PART 4
REFUSAL OF ADMISSION AND REMOVAL ETC

19 Exclusion and removal from the United Kingdom

(1) A person is not entitled to be admitted to the United Kingdom by virtue of regulation 11 if his exclusion is justified on grounds of public policy, public security or public health in accordance with regulation 21.

(2) A person is not entitled to be admitted to the United Kingdom as the family member of an EEA national under regulation 11(2) unless, at the time of his arrival—

(a) he is accompanying the EEA national or joining him in the United Kingdom; and
(b) the EEA national has a right to reside in the United Kingdom under these Regulations.

(3) Subject to paragraphs (4) and (5), a person who has been admitted to, or acquired a right to reside in, the United Kingdom under these Regulations may be removed from the United Kingdom if—

(a) he does not have or ceases to have a right to reside under these Regulations; or
(b) he would otherwise be entitled to reside in the United Kingdom under these Regulations but the Secretary of State has decided that his removal is justified on the grounds of public policy, public security or public health in accordance with regulation 21.

(4) A person must not be removed under paragraph (3) as the automatic consequence of having recourse to the social assistance system of the United Kingdom.

(5) A person must not be removed under paragraph (3) if he has a right to remain in the United Kingdom by virtue of leave granted under the 1971 Act unless his removal is justified on the grounds of public policy, public security or public health in accordance with regulation 21.

Initial Commencement
Specified date: 30 April 2006: see reg 1.

20 Refusal to issue or renew and revocation of residence documentation

(1) The Secretary of State may refuse to issue, revoke or refuse to renew a registration certificate, a residence card, a document certifying permanent residence or a permanent residence card if the refusal or revocation is justified on grounds of public policy, public security or public health.

(2) The Secretary of State may revoke a registration certificate or a residence card or refuse to renew a residence card if the holder of the certificate or card has ceased to have a right to reside under these Regulations.

(3) The Secretary of State may revoke a document certifying permanent residence or a permanent residence card or refuse to renew a permanent residence card if the holder of the certificate or card has ceased to have a right of permanent residence under regulation 15.

(4) An immigration officer may, at the time of a person's arrival in the United Kingdom—

(a) revoke that person's residence card if he is not at that time the family member of a qualified person or of an EEA national who has a right of permanent residence under regulation 15, a family member who has retained the right of residence or a person with a right of permanent residence under regulation 15;

(b) revoke that person's permanent residence card if he is not at that time a person with a right of permanent residence under regulation 15.

(5) An immigration officer may, at the time of a person's arrival in the United Kingdom, revoke that person's EEA family permit if—

(a) the revocation is justified on grounds of public policy, public security or public health; or
(b) the person is not at that time the family member of an EEA national with the right to reside in the United Kingdom under these Regulations or is not accompanying that national or joining him in the United Kingdom.

(6) Any action taken under this regulation on grounds of public policy, public security or public health shall be in accordance with regulation 21.

Initial Commencement
Specified date: 30 April 2006: see reg 1.

21 Decisions taken on public policy, public security and public health grounds

(1) In this regulation a "relevant decision" means an EEA decision taken on the grounds of public policy, public security or public health.

(2) A relevant decision may not be taken to serve economic ends.

(3) A relevant decision may not be taken in respect of a person with a permanent right of residence under regulation 15 except on serious grounds of public policy or public security.

(4) A relevant decision may not be taken except on imperative grounds of public security in respect of an EEA national who—

(a) has resided in the United Kingdom for a continuous period of at least ten years prior to the relevant decision; or
(b) is under the age of 18, unless the relevant decision is necessary in his best interests, as provided for in the Convention on the Rights of the Child adopted by the General Assembly of the United Nations on 20th November 1989.

(5) Where a relevant decision is taken on grounds of public policy or public security it shall, in addition to complying with the preceding paragraphs of this regulation, be taken in accordance with the following principles—

(a) the decision must comply with the principle of proportionality;
(b) the decision must be based exclusively on the personal conduct of the person concerned;
(c) the personal conduct of the person concerned must represent a genuine, present and sufficiently serious threat affecting one of the fundamental interests of society;
(d) matters isolated from the particulars of the case or which relate to considerations of general prevention do not justify the decision;
(e) a person's previous criminal convictions do not in themselves justify the decision.

(6) Before taking a relevant decision on the grounds of public policy or public security in relation to a person who is resident in the United Kingdom the decision maker must take account of considerations such as the age, state of health, family and economic situation of the person, the person's length of residence in the United Kingdom, the person's social and cultural integration into the United Kingdom and the extent of the person's links with his country of origin.

(7) In the case of a relevant decision taken on grounds of public health—

(a) a disease that does not have epidemic potential as defined by the relevant instruments of the World Health Organisation or is not a disease to which section 38 of the Public Health (Control of Disease) Act 1984 applies (detention in hospital of a person with a notifiable disease) shall not constitute grounds for the decision; and

(b) if the person concerned is in the United Kingdom, diseases occurring after the three month period beginning on the date on which he arrived in the United Kingdom shall not constitute grounds for the decision.

Initial Commencement
Specified date: 30 April 2006: see reg 1.

PART 5
PROCEDURE IN RELATION TO EEA DECISIONS

22 Person claiming right of admission

(1) This regulation applies to a person who claims a right of admission to the United Kingdom under regulation 11 as—

(a) a person, not being an EEA national, who is a family member of an EEA national, a family member who has retained the right of residence or a person with a permanent right of residence under regulation 15; or

(b) an EEA national, where there is reason to believe that he may fall to be excluded from the United Kingdom on grounds of public policy, public security or public health.

(2) A person to whom this regulation applies is to be treated as if he were a person seeking leave to enter the United Kingdom under the 1971 Act for the purposes of paragraphs 2, 3, 4, 7, 16 to 18 and 21 to 24 of Schedule 2 to the 1971 Act (administrative provisions as to control on entry etc), except that—

(a) the reference in paragraph 2(1) to the purpose for which the immigration officer may examine any persons who have arrived in the United Kingdom is to be read as a reference to the purpose of determining whether he is a person who is to be granted admission under these Regulations;

(b) the references in paragraphs 4(2A), 7 and 16(1) to a person who is, or may be, given leave to enter are to be read as references to a person who is, or may be, granted admission under these Regulations; and

(c) a medical examination is not be carried out under paragraph 2 or paragraph 7 as a matter of routine and may only be carried out within three months of a person's arrival in the United Kingdom.

(3) For so long as a person to whom this regulation applies is detained, or temporarily admitted or released while liable to detention, under the powers conferred by Schedule 2 to the 1971 Act, he is deemed not to have been admitted to the United Kingdom.

Initial Commencement
Specified date: 30 April 2006: see reg 1.

23 Person refused admission

(1) This regulation applies to a person who is in the United Kingdom and has been refused admission to the United Kingdom—

(a) because he does not meet the requirement of regulation 11 (including where he does not meet those requirements because his EEA family permit, residence card or permanent residence card has been revoked by an immigration officer in accordance with regulation 20); or

(b) in accordance with regulation 19(1) or (2).

(2) A person to whom this regulation applies, is to be treated as if he were a person refused leave to enter under the 1971 Act for the purpose of paragraphs 8, 10, 10A, 11, 16 to 19 and 21 to 24 of Schedule 2 to the 1971 Act, except that the reference in paragraph 19 to a certificate of entitlement, entry clearance or work permit is to be read as a reference to an EEA family permit, residence card or a permanent residence card.

Initial Commencement
Specified date: 30 April 2006: see reg 1.

24 Person subject to removal

(1) This regulation applies to a person whom it has been decided to remove from the United Kingdom in accordance with regulation 19(3).

(2) Where the decision is under regulation 19(3)(a), the person is to be treated as if he were a person to whom section 10(1)(a) of the 1999 Act applied, and section 10 of that Act (removal of certain persons unlawfully in the United Kingdom) is to apply accordingly.

(3) Where the decision is under regulation 19(3)(b), the person is to be treated as if he were a person to whom section 3(5)(a) of the 1971 Act (liability to deportation) applied, and section 5 of that Act (procedure for deportation) and Schedule 3 to that Act (supplementary provision as to deportation) are to apply accordingly.

(4) A person who enters or seeks to enter the United Kingdom in breach of a deportation order made against him pursuant to paragraph (3) shall be removable as an illegal entrant under Schedule 2 to the 1971 Act and the provisions of that Schedule shall apply accordingly.

(5) Where such a deportation order is made against a person but he is not removed under the order during the two year period beginning on the date on which the order is made, the Secretary of State shall only take action to remove the person under the order after the end of that period if, having assessed whether there has been any material change in circumstances since the deportation order was made, he considers that the removal continues to be justified on the grounds of public policy, public security or public health.

(6) A person to whom this regulation applies shall be allowed one month to leave the United Kingdom, beginning on the date on which he is notified of the decision to remove him, before being removed pursuant to that decision except—

(a) in duly substantiated cases of urgency;
(b) where the person is detained pursuant to the sentence or order of any court;
(c) where a person is a person to whom regulation 24(4) applies.

Initial Commencement
Specified date: 30 April 2006: see reg 1.

Part 6
Appeals Under These Regulations

25 Interpretation of Part 6

(1) In this Part—

"Asylum and Immigration Tribunal" has the same meaning as in the 2002 Act;
"Commission" has the same meaning as in the Special Immigration Appeals Commission Act 1997;

"the Human Rights Convention" has the same meaning as "the Convention" in the Human Rights Act 1998; and

"the Refugee Convention" means the Convention relating to the Status of Refugees done at Geneva on 28th July 1951 and the Protocol relating to the Status of Refugees done at New York on 31st January 1967.

(2) For the purposes of this Part, and subject to paragraphs (3) and (4), an appeal is to be treated as pending during the period when notice of appeal is given and ending when the appeal is finally determined, withdrawn or abandoned.

(3) An appeal is not to be treated as finally determined while a further appeal may be brought; and, if such a further appeal is brought, the original appeal is not to be treated as finally determined until the further appeal is determined, withdrawn or abandoned.

(4) A pending appeal is not to be treated as abandoned solely because the appellant leaves the United Kingdom.

Initial Commencement

Specified date: 30 April 2006: see reg 1.

26 Appeal rights

(1) Subject to the following paragraphs of this regulation, a person may appeal under these Regulations against an EEA decision.

(2) If a person claims to be an EEA national, he may not appeal under these Regulations unless he produces a valid national identity card or passport issued by an EEA State.

(3) If a person claims to be the family member or relative of an EEA national he may not appeal under these Regulations unless he produces—

(a) an EEA family permit; or
(b) other proof that he is related as claimed to an EEA national.

(4) A person may not bring an appeal under these Regulations on a ground certified under paragraph (5) or rely on such a ground in an appeal brought under these Regulations.

(5) The Secretary of State or an immigration officer may certify a ground for the purposes of paragraph (4) if it has been considered in a previous appeal brought under these Regulations or under section 82(1) of the 2002 Act.

(6) Except where an appeal lies to the Commission, an appeal under these Regulations lies to the Asylum and Immigration Tribunal.

(7) The provisions of or made under the 2002 Act referred to in Schedule 1 shall have effect for the purposes of an appeal under these Regulations to the Asylum and Immigration Tribunal in accordance with that Schedule.

Initial Commencement

Specified date: 30 April 2006: see reg 1.

27 Out of country appeals

(1) Subject to paragraphs (2) and (3), a person may not appeal under regulation 26 whilst he is in the United Kingdom against an EEA decision—

(a) to refuse to admit him to the United Kingdom;
(b) to refuse to revoke a deportation order made against him;
(c) to refuse to issue him with an EEA family permit; or

(d) to remove him from the United Kingdom after he has entered or sought to enter the United Kingdom in breach of a deportation order.

(2) Paragraph (1)(a) does not apply where—

(a) the person held an EEA family permit, a registration certificate, a residence card, a document certifying permanent residence or a permanent residence card on his arrival in the United Kingdom or can otherwise prove that he is resident in the United Kingdom;
(b) the person is deemed not to have been admitted to the United Kingdom under regulation 22(3) but at the date on which notice of the decision to refuse to admit him is given he has been in the United Kingdom for at least 3 months;
(c) the person is in the United Kingdom and a ground of the appeal is that, in taking the decision, the decision maker acted in breach of his rights under the Human Rights Convention or the Refugee Convention, unless the Secretary of State certifies that that ground of appeal is clearly unfounded.

(3) Paragraph (1)(d) does not apply where a ground of the appeal is that, in taking the decision, the decision maker acted in breach of the appellant's rights under the Human Rights Convention or the Refugee Convention, unless the Secretary of State certifies that that ground of appeal is clearly unfounded.

Initial Commencement
Specified date: 30 April 2006: see reg 1.

28 Appeals to the Commission

(1) An appeal against an EEA decision lies to the Commission where paragraph (2) or (4) applies.

(2) This paragraph applies if the Secretary of State certifies that the EEA decision was taken—

(a) by the Secretary of State wholly or partly on a ground listed in paragraph (3); or
(b) in accordance with a direction of the Secretary of State which identifies the person to whom the decision relates and which is given wholly or partly on a ground listed in paragraph (3).

(3) The grounds mentioned in paragraph (2) are that the person's exclusion or removal from the United Kingdom is—

(a) in the interests of national security; or
(b) in the interests of the relationship between the United Kingdom and another country.

(4) This paragraph applies if the Secretary of State certifies that the EEA decision was taken wholly or partly in reliance on information which in his opinion should not be made public—

(a) in the interests of national security;
(b) in the interests of the relationship between the United Kingdom and another country; or
(c) otherwise in the public interest.

(5) In paragraphs (2) and (4) a reference to the Secretary of State is to the Secretary of State acting in person.

(6) Where a certificate is issued under paragraph (2) or (4) in respect of a pending appeal to the Asylum and Immigration Tribunal the appeal shall lapse.

(7) An appeal against an EEA decision lies to the Commission where an appeal lapses by virtue of paragraph (6).

(8) The Special Immigration Appeals Commission Act 1997 shall apply to an appeal to the Commission under these Regulations as it applies to an appeal under section 2 of that Act to which subsection (2) of that section applies (appeals against an immigration decision) but paragraph (i) of that subsection shall not apply in relation to such an appeal.

Initial Commencement
Specified date: 30 April 2006: see reg 1.

29 Effect of appeals to the Asylum and Immigration Tribunal

(1) This Regulation applies to appeals under these Regulations made to the Asylum and Immigration Tribunal.

(2) If a person in the United Kingdom appeals against an EEA decision to refuse to admit him to the United Kingdom, any directions for his removal from the United Kingdom previously given by virtue of the refusal cease to have effect, except in so far as they have already been carried out, and no directions may be so given while the appeal is pending.

(3) If a person in the United Kingdom appeals against an EEA decision to remove him from the United Kingdom, any directions given under section 10 of the 1999 Act or Schedule 3 to the 1971 Act for his removal from the United Kingdom are to have no effect, except in so far as they have already been carried out, while the appeal is pending.

(4) But the provisions of Part I of Schedule 2, or as the case may be, Schedule 3 to the 1971 Act with respect to detention and persons liable to detention apply to a person appealing against a refusal to admit him or a decision to remove him as if there were in force directions for his removal from the United Kingdom, except that he may not be detained on board a ship or aircraft so as to compel him to leave the United Kingdom while the appeal is pending.

(5) In calculating the period of two months limited by paragraph 8(2) of Schedule 2 to the 1971 Act for—

(a) the giving of directions under that paragraph for the removal of a person from the United Kingdom; and
(b) the giving of a notice of intention to give such directions,

any period during which there is pending an appeal by him under is to be disregarded.

(6) If a person in the United Kingdom appeals against an EEA decision to remove him from the United Kingdom, a deportation order is not to be made against him under section 5 of the 1971 Act while the appeal is pending.

(7) Paragraph 29 of Schedule 2 to the 1971 Act (grant of bail pending appeal) applies to a person who has an appeal pending under these Regulations as it applies to a person who has an appeal pending under section 82(1) of the 2002 Act.

Initial Commencement
Specified date: 30 April 2006: see reg 1.

PART 7
GENERAL

30 Effect on other legislation

Schedule 2 (effect on other legislation) shall have effect.

Initial Commencement
Specified date: 30 April 2006: see reg 1.

31 Revocations, transitional provisions and consequential amendments

(1) The Regulations listed in column 1 of the table in Part 1 of Schedule 3 are revoked to the extent set out in column 3 of that table, subject to Part 2 of that Schedule and to Schedule 4.

(2) Schedule 4 (transitional provisions) and Schedule 5 (consequential amendments) shall have effect.

Initial Commencement
Specified date: 30 April 2006: see reg 1.

SCHEDULE 1
APPEALS TO THE ASYLUM AND IMMIGRATION TRIBUNAL

Regulation 26(7)

The following provisions of, or made under, the 2002 Act have effect in relation to an appeal under these Regulations to the Asylum and Immigration Tribunal as if it were an appeal against an immigration decision under section 82(1) of that Act:

section 84(1), except paragraphs (a) and (f);
sections 85 to 87;
sections 103A to 103E;
section 105 and any regulations made under that section; and
section 106 and any rules made under that section.

Initial Commencement
Specified date: 30 April 2006: see reg 1.

SCHEDULE 2
EFFECT ON OTHER LEGISLATION

Regulation 30

1 Leave under the 1971 Act

(1) In accordance with section 7 of the Immigration Act 1988, a person who is admitted to or acquires a right to reside in the United Kingdom under these Regulations shall not require leave to remain in the United Kingdom under the 1971 Act during any period in which he has a right to reside under these Regulations but such a person shall require leave to remain under the 1971 Act during any period in which he does not have such a right.

(2) Where a person has leave to enter or remain under the 1971 Act which is subject to conditions and that person also has a right to reside under these Regulations, those conditions shall not have effect for as long as the person has that right to reside.

2 Persons not subject to restriction on the period for which they may remain

(1) For the purposes of the 1971 Act and the British Nationality Act 1981, a person who has a permanent right of residence under regulation 15 shall be regarded as a person who is in the United Kingdom without being subject under the immigration laws to any restriction on the period for which he may remain.

(2) But a qualified person, the family member of a qualified person and a family member who has retained the right of residence shall not, by virtue of that status, be so regarded for those purposes.

3 Carriers' liability under the 1999 Act

For the purposes of satisfying a requirement to produce a visa under section 40(1)(b) of the 1999 Act (charges in respect of passenger without proper documents), "a visa of the required kind" includes an EEA family permit, a residence card or a permanent residence card required for admission under regulation 11(2).

4 Appeals under the 2002 Act and previous immigration Acts

(1) The following EEA decisions shall not be treated as immigration decisions for the purpose of section 82(2) of the 2002 Act (right of appeal against an immigration decision)—

- (a) a decision that a person is to be removed under regulation 19(3)(a) by way of a direction under section 10(1)(a) of the 1999 Act (as provided for by regulation 24(2));
- (b) a decision to remove a person under regulation 19(3)(b) by making a deportation order under section 5(1) of the 1971 Act (as provided for by regulation 24(3));
- (c) a decision to remove a person mentioned in regulation 24(4) by way of directions under paragraphs 8 to 10 of Schedule 2 to the 1971 Act.

(2) A person who has been issued with a registration certificate, residence card, a document certifying permanent residence or a permanent residence card under these Regulations or a registration certificate under the Accession (Immigration and Worker Registration) Regulations 2004, or a person whose passport has been stamped with a family member residence stamp, shall have no right of appeal under section 2 of the Special Immigration Appeals Commission Act 1997 or section 82(1) of the 2002 Act. Any existing appeal under those sections of those Acts or under the Asylum and Immigration Appeals Act 1993, the Asylum and Immigration Act 1996 or the 1999 Act shall be treated as abandoned.

(3) Subject to paragraph (4), a person may appeal to the Asylum and Immigration Tribunal under section 83(2) of the 2002 Act against the rejection of his asylum claim where—

- (a) that claim has been rejected, but
- (b) he has a right to reside in the United Kingdom under these Regulations.

(4) Paragraph (3) shall not apply if the person is an EEA national and the Secretary of State certifies that the asylum claim is clearly unfounded.

(5) The Secretary of State shall certify the claim under paragraph (4) unless satisfied that it is not clearly unfounded.

(6) In addition to the national of a State which is a contracting party to the Agreement referred to in section 84(2) of the 2002 Act, a Swiss national shall also be treated as an EEA national for the purposes of section 84(1)(d) of that Act.

(7) An appeal under these Regulations against an EEA decision (including an appeal made on or after 1st April 2003 which is treated as an appeal under these Regulations under Schedule 4 but not an appeal made before that date) shall be treated as an appeal under section 82(1) of the 2002 Act against an immigration decision for the purposes of section 96(1)(a) of the 2002 Act.

(8) Section 120 of the 2002 Act shall apply to a person if an EEA decision has been taken or may be taken in respect of him and, accordingly, the Secretary of State or an immigration officer may by notice require a statement from that person under subsection (2) of that section and that notice shall have effect for the purpose of section 96(2) of the 2002 Act.

(9) In sub-paragraph (1), "family member residence stamp" means a stamp in the passport of a family member of an EEA national confirming that he is the family member of an accession State worker requiring registration with a right of residence under these Regulations as the family member of that worker; and in this sub-paragraph "accession State worker requiring registration" has the same meaning as in regulation 2 of the Accession (Immigration and Worker Registration) Regulations 2004.

Initial Commencement
Specified date: 30 April 2006: see reg 1.

SCHEDULE 3
REVOCATIONS AND SAVINGS

Regulation 31(2)

PART 1
TABLE OF REVOCATIONS

(1)	*(2)*	*(3)*
Regulations revoked	*References*	*Extent of revocation*
The Immigration (European Economic Area) Regulations 2000	SI 2000/2326	The whole Regulations
The Immigration (European Economic Area) (Amendment) Regulations 2001	SI 2001/865	The whole Regulations
The Immigration (Swiss Free Movement of Persons) (No 3) Regulations 2002	SI 2002/1241	The whole Regulations
The Immigration (European Economic Area) (Amendment) Regulations 2003	SI 2003/549	The whole Regulations
The Immigration (European Economic Area) (Amendment No 2) Regulations 2003	SI 2003/3188	The whole Regulations
The Accession (Immigration and Worker Registration) Regulations 2004	SI 2004/1219	Regulations 3 and 6
The Immigration (European Economic Area) and Accession (Amendment) Regulations 2004	SI 2004/1236	Regulation 2
The Immigration (European Economic Area) (Amendment) Regulations 2005	SI 2005/47	The whole Regulations

The Immigration (European Economic Area) (Amendment) (No 2) Regulations 2005	SI 2005/671	The whole Regulations

Initial Commencement
Specified date: 30 April 2006: see reg 1.

PART 2
SAVINGS

1 The—

(a) Immigration (Swiss Free Movement of Persons) (No 3) Regulations 2002 are not revoked insofar as they apply the 2000 Regulations to posted workers; and
(b) the 2000 Regulations and the Regulations amending the 2000 Regulations are not revoked insofar as they are so applied to posted workers;

and, accordingly, the 2000 Regulations, as amended, shall continue to apply to posted workers in accordance with the Immigration (Swiss Free Movement of Persons) (No 3) Regulations 2002.

2 In paragraph 1, "the 2000 Regulations" means the Immigration (European Economic Area) Regulations 2000 and "posted worker" has the meaning given in regulation 2(4)(b) of the Immigration (Swiss Free Movement of Persons) (No 3) Regulations 2002.

Initial Commencement
Specified date: 30 April 2006: see reg 1.

SCHEDULE 4
TRANSITIONAL PROVISIONS

Regulation 31(2)

1 Interpretation

In this Schedule—

(a) the "2000 Regulations" means the Immigration (European Economic Area) Regulations 2000 and expressions used in relation to documents issued or applied for under those Regulations shall have the meaning given in regulation 2 of those Regulations;
(b) the "Accession Regulations" means the Accession (Immigration and Worker Registration) Regulations 2004.

2 Existing documents

(1) An EEA family permit issued under the 2000 Regulations shall, after 29th April 2006, be treated as if it were an EEA family permit issued under these Regulations.

(2) Subject to paragraph (4), a residence permit issued under the 2000 Regulations shall, after 29th April 2006, be treated as if it were a registration certificate issued under these Regulations.

(3) Subject to paragraph (5), a residence document issued under the 2000 Regulations shall, after 29th April 2006, be treated as if it were a residence card issued under these Regulations.

(4) Where a residence permit issued under the 2000 Regulations has been endorsed under the immigration rules to show permission to remain in the United Kingdom indefinitely it shall, after 29th April 2006, be treated as if it were a document certifying permanent residence issued under these Regulations and the holder of the permit shall be treated as a person with a permanent right of residence under regulation 15.

(5) Where a residence document issued under the 2000 Regulations has been endorsed under the immigration rules to show permission to remain in the United Kingdom indefinitely it shall, after 29th April 2006, be treated as if it were a permanent residence card issued under these Regulations and the holder of the permit shall be treated as a person with a permanent right of residence under regulation 15.

(6) Paragraphs (4) and (5) shall also apply to a residence permit or residence document which is endorsed under the immigration rules on or after 30th April 2006 to show permission to remain in the United Kingdom indefinitely pursuant to an application for such an endorsement made before that date.

3 Outstanding applications

(1) An application for an EEA family permit, a residence permit or a residence document made but not determined under the 2000 Regulations before 30 April 2006 shall be treated as an application under these Regulations for an EEA family permit, a registration certificate or a residence card, respectively.

(2) But the following provisions of these Regulations shall not apply to the determination of an application mentioned in sub-paragraph (1)—

- (a) the requirement to issue a registration certificate immediately under regulation 16(1); and
- (b) the requirement to issue a certificate of application for a residence card under regulation 17(3).

4 Decisions to remove under the 2000 Regulations

(1) A decision to remove a person under regulation 21(3)(a) of the 2000 Regulations shall, after 29th April 2006, be treated as a decision to remove that person under regulation 19(3)(a) of these Regulations.

(2) A decision to remove a person under regulation 21(3)(b) of the 2000 Regulations, including a decision which is treated as a decision to remove a person under that regulation by virtue of regulation 6(3)(a) of the Accession Regulations, shall, after 29th April 2006, be treated as a decision to remove that person under regulation 19(3)(b) of these Regulations.

(3) A deportation order made under section 5 of the 1971 Act by virtue of regulation 26(3) of the 2000 Regulations shall, after 29th April 2006, be treated as a deportation made under section 5 of the 1971 Act by virtue of regulation 24(3) of these Regulations.

5 Appeals

(1) Where an appeal against an EEA decision under the 2000 Regulations is pending immediately before 30th April 2006 that appeal shall be treated as a pending appeal against the corresponding EEA Decision under these Regulations.

(2) Where an appeal against an EEA decision under the 2000 Regulations has been determined, withdrawn or abandoned it shall, on and after 30th April 2006, be treated as an appeal against the corresponding EEA decision under these Regulations which has been determined, withdrawn or abandoned, respectively.

(3) For the purpose of this paragraph—

(a) a decision to refuse to admit a person under these Regulations corresponds to a decision to refuse to admit that person under the 2000 Regulations;
(b) a decision to remove a person under regulation 19(3)(a) of these Regulations corresponds to a decision to remove that person under regulation 21(3)(a) of the 2000 Regulations;
(c) a decision to remove a person under regulation 19(3)(b) of these Regulations corresponds to a decision to remove that person under regulation 21(3)(b) of the 2000 Regulations, including a decision which is treated as a decision to remove a person under regulation 21(3)(b) of the 2000 Regulations by virtue of regulation 6(3)(a) of the Accession Regulations;
(d) a decision to refuse to revoke a deportation order made against a person under these Regulations corresponds to a decision to refuse to revoke a deportation order made against that person under the 2000 Regulations, including a decision which is treated as a decision to refuse to revoke a deportation order under the 2000 Regulations by virtue of regulation 6(3)(b) of the Accession Regulations;
(e) a decision not to issue or renew or to revoke an EEA family permit, a registration certificate or a residence card under these Regulations corresponds to a decision not to issue or renew or to revoke an EEA family permit, a residence permit or a residence document under the 2000 Regulations, respectively.

6 Periods of residence under the 2000 Regulations

(1) Any period during which a person carried out an activity or was resident in the United Kingdom in accordance with the 2000 Regulations shall be treated as a period during which the person carried out that activity or was resident in the United Kingdom in accordance with these Regulations for the purpose of calculating periods of activity and residence under these Regulations.

Initial Commencement
Specified date: 30 April 2006: see reg 1.

SCHEDULE 5
CONSEQUENTIAL AMENDMENTS

Regulation 31(2)

STATUTORY INSTRUMENTS

THE CHANNEL TUNNEL (INTERNATIONAL ARRANGEMENTS) ORDER 1993

1 (1) The Channel Tunnel (International Arrangements) Order 1993 is amended as follows.

(2) In Schedule 4, in paragraph 5—

(a) at the beginning of the paragraph, for "the Immigration (European Economic Area) Regulations 2000" there is substituted "the Immigration (European Economic Area) Regulations 2006";
(b) in sub-paragraph (a), for "regulation 12(2)" there is substituted "regulation 11(2)" and for "residence document or document proving family membership" there is substituted "residence card or permanent residence card";
(c) for sub-paragraph (b) there is substituted—
"(b) in regulations 11(4) and 19(2) after the word "arrival" and in regulations 20(4) and (5) after the words "United Kingdom" insert "or the time of his production of the required documents in a control zone or a supplementary control zone".

THE TRAVEL RESTRICTION ORDER (PRESCRIBED REMOVAL POWERS) ORDER 2002

2 (1) The Travel Restriction Order (Prescribed Removal Powers) Order 2002 is amended as follows.

(2) In the Schedule, for "Immigration (European Economic Area) Regulations 2000 (2000/2326)" in the first column of the table there is substituted "Immigration (European Economic Area) Regulations 2006" and for "Regulation 21(3)" in the corresponding row in the second column of the table there is substituted "Regulation 19(3)".

THE IMMIGRATION (NOTICES) REGULATIONS 2003

3 (1) The Immigration (Notices) Regulations 2003 are amended as follows.

(2) In regulation 2, in the definition of "EEA decision"—

(a) at the end of paragraph (b), "or" is omitted;
(b) in paragraph (c), after "residence document;", there is inserted "or"; and
(c) after paragraph (c), there is inserted—
"(d) on or after 30th April 2006, entitlement to be issued with or have renewed, or not to have revoked, a registration certificate, residence card, document certifying permanent residence or permanent residence card;"

THE NATIONALITY, IMMIGRATION AND ASYLUM ACT 2002 (JUXTAPOSED CONTROLS) ORDER 2003

4 (1) The Nationality, Immigration and Asylum Act 2002 (Juxtaposed Controls) Order 2003 is amended as follows.

(2) In article 11(1), for sub-paragraph (e) there is substituted—

"(e) the Immigration (European Economic Area) Regulations 2006.".

(3) In Schedule 2, in paragraph 5—

(a) at the beginning of the paragraph, for "the Immigration (European Economic Area) Regulations 2000" there is substituted "the Immigration (European Economic Area) Regulations 2006";
(b) in sub-paragraph (a), for "in regulation 2, at the beginning insert" there is substituted "in regulation 2(1), after the definition of "civil partner" insert";
(c) in sub-paragraph (b), for "regulation 12(2)" there is substituted "regulation 11(2)" and for "residence document or document proving family membership" there is substituted "residence card or permanent residence card";
(d) for sub-paragraph (c) there is substituted—
"(c) in regulations 11(4) and 19(2) after the word "arrival" and in regulations 20(4) and (5) after the words "United Kingdom" insert "or the time of his production of the required documents in a Control Zone".

THE IMMIGRATION AND ASYLUM ACT 1999 (PART V EXEMPTION: RELEVANT EMPLOYERS) ORDER 2003

5 (1) The Immigration and Asylum Act 1999 (Part V Exemption: Relevant Employers) Order 2003 is amended as follows.

(2) In Article 2, in the definition of "EEA national" and "family member of an EEA national", for "Immigration (European Economic Area) Regulations 2000" there is substituted "Immigration (European Economic Area) Regulations 2006".

THE IMMIGRATION (RESTRICTIONS ON EMPLOYMENT) ORDER 2004

6 (1) The Immigration (Restrictions on Employment) Order 2004 is amended as follows.

(2) In Part 1 of the Schedule (descriptions of documents for the purpose of article 4(2)(a) of the Order)—

(a) for paragraph 4 there is substituted—

"4 A registration certificate or document certifying permanent residence within the meaning of regulation 2 of the Immigration (European Economic Area) Regulations 2006, including a document which is treated as a registration certificate or document certifying permanent residence by virtue of Schedule 4 to those Regulations.";

(b) for paragraph 5 there is substituted—

"5 A residence card or a permanent residence card within the meaning of regulation 2 of the Immigration (European Economic Area) Regulations 2006, including a document which is treated as a residence card or a permanent residence card by virtue of Schedule 4 to those Regulations".

THE ACCESSION (IMMIGRATION AND WORKER REGISTRATION) REGULATIONS 2004

7 (1) The Accession (Immigration and Worker Registration) Regulations 2004 are amended as follows.

(2) In regulation 1(2) (interpretation)—

(a) after paragraph (b) there is inserted—
"(ba)"the 2006 Regulations" means the Immigration (European Economic Area) Regulations 2006;";
(b) in paragraph (j), for "regulation 3 of the 2000 Regulations" these is substituted "regulation 4 of the 2006 Regulations".

(3) In regulation 2 ("accession State worker requiring registration")—

(a) for paragraph (6)(b) there is substituted—
"(b) a family member of a Swiss or EEA national (other than an accession State worker requiring registration) who has a right to reside in the United Kingdom under regulation 14(1) or 15 of the 2006 Regulations;";
(b) paragraph (9)(a) is omitted;
(c) for paragraph (9)(c) there is substituted—
"(c) "family member" has the same meaning as in regulation 7 of the 2006 Regulations.".

(4) In regulation 4 (right of residence of work seekers and workers from relevant acceding States during the accession period)—

(a) in paragraph (1), before "Council Directive" there is inserted "Council Directive 2004/38/EC of the European Parliament and of the Council on the right of citizens of the Union and their family members to move and reside freely within the territory of the Member States, insofar as it takes over provisions of";
(b) in paragraph (3), for "2000 Regulations" there is substituted "2006 Regulations";
(c) in paragraph (4), for "An" there is substituted "A national of a relevant accession State who is seeking employment and an" and for "2000 Regulations" there is substituted "2006 Regulations".

(5) For regulation 5 (application of 2000 Regulations in relation to accession State worker requiring registration) there is substituted—

"5 Application of 2006 Regulations in relation to accession State worker requiring registration

(1) The 2006 Regulations shall apply in relation to a national of a relevant accession State subject to the modifications set out in this regulation.

(2) A national of a relevant accession State who is seeking employment in the United Kingdom shall not be treated as a jobseeker for the purpose of the definition of "qualified person" in regulation 6(1) of the 2006 Regulations and an accession State worker requiring registration shall be treated as a worker for the purpose of that definition only during a period in which he is working in the United Kingdom for an authorised employer.

(3) Subject to paragraph (4), regulation 6(2) of the 2006 Regulations shall not apply to an accession State worker requiring registration who ceases to work.

(4) Where an accession State worker requiring registration ceases working for an authorised employer in the circumstances mentioned in regulation 6(2) of the 2006 Regulations during the one month period beginning on the date on which the work begins, that regulation shall apply to that worker during the remainder of that one month period.

(5) An accession State worker requiring registration shall not be treated as a qualified person for the purpose of regulations 16 and 17 of the 2006 Regulations (issue of registration certificates and residence cards)."

THE ASYLUM AND IMMIGRATION TRIBUNAL (PROCEDURE) RULES 2005

8 (1) The Asylum and Immigration Tribunal (Procedure) Rules 2005 are amended as follows.

(2) In regulation 18(1)(b), after "("the 2000 Regulations")" there is inserted "or, on or after 30th April 2006, paragraph 4(2) of Schedule 2 to the Immigration (European Economic Area) Regulations 2006 ("the 2006 Regulations")".

(3) In regulation 18(2), after "2000 Regulations" there is inserted "or paragraph 4(2) of Schedule 2 to the 2006 Regulations".

Initial Commencement
Specified date: 30 April 2006: see reg 1.

IMMIGRATION (LEAVE TO REMAIN) (PRESCRIBED FORMS AND PROCEDURES) REGULATIONS 2006

SI 2006/1421

Made ...25th May 2006

Laid before Parliament ...1st June 2006

Coming into force ...22nd June 2006

The Secretary of State, in exercise of the powers conferred upon him by section 31A of the Immigration Act 1971 makes the following Regulations:

1 Citation, commencement and interpretation

These Regulations may be cited as the Immigration (Leave to Remain) (Prescribed Forms and Procedures) Regulations 2006 and shall come into force on 22nd June 2006.

Initial Commencement
Specified date: 22 June 2006: see above.

2

In these Regulations:

"asylum claimant" means a person making a claim for asylum (within the meaning given in section 94(1) of the Immigration and Asylum Act 1999) which claim either has not been determined or has been granted;

"dependant", of a person, means—

(a) the spouse, civil partner, unmarried partner or same sex partner, or

(b) a child under the age of eighteen,

of that person; and

"public enquiry office" means a public enquiry office of the Immigration and Nationality Directorate of the Home Office.

Initial Commencement
Specified date: 22 June 2006: see reg 1.

3 Prescribed Forms

(1) Subject to paragraph (2), the form set out in Schedule 1 is prescribed for an application for limited or indefinite leave to remain in the United Kingdom as:

(a) a business person,
(b) a sole representative,
(c) a retired person of independent means,
(d) an investor, or
(e) an innovator,

for the purposes of the immigration rules.

(2) Paragraph (1) does not apply to an application for limited or indefinite leave to remain in the United Kingdom as a business person where the application is made under the terms of a European Community Association Agreement.

Initial Commencement
Specified date: 22 June 2006: see reg 1.

4

The form set out in Schedule 2 is prescribed for an application for limited leave to remain in the United Kingdom:

(a) for work permit employment,
(b) as a highly skilled migrant,
(c) as a seasonal agricultural worker,
(d) for the purpose of employment under the Sectors-Based Scheme, or
(e) for Home Office approved training or work experience,

for the purposes of the immigration rules.

Initial Commencement
Specified date: 22 June 2006: see reg 1.

5

The form set out in Schedule 3 is prescribed for an application for limited leave to remain in the United Kingdom as:

(a) the spouse or civil partner of a person present and settled in the United Kingdom, or
(b) the unmarried partner or same sex partner of a person present and settled in the United Kingdom,

for the purposes of the immigration rules.

Initial Commencement
Specified date: 22 June 2006: see reg 1.

6

The form set out in Schedule 4 is prescribed for an application for limited leave to remain in the United Kingdom:

(a) as a student,
(b) as a student nurse,
(c) to re-sit an examination,
(d) to write up a thesis,
(e) as a student union sabbatical officer, or
(f) as a prospective student,

for the purposes of the immigration rules.

Initial Commencement
Specified date: 22 June 2006: see reg 1.

7

The form set out in Schedule 5 is prescribed for an application for limited leave to remain in the United Kingdom as a participant in the Science and Engineering Graduates Scheme for the purposes of the immigration rules.

Initial Commencement
Specified date: 22 June 2006: see reg 1.

8

The form set out in Schedule 6 is prescribed for an application for limited leave to remain in the United Kingdom as a participant in the Fresh Talent: Working in Scotland Scheme for the purposes of the immigration rules.

Initial Commencement
Specified date: 22 June 2006: see reg 1.

9

(1) The form set out in Schedule 7 is prescribed for an application for limited leave to remain in the United Kingdom as:

(a) a visitor,
(b) a visitor seeking to undergo or continue private medical treatment,
(c) a postgraduate doctor or dentist or a trainee general practitioner,
(d) an au pair,
(e) a teacher or language assistant under an approved exchange scheme,
(f) a representative of an overseas newspaper, news agency or broadcasting organisation,
(g) a private servant in a diplomatic household,
(h) a domestic worker in a private household,
(i) an overseas government employee,
(j) a minister of religion, missionary or member of a religious order,
(k) a visiting religious worker or a religious worker in a non-pastoral role,
(l) a member of the operational ground staff of an overseas-owned airline,
(m) a person with United Kingdom ancestry,
(n) a writer, composer or artist,
(o) an overseas qualified nurse or midwife, or
(p) the spouse, civil partner or child of an armed forces member who is exempt from immigration control under section 8(4) of the Immigration Act 1971,

for the purposes of the immigration rules.

(2) Subject to paragraph (3), the form set out in Schedule 7 is prescribed for an application for limited leave to remain in the United Kingdom for any other reason or purpose for which provision is made in the immigration rules but which is not covered by the forms prescribed in regulations 3 to 8.

(3) Paragraph (2) does not apply to an application for limited leave to remain in the United Kingdom where:

(a) the application is made under the terms of a European Community Association Agreement, or
(b) the basis on which the application is made is that the applicant is an asylum claimant or a dependant of an asylum claimant.

Initial Commencement
Specified date: 22 June 2006: see reg 1.

10

The form set out in Schedule 8 is prescribed for an application for indefinite leave to remain in the United Kingdom as:

(a) the spouse or civil partner of a person present and settled in the United Kingdom, or
(b) the unmarried partner or same sex partner of a person present and settled in the United Kingdom,

for the purposes of the immigration rules.

Initial Commencement
Specified date: 22 June 2006: see reg 1.

11

The form set out in Schedule 9 is prescribed for an application for indefinite leave to remain in the United Kingdom as:

- (a) the child under the age of eighteen of a parent, parents or relative present and settled in the United Kingdom,
- (b) the adopted child under the age of eighteen of a parent or parents present and settled in the United Kingdom, or
- (c) the parent, grandparent or other dependent relative of a person present and settled in the United Kingdom,

for the purposes of the immigration rules.

Initial Commencement
Specified date: 22 June 2006: see reg 1.

12

(1) The form set out in Schedule 10 is prescribed for an application for indefmite leave to remain in the United Kingdom:

- (a) as a work permit holder,
- (b) as a highly skilled migrant,
- (c) as a representative of an overseas newspaper, news agency or broadcasting organisation,
- (d) as a private servant in a diplomatic household,
- (e) as a domestic worker in a private household,
- (f) as an overseas government employee,
- (g) as a minister of religion, missionary or member of a religious order,
- (h) as a member of the operational ground staff of an overseas-owned airline,
- (i) as a person with United Kingdom ancestry,
- (j) as a writer, composer or artist,
- (k) on the basis of long residence in the United Kingdom,
- (l) as a victim of domestic violence, or
- (m) as a foreign or Commonwealth citizen discharged from HM Forces,

for the purposes of the immigration rules.

(2) Subject to paragraph (3), the form set out in Schedule 10 is hereby prescribed for an application for indefinite leave to remain in the United Kingdom for any other reason or purpose for which provision is made in the immigration rules but which is not covered by the forms prescribed in regulations 10 or 11.

(3) Paragraph (2) does not apply to an application for indefinite leave to remain in the United Kingdom where:

- (a) the application is made under the terms of a European Community Association Agreement,
- (b) the basis on which the application is made is that the applicant is an asylum claimant or a dependant of an asylum claimant.

Initial Commencement
Specified date: 22 June 2006: see reg 1.

13

An application for leave to remain in the United Kingdom which is made by a person ("the main applicant") on a form prescribed in any of the regulations 3 to 12 above may include an application in respect of any person applying for leave to remain in the United Kingdom as a dependant of the main applicant, insofar as this is permitted by the immigration rules.

Initial Commencement
Specified date: 22 June 2006: see reg 1.

14 Prescribed procedures

(1) The following procedures are hereby prescribed in relation to an application for which a form is prescribed in regulations 3 to 12:

- (a) the form shall be signed and dated by the applicant, save that where the applicant is under the age of eighteen, the form may be signed and dated by the parent or legal guardian of the applicant on behalf of the applicant;
- (b) the application shall be accompanied by such documents and photographs as specified in the form; and
- (c) each part of the form shall be completed as specified in the form.

(2) The following procedures are hereby prescribed in relation to delivery of an application for which a form is prescribed:

- (a) in relation to an application for which a form is prescribed in regulation 3, the application shall be sent by prepaid post or by courier to the Immigration and Nationality Directorate of the Home Office; it may not be submitted in person at a public enquiry office;
- (b) subject to (3) in relation to an application for which a form is prescribed in regulation 4, the application shall be:
  - (i) sent by prepaid post or by courier to Work Permits (UK) at the Immigration and Nationality Directorate of the Home Office, or
  - (ii) submitted in person at the Croydon public enquiry office (but no other public enquiry office),
- (c) in relation to an application for which a form is prescribed in regulations 5 to 12 above, the application shall be:
  - (i) sent by prepaid post to the Immigration and Nationality Directorate of the Home Office, or
  - (ii) submitted in person at a public enquiry office.

(3) An application for which a form is prescribed in regulation 4(b) (application for limited leave to remain in the United Kingdom as a highly skilled migrant) shall be sent by prepaid post or by courier to Work Permits (UK) at the Immigration and Nationality Directorate of the Home Office, and may not be submitted in person at a public enquiry office.

Initial Commencement
Specified date: 22 June 2006: see reg 1.

15

(1) A failure to comply with any of the requirements of regulation 14(1) to any extent will only invalidate an application if:

- (a) the applicant does not provide, when making the application, an explanation for the failure which the Secretary of State considers to be satisfactory,

(b) the Secretary of State notifies the applicant, or the person who appears to the Secretary of State to represent the applicant, of the failure within 28 days of the date on which the application is made, and
(c) the applicant does not comply with the requirements within a reasonable time, and in any event within 28 days, of being notified by the Secretary of State of the failure.

(2) For the purposes of this regulation, the date on which the application is made is:

(a) in the case of an application sent by post, the date of posting,
(b) in the case of an application submitted in person, the date on which the application is delivered to, and accepted by, a public enquiry office, and
(c) in the case of an application sent by courier, the date on which the application is delivered to Work Permits (UK) at the Immigration and Nationality Directorate of the Home Office.

Initial Commencement
Specified date: 22 June 2006: see reg 1.

16 Revocation and transitional provision

(1) Subject to (2) the Immigration (Leave to Remain) (Prescribed Forms and Procedures) (No 2) Regulations 2005 are hereby revoked.

(2) An application made on a form prescribed in the Immigration (Leave to Remain) (Prescribed Forms and Procedures) (No 2) Regulations 2005 shall be deemed to have been made on the corresponding form prescribed in these Regulations if made within 21 days of these Regulations coming into force for the purposes of section 31A of the Immigration Act 1971.

Initial Commencement
Specified date: 22 June 2006: see reg 1.

SCHEDULES 1–10

Regulations 3–12

[The text of the Schedules has been omitted.]

BRITISH NATIONALITY (PROOF OF PATERNITY) REGULATIONS 2006

SI 2006/1496

Made ...5th June 2006

Laid before Parliament ...9th June 2006

Coming into force ...1st July 2006

The Secretary of State, in exercise of the powers conferred by section 50(9A) and (9B) of the British Nationality Act 1981, makes the following Regulations:

1

These Regulations may be cited as the British Nationality (Proof of Paternity) Regulations 2006 and shall come into force on 1st July 2006.

Initial Commencement
Specified date: 1 July 2006: see above.

2

The following requirements are prescribed as to proof of paternity for the purposes of section 50(9A)(c) of the British Nationality Act 1981—

(a) the person must be named as the father of the child in a birth certificate issued within one year of the date of the child's birth; or
(b) the person must satisfy the Secretary of State that he is the father of the child.

Initial Commencement
Specified date: 1 July 2006: see reg 1.

3

The Secretary of State may determine whether a person is the father of a child for the purpose of regulation 2(b), and for this purpose the Secretary of State may have regard to any evidence which he considers to be relevant, including, but not limited to—

(a) DNA test reports; and
(b) court orders.

Initial Commencement
Specified date: 1 July 2006: see reg 1.

IMMIGRATION (PROVISION OF PHYSICAL DATA) REGULATIONS 2006

SI 2006/1743

Made ...3rd July 2006

Coming into force ...4th July 2006

The Secretary of State makes the following Regulations in exercise of the powers conferred by section 126(1) of the Nationality, Immigration and Asylum Act 2002.

In accordance with section 126(8)(b) of that Act, a draft of this instrument was laid before Parliament and approved by a resolution of each House of Parliament.

1 Citation, commencement and interpretation

These Regulations may be cited as the Immigration (Provision of Physical Data) Regulations 2006 and shall come into force on the day after they are made.

Initial Commencement
Specified date: 4 July 2006: see above.

2

In these Regulations:

"application" means:
- (a) an application for entry clearance; or
- (b) an application for leave to enter the United Kingdom where the person seeking leave to enter presents a Convention travel document endorsed with an entry clearance for that journey to the United Kingdom;

"Convention travel document" means a travel document issued pursuant to Article 28 of the Refugee Convention, except where that travel document was issued by the United Kingdom Government;

"Refugee Convention" means the Convention relating to the Status of Refugees done at Geneva on 28th July 1951 and its Protocol.

Initial Commencement
Specified date: 4 July 2006: see reg 1.

3 Power for an authorised person to require an individual to provide a record of his fingerprints and a photograph of his face

Subject to regulations 4 and 5, an authorised person may require an individual who makes an application to provide a record of his fingerprints and a photograph of his face.

Initial Commencement
Specified date: 4 July 2006: see reg 1.

4 Provision in relation to applicants under the age of sixteen

(1) An applicant under the age of sixteen shall not be required to provide a record of his fingerprints or a photograph of his face except where the authorised person is satisfied that the fingerprints or the photograph will be taken in the presence of a person aged eighteen or over who is—

- (a) the child's parent or guardian; or

(b) a person who for the time being takes responsibility for the child.

(2) The person mentioned in paragraph (1)(b) may not be—

(a) an officer of the Secretary of State who is not an authorised person;
(b) an authorised person; or
(c) any other person acting on behalf of an authorised person as part of a process specified under regulation 6(2).

(3) An authorised person shall not require a person under the age of sixteen to provide a record of his fingerprints or a photograph of his face unless his decision to do so has been confirmed by a person designated for the purpose by the Secretary of State.

(4) This regulation shall not apply if the authorised person reasonably believes that the applicant is aged sixteen or over.

Initial Commencement
Specified date: 4 July 2006: see reg 1.

5 Provision in relation to section 141 of the Immigration and Asylum Act 1999

An applicant shall not be required to provide a record of his fingerprints or a photograph of his face under regulation 3 if he is a person to whom section 141 of the Immigration and Asylum Act 1999 applies, during the relevant period within the meaning of that section.

Initial Commencement
Specified date: 4 July 2006: see reg 1.

6 Process by which the applicant's fingerprints and photograph may be obtained and recorded

(1) An authorised person who requires an individual to provide a record of his fingerprints or a photograph of his face under regulation 3 may require that individual to submit to any process specified in paragraph (2).

(2) A process by which the individual who makes the application:

(a) attends a British Diplomatic mission or British Consular post where a record of his fingerprints or a photograph of his face is taken;
(b) attends a Diplomatic mission or Consular post of another State where a record of his fingerprints or a photograph of his face is taken by an official of that State on behalf of an authorised person; or
(c) attends other premises nominated by an authorised person where a record of his fingerprints or a photograph of his face is taken by a person on behalf of an authorised person.

Initial Commencement
Specified date: 4 July 2006: see reg 1.

7 Consequences of failure to comply with these Regulations

(1) Subject to paragraphs (2) and (3), where an individual does not provide a record of his fingerprints or a photograph of his face in accordance with a requirement imposed under these Regulations, his application may be treated as invalid.

(2) An application shall not be treated as invalid under paragraph (1) if it is for leave to enter the United Kingdom where the person seeking leave to enter presents a Convention travel document endorsed with an entry clearance for that journey to the United Kingdom.

(3) Where an application is of a type described in paragraph (2) and the applicant does not provide a record of his fingerprints or a photograph of his face in accordance with a requirement imposed under these Regulations, that application may be refused.

Initial Commencement
Specified date: 4 July 2006: see reg 1.

8 Destruction of information

Subject to regulation 9, any record of fingerprints, photograph, copy of fingerprints or copy of a photograph held by the Secretary of State pursuant to these Regulations must be destroyed by the Secretary of State at the end of ten years beginning with the date on which the original record or photograph was provided.

Initial Commencement
Specified date: 4 July 2006: see reg 1.

9

If an applicant proves that he is—

(a) a British citizen; or
(b) a Commonwealth citizen who has a right of abode in the United Kingdom as a result of section 2(1)(b) of the Immigration Act 1971,

any record of fingerprints, photograph, copy of fingerprints or copy of a photograph held by the Secretary of State pursuant to these Regulations must be destroyed as soon as reasonably practicable.

Initial Commencement
Specified date: 4 July 2006: see reg 1.

10

(1) The Secretary of State must take all reasonably practicable steps to secure:

(a) that data held in electronic form which relate to any record of fingerprints or photograph which have to be destroyed in accordance with regulation 8 or 9 are destroyed or erased; or
(b) that access to such data is blocked.

(2) The applicant to whom the data relates is entitled, on written request, to a certificate issued by the Secretary of State to the effect that he has taken the steps required by paragraph (1).

(3) A certificate issued under paragraph (2) must be issued within three months of the date on which the request was received by the Secretary of State.

Initial Commencement
Specified date: 4 July 2006: see reg 1.

11 Revocation and transitional provisions

(1) Subject to paragraphs (2) and (3), the Regulations specified in the Schedule are revoked.

(2) For the purposes of paragraph (3) only, "application" means an application within the meaning of regulation 2 of the Immigration (Provision of Physical Data) Regulations 2003 (the "2003 Regulations").

(3) Where a person made an application before these Regulations came into force, the 2003 Regulations will continue to apply for the purposes of that application as if they had not been revoked by paragraph (1).

Initial Commencement
Specified date: 4 July 2006: see reg 1.

SCHEDULE

Regulation 11

(1)	(2)
Orders revoked	*References*
The Immigration (Provision of Physical Data) Regulations 2003	SI 2003/1875
The Immigration (Provision of Physical Data) (Amendment) Regulations 2004	SI 2004/474
The Immigration (Provision of Physical Data) (Amendment) (No 2) Regulations 2004	SI 2004/1834
The Immigration (Provision of Physical Data) (Amendment) Regulations 2005	SI 2005/3127

Initial Commencement
Specified date: 4 July 2006: see reg 1.

IMMIGRATION (CONTINUATION OF LEAVE) (NOTICES) REGULATIONS 2006

SI 2006/2170

Made ...4th August 2006

Laid before Parliament ...10th August 2006

Coming into force ...31st August 2006

The Secretary of State, in the exercise of the powers conferred on him by section 3C(6) of the Immigration Act 1971, makes the following Regulations:

1 Citation and Commencement

These Regulations may be cited as the Immigration (Continuation of Leave) (Notices) Regulations 2006 and shall come into force on 31st August 2006.

Initial Commencement
Specified date: 31 August 2006: see above.

2 Decision on an application for variation of leave

For the purpose of section 3C of the Immigration Act 1971 an application for variation of leave is decided—

(a) when notice of the decision has been given in accordance with regulations made under section 105 of the Nationality, Immigration and Asylum Act 2002; or where no such notice is required,
(b) when notice of the decision has been given in accordance with section 4(1) of the Immigration Act 1971.

Initial Commencement
Specified date: 31 August 2006: see reg 1.

PERSONS SUBJECT TO IMMIGRATION CONTROL (HOUSING AUTHORITY ACCOMMODATION AND HOMELESSNESS) (AMENDMENT) ORDER 2006

SI 2006/2521

Made ...13th September 2006

Laid before Parliament ...18th September 2006

Coming into force ...9th October 2006

The Secretary of State, in exercise of the powers conferred upon him by sections 118, 119 and 166(3) of the Immigration and Asylum Act 1999, makes the following Order:

1 Citation and Commencement

This Order may be cited as the Persons Subject to Immigration Control (Housing Authority Accommodation and Homelessness) (Amendment) Order 2006 and shall come into force on 9th October 2006.

2 Amendment of the Persons subject to Immigration Control (Housing Authority Accommodation and Homelessness) Order 2000

(1) The Persons subject to Immigration Control (Housing Authority Accommodation and Homelessness) Order 2000 is amended as follows.

(2) In article 3 (Housing authority accommodation—England, Scotland and Northern Ireland)—

(a) for sub-paragraph (b)(i) there shall be substituted the following—
"(b)
(i) who has leave to enter or remain in the United Kingdom granted outside the provisions of the immigration rules; and"; and
(b) after paragraph (b) there shall be inserted the following—
"(bb)Class BA—a person who has humanitarian protection granted under the immigration rules;".

(3) In article 7 (Homelessness—Scotland and Northern Ireland) for sub-paragraph (1)(a) there shall be substituted the following—

"(a) the classes specified in article 3(a) to (e) (Class A, Class B, Class BA, Class C, Class D and Class E);".

REFUGEE OR PERSON IN NEED OF INTERNATIONAL PROTECTION (QUALIFICATION) REGULATIONS 2006

SI 2006/2525

Made ...11th September 2006

Laid before Parliament ...18th September 2006

Coming into force ...9th October 2006

The Secretary of State is a Minister designated for the purposes of section 2(2) of the European Communities Act 1972 in relation to measures relating to immigration, asylum, refugees and displaced persons, and in exercise of the powers conferred on him by that section, makes the following Regulations:

1 Citation and commencement

(1) These Regulations may be cited as The Refugee or Person in Need of International Protection (Qualification) Regulations 2006 and shall come into force on 9th October 2006.

(2) These Regulations apply to any application for asylum which has not been decided and any immigration appeal brought under the Immigration Acts (as defined in section 64(2) of the Immigration, Asylum and Nationality Act 2006) which has not been finally determined.

Initial Commencement
Specified date: 9 October 2006: see para (1) above.

2 Interpretation

In these Regulations—

"application for asylum" means the request of a person to be recognised as a refugee under the Geneva Convention;
"Geneva Convention" means the Convention Relating to the Status of Refugees done at Geneva on 28 July 1951 and the New York Protocol of 31 January 1967;
"immigration rules" means rules made under section 3(2) of the Immigration Act 1971;
"persecution" means an act of persecution within the meaning of Article 1(A) of the Geneva Convention;
"person eligible for humanitarian protection" means a person who is eligible for a grant of humanitarian protection under the immigration rules;
"refugee" means a person who falls within Article 1(A) of the Geneva Convention and to whom regulation 7 does not apply;
"residence permit" means a document confirming that a person has leave to enter or remain in the United Kingdom whether limited or indefinite;
"serious harm" means serious harm as defined in the immigration rules;
"person" means any person who is not a British citizen.

Initial Commencement
Specified date: 9 October 2006: see reg 1(1).

3 Actors of persecution or serious harm

In deciding whether a person is a refugee or a person eligible for humanitarian protection, persecution or serious harm can be committed by:

(a) the State;
(b) any party or organisation controlling the State or a substantial part of the territory of the State;
(c) any non-State actor if it can be demonstrated that the actors mentioned in paragraphs (a) and (b), including any international organisation, are unable or unwilling to provide protection against persecution or serious harm.

Initial Commencement
Specified date: 9 October 2006: see reg 1(1).

4 Actors of protection

(1) In deciding whether a person is a refugee or a person eligible for humanitarian protection, protection from persecution or serious harm can be provided by:

(a) the State; or
(b) any party or organisation, including any international organisation, controlling the State or a substantial part of the territory of the State.

(2) Protection shall be regarded as generally provided when the actors mentioned in paragraph (1)(a) and (b) take reasonable steps to prevent the persecution or suffering of serious harm by operating an effective legal system for the detection, prosecution and punishment of acts constituting persecution or serious harm, and the person mentioned in paragraph (1) has access to such protection.

(3) In deciding whether a person is a refugee or a person eligible for humanitarian protection the Secretary of State may assess whether an international organisation controls a State or a substantial part of its territory and provides protection as described in paragraph (2).

Initial Commencement
Specified date: 9 October 2006: see reg 1(1).

5 Act of persecution

(1) In deciding whether a person is a refugee an act of persecution must be:

(a) sufficiently serious by its nature or repetition as to constitute a severe violation of a basic human right, in particular a right from which derogation cannot be made under Article 15 of the Convention for the Protection of Human Rights and Fundamental Freedoms; or
(b) an accumulation of various measures, including a violation of a human right which is sufficiently severe as to affect an individual in a similar manner as specified in (a).

(2) An act of persecution may, for example, take the form of:

(a) an act of physical or mental violence, including an act of sexual violence;
(b) a legal, administrative, police, or judicial measure which in itself is discriminatory or which is implemented in a discriminatory manner;
(c) prosecution or punishment, which is disproportionate or discriminatory;
(d) denial of judicial redress resulting in a disproportionate or discriminatory punishment;
(e) prosecution or punishment for refusal to perform military service in a conflict, where performing military service would include crimes or acts falling under regulation 7.

(3) An act of persecution must be committed for at least one of the reasons in Article 1(A) of the Geneva Convention.

Initial Commencement
Specified date: 9 October 2006: see reg 1(1).

6 Reasons for persecution

(1) In deciding whether a person is a refugee:

- (a) the concept of race shall include consideration of, for example, colour, descent, or membership of a particular ethnic group;
- (b) the concept of religion shall include, for example, the holding of theistic, non-theistic and atheistic beliefs, the participation in, or abstention from, formal worship in private or in public, either alone or in community with others, other religious acts or expressions of view, or forms of personal or communal conduct based on or mandated by any religious belief;
- (c) the concept of nationality shall not be confined to citizenship or lack thereof but shall include, for example, membership of a group determined by its cultural, ethnic, or linguistic identity, common geographical or political origins or its relationship with the population of another State;
- (d) a group shall be considered to form a particular social group where, for example:
  - (i) members of that group share an innate characteristic, or a common background that cannot be changed, or share a characteristic or belief that is so fundamental to identity or conscience that a person should not be forced to renounce it, and
  - (ii) that group has a distinct identity in the relevant country, because it is perceived as being different by the surrounding society;
- (e) a particular social group might include a group based on a common characteristic of sexual orientation but sexual orientation cannot be understood to include acts considered to be criminal in accordance with national law of the United Kingdom;
- (f) the concept of political opinion shall include the holding of an opinion, thought or belief on a matter related to the potential actors of persecution mentioned in regulation 3 and to their policies or methods, whether or not that opinion, thought or belief has been acted upon by the person.

(2) In deciding whether a person has a well-founded fear of being persecuted, it is immaterial whether he actually possesses the racial, religious, national, social or political characteristic which attracts the persecution, provided that such a characteristic is attributed to him by the actor of persecution.

Initial Commencement
Specified date: 9 October 2006: see reg 1(1).

7 Exclusion

(1) A person is not a refugee, if he falls within the scope of Article 1 D, 1E or 1F of the Geneva Convention.

(2) In the construction and application of Article 1F(b) of the Geneva Convention:

- (a) the reference to serious non-political crime includes a particularly cruel action, even if it is committed with an allegedly political objective;
- (b) the reference to the crime being committed outside the country of refuge prior to his admission as a refugee shall be taken to mean the time up to and including the day on which a residence permit is issued.

(3) Article 1F(a) and (b) of the Geneva Convention shall apply to a person who instigates or otherwise participates in the commission of the crimes or acts specified in those provisions.

Initial Commencement
Specified date: 9 October 2006: see reg 1(1).

EUROPEAN LEGISLATION

COUNCIL DIRECTIVE (2004/58/EC)

SI 2006/2525 **of 29 April 2004 on the right of citizens of the Union and their family members to move and reside freely within the territory of the Member States amending Regulation (EEC) No 1612/68 and repealing Directives 64/221/EEC, 68/360/EEC, 72/194/EEC, 73/148/EEC, 75/34/EEC, 75/35/EEC, 90/364/EEC, 90/365/EEC and 93/96/EEC**

OJ L 229, 29 June 2004, p 35

THE EUROPEAN PARLIAMENT AND THE COUNCIL OF THE EUROPEAN UNION,

Having regard to the Treaty establishing the European Community, and in particular Articles 12, 18, 40, 44 and 52 thereof,

Having regard to the proposal from the Commission[1],

Having regard to the opinion of the European Economic and Social Committee[2],

Having regard to the opinion of the Committee of the Regions[3],

Acting in accordance with the procedure laid down in Article 251 of the Treaty[4],

Whereas:

(1) Citizenship of the Union confers on every citizen of the Union a primary and individual right to move and reside freely within the territory of the Member States, subject to the limitations and conditions laid down in the Treaty and to the measures adopted to give it effect.

(2) The free movement of persons constitutes one of the fundamental freedoms of the internal market, which comprises an area without internal frontiers, in which freedom is ensured in accordance with the provisions of the Treaty.

(3) Union citizenship should be the fundamental status of nationals of the Member States when they exercise their right of free movement and residence. It is therefore necessary to codify and review the existing Community instruments dealing separately with workers, self-employed persons, as well as students and other inactive persons in order to simplify and strengthen the right of free movement and residence of all Union citizens.

(4) With a view to remedying this sector-by-sector, piecemeal approach to the right of free movement and residence and facilitating the exercise of this right, there needs to be a single legislative act to amend Council Regulation (EEC) No 1612/68 of 15 October 1968 on freedom of movement for workers within the Community[5], and to repeal the following acts: Council Directive 68/360/EEC of 15 October 1968 on the abolition of restrictions on movement and residence within the Community for workers of Member States and their families[6], Council Directive 73/148/EEC of 21 May 1973 on the abolition of restrictions on movement and residence within the Community for nationals of Member States with regard to establishment and the provision of services[7], Council Directive 90/364/EEC of 28 June 1990 on the right of residence[8], Council Directive 90/365/EEC of 28 June 1990 on the right of residence for employees and self-employed persons who have ceased their occupational activity[9] and Council Directive 93/96/EEC of 29 October 1993 on the right of residence for students[10].

(5) The right of all Union citizens to move and reside freely within the territory of the Member States should, if it is to be exercised under objective conditions of freedom and dignity, be also granted to their family members, irrespective of nationality. For the purposes of this Directive, the definition of 'family

member' should also include the registered partner if the legislation of the host Member State treats registered partnership as equivalent to marriage.

(6) In order to maintain the unity of the family in a broader sense and without prejudice to the prohibition of discrimination on grounds of nationality, the situation of those persons who are not included in the definition of family members under this Directive, and who therefore do not enjoy an automatic right of entry and residence in the host Member State, should be examined by the host Member State on the basis of its own national legislation, in order to decide whether entry and residence could be granted to such persons, taking into consideration their relationship with the Union citizen or any other circumstances, such as their financial or physical dependence on the Union citizen.

(7) The formalities connected with the free movement of Union citizens within the territory of Member States should be clearly defined, without prejudice to the provisions applicable to national border controls.

(8) With a view to facilitating the free movement of family members who are not nationals of a Member State, those who have already obtained a residence card should be exempted from the requirement to obtain an entry visa within the meaning of Council Regulation (EC) No 539/2001 of 15 March 2001 listing the third countries whose nationals must be in possession of visas when crossing the external borders and those whose nationals are exempt from that requirement[11] or, where appropriate, of the applicable national legislation.

(9) Union citizens should have the right of residence in the host Member State for a period not exceeding three months without being subject to any conditions or any formalities other than the requirement to hold a valid identity card or passport, without prejudice to a more favourable treatment applicable to job-seekers as recognised by the case-law of the Court of Justice.

(10) Persons exercising their right of residence should not, however, become an unreasonable burden on the social assistance system of the host Member State during an initial period of residence. Therefore, the right of residence for Union citizens and their family members for periods in excess of three months should be subject to conditions.

(11) The fundamental and personal right of residence in another Member State is conferred directly on Union citizens by the Treaty and is not dependent upon their having fulfilled administrative procedures.

(12) For periods of residence of longer than three months, Member States should have the possibility to require Union citizens to register with the competent authorities in the place of residence, attested by a registration certificate issued to that effect.

(13) The residence card requirement should be restricted to family members of Union citizens who are not nationals of a Member State for periods of residence of longer than three months.

(14) The supporting documents required by the competent authorities for the issuing of a registration certificate or of a residence card should be comprehensively specified in order to avoid divergent administrative practices or interpretations constituting an undue obstacle to the exercise of the right of residence by Union citizens and their family members.

(15) Family members should be legally safeguarded in the event of the death of the Union citizen, divorce, annulment of marriage or termination of a registered partnership. With due regard for family life and human dignity, and in certain conditions to guard against abuse, measures should therefore be taken to ensure that in such circumstances family members already residing within the territory of the host Member State retain their right of residence exclusively on a personal basis.

(16) As long as the beneficiaries of the right of residence do not become an unreasonable burden on the social assistance system of the host Member State

they should not be expelled. Therefore, an expulsion measure should not be the automatic consequence of recourse to the social assistance system. The host Member State should examine whether it is a case of temporary difficulties and take into account the duration of residence, the personal circumstances and the amount of aid granted in order to consider whether the beneficiary has become an unreasonable burden on its social assistance system and to proceed to his expulsion. In no case should an expulsion measure be adopted against workers, self-employed persons or job-seekers as defined by the Court of Justice save on grounds of public policy or public security.

(17) Enjoyment of permanent residence by Union citizens who have chosen to settle long term in the host Member State would strengthen the feeling of Union citizenship and is a key element in promoting social cohesion, which is one of the fundamental objectives of the Union. A right of permanent residence should therefore be laid down for all Union citizens and their family members who have resided in the host Member State in compliance with the conditions laid down in this Directive during a continuous period of five years without becoming subject to an expulsion measure.

(18) In order to be a genuine vehicle for integration into the society of the host Member State in which the Union citizen resides, the right of permanent residence, once obtained, should not be subject to any conditions.

(19) Certain advantages specific to Union citizens who are workers or self-employed persons and to their family members, which may allow these persons to acquire a right of permanent residence before they have resided five years in the host Member State, should be maintained, as these constitute acquired rights, conferred by Commission Regulation (EEC) No 1251/70 of 29 June 1970 on the right of workers to remain in the territory of a Member State after having been employed in that State[12] and Council Directive 75/34/EEC of 17 December 1974 concerning the right of nationals of a Member State to remain in the territory of another Member State after having pursued therein an activity in a self-employed capacity[13].

(20) In accordance with the prohibition of discrimination on grounds of nationality, all Union citizens and their family members residing in a Member State on the basis of this Directive should enjoy, in that Member State, equal treatment with nationals in areas covered by the Treaty, subject to such specific provisions as are expressly provided for in the Treaty and secondary law.

(21) However, it should be left to the host Member State to decide whether it will grant social assistance during the first three months of residence, or for a longer period in the case of job-seekers, to Union citizens other than those who are workers or self-employed persons or who retain their status or their family members, or maintenance assistance for studies, including vocational training, prior to acquisition of the right of permanent residence, to these same persons.

(22) The Treaty allows restrictions to be placed on the right of free movement and residence on grounds of public policy, public security or public health. In order to ensure a tighter definition of the circumstances and procedural safeguards subject to which Union citizens and their family members may be denied leave to enter or may be expelled, this Directive should replace Council Directive 64/221/EEC of 25 February 1964 on the co-ordination of special measures concerning the movement and residence of foreign nationals, which are justified on grounds of public policy, public security or public health[14].

(23) Expulsion of Union citizens and their family members on grounds of public policy or public security is a measure that can seriously harm persons who, having availed themselves of the rights and freedoms conferred on them by the Treaty, have become genuinely integrated into the host Member State. The scope for such measures should therefore be limited in accordance with the principle of proportionality to take account of the degree of integration of the

persons concerned, the length of their residence in the host Member State, their age, state of health, family and economic situation and the links with their country of origin.

(24) Accordingly, the greater the degree of integration of Union citizens and their family members in the host Member State, the greater the degree of protection against expulsion should be. Only in exceptional circumstances, where there are imperative grounds of public security, should an expulsion measure be taken against Union citizens who have resided for many years in the territory of the host Member State, in particular when they were born and have resided there throughout their life. In addition, such exceptional circumstances should also apply to an expulsion measure taken against minors, in order to protect their links with their family, in accordance with the United Nations Convention on the Rights of the Child, of 20 November 1989.

(25) Procedural safeguards should also be specified in detail in order to ensure a high level of protection of the rights of Union citizens and their family members in the event of their being denied leave to enter or reside in another Member State, as well as to uphold the principle that any action taken by the authorities must be properly justified.

(26) In all events, judicial redress procedures should be available to Union citizens and their family members who have been refused leave to enter or reside in another Member State.

(27) In line with the case-law of the Court of Justice prohibiting Member States from issuing orders excluding for life persons covered by this Directive from their territory, the right of Union citizens and their family members who have been excluded from the territory of a Member State to submit a fresh application after a reasonable period, and in any event after a three year period from enforcement of the final exclusion order, should be confirmed.

(28) To guard against abuse of rights or fraud, notably marriages of convenience or any other form of relationships contracted for the sole purpose of enjoying the right of free movement and residence, Member States should have the possibility to adopt the necessary measures.

(29) This Directive should not affect more favourable national provisions.

(30) With a view to examining how further to facilitate the exercise of the right of free movement and residence, a report should be prepared by the Commission in order to evaluate the opportunity to present any necessary proposals to this effect, notably on the extension of the period of residence with no conditions.

(31) This Directive respects the fundamental rights and freedoms and observes the principles recognised in particular by the Charter of Fundamental Rights of the European Union. In accordance with the prohibition of discrimination contained in the Charter, Member States should implement this Directive without discrimination between the beneficiaries of this Directive on grounds such as sex, race, colour, ethnic or social origin, genetic characteristics, language, religion or beliefs, political or other opinion, membership of an ethnic minority, property, birth, disability, age or sexual orientation,

[1] OJ C 270 E, 25.9.2001, p 150.

[2] OJ C 149, 21.6.2002, p 46.

[3] OJ C 192, 12.8.2002, p 17.

[4] Opinion of the European Parliament of 11 February 2003 (OJ C 43 E, 19.2.2004, p 42), Council Common Position of 5 December 2003 (OJ C 54 E, 2.3.2004, p 12) and Position of the European Parliament of 10 March 2004 (not yet published in the Official Journal at time of going to press).

[5] OJ L 257, 19.10.1968, p 2. Regulation as last amended by Regulation (EEC) No 2434/92 (OJ L 245, 26.8.1992, p 1).

[6] OJ L 257, 19.10.1968, p 13. Directive as last amended by the 2003 Act of Accession.

[7] OJ L 172, 28.6.1973, p 14.

[8] OJ L 180, 13.7.1990, p 26.

[9] OJ L 180, 13.7.1990, p 28.

[10] OJ L 317, 18.12.1993, p 59.
[11] OJ L 81, 21.3.2001, p 1. Regulation as last amended by Regulation (EC) No 453/2003 (OJ L 69, 13.3.2003, p 10).
[12] OJ L 142, 30.6.1970, p 24.
[13] OJ L 14, 20.1.1975, p 10.
[14] OJ 56, 4.4.1964, p 850. Directive as last amended by Directive 75/35/EEC (OJ 14, 20.1.1975, p 14).

Has adopted this Directive,

CHAPTER I
GENERAL PROVISIONS

Article 1
Subject

This Directive lays down:

(a) the conditions governing the exercise of the right of free movement and residence within the territory of the Member States by Union citizens and their family members;
(b) the right of permanent residence in the territory of the Member States for Union citizens and their family members;
(c) the limits placed on the rights set out in (a) and (b) on grounds of public policy, public security or public health.

Article 2
Definitions

For the purposes of this Directive:

1. 'Union citizen' means any person having the nationality of a Member State;
2. 'family member' means:
   (a) the spouse;
   (b) the partner with whom the Union citizen has contracted a registered partnership, on the basis of the legislation of a Member State, if the legislation of the host Member State treats registered partnerships as equivalent to marriage and in accordance with the conditions laid down in the relevant legislation of the host Member State;
   (c) the direct descendants who are under the age of 21 or are dependants and those of the spouse or partner as defined in point (b);
   (d) the dependent direct relatives in the ascending line and those of the spouse or partner as defined in point (b);
3. 'host Member State' means the Member State to which a Union citizen moves in order to exercise his/her right of free movement and residence.

Article 3
Beneficiaries

1. This Directive shall apply to all Union citizens who move to or reside in a Member State other than that of which they are a national, and to their family members as defined in point 2 of Article 2 who accompany or join them.

2. Without prejudice to any right to free movement and residence the persons concerned may have in their own right, the host Member State shall, in accordance with its national legislation, facilitate entry and residence for the following persons:

(a) any other family members, irrespective of their nationality, not falling under the definition in point 2 of Article 2 who, in the country from which they have come, are dependants or members of the household of the Union citizen having the primary right of residence, or where serious health grounds strictly require the personal care of the family member by the Union citizen;

(b) the partner with whom the Union citizen has a durable relationship, duly attested.

The host Member State shall undertake an extensive examination of the personal circumstances and shall justify any denial of entry or residence to these people.

CHAPTER II
RIGHT OF EXIT AND ENTRY

Article 4
Right of exit

1. Without prejudice to the provisions on travel documents applicable to national border controls, all Union citizens with a valid identity card or passport and their family members who are not nationals of a Member State and who hold a valid passport shall have the right to leave the territory of a Member State to travel to another Member State.

2. No exit visa or equivalent formality may be imposed on the persons to whom paragraph 1 applies.

3. Member States shall, acting in accordance with their laws, issue to their own nationals, and renew, an identity card or passport stating their nationality.

4. The passport shall be valid at least for all Member States and for countries through which the holder must pass when travelling between Member States. Where the law of a Member State does not provide for identity cards to be issued, the period of validity of any passport on being issued or renewed shall be not less than five years.

Article 5
Right of entry

1. Without prejudice to the provisions on travel documents applicable to national border controls, Member States shall grant Union citizens leave to enter their territory with a valid identity card or passport and shall grant family members who are not nationals of a Member State leave to enter their territory with a valid passport.

No entry visa or equivalent formality may be imposed on Union citizens.

2. Family members who are not nationals of a Member State shall only be required to have an entry visa in accordance with Regulation (EC) No 539/2001 or, where appropriate, with national law. For the purposes of this Directive, possession of the valid residence card referred to in Article 10 shall exempt such family members from the visa requirement.

Member States shall grant such persons every facility to obtain the necessary visas. Such visas shall be issued free of charge as soon as possible and on the basis of an accelerated procedure.

3. The host Member State shall not place an entry or exit stamp in the passport of family members who are not nationals of a Member State provided that they present the residence card provided for in Article 10.

4. Where a Union citizen, or a family member who is not a national of a Member State, does not have the necessary travel documents or, if required, the necessary visas, the Member State concerned shall, before turning them back, give such persons every reasonable opportunity to obtain the necessary documents or have them brought to them within a reasonable period of time or to corroborate or prove by other means that they are covered by the right of free movement and residence.

5. The Member State may require the person concerned to report his/her presence within its territory within a reasonable and non-discriminatory period of time. Failure to comply with this requirement may make the person concerned liable to proportionate and non-discriminatory sanctions.

CHAPTER III
RIGHT OF RESIDENCE

Article 6
Right of residence for up to three months

1. Union citizens shall have the right of residence on the territory of another Member State for a period of up to three months without any conditions or any formalities other than the requirement to hold a valid identity card or passport.

2. The provisions of paragraph 1 shall also apply to family members in possession of a valid passport who are not nationals of a Member State, accompanying or joining the Union citizen.

Article 7
Right of residence for more than three months

1. All Union citizens shall have the right of residence on the territory of another Member State for a period of longer than three months if they:

(a) are workers or self-employed persons in the host Member State; or
(b) have sufficient resources for themselves and their family members not to become a burden on the social assistance system of the host Member State during their period of residence and have comprehensive sickness insurance cover in the host Member State; or
(c)
- are enrolled at a private or public establishment, accredited or financed by the host Member State on the basis of its legislation or administrative practice, for the principal purpose of following a course of study, including vocational training; and
- have comprehensive sickness insurance cover in the host Member State and assure the relevant national authority, by means of a declaration or by such equivalent means as they may choose, that they have sufficient resources for themselves and their family members not to become a burden on the social assistance system of the host Member State during their period of residence; or

(d) are family members accompanying or joining a Union citizen who satisfies the conditions referred to in points (a), (b) or (c).

2. The right of residence provided for in paragraph 1 shall extend to family members who are not nationals of a Member State, accompanying or joining the Union citizen in the host Member State, provided that such Union citizen satisfies the conditions referred to in paragraph 1(a), (b) or (c).

3. For the purposes of paragraph 1(a), a Union citizen who is no longer a worker or self-employed person shall retain the status of worker or self-employed person in the following circumstances:

(a) he/she is temporarily unable to work as the result of an illness or accident;
(b) he/she is in duly recorded involuntary unemployment after having been employed for more than one year and has registered as a job-seeker with the relevant employment office;
(c) he/she is in duly recorded involuntary unemployment after completing a fixed-term employment contract of less than a year or after having become

involuntarily unemployed during the first twelve months and has registered as a job-seeker with the relevant employment office. In this case, the status of worker shall be retained for no less than six months;

(d) he/she embarks on vocational training. Unless he/she is involuntarily unemployed, the retention of the status of worker shall require the training to be related to the previous employment.

4. By way of derogation from paragraphs 1(d) and 2 above, only the spouse, the registered partner provided for in Article 2(2)(b) and dependent children shall have the right of residence as family members of a Union citizen meeting the conditions under 1(c) above. Article 3(2) shall apply to his/her dependent direct relatives in the ascending lines and those of his/her spouse or registered partner.

Article 8
Administrative formalities for Union citizens

1. Without prejudice to Article 5(5), for periods of residence longer than three months, the host Member State may require Union citizens to register with the relevant authorities.

2. The deadline for registration may not be less than three months from the date of arrival. A registration certificate shall be issued immediately, stating the name and address of the person registering and the date of the registration. Failure to comply with the registration requirement may render the person concerned liable to proportionate and non-discriminatory sanctions.

3. For the registration certificate to be issued, Member States may only require that:

- Union citizens to whom point (a) of Article 7(1) applies present a valid identity card or passport, a confirmation of engagement from the employer or a certificate of employment, or proof that they are self-employed persons,
- Union citizens to whom point (b) of Article 7(1) applies present a valid identity card or passport and provide proof that they satisfy the conditions laid down therein,
- Union citizens to whom point (c) of Article 7(1) applies present a valid identity card or passport, provide proof of enrolment at an accredited establishment and of comprehensive sickness insurance cover and the declaration or equivalent means referred to in point (c) of Article 7(1). Member States may not require this declaration to refer to any specific amount of resources.

4. Member States may not lay down a fixed amount which they regard as 'sufficient resources', but they must take into account the personal situation of the person concerned. In all cases this amount shall not be higher than the threshold below which nationals of the host Member State become eligible for social assistance, or, where this criterion is not applicable, higher than the minimum social security pension paid by the host Member State.

5. For the registration certificate to be issued to family members of Union citizens, who are themselves Union citizens, Member States may require the following documents to be presented:

(a) a valid identity card or passport;
(b) a document attesting to the existence of a family relationship or of a registered partnership;
(c) where appropriate, the registration certificate of the Union citizen whom they are accompanying or joining;
(d) in cases falling under points (c) and (d) of Article 2(2), documentary evidence that the conditions laid down therein are met;

(e) in cases falling under Article 3(2)(a), a document issued by the relevant authority in the country of origin or country from which they are arriving certifying that they are dependants or members of the household of the Union citizen, or proof of the existence of serious health grounds which strictly require the personal care of the family member by the Union citizen;
(f) in cases falling under Article 3(2)(b), proof of the existence of a durable relationship with the Union citizen.

Article 9
Administrative formalities for family members who are not nationals of a Member State

1. Member States shall issue a residence card to family members of a Union citizen who are not nationals of a Member State, where the planned period of residence is for more than three months.

2. The deadline for submitting the residence card application may not be less than three months from the date of arrival.

3. Failure to comply with the requirement to apply for a residence card may make the person concerned liable to proportionate and non-discriminatory sanctions.

Article 10
Issue of residence cards

1. The right of residence of family members of a Union citizen who are not nationals of a Member State shall be evidenced by the issuing of a document called 'Residence card of a family member of a Union citizen' no later than six months from the date on which they submit the application. A certificate of application for the residence card shall be issued immediately.

2. For the residence card to be issued, Member States shall require presentation of the following documents:

(a) a valid passport;
(b) a document attesting to the existence of a family relationship or of a registered partnership;
(c) the registration certificate or, in the absence of a registration system, any other proof of residence in the host Member State of the Union citizen whom they are accompanying or joining;
(d) in cases falling under points (c) and (d) of Article 2(2), documentary evidence that the conditions laid down therein are met;
(e) in cases falling under Article 3(2)(a), a document issued by the relevant authority in the country of origin or country from which they are arriving certifying that they are dependants or members of the household of the Union citizen, or proof of the existence of serious health grounds which strictly require the personal care of the family member by the Union citizen;
(f) in cases falling under Article 3(2)(b), proof of the existence of a durable relationship with the Union citizen.

Article 11
Validity of the residence card

1. The residence card provided for by Article 10(1) shall be valid for five years from the date of issue or for the envisaged period of residence of the Union citizen, if this period is less than five years.

2. The validity of the residence card shall not be affected by temporary absences not exceeding six months a year, or by absences of a longer duration for compulsory

military service or by one absence of a maximum of 12 consecutive months for important reasons such as pregnancy and childbirth, serious illness, study or vocational training, or a posting in another Member State or a third country.

Article 12
Retention of the right of residence by family members in the event of death or departure of the Union citizen

1. Without prejudice to the second subparagraph, the Union citizen's death or departure from the host Member State shall not affect the right of residence of his/her family members who are nationals of a Member State.

Before acquiring the right of permanent residence, the persons concerned must meet the conditions laid down in points (a), (b), (c) or (d) of Article 7(1).

2. Without prejudice to the second subparagraph, the Union citizen's death shall not entail loss of the right of residence of his/her family members who are not nationals of a Member State and who have been residing in the host Member State as family members for at least one year before the Union citizen's death.

Before acquiring the right of permanent residence, the right of residence of the persons concerned shall remain subject to the requirement that they are able to show that they are workers or self-employed persons or that they have sufficient resources for themselves and their family members not to become a burden on the social assistance system of the host Member State during their period of residence and have comprehensive sickness insurance cover in the host Member State, or that they are members of the family, already constituted in the host Member State, of a person satisfying these requirements. 'Sufficient resources' shall be as defined in Article 8(4).

Such family members shall retain their right of residence exclusively on a personal basis.

3. The Union citizen's departure from the host Member State or his/her death shall not entail loss of the right of residence of his/her children or of the parent who has actual custody of the children, irrespective of nationality, if the children reside in the host Member State and are enrolled at an educational establishment, for the purpose of studying there, until the completion of their studies.

Article 13
Retention of the right of residence by family members in the event of divorce, annulment of marriage or termination of registered partnership

1. Without prejudice to the second subparagraph, divorce, annulment of the Union citizen's marriage or termination of his/her registered partnership, as referred to in point 2(b) of Article 2 shall not affect the right of residence of his/her family members who are nationals of a Member State.

Before acquiring the right of permanent residence, the persons concerned must meet the conditions laid down in points (a), (b), (c) or (d) of Article 7(1).

2. Without prejudice to the second subparagraph, divorce, annulment of marriage or termination of the registered partnership referred to in point 2(b) of Article 2 shall not entail loss of the right of residence of a Union citizen's family members who are not nationals of a Member State where:

(a) prior to initiation of the divorce or annulment proceedings or termination of the registered partnership referred to in point 2(b) of Article 2, the marriage or registered partnership has lasted at least three years, including one year in the host Member State; or

(b) by agreement between the spouses or the partners referred to in point 2(b) of Article 2 or by court order, the spouse or partner who is not a national of a Member State has custody of the Union citizen's children; or

(c) this is warranted by particularly difficult circumstances, such as having been a victim of domestic violence while the marriage or registered partnership was subsisting; or
(d) by agreement between the spouses or partners referred to in point 2(b) of Article 2 or by court order, the spouse or partner who is not a national of a Member State has the right of access to a minor child, provided that the court has ruled that such access must be in the host Member State, and for as long as is required.

Before acquiring the right of permanent residence, the right of residence of the persons concerned shall remain subject to the requirement that they are able to show that they are workers or self-employed persons or that they have sufficient resources for themselves and their family members not to become a burden on the social assistance system of the host Member State during their period of residence and have comprehensive sickness insurance cover in the host Member State, or that they are members of the family, already constituted in the host Member State, of a person satisfying these requirements. 'Sufficient resources' shall be as defined in Article 8(4).

Such family members shall retain their right of residence exclusively on personal basis.

Article 14
Retention of the right of residence

1. Union citizens and their family members shall have the right of residence provided for in Article 6, as long as they do not become an unreasonable burden on the social assistance system of the host Member State.

2. Union citizens and their family members shall have the right of residence provided for in Articles 7, 12 and 13 as long as they meet the conditions set out therein.

In specific cases where there is a reasonable doubt as to whether a Union citizen or his/her family members satisfies the conditions set out in Articles 7, 12 and 13, Member States may verify if these conditions are fulfilled. This verification shall not be carried out systematically.

3. An expulsion measure shall not be the automatic consequence of a Union citizen's or his or her family member's recourse to the social assistance system of the host Member State.

4. By way of derogation from paragraphs 1 and 2 and without prejudice to the provisions of Chapter VI, an expulsion measure may in no case be adopted against Union citizens or their family members if:

(a) the Union citizens are workers or self-employed persons, or
(b) the Union citizens entered the territory of the host Member State in order to seek employment. In this case, the Union citizens and their family members may not be expelled for as long as the Union citizens can provide evidence that they are continuing to seek employment and that they have a genuine chance of being engaged.

Article 15
Procedural safeguards

1. The procedures provided for by Articles 30 and 31 shall apply by analogy to all decisions restricting free movement of Union citizens and their family members on grounds other than public policy, public security or public health.

2. Expiry of the identity card or passport on the basis of which the person concerned entered the host Member State and was issued with a registration certificate or residence card shall not constitute a ground for expulsion from the host Member State.

3. The host Member State may not impose a ban on entry in the context of an expulsion decision to which paragraph 1 applies.

CHAPTER IV
RIGHT OF PERMANENT RESIDENCE

SECTION I
ELIGIBILITY

Article 16
General rule for Union citizens and their family members

1. Union citizens who have resided legally for a continuous period of five years in the host Member State shall have the right of permanent residence there. This right shall not be subject to the conditions provided for in Chapter III.

2. Paragraph 1 shall apply also to family members who are not nationals of a Member State and have legally resided with the Union citizen in the host Member State for a continuous period of five years.

3. Continuity of residence shall not be affected by temporary absences not exceeding a total of six months a year, or by absences of a longer duration for compulsory military service, or by one absence of a maximum of 12 consecutive months for important reasons such as pregnancy and childbirth, serious illness, study or vocational training, or a posting in another Member State or a third country.

4. Once acquired, the right of permanent residence shall be lost only through absence from the host Member State for a period exceeding two consecutive years.

Article 17
Exemptions for persons no longer working in the host Member State and their family members

1. By way of derogation from Article 16, the right of permanent residence in the host Member State shall be enjoyed before completion of a continuous period of five years of residence by:

(a) workers or self-employed persons who, at the time they stop working, have reached the age laid down by the law of that Member State for entitlement to an old age pension or workers who cease paid employment to take early retirement, provided that they have been working in that Member State for at least the preceding twelve months and have resided there continuously for more than three years.

If the law of the host Member State does not grant the right to an old age pension to certain categories of self-employed persons, the age condition shall be deemed to have been met once the person concerned has reached the age of 60;

(b) workers or self-employed persons who have resided continuously in the host Member State for more than two years and stop working there as a result of permanent incapacity to work.

If such incapacity is the result of an accident at work or an occupational disease entitling the person concerned to a benefit payable in full or in part by an institution in the host Member State, no condition shall be imposed as to length of residence;

(c) workers or self-employed persons who, after three years of continuous employment and residence in the host Member State, work in an employed or self-employed capacity in another Member State, while retaining their place of residence in the host Member State, to which they return, as a rule, each day or at least once a week.

For the purposes of entitlement to the rights referred to in points (a) and (b), periods of employment spent in the Member State in which the person concerned is working shall be regarded as having been spent in the host Member State.

Periods of involuntary unemployment duly recorded by the relevant employment office, periods not worked for reasons not of the person's own making and absences from work or cessation of work due to illness or accident shall be regarded as periods of employment.

2. The conditions as to length of residence and employment laid down in point (a) of paragraph 1 and the condition as to length of residence laid down in point (b) of paragraph 1 shall not apply if the worker's or the self-employed person's spouse or partner as referred to in point 2(b) of Article 2 is a national of the host Member State or has lost the nationality of that Member State by marriage to that worker or self-employed person.

3. Irrespective of nationality, the family members of a worker or a self-employed person who are residing with him in the territory of the host Member State shall have the right of permanent residence in that Member State, if the worker or self-employed person has acquired himself the right of permanent residence in that Member State on the basis of paragraph 1.

4. If, however, the worker or self-employed person dies while still working but before acquiring permanent residence status in the host Member State on the basis of paragraph 1, his family members who are residing with him in the host Member State shall acquire the right of permanent residence there, on condition that:

(a) the worker or self-employed person had, at the time of death, resided continuously on the territory of that Member State for two years; or
(b) the death resulted from an accident at work or an occupational disease; or
(c) the surviving spouse lost the nationality of that Member State following marriage to the worker or self-employed person.

Article 18
Acquisition of the right of permanent residence by certain family members who are not nationals of a Member State

Without prejudice to Article 17, the family members of a Union citizen to whom Articles 12(2) and 13(2) apply, who satisfy the conditions laid down therein, shall acquire the right of permanent residence after residing legally for a period of five consecutive years in the host Member State.

SECTION II
ADMINISTRATIVE FORMALITIES

Article 19
Document certifying permanent residence for Union citizens

1. Upon application Member States shall issue Union citizens entitled to permanent residence, after having verified duration of residence, with a document certifying permanent residence.

2. The document certifying permanent residence shall be issued as soon as possible.

Article 20
Permanent residence card for family members who are not nationals of a Member State

1. Member States shall issue family members who are not nationals of a Member State entitled to permanent residence with a permanent residence card within six months of the submission of the application. The permanent residence card shall be renewable automatically every 10 years.

2. The application for a permanent residence card shall be submitted before the residence card expires. Failure to comply with the requirement to apply for a permanent residence card may render the person concerned liable to proportionate and non-discriminatory sanctions.

3. Interruption in residence not exceeding two consecutive years shall not affect the validity of the permanent residence card.

Article 21
Continuity of residence

For the purposes of this Directive, continuity of residence may be attested by any means of proof in use in the host Member State. Continuity of residence is broken by any expulsion decision duly enforced against the person concerned.

CHAPTER V
PROVISIONS COMMON TO THE RIGHT OF RESIDENCE AND THE RIGHT OF PERMANENT RESIDENCE

Article 22
Territorial scope

The right of residence and the right of permanent residence shall cover the whole territory of the host Member State. Member States may impose territorial restrictions on the right of residence and the right of permanent residence only where the same restrictions apply to their own nationals.

Article 23
Related rights

Irrespective of nationality, the family members of a Union citizen who have the right of residence or the right of permanent residence in a Member State shall be entitled to take up employment or self-employment there.

Article 24
Equal treatment

1. Subject to such specific provisions as are expressly provided for in the Treaty and secondary law, all Union citizens residing on the basis of this Directive in the territory of the host Member State shall enjoy equal treatment with the nationals of that Member State within the scope of the Treaty. The benefit of this right shall be extended to family members who are not nationals of a Member State and who have the right of residence or permanent residence.

2. By way of derogation from paragraph 1, the host Member State shall not be obliged to confer entitlement to social assistance during the first three months of residence or, where appropriate, the longer period provided for in Article 14(4)(b), nor shall it be obliged, prior to acquisition of the right of permanent residence, to grant maintenance aid for studies, including vocational training, consisting in student grants or student loans to persons other than workers, self-employed persons, persons who retain such status and members of their families.

Article 25
General provisions concerning residence documents

1. Possession of a registration certificate as referred to in Article 8, of a document certifying permanent residence, of a certificate attesting submission of an application for a family member residence card, of a residence card or of a permanent residence card, may under no circumstances be made a precondition for the exercise of a right or the completion of an administrative formality, as entitlement to rights may be attested by any other means of proof.

2. All documents mentioned in paragraph 1 shall be issued free of charge or for a charge not exceeding that imposed on nationals for the issuing of similar documents.

Article 26
Checks

Member States may carry out checks on compliance with any requirement deriving from their national legislation for non-nationals always to carry their registration certificate or residence card, provided that the same requirement applies to their own nationals as regards their identity card. In the event of failure to comply with this requirement, Member States may impose the same sanctions as those imposed on their own nationals for failure to carry their identity card.

CHAPTER VI
RESTRICTIONS ON THE RIGHT OF ENTRY AND THE RIGHT OF RESIDENCE ON GROUNDS OF PUBLIC POLICY, PUBLIC SECURITY OR PUBLIC HEALTH

Article 27
General principles

1. Subject to the provisions of this Chapter, Member States may restrict the freedom of movement and residence of Union citizens and their family members, irrespective of nationality, on grounds of public policy, public security or public health. These grounds shall not be invoked to serve economic ends.

2. Measures taken on grounds of public policy or public security shall comply with the principle of proportionality and shall be based exclusively on the personal conduct of the individual concerned. Previous criminal convictions shall not in themselves constitute grounds for taking such measures.

The personal conduct of the individual concerned must represent a genuine, present and sufficiently serious threat affecting one of the fundamental interests of society. Justifications that are isolated from the particulars of the case or that rely on considerations of general prevention shall not be accepted.

3. In order to ascertain whether the person concerned represents a danger for public policy or public security, when issuing the registration certificate or, in the absence of a registration system, not later than three months from the date of arrival of the person concerned on its territory or from the date of reporting his/her presence within the territory, as provided for in Article 5(5), or when issuing the residence card, the host Member State may, should it consider this essential, request the Member State of origin and, if need be, other Member States to provide information concerning any previous police record the person concerned may have. Such enquiries shall not be made as a matter of routine. The Member State consulted shall give its reply within two months.

4. The Member State which issued the passport or identity card shall allow the holder of the document who has been expelled on grounds of public policy, public security, or public health from another Member State to re-enter its territory without any formality even if the document is no longer valid or the nationality of the holder is in dispute.

Article 28
Protection against expulsion

1. Before taking an expulsion decision on grounds of public policy or public security, the host Member State shall take account of considerations such as how long the individual concerned has resided on its territory, his/her age, state of health, family and economic situation, social and cultural integration into the host Member State and the extent of his/her links with the country of origin.

2. The host Member State may not take an expulsion decision against Union citizens or their family members, irrespective of nationality, who have the right of permanent residence on its territory, except on serious grounds of public policy or public security.

3. An expulsion decision may not be taken against Union citizens, except if the decision is based on imperative grounds of public security, as defined by Member States, if they:

(a) have resided in the host Member State for the previous 10 years; or
(b) are a minor, except if the expulsion is necessary for the best interests of the child, as provided for in the United Nations Convention on the Rights of the Child of 20 November 1989.

Article 29
Public health

1. The only diseases justifying measures restricting freedom of movement shall be the diseases with epidemic potential as defined by the relevant instruments of the World Health Organisation and other infectious diseases or contagious parasitic diseases if they are the subject of protection provisions applying to nationals of the host Member State.

2. Diseases occurring after a three-month period from the date of arrival shall not constitute grounds for expulsion from the territory.

3. Where there are serious indications that it is necessary, Member States may, within three months of the date of arrival, require persons entitled to the right of residence to undergo, free of charge, a medical examination to certify that they are not suffering from any of the conditions referred to in paragraph 1. Such medical examinations may not be required as a matter of routine.

Article 30
Notification of decisions

1. The persons concerned shall be notified in writing of any decision taken under Article 27(1), in such a way that they are able to comprehend its content and the implications for them.

2. The persons concerned shall be informed, precisely and in full, of the public policy, public security or public health grounds on which the decision taken in their case is based, unless this is contrary to the interests of State security.

3. The notification shall specify the court or administrative authority with which the person concerned may lodge an appeal, the time limit for the appeal and, where applicable, the time allowed for the person to leave the territory of the Member State. Save in duly substantiated cases of urgency, the time allowed to leave the territory shall be not less than one month from the date of notification.

Article 31
Procedural safeguards

1. The persons concerned shall have access to judicial and, where appropriate, administrative redress procedures in the host Member State to appeal against or seek review of any decision taken against them on the grounds of public policy, public security or public health.

2. Where the application for appeal against or judicial review of the expulsion decision is accompanied by an application for an interim order to suspend enforcement of that decision, actual removal from the territory may not take place until such time as the decision on the interim order has been taken, except:

- where the expulsion decision is based on a previous judicial decision; or
- where the persons concerned have had previous access to judicial review; or
- where the expulsion decision is based on imperative grounds of public security under Article 28(3).

3. The redress procedures shall allow for an examination of the legality of the decision, as well as of the facts and circumstances on which the proposed measure is based. They shall ensure that the decision is not disproportionate, particularly in view of the requirements laid down in Article 28.

4. Member States may exclude the individual concerned from their territory pending the redress procedure, but they may not prevent the individual from submitting his/her defence in person, except when his/her appearance may cause serious troubles to public policy or public security or when the appeal or judicial review concerns a denial of entry to the territory.

Article 32
Duration of exclusion orders

1. Persons excluded on grounds of public policy or public security may submit an application for lifting of the exclusion order after a reasonable period, depending on the circumstances, and in any event after three years from enforcement of the final exclusion order which has been validly adopted in accordance with Community law, by putting forward arguments to establish that there has been a material change in the circumstances which justified the decision ordering their exclusion.
The Member State concerned shall reach a decision on this application within six months of its submission.

2. The persons referred to in paragraph 1 shall have no right of entry to the territory of the Member State concerned while their application is being considered.

Article 33
Expulsion as a penalty or legal consequence

1. Expulsion orders may not be issued by the host Member State as a penalty or legal consequence of a custodial penalty, unless they conform to the requirements of Articles 27, 28 and 29.

2. If an expulsion order, as provided for in paragraph 1, is enforced more than two years after it was issued, the Member State shall check that the individual concerned is currently and genuinely a threat to public policy or public security and shall assess whether there has been any material change in the circumstances since the expulsion order was issued.

CHAPTER VII
FINAL PROVISIONS

Article 34
Publicity

Member States shall disseminate information concerning the rights and obligations of Union citizens and their family members on the subjects covered by this Directive, particularly by means of awareness-raising campaigns conducted through national and local media and other means of communication.

Article 35
Abuse of rights

Member States may adopt the necessary measures to refuse, terminate or withdraw any right conferred by this Directive in the case of abuse of rights or fraud, such as marriages of convenience. Any such measure shall be proportionate and subject to the procedural safeguards provided for in Articles 30 and 31.

Article 36
Sanctions

Member States shall lay down provisions on the sanctions applicable to breaches of national rules adopted for the implementation of this Directive and shall take the measures required for their application. The sanctions laid down shall be effective and proportionate. Member States shall notify the Commission of these provisions not later than 30 April 2006 and as promptly as possible in the case of any subsequent changes.

Article 37
More favourable national provisions

The provisions of this Directive shall not affect any laws, regulations or administrative provisions laid down by a Member State which would be more favourable to the persons covered by this Directive.

Article 38
Repeals

1. Articles 10 and 11 of Regulation (EEC) No 1612/68 shall be repealed with effect from 30 April 2006.

2. Directives 64/221/EEC, 68/360/EEC, 72/194/EEC, 73/148/EEC, 75/34/EEC, 75/35/EEC, 90/364/EEC, 90/365/EEC and 93/96/EEC shall be repealed with effect from 30 April 2006.

3. References made to the repealed provisions and Directives shall be construed as being made to this Directive.

Article 39
Report

No later than 30 April 2006 the Commission shall submit a report on the application of this Directive to the European Parliament and the Council, together with any necessary proposals, notably on the opportunity to extend the period of time during which Union citizens and their family members may reside in the territory of the host Member State without any conditions. The Member States shall provide the Commission with the information needed to produce the report.

Article 40
Transposition

1. Member States shall bring into force the laws, regulations and administrative provisions necessary to comply with this Directive by 30 April 2006.

When Member States adopt those measures, they shall contain a reference to this Directive or shall be accompanied by such a reference on the occasion of their official publication. The methods of making such reference shall be laid down by the Member States.

2. Member States shall communicate to the Commission the text of the provisions of national law which they adopt in the field covered by this Directive together with a table showing how the provisions of this Directive correspond to the national provisions adopted.

Article 41
Entry into force

This Directive shall enter into force on the day of its publication in the Official Journal of the European Union.

Article 42
Addressees

This Directive is addressed to the Member States.

Done at Strasbourg, 29 April 2004.